Multimedia: Making It Work, Fifth Edition

Multimedia is any combination of text, graphic art, sound, animation and video

Tay Vaughan

Osborne/**McGraw-Hill**

New York   Chicago   San Francisco   Lisbon   London   Madrid   Mexico City
Milan   New Delhi   San Juan   Seoul   Singapore   Sydney   Toronto

Publisher
Brandon A. Nordin

Vice President & Associate Publisher
Scott Rogers

Editorial Director
Roger Stewart

Project Editor
Madhu Prasher

Acquisitions Coordinators
Alissa Larson and Tim Madrid

Copy Editor
Judith Brown

Proofreader
Pamela Vevea

Indexer
Valerie Robbins

Computer Designers
Tara A. Davis
Elizabeth Jang
Lauren McCarthy

Illustrators
Michael Mueller
Alex Putney
Lyssa Sieben-Wald
Beth E. Young

Series Design
Seventeenth Street Studios

Osborne/**McGraw-Hill**
2600 Tenth Street
Berkeley, California 94710
U.S.A.

To arrange bulk purchase discounts for sales promotions, premiums, or fund-raisers, please contact Osborne/**McGraw-Hill** at the above address. For information on translations or book distributors outside the U.S.A., please see the International Contact Information page immediately following the index of this book.

Multimedia: Making It Work, Fifth Edition

234567890 CUS CUS 01987654321

Book p/n 0-07-219096-5 and CD p/n 0-07-219097-3
parts of
ISBN 0-07-219095-7

This book was composed with Corel VENTURA™ Publisher.

CONTENTS AT A GLANCE

Multimedia and the Internet

Assembling and Delivering a Project

Contents

Introduction

Multimedia Hardware and Software

Multimedia Building Blocks

IV   Multimedia and the Internet

V   Assembling and Delivering a Project

Acknowledgments

This fifth edition of *Multimedia: Making It Work* includes the cumulated input and advice of many colleagues and friends over a ten-year period. Each time I revise and update this book, I am pleased to see that the acknowledgments section grows. Indeed, it is difficult to delete people from this (huge) list because, like the stones of a medieval castle, new and revised material relies upon the older foundation. I will continue accumulating the names of the good people who have helped me build this castle and list them here, at least until my publisher cries "Enough!" and provides substantial reason to press the Delete key.

Roger Stewart, Madhu Prasher, Judith Brown, Alissa Larson, Cindy Wathen, Eileen Corcoran, Chris Johnson, Lyssa Wald, Elizabeth Jang, Kelly Stanton-Scott, and others carried the Osborne/McGraw-Hill flag for this edition. In past editions, Megg Bonar, Robin Small, Scott Rogers, Stephane Thomas, Bob Myren, Heidi Poulin, Mark Karmendy, Joanne Cuthbertson, Bill Pollock, Jeff Pepper, Kathy Hashimoto, Marla Shelasky, Linda Medoff, Valerie Robbins, Cindy Brown, Larry Levitsky, Frances Stack, Jill Pisoni, Carol Henry, and Linda Beatty went out of their way to keep me on track. Chip Harris, Donna Booher, Takis Metaxas, Dan Hilgert, Helayne Waldman, Hank Duderstadt, Dina Medina, Joyce Edwards, Theo Posselt, Ann Stewart, Graham Arlen, Kathy Gardner, Steve Goeckler, Steve Peha, Christine Perey, Pam Sansbury, Terry Schussler, Alden Trull, Eric Butler, and Michael Allen have contributed to making the work more complete since its first edition.

This fifth edition has been greatly improved by considered input and criticism from a circle of knowledgeable educators—multimedia experts who use this book in the trenches, in the real world. To them, for their valuable time, their expertise, and their willingness to share, I am deeply indebted:

J. Wesley Baker, Cedarville University, Cedarville,OH

Celina Byers, Oakland University, Rochester, MI

Nancy Doubleday, Rochester Institute of Technology, Rochester, NY

Tom Duff, University of Paisley, Paisley, UK

Chris Hand, mungbean media, Edinburgh, UK

Scott Herd, Salt Lake Community College, Salt Lake City, UT

Kenneth Hoffman, Seton Hall University, South Orange, NJ

Sherry Hutson, University of Illinois at Springfield, Springfield, IL

Judith Junger, Open University of the Netherlands, Amsterdam, Netherlands

Ari Kissiloff, Ithaca College, Ithaca, NY

Peter Korovessis, The American College of Greece, Athens, Greece

Sallie Kravetz, Annapolis High School, Annapolis, MD

Jeff Kushner, James Madison University, Harrisonburg, VA

Theresa McHugh, BIHE, Bolton, Gtr. Manchester, UK

Ken Messersmith, University of Nebraska at Kearney, Kearney, NE

Marianne Nilsson, School of Mathematics and Systems Engineering, Växjö, Sweden

Lyn Pemberton, University of Brighton, Brighton, UK

Samuel Shiffman, Seton Hall University, South Orange, NJ

Dennis Woytek, Duquesne University, Pittsburgh, PA

I would also like to acknowledge many friends in the computer and publishing industries who continue to make this book possible. They send me quotes and multimedia anecdotes to enliven the book; many arranged for me to review and test software and hardware; many have been there when I needed them. Some from editions past have changed companies or left the industry; my friend Dana Atchley, the well-known digital storyteller, has died. Whole companies in the list below have died, too, since the first edition of this book, but their passing is mourned differently from the heartfelt loss of the real people and real creators who have launched the information age. I would like to thank them all for the time and courtesy they have afforded me on this long-legged project:

Grace Abbett, Adobe Systems

Jennifer Ackman, Edelman Worldwide

Eric Alderman, HyperMedia Group

Heather Alexander, Waggener/Edstrom

Laura Ames, Elgin/Syferd PR

Kurt Andersen, Andersen Design

Ines Anderson, Claris

Travis Anton, BoxTop Software

David Antoniuk, Live Oak Multimedia

Yasemin Argun, Corel Systems

Cornelia Atchley, Comprehensive Technologies

Dana Atchley, Network Productions

Pamela Atkinson, Pioneer Software

Paul Babb, Maxon Computer

Ann Bagley, Asymetrix

Patricia Baird, Hypermedia Journal

Gary Baker, Technology Solutions

Richard Bangs, Mountain Travel-Sobek

Sean Barger, Equilibrium

Jon Barrett, Dycam

Kathryn Barrett, O'Reilly

Heinz Bartesch, The Search Firm

Bob Bauld, Bob Bauld Productions

Thomas Beinar, Add-On America/Rohm

Bob Bell, SFSU Multimedia Studies Program

George Bell, Ocron

Mike Bellefeuille, Corel Systems

Andrew Bergstein, Altec Lansing

Kathy Berlan, Borland International

Camarero Bernard, mFactory

Brian Berson, Diamondsoft

Bren Besser, Unlimited Access

Time Bigoness, Equilibrium

Nancy Blachman, Variable Symbols

Dana Blankenhorn, Have Modem Will Travel

Brian Blum, The Software Toolworks

Sharon Bodenschatz, International Typeface

Michele Boeding, ICOM Simulations

Donna Booher, Timestream

Brad Borch, Activa Digital Media

Gail Bower, TMS

Kellie Bowman, Adobe

Susan Boyer, Blue Sky Software

Deborah Brown, Technology Solutions

Eric Brown, NewMedia Magazine

Russell Brown, Adobe Systems

Tiffany Brown, Network Associates

Stephanie Bryan, SuperMac

Ann Marie Buddrus, Digital Media Design

David Bunnell, NewMedia Magazine

Jeff Burger, Creative Technologies

Bridget Burke, Gryphon Software

Dominique Busso, OpenMind

Ben Calica, Tools for the Mind

Doug Campbell, Spinnaker Software

Teri Campbell, MetaCreations

Doug Camplejohn, Apple Computer

Norman Cardella, Best-Seller

Tim Carrigan, Multimedia Magazine

Herman Chin, Computer Associates International

Jane Chuey, Macromedia

Curtis Christiansen, Deneba Software

Angie Ciarloni, Hayes

Kevin Clark, Strata

Cathy Clarke, DXM Productions

Frank Colin, Equilibrium

David Collier, decode communications
David Conti, AimTech
Freda Cook, Aldus
Renee Cooper, Miramar Systems
Wendy Cornish, Vividus
Patrick Crisp, Caere
Michelle Cunningham, Symantec
Lee Curtis, CE Software
Eric Dahlinger, Newer Technology
John deLorimier, Kallisto Productions
Jeff Dewey, Luminaria
Jennifer Doettling, Delta Point
Hank Duderstadt, Timestream
Mike Duffy, The Software Toolworks
Eileen Ebner, McLean Public Relations
Dawn Echols, Oracle
Dorothy Eckel, Specular International
Joyce Edwards, Timestream
Kevin Edwards, c|net
Mark Edwards, Independent Multimedia Developer
Dan Elenbaas, Amaze!
Ellen Elias, O'Reilly & Associates
Shelly Ellison, Tektronix
Heidi Elmer, Sonic Foundry
Kathy Englar, RayDream
Jonathan Epstein, MPC World
Jeff Essex, Audio Synchrosy
Sharron Evans, Graphic Directions
Kiko Fagan, Attorney at Law
Joe Fantuzzi, Macromedia
Lee Feldman, Voxware
Laura Finkelman, S & S Communications
Holly Fisher, MetaTools
Terry Fleming, Timeworks
Patrick Ford, Microsoft
Marty Fortier, Prosonus
Robin Galipeau, Mutual/Hadwen Imaging
Kathy Gardner, Gardner Associates
Peter Gariepy, Zedcor
Bill Gates, Microsoft
Petra Gerwin, Mathematica
John Geyer, Terran Interactive
Jonathan Gibson, Form and Function
Karen Giles, Borland
Amanda Goodenough, AmandaStories

Danny Goodman, Concentrics Technology
Howard Gordon, Xing Technology
Jonathan Graham, Iomega
Catherine Greene, LightSource
Fred Greguras, Fenwick & West
Maralyn Guarino, Blue Sky Software
Cari Gushiken, Copithorne & Bellows
Kim Haas, McLean Public Relations
Marc Hall, Deneba Software
Johan Hamberg, Timestream
Lynda Hardman, CWI - Netherlands
Tom Hargadon, Conference Communications
Chip Harris, InHouse Productions
Sue Hart, FileMaker
Trip Hawkins, 3DO/Electronic Arts
Randy Haykin, Apple Computer
Jodi Hazzan, SoftQuad
Ray Heizer, Heizer Software
Dave Heller, Salient Software
Josh Hendrix, CoSA
Maria Hermanussen, Gold Disk
Allan Hessenflow, HandMade Software
Lars Hidde, The HyperMedia Group
Dave Hobbs, LickThis
Petra Hodges, Mathematica
John Holder, John V. Holder Software
Elena Holland, Traveling Software
Mike Holm, Apple Computer
Robert Hone, Red Hill Studios
Kevin Howat, MacMillan Digital
Joy Hsu, Sonnet Technologies
Tom Hughes, PhotoDisc
Claudia Husemann, Cunningham Communications
Les Inanchy, Sony CD-ROM Division
Tom Inglesby, Manufacturing Systems
Carl Jaffe, Yale University School of Medicine
Farrah Jinha, Vertigo 3D
Cynthia Johnson, BoxTop Software
Scott Johnson, NTERGAID
JoAnn Johnston, Regis McKenna
Neele Johnston, Autodesk
Jedidah Karanja, Genealogy.com
Dave Kaufer, Waggener/Edstrom
David Kazanjian, AFTRA Actor
Jenna Keller, Alexander Communications

Helen Kendrick, Software Publishing

Benita Kenn, Creative Labs

Trudy Kerr, Alexander Communications

Gary Kevorkian, ULead Systems

Deirdre Kidd, Nemetschek

David Kleinberg, NetObjects

Jeff Kleindinst, Turtle Beach Systems

Kevin Klingler, Sonic Desktop Software

Sharon Klocek, Visual In-Seitz

Christina Knighton, Play Incorporated

Lewis Kraus, InfoUse

Katrina Krebs, Micrografx

Kevin Krejci, Pop Rocket

Larry Kubo, Ocron

Howard Kwak, Multimedia SourceBook

Irving Kwong, Waggener/Edstrom

Craig LaGrow, Morph's Outpost

Kimberly Larkin, Alexander Communications

Kevin LaRue, Allegiant Technologies

Mark Law, Extensis

Nicole Lazzaro, ONYX Productions

Alan Levine, Maricopa Community Colleges

Bob LeVitus, LeVitus Productions

Steven Levy, MacWorld

Leigh-Ann Lindsey, Mathematica

Rob Lippincott, Lotus

Mark Lissick, C-Star Technology

Jason Lockhart, G3 Systems

Elliot Luber, Technology Solutions

David Ludwig, Interactive Learning Designs

Kirk Lyford, Vivid Details

Jennifer Lyng, Aladdin Systems

John MacLeod, FastForward

Philip Malkin, Passport Designs

Kevin Mallon, FileMaker

Basil Maloney, Winalysis

Kathy Mandle, Adobe

Audrey Mann, Technology Solutions

Lisa Mann, O'Reilly

Nicole Martin, Netopia/Farallon Division

Robert May, Ikonic

Georgia McCabe, Applied Graphics Technologies

Russ McCann, Ares Software

Kevin McCarthy, Medius IV

Charles McConathy, MicroNet Technology

Carol McGarry, Schwartz Communications

Laurie McLean, McLean Public Relations

Amy McManus, Delta Point

Bert Medley, "The NBC Today Show"

Art Metz, Metz

Steve Michel, Author

Aline Mikaelian, Screenplay Systems

Nancy Miller, Canto Software

Doug Millison, Morph's Outpost

Karen Milne, Insignia Solutions

Brian Molyneaux, Heizer Software

Molly Morelock, Macromedia

Jeff Morgan, Radmedia

Rob Morris, VGraph

Glenn Morrisey, Asymetrix

Terry Morse, Terry Morse Software

Rachel Muñoz, Caere

Philip Murray, Knowledge Management Associates

Chuck Nakell, Inspiration Software

Kee Nethery, Kagi Engineering

Chris Newell, Musitek

Mark Newman, Photographer

Wendy Woods Newman, Newsbytes

Terry Nizko, AimTech

Glenn Ochsenreiter, MPC Marketing Council

Maureen O'Conell, Apple Computer

Jim O'Gara, Altsys

Eric Olson, Virtus

Karen Oppenheim, Cunningham Communications

Kim Osborne, Symantec

Nicole DeMeo Overson, GoLive Systems

Andy Parng, PixoArts

David Pawlan, Timestream

Susan Pearson, Waggener/Edstrom

Lorena Peer, Chroma Graphics

Steve Peha, Music Technology Associates

Sylvester Pesek, Optical Media International

Christiane Petite, Symantec

Paul Phelan, INESC (Portugal)

Scott Pink, Bronson

Audrey Pobre, Quarterdeck

Dave Pola, Equilibrium

JB Popplewell, Alien Skin Software

Melissa Rabin, Miramar

Shirley Rafieetary, Medius IV

Tom Randolph, FM Towns/Fujitsu
Steven Rappaport, Interactive Records
Ronelle Reed, Switzer Communications
David Reid, Author
Diane Reynolds, Graphsoft
Laurie Robinson, Gold Disk
Connie Roloff, Software Products International
John Rootenberg, Paceworks
Steve Rubenstein, San Francisco Chronicle
Jill Ryan, McLean Public Relations
Marie Salerno, AFTRA/SAG
John Sammis, DataDescription
Jay Sandom, Einstein & Sandom
Pam Sansbury, Disc Manufacturing
Richard Santalesa, R&D Technologies
Anne Sauer, Fast Electronic U.S.
Joe Scarano, DS Design
Sonya Schaefer, Adobe
Rochelle Schiffman, Electronics for Imaging
Rachel Schindler, Macromedia
Melissa Scott, Window Painters
Sandy Scott, Soft-Kat
Brigid Sealy, INESC (Portugal)
Karl Seppala, Gold Disk
Chip Shabazian, Ocron
Ashley Sharp, Virtus
Elizabeth Siedow, Macromedia
Adam Silver, Videologic
Stephanie Simpson, Adaptec
Marlene Sinicki, Designer
Chris Smith, VideoLabs
Brian Snook, Visual In-Seitz
Kent Sokoloff, Timestream
Simone Souza, Roxio
David Spitzer, Hewlett-Packard
Domenic Stansberry, Author
Ann Stewart, Interactive Dimensions
Polina Sukonik, Xaos Tools
Lisa Sunaki, Autodesk
Lee Swearingen, DXM Productions
Joe Taglia, Insignia Solutions

Meredith Taitz, Bare Bones Software
Marty Taucher, Microsoft
Bill Tchakirides, U-Design Type Foundry
Toni Teator, NetObjects
Amy Tenderich, Norton-Lambert
Lori Ternacole, SoftQuad
Dave Terran, WordPerfect
Leo Thomas, Eastman Kodak
Terry Thompson, Timestream
Bill Thursby, Thursby Software Systems
Alexandrea Todd, McLean Public Relations
Kim Tompkins, Micrografx
Tom Toperczer, Imspace Systems
Cara Ucci, Autodesk
Ross Uchimura, GC3
Jane Van Saun, Scansoft
David Vasquez, SFSU Multimedia Studies Program
Sally von Bargen, 21st Century Media
Dan Wagner, Miramar Systems
Helayne Waldman, SFSU Multimedia Studies Program
James J. Waldron, Visage
Arnold Waldstein, Creative Labs
Keri Walker, Apple Computer
Brad Walter, Leister Productions
Stefan Wennik, Bitstream
Chris Wheeler, TechSmith
Tom White, Roland
John Wilczak, HSC Software
Darby Williams, Microsoft
Laura Williams, Waggener/Edstrom
Mark Williams, Microsoft
Shelly Williams, Prosonus
Hal Wine, Programmer
Sara Winge, O'Reilly & Associates
Warren Witt, Thursby Software Systems
Marcus Woehrmann, Handmade Software
Sandy Wong, Fenwick & West
Chris Yalonis, Passport Designs
Alexandra Yessios, auto*des*sys
Barbara Zediker, Pioneer
Frank Zellis, KyZen

Introduction

In the four editions of this book since 1992, I have begun its introduction with the following sentence:

> "In a few years, multimedia computers will be an anachronism because all computers will readily deal with images, sounds, and motion video, seamlessly and smoothly integrated into what a computer *is*."

Now, after almost ten years, this prophecy has been fulfilled! Catalogs and e-commerce sites offer affordable desktop and laptop systems with high-powered processors, gigabytes of hard drive memory, DVD-ROM drives, high-resolution monitors showing millions of colors, stereo and surround sound, and built-in video cameras. So the specialness of multimedia computer hardware has disappeared, and we can take sound, animation, and video features for granted. This is what a computer *does*.

Happily for the longevity of this book, however, the fundamental concepts and techniques required to work with the elements of multimedia remain unchanged, and there are serious learning curves to climb before you can make your new multimedia-capable computer stand up and dance!

This is a book about the basic parts of multimedia as much as about how to sew these parts together with current technology and tools. It is a book that shows you how to use text, images, sound, and video to deliver your messages and content in meaningful ways. It is about designing, organizing, and producing multimedia projects of all kinds and avoiding technical and legal pitfalls along the way. Above all, it is a practical guide to making multimedia, complete with tips, pointers, and answers.

The first part deals with the basic elements of multimedia. Hardware and software tools are described in detail. You will learn about the importance of text and how to make characters look pretty, about making graphic art on your computer and how to choose colors, and about how to digitize sound and video segments. You will learn about human interaction and how to design a user-friendly computer interface. Then you will be introduced to the step-by-step creative and organizing process that results in a finished multimedia project. You will even learn how to deliver your multimedia projects on the Web.

I have written this book for people who make or want to make multimedia, for people who gladly take up new challenges and are unafraid of intensely creative work. The words and ideas of this book are the harvest of many years in the computer industry and of hands-on experience deep in the factory where multimedia is being made daily. The book is intended to be, above all, useful.

For focus, I chose two well-known computer environments to discuss in detail throughout the book: Microsoft's Windows and Apple's Macintosh—the most widely used platforms for making and delivering multimedia today. But multimedia is by no means limited to these platforms, and most of the ideas discussed in the book are translatable to the Macintosh OS-X and Linux/Unix operating systems. Today, the fastest moving wavefront in multimedia may be seen on the Internet, so I have updated and enlarged the chapters about designing, creating, and delivering multimedia for the Web.

I have made a great effort to include in this book references to as much multimedia software and hardware as I could, trying not to miss any players. But because the industry is fast paced and rapidly evolving, and because, while writing this book, I have rediscovered the finite limits of my own time, I am sure some have fallen into the bit bucket anyway. Immutable physical laws have prevented me from including the fine details of 40 or 50 hardware and software manuals and technical resources into the pages allowed for this book. The distillation presented here should, however, point you toward further information and study. I have also made a great effort to double-check my words and statements for accuracy; if errors have slipped past, they are mine alone.

Some years ago, after completing a book about HyperCard, I swore never to write another. Writing a book is much like childbirth, I believe. In the beginning, it gestates slowly, usually over a few months. Then it ramps up inexorably and quickly toward deadline, until all attention is focused upon the delivery itself, and the pain and workload are great. Editors cry, "Push." Afterwards, you remember it was rough, but memories of the pain itself become diffused, and one is only too easily persuaded to do it again. I am glad to share my multimedia experiences with you, and hope that in reading this book you will become better at what you do.

Tay Vaughan
Appleton, Maine
June 2001

About the Author...

Tay Vaughan is a widely renowned multimedia authority. He has developed and produced award-winning projects for clients such as Apple, Microsoft, Lotus, Novell, and Sun. He is president of Timestream®, a multi-format CD-ROM and Internet design and development company.

Multi

Multimedia is any combination

> Multimedia excites
> eyes, ears, fingertips,
> and, most importantly,
> the head.

When you **weave** together the sensual elements of multmedia -

interactive control

media

text, graphic art, sound, animation and video

part

I

Introduction

■ — dazzling
pictures
and
animations,
engaging
sounds,
compelling
video clips —
you can electrify the thought and action centers of people's minds.

in·for·ma·tion

Multimedia is any combination

[
A revolution is taking place
today in the way humans
access, learn, and interact
with information.
]

When you **weave** together the sensual elements of multmedia -

interactive control

media

chapter

I

What Is Multimedia?

■ — dazzling
pictures
and
animations,
engaging
sounds,
compelling
video clips —
you can electrify the thought and action centers of people's minds.

in·for·ma·tion

M

ULTIMEDIA is an eerie wail as two cat's eyes appear on a dark screen. It's the red rose that dissolves into a little girl's face when you press "Valentine's Day." It's a small window of video laid onto a map of India, showing an old man recalling his dusty journey to meet a rajah there. It's a catalog of fancy cars with a guide to help you buy one. It's a real-time video conference with colleagues in Paris, London, and Hong Kong on your office computer. At home, it's an algebra or geography lesson for a fifth-grader. At the arcade, it's goggle-faced kids flying fighter planes in sweaty virtual reality.

Multimedia is any combination of text, graphic art, sound, animation, and video delivered to you by computer or other electronic means. It is richly presented sensation. When you weave together the sensual elements of multimedia—dazzling pictures and animations, engaging sounds, compelling video clips, and raw textual information—you can electrify the thought and action centers of people's minds. When you give them interactive control of the process, they can be enchanted. Multimedia excites eyes, ears, fingertips, and, most importantly, the head.

This book is about creating each of the elements of multimedia and about how you can weave them together for maximum effect. This book is for computer beginners and computer experts. It is for serious multimedia producers and their clients, as well. It is for desktop publishers and video producers who may need a leg-up as they watch traditional methods for delivery of information and ideas evolve into new, technology-driven formats. This book is also for hobbyists, who want to make albums and family histories on the World Wide Web; for mainstream businesses, where word-processed documents and spreadsheets are illustrated with audio, video, and graphic animations; for public speakers, who use animation and sound on large monitors and auditorium projection systems to present ideas and information to an audience; for information managers, who organize and distribute digital images, sound, video, and text; and for educators and trainers, who design and present information for learning.

The implementation of multimedia capabilities in computers is just the latest episode in a long series: cave painting, hand-crafted manuscripts, the printing press, radio and television... These advances reflect the innate desire of man to create outlets for creative expression, to use technology and imagination to gain empowerment and freedom for ideas.

Glenn Ochsenreiter, Director, Multimedia PC Council

If you are new to multimedia and are facing a major investment in hardware, software, and the time to learn each new tool, take a gradual approach to these challenges. Begin by studying each element of multimedia and learning one or more tools for creating and editing that element. Get to know how to use text and fonts, how to make and edit colorful graphic images and animate them into movies, and how to record and edit digital sound. Read the computer trade periodicals that contain the most up-to-date information. Your skills will be most valuable if you develop a broad foundation of knowledge about each of the basic elements of multimedia.

Producing a multimedia project or a Web site requires more than creative skill and high technology. You need organizing and business talent as well. For example, issues of ownership and copyright will be attached to some elements that you wish to use: text from books, scanned images from magazines, audio and video clips. These require permission and often payment of a fee to the owner. Indeed, the management and production infrastructure of a multimedia project may be as intense and complicated as the technology and creative skills you bring to bear in rendering it.

Definitions

Multimedia is, as described above, woven combinations of text, graphic art, sound, animation, and video elements. When you allow an end user—the viewer of a multimedia project—to control what and when the elements are delivered, it is *interactive multimedia*. When you provide a structure of linked elements through which the user can navigate, interactive multimedia becomes *hypermedia*.

Although the definition of multimedia is a simple one, making it work can be complicated. Not only do you need to understand how to make each multimedia element stand up and dance, but you also need to know how to use multimedia computer tools and technologies to weave them together. The people who weave multimedia into meaningful tapestries are *multimedia developers*.

The software vehicle, the messages, and the content presented on a computer or television screen—together constitute a *multimedia project*. If the project will be shipped or sold to consumers or end users, typically in a box or sleeve or on the Internet, with or without instructions, it is a *multimedia title*. Your project may also be a *page* or *site* on the World Wide Web, where you can weave the elements of multimedia into HTML (Hypertext Markup Language) or DHTML (Dynamic Hypertext Markup Language) documents and use plug-ins like Macromedia's Flash, Adobe's LiveMotion, or Apple's QuickTime to display your multimedia work using a *browser* application such as Internet Explorer or Netscape Navigator. See Chapter 14 for more about multimedia and the Web.

A multimedia project need not be interactive to be called multimedia: users can sit back and watch it just as they do a movie or the television. In such cases a project is *linear*, starting at a beginning and running through to an end. When users are given navigational control and can wander through the content at will, multimedia becomes *nonlinear* and interactive, and is a powerful personal gateway to information.

Determining how a user will interact with and navigate through the content of a project requires great attention to the message, the *scripting* or *storyboarding*, the artwork, and the programming. You can break an entire project with a badly designed interface. You can also break a project with inadequate or inaccurate content.

Multimedia elements are typically sewn together into a project using *authoring tools*. These software tools are designed to manage individual multimedia elements and provide user interaction. In addition to providing a method for users to interact with the project, most authoring tools also offer facilities for creating and editing text and images, and they have extensions to drive videodisc players, videotape players, and other relevant hardware peripherals. Sounds and movies are usually created with editing tools dedicated to these media, and then the elements are imported into the authoring system for playback. The sum of what gets played back and how it is presented to the viewer is the *graphical user interface*, or GUI (pronounced "gooey"). This interface is just as much the rules for what happens to the user's input as it is the actual graphics on the screen. The hardware and software that govern the limits of what can happen are the multimedia *platform* or *environment*.

CD-ROM and the Multimedia Highway

Multimedia requires large amounts of digital memory when stored in an end user's library, or large amounts of *bandwidth* when distributed over wires or glass fiber on a network.

CD-ROM and Multimedia

CD-ROM (compact disc read-only memory, see Chapter 19) has emerged during the last few years as the most cost-effective distribution medium for multimedia projects: a CD-ROM disc can be mass-produced for pennies and can contain up to 84 minutes of full-screen video or sound. Or it can contain unique mixes of images, sounds, text, video, and animations controlled by an authoring system to provide unlimited user interaction.

Discs can be stamped out of polycarbonate plastic as fast as cookies on a baker's production line. Most personal computers sold today include a CD-ROM player, and the software that drives these computers is commonly available on a CD-ROM disc—applications that required inserting as many as 16 or more floppy disks one after another are now installed from a CD-ROM without muss or fuss. Multilayered Digital Versatile Disc (DVD) technology is on the way toward general usage and will increase the capacity and multimedia capability of current CD-ROM optical technology. CD *burners* are used for reading CDs and for making them too, in both audio and data formats.

In the very long term, however, CD-ROM and DVD are but interim memory technologies that will be replaced by new devices that do not require moving parts. As the data highway described below becomes more and more pervasive and users become more easily "connected," copper wire, glass fiber, and radio/cellular technologies may prevail as the most commonly used delivery means for interactive multimedia.

The Multimedia Highway

Now that telecommunications networks are global, and when information providers and content owners determine the worth of their products and how to charge money for them, information elements will ultimately link up online as distributed resources on a data highway (actually more like a toll road), where you will pay to acquire and use multimedia-based information.

Curiously, the actual glass fiber cables that make up much of the physical backbone of the data highway are, in many cases, owned by railroads and pipeline companies who simply buried the cable on existing rights of way where no special permits and environmental reports are necessary. One railroad in the United States invested more than a million dollars in a special cable-laying trenching car; in Great Britain, there is talk of placing a fiber-optic cable backbone along the decaying 19th-century canal and barge system. Bandwidth on these lines is leased to others, so competing retailers such as AT&T, MCI, and Sprint may even share the same cable.

Full-text content from books and magazines will be accessible by modem and electronic link; feature movies will be played at home; real-time news reports from anywhere on earth will be available; lectures from participating universities will be monitored for education credits; street maps of any city will be viewable—with recommendations for restaurants, in any language—and online travelogues will include testimonials and video tracks. This is not science fiction; it is happening now. Each of these interfaces or gateways to information is a multimedia project just waiting to be developed.

http://www.moviefone.com
http://www.nyfood.com
http://www.travelocity.com
http://www.nytimes.com

Show times for many major cities, restaurants, vacation trips, and current news items are quickly available on the Web

In a few years, interactive multimedia will be delivered to many homes throughout the world. Interest from a confluence of entertainment megacorps, information publishers and providers, cable and telephone companies, and hardware and software manufacturers is already driving this inevitable evolution, and profound changes in global communications strategy are on the drawing boards. What will be piped through this new system are the very multimedia elements discussed in the chapters of this book: text, graphics, animation, sound, and video. The software tools for making and editing these elements are discussed in Part 3; the methods for delivering these elements on the Internet are described in Chapter 14.

Entertainment companies that own content easily converted to multimedia projects are teaming up with cable TV companies such as QVC or Viacom (owner of MTV, Showtime, and Nickelodeon). Film studios such as Disney and Warner Brothers are creating new divisions to produce interactive multimedia, and wealthy talents like Spielberg, Katzenberg, and Geffen (DreamWorks) have formed new companies to join the action. Already, large media corporations are uniting to create huge conglomerates that will control the content of tomorrow's information. Disney has merged with Capital Cities/ABC, Time Warner has purchased Turner Broadcasting, and Microsoft has joined forces with NBC. Indeed, Microsoft's interests in the growing Internet are so pervasive that it risks breakup and reorganization by the government under antitrust and monopoly laws, as was required of AT&T, the telephone giant.

Some companies will own the routes for carrying data, other companies will own the hardware and software interfaces at the end of the line, at offices and homes. Some will knit it all together and provide supply-on-demand and billing services. Regardless of who owns the roadways and the hardware boxes, multimedia producers will create the new literature and the rich content sent along it. This is a fresh and exciting industry coming of age, but one still faced with many growing pains.

Where to Use Multimedia

Multimedia is appropriate whenever a human interface connects a human user to electronic information of any kind. Multimedia enhances minimalist text-only computer interfaces and yields measurable benefit by gaining and holding attention and interest; multimedia improves information retention. When properly woven, multimedia can also be profoundly entertaining.

Multimedia is a very effective presentation and sales tool. If you're being driven somewhere in the back seat of a car, you may not remember how you got to your destination; but if you had been driving the car yourself, chances are you could get there again. Studies indicate that if you're stimulated with audio, you will have about a 20 percent retention rate, audiovisual is up to 30 percent, and in interactive multimedia presentations where you are really involved, the retention rate is as high as 60 percent.

Jay Sandom, Einstein & Sandom

Multimedia in Business

Business applications for multimedia include presentations, training, marketing, advertising, product demos, databases, catalogues, and networked communications. Voice mail and video conferencing will soon be provided on many local and wide area networks (LANs and WANs) using Internet protocols.

After a morning of mind-numbing 35 mm slide and overhead presentations delivered from the podium of a national sales conference, a multimedia presentation can make an audience come alive. Most presentation software packages let you add audio and video clips to the usual "slide show" of graphics and text material (see Chapter 6).

Multimedia is enjoying widespread use in training programs. Flight attendants learn to manage international terrorism and security through simulation. Mechanics learn to repair engines. Salespeople learn about product lines and leave behind software to train their customers. Fighter pilots practice full-terrain sorties before spooling up for the real thing. Figure 1-1 is from an animated project made with Macromedia's Director that describes the process of making steel.

Multimedia around the office has become more commonplace. Figure 1-2 shows VideoLabs' FlexCam, an inexpensive add-on video camera and stereo microphone unit. Connectix's popular QuickCam lets you add a gray-scale camera to your PC or Mac for less than $100, and Nokia sells a high-resolution Trinitron monitor (the "447K") that integrates a video camera, a microphone, and full-range stereo speakers. Such video capture hardware can be used for building employee ID and badging databases, for video annotation,

FIGURE 1-1

Animated instructional and training multimedia can simulate the real thing, allowing trainees to actually turn valves and flip switches

and for real-time teleconferencing. Laptop computers equipped with the fastest processors come complete with CD-ROM drives and are ready for multimedia presentations on the road.

As companies and businesses catch on to the power of multimedia, and the cost of installing multimedia capability decreases, more applications will be developed both in-house and by third parties to allow businesses to run more smoothly and efficiently.

Multimedia in Schools

Schools are perhaps the most needy destination for multimedia. Many schools in the United States today are chronically underfunded and occasionally slow to adopt new technologies, but it is here that the power of multimedia can be maximized for the greatest long-term benefit to all.

In March 1995, the White House challenged the telecommunications industry to connect every classroom, library, clinic, and hospital to the information superhighway by the year 2000. The White House has also taken steps to provide governmental support for state-of-the-art technology in low-income rural and urban school districts.

FIGURE 1-2

VideoLabs' FlexCam (neatly implemented by Worrell Design of Minneapolis, MN) can be used for video capture and videoconferencing

Technological literacy must become the standard in our country. Preparing children for a lifetime of computer use is just as essential today as teaching them the basics of reading, writing, and arithmetic.

Bill Clinton, Former President of the United States

http://www.wvaworldschool.org
http://www.svi.org/

Verizon's WORLD SCHOOL Project is connecting more than 700 West Virginia schools to the Internet; Smart Valley, Inc., is a nonprofit Silicon Valley consortium providing advice and technical support to schools on the Internet

Multimedia will provoke radical changes in the teaching process during the coming decades, particularly as smart students discover they can go beyond the limits of traditional teaching methods. Indeed, in some instances, teachers may become more like guides and mentors along a learning path, not the primary providers of information and understanding—the students, not teachers, become the core of the teaching and learning process. This is a sensitive and highly politicized subject among educators, so educational software is often positioned as "enriching" the learning process, not as a potential substitute for traditional teacher-based methods.

An interactive episode of Wild Kingdom might start out with normal narration. "We're here in the Serengeti to learn about the animals." I see a lion on the screen and think, "I want to learn about the lion." So I point at the lion, and it zooms up on the screen. The narration is now just about the lion. I say, "Well that's really interesting, but I wonder how the lion hunts." I point at a hunt icon. Now the lion is hunting, and the narrator tells me about how it hunts. I dream about being the lion. I select another icon and now see the world from the lion's point of view, making the same kinds of decisions the lion has to make—with some hints as I go along. I'm told how I'm doing and how well I'm surviving. Kids could get very motivated from experiencing what it's like to be a lion and from wanting to be a competent lion. Pretty soon they'd be digging deeper into the information resource, finding out about animals in different parts of the world, studying geography from maps displayed on the screen, learning which animals are endangered species...

Trip Hawkins, Chairman & CEO, 3DO Company

Multimedia for learning takes many forms. Figure 1-3 shows Mercer Meyer's pioneering and award-winning classic "Just Grandma and Me," aimed at three- to eight-year-olds. Reading skills grow through word recognition: a mouse click on any word plays it back. The computer reads the story aloud, sometimes spelling words individually. Click on the mailbox and a frog jumps out; the chimney coughs smoke; the telephone rings, but nobody is home, and you hear Grandma's answering machine. Wait 'til you get to the beach! Figure 1-4, at the other end of the educational continuum, shows the title screen from an advanced electronic teaching tool prepared by Yale University School of Medicine. It provides physicians with over 100 case presentations and gives cardiologists, radiologists, medical students, and fellows an opportunity for in-depth learning of new clinical techniques in nuclear cardiac perfusion imaging. Adults, as well as children, learn well by exploration and discovery.

An interesting use of multimedia in schools involves the students themselves. Students put together interactive magazines and newsletters, they make original art using image editing tools (see Chapter 10), they interview students and townspeople and coaches and teachers, and they make QuickTime movies (see Chapter 5). They design and run Web sites.

FIGURE 1-3

"Just Grandma and Me" is aimed at developing reading skills, but it also entertains with interactive sights and sounds

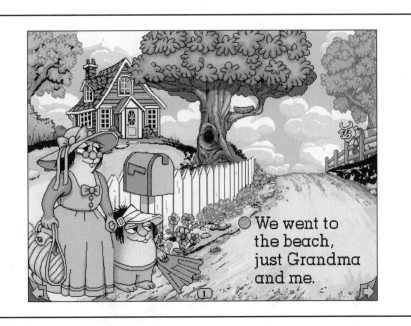

FIGURE 1-4

This multimedia project from Yale University School of Medicine lets physicians and radiology professionals learn new technologies at their own pace
■

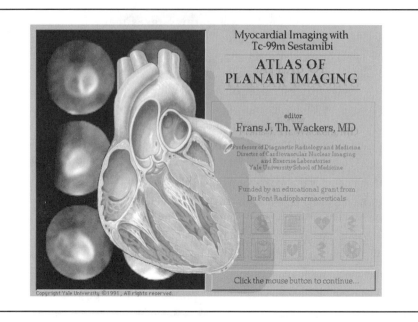

http://www.elibrary.com
http://www.lib.umich.edu/chhome.html
http://sunsite.unc.edu/cisco/cisco-home.html
http://www.ucalgary.ca/~dkbrown/index.html
http://web66.coled.umn.edu/schools.html
http://gda.org

From homework helpers to literature guides to school registries to home pages and information servers, education is finding a place on the World Wide Web

At one time, laserdiscs brought the greatest amount of multimedia to the classroom—in 1994, there were more than 2,500 educational titles available on laserdisc for grades K–12, the majority aimed at science and social science curricula. Use of laserdiscs has been supplanted as schools have purchased more computers with CD-ROM players. And as schools become part of the Internet, multimedia arrives by glass fiber and network.

Multimedia at Home

From gardening to cooking to home design, remodeling, and repair to genealogy software (see Figure 1-5), multimedia has entered the home. Eventually, most multimedia projects will reach the home via television sets or monitors with built-in interactive user inputs—either on old-fashioned color TVs or on new high-definition sets (see Chapter 12). The multimedia viewed on these sets will likely arrive on a pay-for-use basis along the data highway.

Today, home consumers of multimedia either own a computer with an attached CD-ROM drive or a set-top player that hooks up to the television, such as a Sega or Nintendo or Sony game machine. There is increasing convergence of computer-based multimedia with entertainment and games-based media traditionally described as "shoot-em-up." Nintendo alone has sold over 100 million game players worldwide and more than 750 million games.

Live Internet pay-for-play gaming with multiple players has become popular, bringing multimedia to homes on the data highway, often in combination with locally inserted CD-ROMs. Microsoft's Internet Gaming Zone and Sony's Station Web site boast more than a million registered users each—Microsoft claims to be the most successful, with tens of thousands of people logged on and playing every evening.

The home of the future will be very different when the cost of computer hardware and multimedia televisions becomes mass-market affordable and the multimedia connection to the data highway is widely available. When the number of multimedia households increases from hundreds of thousands to many millions, a vast selection of multimedia titles and material will be required to satisfy the demands of this market, and vast amounts of money will be earned producing and distributing these multimedia products.

FIGURE   1-5

Genealogy software such as Reunion from Leister Productions lets families add text, images, sounds, and video clips as they build their family trees

Multimedia in Public Places

In hotels, train stations, shopping malls, museums, and grocery stores, multimedia will become available at stand-alone terminals or kiosks to provide information and help. Such installations reduce demand on traditional information booths and personnel, add value, and they can work round the clock, even in the middle of the night, when live help is off duty.

Figure 1-6 shows a menu screen from a supermarket kiosk that provides services ranging from meal planning to coupons. Hotel kiosks list nearby restaurants, maps of the city, airline schedules, and provide guest services such as automated checkout. Printers are often attached so users can walk away with a printed copy of the information. Museum kiosks are not only used to guide patrons through the exhibits, but when installed at each exhibit, provide great added depth, allowing visitors to browse through richly detailed information specific to that display.

The power of multimedia has been part of the human experience for many thousands of years: the mystical chants of monks, cantors, and shamans accompanied by potent visual cues, raised icons, and persuasive text has long been known to produce effective responses in public places. Scriabin, the 19th-century Russian composer, used an orchestra, a piano, a chorus, and a special color organ to synthesize music and color in his Fifth Symphony, *Prometheus*. Probably suffering from synesthesia (a strange condition where a

FIGURE 1-6

Kiosks in public places can make everyday life simpler

sensory stimulus, such as a color, evokes a false response, such as a smell), Scriabin talked of tactile symphonies with burning incense scored into the work. He also claimed that colors can be heard; Table 1-1 lists the colors of his color organ.

Prometheus premiered before a live audience in Moscow in 1911, but the color organ had proved technologically too complicated and was eliminated from the program. Then Scriabin died suddenly of blood poisoning from a boil on his lip, so his ultimate multimedia vision, the Mysterium, remained unwritten. He would have reveled in today's world of MIDI synthesizers (see Chapter 9), rich computer colors, and video digitizers, and, though smell is not yet part of any multimedia standard, he would surely have researched that concept, too. The platforms for multimedia presentation have much improved since Scriabin's time.

Virtual Reality

At the convergence of technology and creative invention in multimedia is virtual reality, or VR. Goggles, helmets, special gloves, and bizarre human interfaces attempt to place you "inside" a lifelike experience. Take a step forward, and the view gets closer, turn your head, and the view rotates.

Frequency (Hz)	Note	Scriabin's Color
256	C	Red
277	C#	Violet
298	D	Yellow
319	D#	Glint of steel
341	E	Pearly white shimmer of moonlight
362	F	Deep red
383	F#	Bright blue
405	G	Rosy orange
426	G#	Purple
447	A	Green
469	A#	Glint of steel
490	B	Pearly blue

TABLE 1-1   *Scriabin's Color Organ* ∎

Reach out and grab an object; your hand moves in front of you. Maybe the object explodes in a 90-decibel crescendo as you wrap your fingers around it. Or it slips out from your grip, falls to the floor, and hurriedly escapes through a mouse hole at the bottom of the wall.

VR requires terrific computing horsepower to be realistic. In VR, your cyberspace is made up of many thousands of geometric objects plotted in three-dimensional space: the more objects and the more points that describe the objects, the higher the resolution and the more realistic your view. As you move about, each motion or action requires the computer to recalculate the position, angle, size, and shape of *all* the objects that make up your view, and many thousands of computations must occur as fast as 30 times per second to seem smooth.

On the World Wide Web, standards for transmitting virtual reality worlds or "scenes" in VRML (Virtual Reality Modeling Language) documents (with the file name extension .wrl) have been developed. Intel and software makers such as Macromedia and Adobe have announced support for new 3-D technologies. See Chapter 14 for more about 3-D on the Internet.

Using high-speed dedicated computers, multi-million-dollar flight simulators built by Singer, RediFusion, and others have led the way in commercial application of VR. Pilots of F-16s, Boeing 777s, and Rockwell space shuttles have made many dry runs before doing the real thing. At the California Maritime Academy and other merchant marine officer training schools, computer-controlled simulators teach the intricate loading and unloading of oil tankers and container ships.

Specialized public game arcades have been built recently to offer VR combat and flying experiences for a price. From Virtual World Entertainment in Walnut Creek, California, and Chicago, for example, BattleTech is a ten-minute interactive video encounter with hostile robots. You compete against others, perhaps your friends, who share couches in the same Containment Bay. The computer keeps score in a fast and sweaty firefight. Similar "attractions" will bring VR to the public, particularly a youthful public, with increasing presence.

....

BattleTech is pretty cool. I've played the one in Chicago. The key to winning is getting a unit where the controls work smoothly, otherwise you wind up running in circles until someone puts you out of your misery.

....

Rich Santalesa, Editor, *NetGuide* Magazine

The technology and methods for working with three-dimensional images and for animating them are discussed in Chapters 10 and 11. VR is an extension of multimedia—it uses the basic multimedia elements of imagery, sound, and animation. Because it requires instrumented feedback from a wired-up person, VR is perhaps interactive multimedia at its fullest extension.

People who work in VR do not see themselves as part of "multimedia." VR deals with goggles and gloves and is still a research field where no authoring products are available, and you need a hell of a computer to develop the real-time 3-D graphics. Although there is a middle ground covered by such things as QuicktimeVR and VRML that gives multimedia developers a "window" into VR, people often confuse multimedia and VR and want to create futuristic environments using multimedia authoring tools not designed for that purpose.

Takis Metaxis, Assistant Professor of Computer Science, Wellesley College

Multi

You have to have a real yearning
to communicate because multimedia
is creating, essentially, an entirely
new syntax for communication.

good ideas

media

2

Introduction to Making Multimedia

You need hardware, software, and good ideas to make multimedia.

To make *good* multimedia, you need talent and skill.

I n Chapter 1, you learned what multimedia is, what it may become, and where you can experience it. In this chapter, you will be introduced to the workshop where it is made. This chapter provides guidance and suggestions for getting started. Later, more detail about planning a project is provided in Chapter 16. Chapters 4 through 14 deal with the basic concepts and the tools required. In Chapter 17, you will learn about producing, managing, and designing a project. In Chapter 18, you will learn about where to get material and content for your project, and in Chapter 19, you will learn how to test your work and ship it to end users or post it to the Web. If you want to create multimedia yourself, from your own ideas and talents, check your skills against those described in Chapter 3. Chapters 14 and 15 discuss the tools and tricks for making multimedia for the Internet and the World Wide Web.

The Stages of a Project

Most multimedia and Web projects must be undertaken in stages. Some stages should be completed before other stages begin, and some stages may be skipped or combined. Here are the four basic stages in a multimedia project:

1. **Planning and costing:** A project always begins with an idea or a need that you refine by outlining its messages and objectives. Identify how you will make each message and objective work within your authoring system. Before you begin developing, plan what writing skills, graphic art, music, video, and other multimedia expertise will be required. Develop a creative graphic look and feel, as well as a structure and navigation system that will let the viewer visit

the messages and content. Estimate the time needed to do all elements, and prepare a budget. Work up a short prototype or proof-of-concept. The more time you spend getting your arms around your project and defining its content and structure, the faster you can later build it, and less reworking and rearranging will be required midstream. Think it through before you start!

2. **Designing and producing:** Perform each of the planned tasks to create a finished product.

3. **Testing:** Always test your programs to make sure they meet the objectives of your project, they work properly on the intended delivery platforms, and they meet the needs of your client or end user.

4. **Delivering:** Package and deliver the project to the end user.

What You Need

You need hardware, software, and good ideas to make multimedia. To make *good* multimedia, you need talent and skill. You also need to stay organized, because as the construction work gets under way, all the little bits and pieces of multimedia content—the six audio recordings of Alaskan Eskimos, the Christmas-two-years-ago snapshot of your niece, the 41 articles still to scan with your optical character recognition (OCR) program—will get lost under growing piles of paper, cassettes, videotapes, disks, phone messages, permissions and releases, cookie crumbs, Xerox copies, and yesterday's mail. Even in serious offices, where people sweep all flat surfaces of paperwork and rubber bands at five o'clock, there will be mess.

You will need time and money (for consumable resources such as disks and other memory, for telephoning and postage, and possibly for paying for special services and time, yours included), and you will need to budget these precious commodities (see Chapter 16).

You may also need the help of other people. Multimedia is often a team effort: artwork is performed by graphic artists, video shoots by video producers, sound editing by audio producers, and programming by programmers (see Chapter 3). You will certainly wish to provide plenty of coffee and snacks, whether working alone or as a team. Late nights are often involved in the making of multimedia.

You have to have a real yearning to communicate because multimedia is creating, essentially, an entirely new syntax for communication. You must have an interest in human psychology because you need to anticipate the brainwaves of all the potential end users. What will they expect from the program now? What will they want to do with the program now? How can you integrate all the multimedia elements in a really elegant and powerful way? You should adopt a strategy that allows you to prototype and test your interactive design assumptions.

Ann Marie Buddrus, President, Digital Media Design

Hardware

This book will help you understand the two most significant platforms for producing and delivering multimedia projects: the Macintosh OS from Apple and any Intel-based IBM PC or PC clone running Microsoft Windows. These computers, with their graphical user interfaces and huge installed base of many millions of users throughout the world, are the most commonly used platforms today for the development and delivery of multimedia.

Certainly, detailed and animated multimedia is also created on specialized workstations from Silicon Graphics, Sun Microsystems, and even on mainframes, but the Macintosh and the PC offer a compelling combination of affordability, software availability, and worldwide availability. Regardless of the delivery vehicle for your multimedia—whether it is destined to play on a computer, on a television set-top box such as Sega, Nintendo, or Sony, or as bits moving down the data highway—most multimedia will probably be made on a Macintosh or on a PC.

When Windows is discussed in this book, it means *Windows 95/98/ME/2000.* Microsoft introduced Windows 95 with great fanfare in August 1995 to supersede Windows 3.1, and significant enhancements were made for managing multimedia elements. Win95 was then upgraded by Win98, WinME, and Win2000. While it is difficult to conceive of a million of anything (pennies in a drawer, people in a city, bytes on a floppy disk), there are tens of millions of copies of Windows now in use around the world. While the Macintosh platform has been steadily losing market share to Windows, its operating system is in many ways more friendly for multimedia production, and the hardware platforms provided by Apple are better equipped to manage both sound and video editing (see Chapter 4). Hardware and peripherals such as monitors, disk drives, scanners, and network gear are described in Chapter 4. Audio hardware is discussed in Chapter 9, and video hardware is discussed in Chapter 12. The workings and requisite tools of the Internet are discussed in Chapters 13, 14, and 15.

2

The basic principles for creating and editing multimedia elements are the same for Macintoshes and PCs. A bitmap is a bitmap, a digitized sound is a digitized sound, regardless of the methods or tools used to make and display it or play it back. Indeed, many software tools readily convert picture, sound, and other multimedia files (and even whole functioning projects) from Macintosh to Windows format, and vice versa, using known file formats or even *binary compatible* files that require no conversion at all. While there is a lot of talk about platform-independent delivery of multimedia on the Internet, with every new version of a browser there remain annoying failures on both platforms. In this book, the icon shown below will flag complicated or difficult cross-platform issues that may warrant your special attention:

Software

Multimedia software tells the hardware what to do. Display the color red. Move that tiger three leaps to the left. Slide in the words "Now You've Done It!" from the right and blink them on and off. Play the sound of cymbals crashing. Run the digitized movie of Captain Hook. Turn down the volume on that MP3 file!

In this book, the discussion of software is divided into several parts, based on what the software is designed to do for you.

Chapter 5 teaches you about the basic software tools used to work with text, images, sounds, and video; you will also learn about handy tools for capturing screen images, translating between file formats, and editing your resources.

Chapter 6 shows you how to use common tools, such as word processors, spreadsheets, and databases, for presenting instant multimedia—no special authoring systems are required.

In Chapter 7, you'll meet the increasingly wide selection of specialized multimedia authoring tools in detail.

Chapters 14 and 15 discuss techniques and methods for designing and delivering multimedia on the Web.

You do not have to be a programmer or a computer scientist to make multimedia work for you, but you do need some familiarity with terms and building blocks; even the simplest multimedia tools require a modicum of knowledge to operate. If someone asks to borrow a metric 13 mm wrench, you should know they are probably working with a nut or a bolt. If someone

After getting my pilot's license for flying small, single-engine airplanes, I traveled from San Francisco to New York on a Boeing 747. Looking out the window at those pesrfectly circular irrigated farms in Nebraska and Iowa, my lazy thoughts drifted from corn to water to Chevys on levies to girls to football to rope swings splashing into summer rivers. There was a small airport below. Would that make a good emergency field for a dead-stick Cessna? Mmmmm, I drifted.

What if this plane had an emergency? Mmmmm. What if the crew were poisoned and we were on autopilot, and a flight attendant interrupted the movie to ask if there were a pilot on board? Mmmmm. I knew that if I had to sit in the left seat of that 747 I wouldn't have a clue, and the plane would go down. Thousands of switches, glass screens, levers, pedals, blinking lights, and somewhere a radio. Hollywood's version, with the "tower" talking us down, would never work because I couldn't even turn on the radio.

It's like that when you learn multimedia. That sinking feeling. That frustration. That not knowing. But because you have this book in hand, you are already in the pilot's seat and on the learning curve. Relax. Step by step it will get easier. Manuals, online help systems, and instructors are your tower, and you have plenty of fuel. In the same way tens of thousands of pilots have learned to fly, you will learn to make multimedia!

sends you a file in Macintosh AIF format, you should know that you're getting digitized sound. Don't be afraid of the little things that so easily depress the uninformed. From plumbing to nuclear physics, learning is a matter of time and practice. You will be frustrated as you work your way up the learning curves of multimedia. There will be things you want to do, but you will not know how to work the tools. Take the time to learn the fundamentals about computers and multimedia taught in this book. Then load up your tools and open the help files; your learning curve will be easier to manage because you have the bigger picture.

The CD-ROM from Macromedia that is included with this book contains examples and demonstrations of multimedia software applications and projects. Most products on this CD-ROM are "fully functioning" versions of currently shipping software. In most cases, however, the Save command is disabled, so you can experiment with these applications, but you cannot save your work.

From time to time, you will be referred to a site or a number of sites on the World Wide Web for more detailed information or for material that illustrates a point or topic in the book:

http://www.vaughan.org/biotay/biotay1.html

The author's overly long biography

2

You should also know that Web addresses are not guaranteed to be permanent, but like real people's addresses, they disappear when the house burns down or floats away in a flood.

Microsoft.com, walmart.com, mcdonalds.com, and visa.com, however, are such monoliths that it is unlikely they will float away, at least soon, in the river of time. If, when trying to connect to a URL, you receive a "404 - unable to find" error message, try stripping away the directories and subdirectories and file names from the URL and connecting to the domain name itself. If you can connect to the domain name, you may find a menu that will then take you to the relocated document. If, for example, you are looking for a list of tools useful to Web service providers at *http://www.w3.org/hypertext/WWW/Tools/* and the document is not there, try to connect to *http://www.w3.org/*, then follow the hypertext menus provided. If none of these efforts brings you to your destination, you can try a search engine.

http://www.yahoo.com
http://www.lycos.com
http://www.infoseek.com
http://www.ask.com
http://www.excite.com
http://www.google.com
http://www.hotbot.com
http://www.looksmart.com
http://www.altavista.com

Some search engines for the Web

Creativity

Before beginning a multimedia project, you must first develop a sense of its scope and content. Let the project take shape in your head as you think through the various methods available to get your message across to your viewers.

The most precious asset you can bring to the multimedia workshop is your creativity. It's what separates run-of-the-mill and "underwhelming" multimedia from compelling, engaging, and award-winning products, whether for a short sales presentation viewed solely by colleagues within your firm or for a full-blown CD-ROM title.

You have a lot of room for creative risk taking, because the rules for what works and what doesn't work are still being empirically discovered; there are few known formulas for the success of multimedia. Indeed, companies that produce a terrific multimedia title are usually rewarded in the marketplace, but their competitors reverse engineer the product, and six months later knockoffs using similar approaches and techniques appear on the market. Good Web site ideas are easily cloned.

The evolution of multimedia is evident when you look at some of the first multimedia projects done on computers and compare them to today's titles. Taking inspiration from earlier experiments, developers modify and add their own creative touches to design their own unique multimedia projects. For example, "Just Grandma and Me" (see Figure 1-3 in Chapter 1) is an extension of techniques used in an earlier HyperCard children's game (Cosmic Osmo), which in turn is an extension of experiments with interactive virtual desktops in HyperCard. Click on the telephone and up pops a dialing directory, click on the calendar and see your schedule. Click on a flower and it grows. Click on Grandma, and she may warn you about sunscreen. Click on the umbrella, and it blows away in the wind.

It is very difficult to learn creativity. Some might say it's impossible—you have to be born with it. But like classical artists who work in paint, marble, or bronze, the better you know your medium, the better able you are to express your creativity. For multimedia, this means you need to know your hardware and software first. Once you are proficient with the hardware and software tools, what then can you build that will look great, sound great, and knock the socks off the viewer? The rhetorical answer is simply, "How creative are you?"

---

warning   *If you are managing a multimedia project, remember that creative talent is priceless, so be certain to reward it well. If you don't, you may find that your talent takes a job elsewhere, even at lower pay!*

First Person

The Credit Alligator usually appears late in a multimedia project and has nothing to do with MasterCard or Visa. This gnarly animal typically lives unseen in the delicate fringes of workgroup politics, but can appear with great distraction during beta testing, adding moments of personal tension and occasionally destroying friendships and business relationships.

After hard cash, the most satisfying remuneration for your sweaty effort and late-night creative contributions to a multimedia project is to see your name on the credit screen. Indeed, this visible credit is a special high-value currency because it can be added to your portfolio to help you land the next job; the more of this currency, the higher your potential wage. And the more likely you will remain employed doing what you like to do.

Start building defenses against this alligator up front. When you negotiate the original contract with whoever pays the multimedia bill, be sure to include wording such as: "We shall be allowed to include a production credit display on the closing screen or in another *mutually agreeable position in the finished work." If you are an individual who is contracting to a producer, be sure it is understood that if there is a credit screen, your name will be on it.*

Not all clients will stand for a credit screen. Large companies, for example, use many outside contractors to produce multimedia, but as a policy rarely allow contributors to be credited by name. Some contractors and frustrated employees develop ingenious work-arounds and indirections to bury these important intellectual credits within their work.

The Credit Alligator raises its head over the little things, too, and there are often no defenses. If your name begins with a letter that is toward the end of the alphabet, it may never appear first on the list of contributors, even if your contribution was major. Of course, if your name is Walsh or Young, you have endured this ordering system since first-grade lineups.

Warning: reversing an alphabetic credit list from last to first will only create or heighten tension; to propose such a list is, in itself, ego-driven and self-serving. Learn to live with it.

The most treacherous place where the Credit Alligator lives is in the busy time of finalizing a project and "going gold" by producing a final master. If you are not participating in the final mastering but have contributed a piece or pieces to the project, you must trust the masterer to do it right. But it doesn't always happen that way.

One company recently consulted on a job where their work represented the second-greatest contribution from a group of about 15 contributors, all of whom had credit screens. Their contract required credit, but in the final version of the storyboard, they discovered their screen buried at the end of a four-minute linear sequence of all the other credits and advertisements. They asked the producer to move it up. "Sorry,"

said the producer, "it was an oversight." Then in the last-minute process of resequencing, the producer also switched that company's custom music to his own company's credit screen, leaving our friend's screen attached to a pretty ugly leftover sound byte. Because the company was not included in the final feedback and approval loop, they discovered this "little mistake" only after mass replication. It's tough to change 50,000 shrink-wrapped CD-ROMs, so there was nothing to say.

Crediting creative talent is sensitive stuff. Avoid recurring bouts with the Credit Alligator by publicizing among your people your policy about credit screens. Talk about intellectual credit openly, not as a last-minute thing. Negotiate hard for inclusion of credit in all the projects you undertake for clients. Indeed, multimedia doesn't spring from the bankrolls of investors and publishers, but is the result of the hard work of talented real people.

Organization

It's essential that you develop an organized outline and a plan that rationally details the skills, time, budget, tools, and resources you will need for a project. These should be in place before you start to render graphics, sounds, and other components, and they should continue to be monitored throughout the project's execution. Chapter 16 provides planning and costing models for a multimedia project, and Chapter 17 discusses the details of multimedia project management.

Multi

[
Multimedia developers
come from all corners of
the computer, art, literary,
film, and audio worlds.
]

Are multimedia developers computer scientists?

no traditional mold

media

chapter

3

Or are they programmers,
graphic artists, animators,
storyboard
craftspeople,

musicians,

instructional designers,
or Renaissance authors?

Multimedia Skills

Computer scientists, physicians, and dentists share highest honors as the most respected professions in the United States, according to a recent study of occupations. Are multimedia developers computer scientists? Or are they programmers, graphic artists, musicians, animators, storyboard craftspeople, information specialists, instructional designers, and/or Renaissance authors? However you define them, they come from all corners of the computer, art, literary, film, and audio worlds. Video producers become expert with computer-generated animations and MIDI controls for their edit suites. Architects become bored with two-dimensional drafting and create three-dimensional animated walk-throughs. Oil field engineers get tired of FORTRAN and design mouse-driven human interfaces. Classical painters learn the electronic elements of red, green, and blue and create fantastic computer-based artwork. A multimedia developer might be any or all of these and typically fits no traditional management information system (MIS) or computer science mold; many have never seen a line of COBOL code or booted up an IBM 3090 mainframe. Perhaps, in the broadest definition, multimedia developers might simply be called information technology workers.

Consider Leonardo da Vinci, the Renaissance man who was scientist, architect, builder, creative designer, craftsman, and poet folded into one. To produce good multimedia, you will need a similar diverse range of skills—detailed knowledge of computers, text, graphic arts, sound, and video. These skills, the *multimedia skillset*, may be available in a single individual or, more likely, in a composite of individuals working as a team. Complex multimedia projects are, indeed, often assembled by teams of artists and computer craftspeople, where tasks can be delegated to those most skilled and competent in a particular discipline or craft. Many job titles and collaborative team roles for multimedia development are being adapted from a mix of motion picture industry, radio and television broadcasting, and computer software industry experiences.

warning *A multimedia expert working alone will be hard-pressed to compete with a team of experts and may be overwhelmed by the sheer amount of effort required to build a complex project single-handedly.*

When I was young, I started in "media" as a disc jockey and news director on radio. It was one medium. I then progressed to doing movies and slide shows with audio, calling it multiple media. When video took over from film, I moved into print media and paper, the original medium for mass communications when people knew how to read. Now, much of what I do starts out in electronic form on the PC, so I guess I'm into yet another medium. What I see being called "multimedia" seems to be all of the above displayed on a CRT, and it all looks vaguely familiar as what I was doing years ago with projectors on walls. So I guess you might say that multimedia today is the same old stuff packaged in a modern box, it just doesn't use the walls...

Tom Inglesby, Senior Editor, *Software Strategies* Magazine

The Team

A typical team for developing multimedia for CD-ROM or the Web consists of people who bring various capabilities to the table. Often, individual members of multimedia production teams wear several hats: graphic designers may also do interface design, scanning, and image processing. A project manager or producer may also be the video producer or script writer. Depending upon the scope and content of your project and the mix of people required, according to Wes Baker, a professor at Cedarville University in Cedarville, Ohio, a multimedia production team may require as many as 18 discrete roles:

Executive Producer
Producer/Project Manager
Creative Director/Multimedia Designer
Art Director/Visual Designer
Artist
Interface Designer
Game Designer
Subject Matter Expert
Instructional Designer/Training Specialist
Script Writer
Animator (2-D/3-D)
Sound Producer
Music Composer
Video Producer

Multimedia Programmer
HTML Coder
Lawyer/Media Acquisition
Marketing Director

Mere possession of the equipment does not make one into a videographer, film editor, set designer, scriptwriter, audio engineer, animator, and programmer. Some people do possess all of the innate talents required to produce decent multimedia, but few have mastered all the skills required to bring a major project to fruition. More typically, world-class productions are realized through the teamwork of a variety of talented people with specialized experience.

Jeff Burger, Contributing Editor, *NewMedia* Magazine

Project Manager

A project manager's role is at the center of the action. He or she is responsible for overall development and implementation of a project as well as for day-to-day operations. Budgets, schedules, creative sessions, time sheets, illness, invoices, team dynamics—the project manager is the glue that holds it together.

> **Project Manager/Interface Expert**
> Multimedia company looking to immediately fill position on interactive television project for major telecommunications company. Project manager needed to manage production and design efforts on large-scale interactive television project for air in western United States.
>
> - Must be adept and experienced at managing complex projects, preferably with large corporate accounts.
> - Must have solid understanding of interactivity and experience with interactive media—ideally, interactive television.
> - Must have several years experience with interface design or management thereof and have good design sensibilities.
> - Communication skills a must; must be an articulate and effective communicator, an excellent listener, and act as a conduit for information between our team and the client's teams.
> - Superior attention to detail and ability to coordinate large amounts of information a must.
> - Prefer entertainment experience—ideally, television or video production.
> - Solid computer or digital media experience and knowledge a must.
> - Travel required to visit focus groups and gather consumer information.
> - Must function well in fast-paced, team-oriented environment.
> - Position must be filled immediately.

Mark Williams
....

Microsoft's Cinemania CD-ROM is a comprehensive, authoritative guide to the movies and the people who make them, designed for computer-owning film lovers. Producing Cinemania involved a core team headed by project manager Mark Williams, with additional specialists, technicians, and assistants brought on board as needed.

 At Microsoft, project managers are called program managers, but it means exactly the same thing. The program manager has two major areas of responsibility: design and management. Design consists of devising a vision for the product and working out the complete functionality with the design team, and then putting that into a complete functional spec and adjusting it as necessary throughout the development of the product. The management side consists of scheduling and assigning tasks, running meetings, managing milestones—essentially overseeing all aspects of product development from beginning to end.

Our core team consisted of myself, a subject matter expert—which at Microsoft we call an editor—a graphic designer, and a programmer called a software development engineer. Another important team member was the product manager—the marketing person who represents the product to the outside world. We also found that it was very valuable to get early design input from the person who creates the online and printed help for the product and from the person who eventually manages the testing of the product.

In the production phase we brought in additional talent for scanning images, digitizing sound, proofreading, and other production tasks. We also utilized numerous specialists along the way, such as an audio producer to secure sound track material and, crucially, acquisitions specialists.

The acquisitions folks were vital to the effort because we were trying to get a variety of media from people who really didn't understand what we were doing. The second version has been much easier because the studios and license holders saw the product and can now visualize how it works.

Speccing the right content and being able to acquire it was critical. Our pictures and content are all of the highest quality, and the design is clear and easy to use. Keeping a vision of the product in mind—making sure that the design really meets the needs of the end user—is very important. Constant usability testing gives us a way to keep the end user involved in the design process.

A good project manager must completely understand the strengths and limitations of hardware and software so that he or she can make good decisions about what to do and what not to do. Aside from that I'd say the most important skills are people skills (keeping your team happy and motivated), organizational skills, and attention to all the myriad details of a project. At the same time it's critical to keep the big picture, the vision, in mind so that everything that needs to get done does in fact get done.

Multimedia Designer

The look and feel of a multimedia project should be pleasing and aesthetic, inviting and engaging. Screens should present an appealing mix of color, shape, and type. The project should maintain visual consistency, using only those elements that support the overall message of the program. Navigation clues should be clear and consistent, icons should be meaningful, and screen elements should be simple and straightforward. If the project is instructional, its design should be sensitive to the needs and styles of its learner population, demonstrate sound instructional principles, and promote mastery of subject matter. Who puts it all together?

Graphic designers, illustrators, animators, and image processing specialists deal with the visuals. Instructional designers make sure that the subject matter is clear and properly presented. Interface designers devise the navigation pathways and content maps. Information designers structure content, determine user pathways and feedback, and select presentation media based on an awareness of the strengths of the many separate media that make up multimedia.

Multimedia Designer/Producer

Seeking an experienced new-media professional who loves inventing the future and enjoys the challenge of integrating complex information and media systems.

Our ideal candidate has solid experience in interface design, product prototyping, and marketing communication. A knowledge of image manipulation is critical, as well as proven skills in Lingo scripting and the use of digital time-based authoring tools. We seek a team player with excellent communication skills and grace under pressure.

- Must have experience designing large information and/or entertainment systems.
- Must have experience creating system flows and program architectures.
- Must have solid organizational skills and attention to detail.

Kurt Andersen

Kurt Andersen has been an instructional designer for the past six years. Most recently, he was a senior designer at the George Lucas Educational Foundation, where he designed multimedia prototypes for middle school math and science curricula. Currently he is a consultant in the fields of multimedia and information design and development.

 A multimedia designer often wears many hats, but most importantly he or she looks at the overall content of a project, creates a structure for the content, determines the design elements required to support that structure, and decides which media are appropriate for presenting which pieces of content. In essence, the multimedia designer (sometimes called an information designer) prepares the blueprint for the entire project: content, media, and interaction.

From an interactive standpoint, many multimedia projects are too passive—you click and watch. The challenge is to get beyond what is appealing visually and design products to be activity-based. A multimedia project needs to be truly interactive, and this means you have to have a clear picture of what goes on whenever the user interacts with the program.

Advances in technology are bringing us closer to this. For example, one of the most interesting things going on is the development of adaptive systems, which accept user input and modify themselves based on this input. In training projects, they're called intelligent tutors. Right now, we're working on a medical application that will analyze a patient's history and background to present information that is personalized to that particular patient.

I was recently a member of two different teams that developed multimedia prototypes for middle school science and mathematics at the George Lucas Educational Foundation. Our approach was to develop prototypes that might be distributed as exemplars of rigorous, engaging, effective multimedia design using leading-edge technology. The real challenge was to create a program that presented mathematics so that users could play, explore, and develop their own conceptual schema around the concepts we were developing. We were also challenged to implement our ideas from a technological standpoint. For example, we wound up hooking up a high-end rendering machine so that we could do 3-D graphics on the fly.

3

Multimedia designers need a variety of skills. You need to be able to analyze content structurally and match it up with effective presentation methods. You need to be an expert on different media types, and a capable media integrator, in order to create an overall vision. The ability to look at information from different points of view and a willingness to shift your own point of view to be empathetic with end users are absolutely essential. So are interpersonal skills, because you spend so much of your time interacting with other team members, with clients, and extracting information from subject matter experts. You must be able to "talk the talk" with all of them. Finally, you must understand the capabilities of your resources, both technological and human, and know when to push ahead and when to stop.

Interface Designer

Like a good film editor, an interface designer's best work is never seen by the viewer; it's "transparent." In its simplest form, an interface provides control to the people who use it. It also provides access to the "media" of multimedia—the text, graphics, animation, audio, and video—without calling attention to itself. The elegant simplicity of a multimedia title screen, the ease with which a user can move about within a project, effective use of windows, backgrounds, icons, and control panels—these are the result of an interface designer's work.

> **Artist/Designer** needed to create graphics for interactive multimedia titles aimed at children. Solid experience in graphic design, including knowledge of Adobe Photoshop and Adobe Premiere. Must have superior illustration ability. Must have experience in animation. Experience in video graphics and editing (Premiere, Avid, Media100, etc.) a plus.

Nicole Lazzaro

Nicole Lazzaro is an interface designer with ONYX Productions in Oakland, California, and teaches interface design at San Francisco State University's Multimedia Studies Program. She spends her days thinking of new ways to design multimedia interfaces that feel more like real life.

The role of an interface designer is to create a software device that organizes the multimedia content, that lets the user access or modify that content, and that presents the content on screen. These three areas—information design, interactive design, and media design—are central to the creation of any interface, but of course they overlap.

In the real world, design responsibilities are often assigned differently depending on the project. An interface designer may also be the multimedia designer or the graphic designer. Sometimes all of the design is given to one person; sometimes it is divided among group members; and sometimes the interface springs from the group as a whole. In the best of all worlds everyone has input into the final vision, but realistically, everyone also has other responsibilities outside of interface design. The advantage of dedicating one team member experienced in a number of interface solutions to this particular task is to make sure the end user does not get left out of the equation. A good interface designer will create a product that rewards exploration and encourages use. You have to design the interface from the ground up, not just slap on some graphics and fancy icons after most of the programming is done.

A crucial skill is being familiar with a lot of multimedia interfaces so that you are able to visualize ideas as they are discussed. What is the best way to represent this function? Will this program look better using a hierarchical menu or a book metaphor? What will be the user's experience? Being familiar with film or video editing can be helpful, because telling a story with sounds and images is what most multimedia experiences are all about. From a visual perspective, cinematography and film editing are, I think, the closest parallels to what we would call interface design. These techniques can seamlessly change a point of view or tell a story more effectively, and they are being used by interface designers today. Knowing an authoring system is also crucial, so you can develop your ideas in some interactive fashion and be able to present them to your design group. Having basic drawing skills also helps, because then you can describe how a screen looks using pencil and paper. Also, know how to do user testing, and do lots of it!

Writer

Multimedia writers do everything writers of linear media do, and more. They create character, action, and point of view—a traditional scriptwriter's tools of the trade—and they also create interactivity. They write proposals, they script voice-overs and actors' narrations, they write text screens to deliver messages, and they develop characters designed for an interactive environment.

Writers of text screens are sometimes referred to as content writers—they glean information from content experts, synthesize it, and then communicate it in a clear and concise manner. Scriptwriters write dialog, narration, and voice-overs. Both often get involved in overall design.

> **Multimedia Writer** needed for multimedia kiosk in retail outlet. Must be familiar with interactive design and user interface issues. Background in marketing or copywriting a plus. Ability to work under tight deadlines in a team environment essential. Candidates will be asked to provide writing samples.

Domenic Stansberry

Domenic Stansberry is a writer/designer who has worked on interactive multimedia dramas for commercial products. He has also written for documentary film and published two books of fiction.

The role of the writer changes with each different project, depending on the people you're working with. But multimedia writing is always different from writing a film or video script. In a film or video, you're plotting a story the way a dramatist or novelist would. With multimedia, it can be more difficult: you're still thinking dramatically, but in smaller, more discrete units that have to interrelate to each other, that have to be compiled into a puzzle of sorts.

In traditional drama there are characters and an inevitability about what happens to those characters. You build circumstances that have certain significance for your characters as they go on to meet their destiny. In multimedia, we plot out stories that can go many different ways. This is inherently contradictory to the way we've thought about dramatic structure. Intelligent writers are still working hard to invent interactive dramatic structures: we see some attempts in games, which are obstacle driven. The user needs to perform a task and is presented with an obstacle—a need to overcome the obstacle and move on. This is not unlike the position a character takes in a story or movie where characters are presented with physical or psychological obstacles and must find a way to get beyond them. It's really too bad that writers are not brought in on more game projects...the quality of the interaction would be much higher.

I work best when I am involved at the conceptual level of a project, but in many projects, it is the flowcharts that are generated first. Then as the writing process unfolds, you find that the flowchart doesn't work because the material isn't what the flowchart wants it to be. When you're working on a dramatic script, you have to make the characters and the drama work first, before you start doing flowcharts. So if the writer is invited into the process at Step 7 and handed a flowchart, you're going to run into a problem. Another problem lies in working with people who are mainly from computer backgrounds. They are used to the writer as a writer of documentation—someone who comes in at the end of a project and writes a manual about how the product works. Computer people are often very uncomfortable with media people playing a role at the heart of the creative process. You need to develop a sense about where other team members are coming from when you are brought on to a project, and try to educate them if necessary.

But in the final analysis, the producer or project manager has to be the person to handle conflict in differing team members' visions. A good producer will get the most out of the team members by getting team members to work not against each other, but together toward their strengths. There are bound to be competing visions on a project, and in the best case scenario, the team members will work out their differences through a consensus process. But if they can't, the producer has to have a guiding vision.

Video Specialist

A video specialist on a multimedia project may be just one person and a camcorder. Or, for projects requiring extensive amounts of sophisticated video, a video specialist may be responsible for an entire team of videographers, sound technicians, lighting designers, set designers, script supervisors, gaffers, grips, production assistants, and actors. In a multimedia project, a video specialist must be a seasoned professional, skilled in managing all phases of production, from concept to final edit. Team production of video can be very expensive and may be more than might actually be required to produce your own project.

Since the early 1990s, digital video presentation methods such as Apple's QuickTime or Microsoft's Video for Windows (see Chapter 12) have married increasingly capable hardware and software so that editing and preparing video on Macintoshes and PCs has become affordable to multimedia developers. In addition to knowing the basics about shooting good video, multimedia video specialists must also be thoroughly familiar with the tools and techniques used for digital editing on computers.

> **Video Specialist** wanted for multimedia production.
> Must have strong background in video direction and
> editing. Good understanding of shooting for interactive
> programming required. Strong background working
> with blue screen a plus.

Hank Duderstadt

Hank Duderstadt has worked as an independent video producer, director, and video editor specializing in promotions/commercials, corporate marketing, education, broadcast programming, and multimedia production.

A multimedia video specialist does much more than just shoot and edit video. He or she must understand the potentials and limitations of the medium, how these limitations affect the video production itself, and how to get the most out of the video. He or she must also understand interactivity and how it will affect the video. Shooting in traditional styles, you will end up with footage that doesn't work, and there is always a tendency to overcompensate, ending up with video that is little more than gimmicky. With experience, you learn the tricks that make a video look larger than it really is without looking gimmicky.

When you are shooting footage that will end up on CD-ROM, you have to realize in all probability it won't be full screen, full motion. At best it could be half-screen size at 20 frames per second; or at worst, the size of a postage stamp, with 10 frames per second. Wide panoramas and complex camera moves get lost or don't work. The best shots are medium to close-ups. While video may play back in a limited screen size using today's technology, full-screen video will soon become a reality, so shoot your material on the best format available—Beta-SP is ideal—and allow time to grab library shots that also work with larger screen displays.

Another thing to decide is whether to build sets or just shoot your talent in front of a blue screen, compositing later with computer-generated environments. If this is the case, it's important to know exactly what the environment looks like before you shoot, so the talent can be easily incorporated into the scene.

Programs like Premiere, MetaFlo, Video Graffiti, and After FX equal, and often surpass, what you might find at a traditional video production facility, but don't let the ability to do all these incredible things overwhelm your vision. It's very easy to create video that loses the viewer because the editor became so thrilled with all the fancy effects!

Audio Specialist

The quality of audio elements can make or break a multimedia project. Audio specialists are the wizards who make a multimedia program come alive, designing and producing music, voice-over narrations, and sound effects. They perform a variety of functions on the multimedia team and may enlist help from one or many others: composers, audio engineers, or recording technicians. Audio specialists may be responsible for locating and selecting suitable music and talent, scheduling recording sessions, and digitizing and editing recorded material into computer files (see Chapter 9).

3

Chip Harris

Chip Harris studied trumpet and electronic music composition at the Peabody Conservatory of Music, and he has worked with the noted composer Jean Eichelberger Ivy. He has recorded releases on major and independent labels, including Atlantic, RCA, and Warner Brothers, has composed music for CD-ROM titles for Virgin Games, Accolade, and E-greetings, and has created soundtracks for Clio and Joey award-winning spots.

> **Multimedia Audio Specialist**
> Audio specialist needed for multimedia project.
>
> Must have strong background in studio recording techniques—preferably with time spent in the trenches as an engineer in a commercial studio working on a wide range of projects. Must be comfortable working with computers and be open and able to learn new technology and make it work, with high-quality results. Familiarity with standard recording practices, knowledge of music production, and the ability to work with artists a definite plus. Requires fluency in MIDI; experience with sequencing software, patch librarians, and synth programming; and knowledge of sampling/samplers, hard disk recording, and editing. In addition to having a solid technical foundation, you must be able to survive long hours in the studio riding faders and pushing buttons.

An audio specialist working in multimedia should have a thorough understanding of the needs and requirements involved in producing a successful sound track. Most often this person will be either an engineer, technician, composer, sound designer, or any combination of the above. On the rare occasion where all of these skills are requisite for employment, the position would most likely be for an audio department manager for a good-sized and well-funded multimedia company with in-house production facilities. However, even though positions such as this are not plentiful, the skills and talents necessary for quality multimedia audio production are needed every day by companies who have opted to outsource their audio to independent contractors.

Whether it's recording voice-over talent for a business application, or composing a musical score for a shoot-'em-up game, or designing sound effects that reflect the particular feel of a product, the end result will rely on knowing the medium going in. By this I mean, at what sampling rate will the audio be delivered? How much space is available for *all* audio combined? Can different sampling rates be applied to voice-over and music to save space and enhance overall quality? In composition will looping be required of individual pieces to provide a seamless score, but again, to save valuable space? And who will do the looping, the composer or the engineer? Will some voice-over talents sound presentable at higher sampling rates but not at lower? Will the producer understand the difference?

Of course, these are only a few examples of questions and problems to be dealt with in multimedia audio production. But attention to detail, listening for a cohesive presentation, and quality recording techniques are the strong glue that successfully binds the diverse audio components together.

Multimedia Programmer

A multimedia programmer or software engineer integrates all the multimedia elements of a project into a seamless whole using an authoring system or programming language (see Chapter 7). Multimedia programming functions range from coding simple displays of multimedia elements to controlling peripheral devices such as laserdisc players and managing complex timing, transitions, and record keeping. Creative multimedia programmers can coax extra (and sometimes unexpected) performance from multimedia authoring and programming systems. Without programming talent, there can be no multimedia. Code, whether written in JavaScript, OpenScript, Lingo, Authorware, Java, or C++, is the sheet music played by a well-rehearsed orchestra.

Interactive Programmer (Lingo, Java, and C/C++) needed to work on multimedia prototyping and authoring tools for CD-ROM and interactive television projects.

- Thorough knowledge of Lingo, ActionScript, Java, and C/C++, Macintosh and Windows environments required.
- Must have working familiarity with digital media, particularly digital video.
- Must have a demonstrated track record of delivering quality programming on tight schedules.
- Must function well in fast-paced, team-oriented environment.
- Knowledge of HTML, Flash.

Hal Wine

Hal Wine is a programmer familiar with both the Macintosh and Windows environments. In his many years of experience, he has worked in most of the important areas of computing and for many of the leading computing companies.

The programmer on a multimedia team is called on to perform a number of tasks, from assisting producers in organizing their code more effectively to enhancing the production and playback tools. The most important skill a multimedia programmer can bring to a team is the ability to quickly learn and understand systems—and not just understand the various calls, but know why those calls are needed. In other words, to be able to read between the lines of the technical manuals, so that your solutions are harmonious with the philosophy and intent of the system designers.

Multimedia products are displayed on a large variety of display systems, and the enhancement needed often requires going behind the normal system safeguards to meet the objective. Such programming requires a thorough understanding of the target operating system and device capabilities to produce a robust solution.

While multimedia authoring tools are continually improving, they are still evolving. Many times a producer will want to do something slightly beyond the built-in capabilities of the tools, and the programmer will build extensions to the authoring and presentation suite in order to add the desired capability or effect.

Many of the workers on a multimedia team have come to computing from a background in another discipline such as graphic art or journalism, and while they may have strong creative skills, most can benefit from learning more about computing techniques. Often, a multimedia programmer acts as a teacher and technical coach to the team. This implies having better than average communication and comprehension skills, both verbal and written, and the ability to listen!

I often come in to handle "emergencies" in multimedia projects, rather than participate in the whole project's life cycle. This provides me with maximum variety in my own work, which really keeps me on my toes. Sometimes, I'll be working for several clients simultaneously. The downside is that I miss out on a lot of the creative synergy; but even so, coming in on the spur of the moment, trying to understand the parameters of the problem, and producing robust solutions quickly leads to quite a bit of creativity, too! Knowing how to make your own latte is also useful.

3

Producer, Multimedia for the Web

Web site producer is a new occupation, but putting together a coordinated set of pages for the World Wide Web requires the same creative process, skillsets, and often teamwork as the making of any kind of multimedia (see Chapters 15 and 17). There is a great difference, however, between putting up a simple Web page with a few links and designing, implementing, and maintaining a complex site with many areas of content and many messages. A Web site is never finished, but should, indeed, remain dynamic, fluid, and alive. Unlike a CD-ROM multimedia product replicated many times over in permanent plastic, the work product at a Web site is available for tweaking at any time.

Web Site Producer Excellent full-time opportunity with a large manufacturing firm. Responsible for developing Web projects from concept through implementation for internal and external clients. Interact with all levels of management, network teams, and development teams to provide efficient project solutions. Knowledge of HTML coding of tables, frames, and forms, knowledge of CGI scripting, knowledge of Photoshop. Exciting opportunity for a self-motivated individual looking for a career in new media. This new entry-level position in the firm's national marketing department requires a team player with creative ideas who is interested in gaining experience and knowledge in every aspect of Web site development. Job responsibilities include maintaining/updating site content, managing documents, developing new site features.

Kevin Edwards

Kevin Edwards is Senior Multimedia Producer for CNET, a publicly traded media company (NASDAQ: CNWK) that integrates television programming with a network of sites on the World Wide Web. In both media, CNET provides information about computers, the Internet, and future technology using engaging content and design. CNET has about 2 million members on the Internet, and its television programming—which airs on the USA Network, the Sci-Fi Channel, and in national syndication—reaches an estimated weekly audience of more than 8 million viewers.

Back in the summer of 1995, after graduating from NYU with a master's degree in interactive telecommunications, I headed out to San Francisco to join CNET. I wore a lot of different hats at CNET, but my primary responsibility was with the company's online foray into multimedia. For example, early on we did Mediadome, a year-long project with Intel, where I was involved from original concept through implementation. Mediadome (http://www.mediadome.com) merges hot media properties with cutting-edge technology to create a brand-new experience in Web-based browsing, allowing users to become participants in the experience rather than just observers.

What helped me keep this project in focus was my rounded knowledge and ability to perform in all of the different roles required to produce the site, whether graphics, HTML, editorial, support, audio/video, or other. While it's a lot of fun to change hats and do many different tasks, it can be a lot of responsibility and pretty stressful. For me, building the original Mediadome site meant that for a year and a half I was totally plugged into the Net, checking on our site, looking at stats, and analyzing what was going on in the entertainment/technology industries. This meant keeping Web-profession hours rather than banker's hours, so it was pretty rare for me to take a day off, even on weekends, and my office became more my living space than my apartment. To keep from burning out, you have to have a sense of ownership and a passion for what you're doing.

The best is when your team is composed of people who also turn into close friends. During this project we worked incredibly well together: each knew his or her particular field 100 percent and respected the other team members. We worked hard, played hard, and were able to really rock when put to the test. In fact, there were a couple of people who started the project with very little experience, but their eagerness and ability to learn, and the group's willingness to teach, made it happen.

The Sum of Parts

Successful multimedia projects begin with selecting "team players." But selection is only the beginning of a team-building process that must continue through a project's duration. *Team building* refers to activities that help a group and its members function at optimum levels of performance by creating a work culture incorporating the styles of its members: you should encourage communication styles that are fluid and inclusive, and you should develop models for decision making that respect individual talents, expertise, and personalities. This is not easy, but repeated studies have shown that workgroup managers with well-developed "team" skills are more successful than managers who dive headlong into projects without attention to team dynamics. While it is usually a project manager who initiates team building, all team members should recognize their role; gentle collaboration is a key element of successful projects.

:::::::::::::::::::::::::::::::::::::

Computer Programmers

Computer programmers write, test, and maintain the detailed instructions, called programs or software, that computers must follow to perform their functions. They also conceive, design, and test logical structures for solving problems by computer. Many technical innovations in programming—advanced computing technologies and sophisticated new languages and programming tools—have redefined the role of a programmer and elevated much of the programming work done today. As a result, it is becoming more difficult to distinguish different computer specialists—including programmers—since job titles shift so rapidly, reflecting new areas of specialization or changes in technology. Job titles and descriptions also may vary, depending on the organization. In this occupational statement, computer programmer refers to individuals whose main job function is programming; this group has a wide range of responsibilities and educational backgrounds.

Employment of programmers is expected to grow faster than the average for all occupations through 2008. Jobs for both systems and applications programmers should be plentiful in data processing service firms, software houses, and computer consulting businesses. These types of establishments are part of computer and data processing services, which is projected to be the fastest growing industry in the economy.

Programmers generally work in offices in comfortable surroundings. Many programmers may work long hours or weekends, to meet deadlines or fix critical problems that occur during off hours. Given the technology available, telecommuting is becoming common for a wide range of computer professionals—including computer programmers. Programmers can access a system from remote locations, to make corrections or fix problems. Like other workers who spend long periods of time in front of a computer terminal typing at a keyboard, programmers are susceptible to eyestrain, back discomfort, and hand and wrist problems, such as carpal tunnel syndrome.

A growing number of computer programmers are employed on a temporary or contract basis or work as independent consultants, as companies demand expertise with new programming languages or specialized areas of application. Rather than hiring programmers as permanent employees and then laying them off after a job is completed, employers can contract with temporary help agencies, consulting firms, or directly with programmers themselves.

When hiring programmers, employers look for people with the necessary programming skills who can think logically and pay close attention to detail. The job calls for patience, persistence, and the ability to work on exacting analytical work, especially under pressure.

Ingenuity and imagination are also particularly important, when programmers design solutions and test their work for potential failures. Since programmers are expected to work in teams and interact directly with users, employers want programmers who are able to communicate with nontechnical personnel.

From *The Occupational Outlook Handbook*, U.S. Department of Labor, Bureau of Labor Statistics
(http://stats.bls.gov/oco/ocos110.htm)

3

Multi

> The environment will improve; good ideas, not hardware, will drive the multimedia industry.

Selection of the proper platform
for developing your multimedia project may be based on

environment

media

part

2

Multimedia Hardware and Software

personal preference,
budget constraints,
delivery requirements,
type of material and
content in the project.

Multi

[Since its inception,
the Macintosh has
been, by definition, a
multimedia computer.]

Selection of the proper platform
for developing your multimedia project may be based on ▬

environment

media

4

Macintosh and
Windows Production
Platforms

personal preference,
budget constraints,
delivery requirements,
type of material and
content in the project.

S ELECTION of the proper platform for developing your multimedia project may be based on your personal preference of computer, your budget constraints, project delivery requirements, and the type of material and content in the project. Many developers believe that multimedia project development is smoother and easier on the Macintosh than in Windows, even though projects destined to run in Windows must then be ported across platforms. But hardware and authoring software tools for Windows have improved: today you can produce many multimedia projects with equal ease in either the Windows or Macintosh environment.

Vaughan's Rule for Keeping Up

Upgrade to proven products that lie in the calm water slightly behind the leading edge of the wave

1993

The rationale for trading in my workhorse Macintosh IIci for a Quadra 840AV in 1993 was that I will get at least three years of good use out of a computer that will remain at or near the top of the line long enough to justify its cost. Apple's RISC-based PowerMacs will begin shipping in 1994, and they will be more than twice as powerful as my Quadra. But that power will be available mainly to applications that have been written specifically for the PowerPC chip in native code. Indeed, it is rumored that some applications, until they are redesigned by their vendors, will actually run slower on the PowerPC than on my Quadra. You can capsize at the frothy leading edge of technology, where the Surf Alligators live.

1996

My Quadra 840AV continues to perform just fine and is still well supported by software vendors. While writing the third edition of this book, however, Apple kindly loaned me a top-of-the-line Power Macintosh 9500 with all the

(continued)

Vaughan's Rule for Keeping Up (continued)

bells and whistles—some heavy-duty authoring packages now *require* the PowerMac's capabilities, and I wanted to test them. My assistant uses that PowerMac; if I tried it and liked it, I know I wouldn't be able to go back (see "Vaughan's One-Way Rule" later in this chapter), and I know I can still get at least another year of good service out of my 840AV, on which I write these words.

1998

Too many applications just wouldn't run on my Quadra 840AV, and I was too far behind the curve. I bought a 7500 PowerMac, boosted the processor and cache, and added a second hard drive. It screams, compared to the old Quadra, which was relegated to my 10-year-old's bedroom. But now the G3 Macintosh is out, and with an entirely new operating system from Apple on the horizon, perhaps I have purchased only a year or two's grace before the leading edge of technology pinches again. However, I'm safely behind what some call the "bleeding edge."

2001

Whoa, with the Mac 7500 I was way behind the edge! Too little RAM, no speed. G4s were out and OS-X was shipping. When the new Photoshop 6 worked *slower* than Photoshop 5, I knew it was time, but I didn't have an extra $3,000 for fresh hardware. Instead of buying a new Mac, for about $500 I installed a Sonnet G4 Crescendo card and a stick of RAM into my old 7500. Bingo! In the game again. There are more than a few upgrade paths that will keep you going.

Macintosh Versus Windows

Since its inception, the Macintosh has been, by definition, a multimedia computer: at the famous rollout of the Macintosh in January 1984 at Apple's annual shareholders' meeting, the new device actually introduced itself in a crudely synthesized voice:

"Hello. I'm Macintosh. It sure is great to get out of that bag... Unaccustomed as I am to public speaking, I'd like to share with you a maxim I thought of the first time I met an IBM mainframe: Never trust a computer you can't lift! Obviously, I can talk, but right now I'd like to sit back and listen. So it is with considerable pride that I introduce the man who's been like a father to me, Steven Jobs."

Whereas the Macintosh had good built-in audio right from the start, in 1984 IBM personal computers could not process sound without very expensive add-on components. With its focus on business computing, the PC remained for many years able to provide only system beeps and limited sound effects on a tiny (and tinny) onboard speaker. That situation has changed, and today the Intel-based PC running Windows readily challenges the Macintosh in delivering excellent multimedia presentations. Even so, a market research firm studied the comparative advantages of Macintosh versus Windows/Intel computers and discovered that Macintosh users:

- Spend 38 fewer hours per year "futzing" with files
- Save $4,950 annually on support and training
- Use more tools (14.3 versus 8.3)
- Save $2,211 in three-year cost of ownership
- Earn $5.01 more per hour
- Earn $12.22 more revenue per hour of labor
- Create $14,550 more profits per year per person
- Earn 32 percent more net profit per project
- Achieve platform payback in 7.2 months (versus 13.9)

The Macintosh Platform

All Macintoshes can record and play sound. Many include hardware and software for digitizing and editing video and producing DVD discs. High-quality graphics capability is available "out of the box." Unlike the Windows environment, where users can operate any application with keyboard input, the Macintosh *requires* a mouse.

Nevertheless, there is significant variation in the ways you can set up your Macintosh hardware and software. The Macintosh computer you will need for developing a project depends entirely upon the project's delivery requirements, its content, and the tools you will need for production. Of course, the ideal production station is the newest, fastest, and most flexible computer you can get your hands on, but such a configuration may be beyond the scope of your budget. Thankfully, acceptable performance is not limited to the top-of-the-line configuration: all Macintosh models sold today are sufficient for multimedia development.

Apple introduced the first Power Macintosh computers based on reduced instruction-set computing (RISC) microprocessors during 1994. RISC technology was typically used in engineering workstations and commercial database servers designed for raw computational power, but in an alliance with IBM and Motorola, Apple designed and built this new line of RISC-based models. They supplanted earlier models based upon the Motorola 68000, 68030, and 68040 processors. In 1997, the G3 series was introduced with clock speeds greater than 233 MHz and offering higher performance than existing Pentium-based Windows machines. By 2001, the G4 computers offered 733 MHz speeds and even a dual processor arrangement with a 20-times performance increase over the G3 when running applications like Photoshop.

4

Vaughan's One-Way Rule

Once you've tried it, you can't go back

In 1987, a few weeks after HyperCard was released by Apple, I went to work there, designing and building the guided tour for an information management tool used in-house by Apple. I said I didn't know the software; they said that's OK, nobody else does, either. They gave me a cubicle with my name on it, a Macintosh Plus with a 20MB hard disk, and I was up and running. The Macintosh II had been shipping for a short while, and every department at Apple was attempting to get this latest and hottest CPU—but most units were going to the retail channel. There were three Macintosh IIs among about 40 of us.

One afternoon, I sat at a Macintosh II, inserted my 800K disk, and ran my HyperCard stack. I couldn't believe it! The screen-to-screen dissolves and special effects I had carefully programmed on the Macintosh Plus went by so fast I couldn't see them. I had to reprogram everything, with a special test to check for CPU speed. If it was a fast machine, I programmed the visual effects to run slower; on a slow machine, faster. But the sad part was that I not only wanted this faster machine, I felt I needed it! I had had the same experience moving

(continued)

Vaughan's One-Way Rule (continued)

from a 300-baud modem to a 1200-baud modem and, later, from a 14-inch monitor to a 21-inch monitor.

When you upgrade from a 56KB modem using plain old telephone lines to a wireless or cable connection to the Internet, you will experience the One-Way Rule firsthand as you slide into high bandwidth, and Web pages download immediately to your monitor in complete and finished chunks. Recently, tens of thousands of subscribers to a DSL provider in San Francisco went beserk when that company crashed into bankruptcy and pulled the plug without warning—the chalkboard screech of those users going the wrong way was deafening!

The Windows Platform

Unlike the Apple Macintosh computer, a Windows computer is not a computer per se, but rather a collection of parts that are tied together by the requirements of the Windows operating system. Power supplies, processors, hard disks, CD-ROM players, video and audio components, monitors, keyboards and mice—it doesn't matter where they come from or who makes them. Made in Texas, Taiwan, Indonesia, Ireland, Mexico, or Malaysia by widely known or little-known manufacturers, these components are assembled and branded by Dell, IBM, Gateway, and others into computers that run Windows. If you are handy with a Phillips screwdriver and can read instructions, you can even order the parts and assemble your own computer to run Windows—at a considerable cost savings!

In the early days, Microsoft organized the major PC hardware manufacturers into the Multimedia PC Marketing Council to develop a set of specifications that would allow Windows to deliver a dependable multimedia experience. (The fanfare rollout for this effort is described in a First Person in Chapter 11.) Since then, the MPC specification has evolved into "what a computer does." Today, you would need to special order a retrograde computer that did not have audio, a CD-ROM drive, plenty of RAM and processor speed, and a high-resolution monitor.

> ## First Person
>
> *In November 1985, during the COMDEX trade show in Las Vegas, members of the computer press were invited to the birthing party for a new Microsoft product called Windows. A crowd of journalists and friends of Microsoft had gathered in a small low-ceilinged hotel ballroom and were munching on hors d'oeuvres and sipping wine when the swinging doors to the pantry opened suddenly, and Bill Gates drove a golf cart onto the floor, towing a small trailer loaded down with hundreds of blue boxes filled with the new product. A cheer went up, and the boxes disappeared into waiting hands. It was a fun party held in the time before Gates had become the richest man in the world and necessarily employed a personal security force, before his personal income would skew by two dollars the difference between the mean and median income of all Americans. He chatted with a few of us and proudly autographed some User Guides. Mine says "I hope you like the product; thanks for coming, Tay."*
>
> *Back in my office after the show, I loaded the software onto my XT from the five 5.25-inch floppy disks in the box and ran it. Windows was a dog. Indeed, during the ensuing days and months, Windows had a very hard time in the "operating environment" popularity contest and dropped to low-visibility status. But Gates seemed to have a vision, and while we didn't hear too much about Windows during the next years, Gates and Microsoft worked on the product steadily and didn't give up. Windows 3.0, released many years later, changed the world.*

Networking Macintosh and Windows Computers

If you are working in a multimedia development environment consisting of a mixture of Macintosh and Windows computers, you will want them to communicate with each other. You will also wish to share other resources among them, such as printers.

Local area networks (LANs) and wide area networks (WANs) can connect the members of a workgroup. In a LAN, workstations are usually located within a short distance of one another, on the same floor of a building, for example. WANs are communication systems spanning great distances, typically set up and managed by large corporations and institutions for their own use, or to share with other users.

LANs allow direct communication and sharing of peripheral resources such as file servers, printers, scanners, and network modems. They use a variety of proprietary technologies, most commonly Ethernet or TokenRing, to perform the connections. They can usually be set up with twisted-pair telephone wire, but be sure to use "data-grade level 5" or "cat-5" wire—it makes a real difference, even if it's a little more expensive! Bad wiring will give you a never-ending headache of intermittent and often untraceable crashes and failures.

WANs are expensive to install and maintain, but other methods for long-distance communication are available without a dedicated telephone or wireless network: dial-up connections to the Internet through an Internet Service Provider (ISP), CompuServe, America Online, MSN, Prodigy, or MCI Mail allow messages and files to be uploaded to private electronic (e-mail) mailbox addresses and downloaded later by the recipient. You pay for a local telephone call and the length of time you are connected to the service (usually at a reasonable hourly rate). If you are working with people in various time zones (an artist in New York, a programmer in San Francisco, and a client in Singapore), all can communicate and share information with other locations at any time of day or night.

If you are operating a cross-platform multimedia development shop, you should install an Ethernet system so your PCs can talk with your Macintoshes and your network printers as well. This is many times more efficient than carrying removable media among your machines. Macintoshes have Ethernet networking built in; your PCs will require inexpensive Ethernet cards. Ethernet is only a *method* for wiring up computers, so you still will need *client/server* software to enable the computers to speak with each other and pass files back and forth. Here you have two options: you can add software to your Macintosh to allow it to connect to a network of Windows PCs that use the Microsoft Client TCP/IP protocols, or you can add software to your Windows PC that allows it to connect to a network of Macintoshes that uses AppleTalk. Both require Ethernet as the connection method.

With DAVE from Thursby Systems (http://www.thursby.com), software is installed on the Macintosh to enable a Macintosh to connect to the Microsoft TCP/IP network. Users can then mount shared Macintosh hard drives and PostScript printers that are connected to the Macintosh's AppleTalk network so they can be used by the PCs in the network. DAVE uses the industry standard TCP/IP protocol with a NetBIOS driver (see Figure 4-1).

To connect a PC to a network of Macintoshes, you can use MACLAN Connect from Miramar (http://www.miramarsys.com) to share the directories and files on all your computers using AppleTalk protocols—you do not have to install a dedicated server workstation (see Figure 4-2).

Connections

When you attend a conference where multimedia presentations are being shown, the human speakers usually sit facing the audience, which is treated

FIGURE 4-1

Thursby Software Systems' DAVE lets you network a Macintosh into a Windows workgroup using TCP/IP protocols

to a view of the backside of the speakers' computers. Among the many devices—computers, monitors, disk drives, video projectors, light-valves, videodisc players, VCRs, mixers, sound speakers, and power strips—there are enough wires and connections to resemble the intensive-care ward of a hospital. Sometimes an attempt is made to drape these power and data hoses with a curtain.

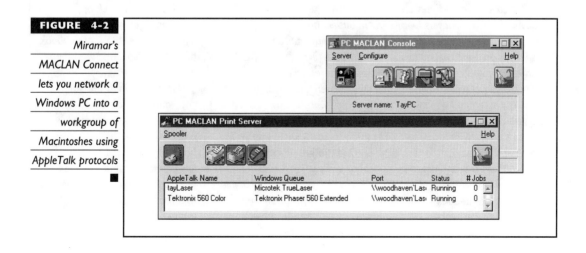

FIGURE 4-2

Miramar's MACLAN Connect lets you network a Windows PC into a workgroup of Macintoshes using AppleTalk protocols

The equipment required for developing your multimedia project will depend on the content of the project as well as its design. You will certainly need as fast a computer as you can lay your hands on, with lots of RAM and disk storage space. If you can find content such as sound effects, music, graphic art, clip animations, and QuickTime or AVI movies to use in your project, you may not need the extra tools for making your own. Typically, however, multimedia developers have separate equipment for digitizing sound from tapes or microphone, scanning photographs or other printed matter, and making digital still or movie images from videotape.

SCSI

The Small Computer System Interface (SCSI—spoken as "scuzzy") was built into all models of the Macintosh before Apple switched over to the less-expensive IDE bus starting with G3 Macs and iMacs. SCSI lets you add peripheral equipment such as disk drives, scanners, CD-ROM players, and other peripheral devices that conform to the SCSI standard. You can connect as many as eight devices (ID numbers from 0 to 7) to a SCSI bus, but one of

First Person

A few years ago I was on a flight from Dallas to Frankfurt and became involved in an unusual but gentlemanly competition. At Mach .75 and 40,000 above the sea, six of us contended for the two available 110-volt "Shavers Only" electrical outlets in the lavatories. Every hour or so we needed to charge our laptop computers, and in the manner of fellow travelers, we quietly negotiated a round-robin power schedule.

More recently, on an overnight flight across that same ocean aboard a brand-new aircraft, mine was the only seat showing its overhead light while I put the finishing touches on a multimedia presentation. After a few hours, I needed to charge batteries, and with the small charger, power cord, and batteries in hand, I went forward to the lavatory. There was no 110-volt outlet. With increasing alarm, I checked the other lavatories. No outlets anywhere.

Behind the curtain of the galley, the flight attendants had gathered to chat while their passengers slept; no, there probably weren't any outlets on this plane, they responded ambivalently. I looked furtively around the galley; none there, either.

It would seem that 110-volt conveniences for passengers with shavers and laptops have gone to that same graveyard of services where you can find Channel 12 for listening to Air Traffic Control while en route, first-person televised views from the cockpit of takeoffs and landings, a catered piano bar and lounge aft, and (in the real old days) a tiny pack of four Winston cigarettes on your dinner tray next to a matchbook proudly emblazoned with the airline's logo.

No doubt there are safety, cost, and general reduction-of-hassle-from-passengers reasons, though airlines are beginning to install special low-voltage computer power outlets for laptops at business and first-class seats. I was, in the end, better off for the extra sleep.

them must be the computer itself with ID 7, and one is usually your internal hard disk with ID 0. High-end Macintoshes (pre-G3) had two SCSI buses, internal and external, and so could hook up twice as many devices.

SCSI cards can also be installed in PCs, and external peripheral devices such as hard disks, CD-ROM drives, tape drives, printers, scanners, rewritable cartridge drives, and magneto-optical drives can be connected to the installed card. When a SCSI device is connected to the interface card in a PC, it is mounted to the system as another drive letter. Thus you may have floppy disk drives mounted as drives A: and B:, a hard disk as drive C:, a CD-ROM drive as D:, and SCSI-based external devices as drives E:, F:, G:, and so on. While usually connected to a hard disk controller card in the PC, the internal disk drive C: can also be a SCSI device, connected to a SCSI card. With Ultra SCSI, you can hook up as many as 32 devices to your computer.

---

cross platform   *Not all PC SCSI cards and software drivers will recognize Macintosh-formatted removable media such as Zip, Jaz, and Syquest cartridges or magneto-optical discs. The Macintosh, however, will usually recognize PC-formatted disks and devices; so many developers working in cross-platform environments use PC formatting for their removable media.*

You will need to set up your SCSI devices carefully, because SCSI cabling is very sensitive to length and to resistance. Follow the instructions in your SCSI user's guide for proper termination and ID number assignment for SCSI devices. Having more than one external SCSI device can make your system "delicate," and even more will make it "fragile." The following configuration, which includes several external disk drives, a CD-ROM player, and a flat-bed scanner, took several hours to hook up and is fragile:

When your computer is not happy with your chain of SCSI peripherals, it is not forgiving and will refuse to boot up. Often you will need to adjust cable lengths and reconfigure terminating resistors, and try again. Make sure that IDs assigned to peripherals are neither 0 nor 7, and that the same ID number is not assigned to two different devices. If you are likely to move different peripheral devices among several computers, it is good practice to put a sticker with that device's assigned SCSI ID on each and also label all devices connected to the computer. Always connect external devices with computer and device power off. By clearly paying attention to the SCSI IDs of your peripherals, you can avoid dangerous ID conflicts (setting two devices to the same ID) when you boot up.

The hardware and the drivers for SCSI have improved over the years to provide faster data transfers across wider buses: SCSI-1 transfers data at a rate of 5MB per second and supports up to seven devices. The newer SCSI-2 is divided into two classifications: Fast SCSI (10MB per second) and Wide SCSI (with an increased bus width to 16-bit). A composite of these two (Fast/Wide SCSI) can achieve data transfer rates of 20MB per second. The latest SCSI-3 (Ultra SCSI) can support up to 32 devices and achieve speeds of 40MB per second. Unlike the less-expensive IDE scheme, a SCSI controller does not demand CPU time, and because it can support as many as 32 devices, it is preferred for real-time video editing, network servers, and situations in which writing simultaneously to two or more disks (*mirroring*) is required.

SCSI devices may be installed (and interchanged) on both your PC and your Macintosh: the PC will *not* read Macintosh-formatted hard disks and other data storage cartridges, but the Macintosh (usually) will read PC-formatted media.

IDE, EIDE, Ultra-IDE, ATA, Ultra-ATA

SCSI connections may connect both *internal* devices, which are inside the chassis of your computer and use the computer's power supply, and *external* devices, which are outside the chassis, use their own power supply, and are plugged into the computer by cable. Integrated Drive Electronics (IDE) connections, also known as Advanced Technology Attachment (ATA) connections, are typically only internal, and they connect hard disks, CD-ROM drives, and other peripherals mounted inside the PC.

A PC motherboard can support two IDE controllers, and each controller in turn can support two devices (a master and a slave). Thus, with IDE, you can install a combination of four hard disks, CD-ROM drives, or other devices in your PC. The floppy disk doesn't count because it is operated by a separate controller. The circuitry for IDE is typically much less expensive than for SCSI, but comes with limitations: IDE requires time from the main processor chip, only one drive in a master/slave pair can be active at once, and because a master drive manages the operations of both drives attached to a controller, a failure of the master drive will disable both drives.

As with SCSI, there are various flavors: plain IDE, which can transfer data at 2.5MB per second; EIDE (Enhanced IDE), which can transfer data at 16.6MB per second; and Ultra IDE (also known as Ultra DMA33), which can transfer data at 33MB per second. As the need has increased for faster interface or external "burst" transfer rates, UltraATA/66, and more recently Ultra ATA/100 connections have become available. A Serial ATA interface supports data transfer rates of up to 150 MB/sec.

Memory and Storage Devices

As you add more memory and storage space to your computer, you can expect your computing needs and habits to keep pace, filling the new capacity. So enjoy the weeks that follow a memory storage upgrade or the addition of a gigabyte hard disk; the honeymoon will eventually end.

Vaughan's Law of Capacity

You never have enough memory or disk space

Somewhere in my basement is an old drive that used 256K, 8-inch floppy disks. I often carried these big floppies from workplace to workplace in a sneaker network (by tennis shoe, that is, not wire or glass fiber). I was astounded and pleased when the new 5.25-inch disks came out, and then amazed by the high technology of 3.5-inch disks that fit in a shirt pocket... The higher-density floppies kept pace with the growing sizes of my project files, until I switched to color and began including sound and animation. For a while, segmenting and joining large files across several disks worked around the constraint, but it was tedious and inadequate for large digital video files. So I went to 44MB Syquest cartridges, then to 128MB magneto-optical disks and to Zip disks, then to 1–2GB Jaz cartridges. Now I burn a quick 640MB CD-R on the Philips recorder; my projects are measured in the tens and hundreds of megabytes.

To estimate the memory requirements of a multimedia project—the space required on a floppy disk, hard disk, or CD-ROM, not the random access memory (RAM) used while your computer is running—you must have a sense of the project's content and scope. Color images, text, sound bites, video clips, and the programming code that glues it all together require memory; if there are many of these elements, you will need even more. If you are *making* multimedia, you will also need to allocate memory for storing and archiving working files used during production, original audio and video clips, edited pieces, and final mixed pieces, production paperwork and correspondence, and at least one backup of your project files, with a second backup stored at another location.

It is said that when John von Neuman, often called "the father of the computer," was designing the ENIAC computer in 1945, there was an argument about how much memory this first computer should have. His colleagues appealed for more than the 2K Dr. von Neuman felt was sufficient. In the end, he capitulated and agreed to install 4K in the ENIAC, commenting "...but this is more memory than you will ever need."

Random Access Memory (RAM)

If you are faced with budget constraints, you can certainly produce a multimedia project on a slower or limited-memory computer. On the other hand, it is profoundly frustrating to face memory (RAM) shortages time after time, when you're attempting to keep multiple applications and files open simultaneously. It is also frustrating to wait the extra seconds required of each editing step when working with multimedia material on a slow processor.

On the Macintosh, the minimum RAM configuration for serious multimedia production is about 32MB; but even 64MB and 256MB systems are becoming common, because while digitizing audio or video, you can store much more data much more quickly in RAM. And when you're using some software, you can quickly chew up available RAM—for example, Photoshop (16MB minimum, 20MB recommended); AfterEffects (32MB required); Director (8MB minimum, 20MB better); Pagemaker (24MB recommended); Illustrator (16MB recommended); Microsoft Office (12MB recommended). Figure 4-3 illustrates the allocation of RAM in a Macintosh system with many applications open simultaneously.

In spite of all the marketing hype about processor speed, this speed is ineffective if not accompanied by sufficient RAM. A fast processor without enough RAM may waste processor cycles while it swaps needed portions of program code into and out of memory. In some cases, increasing available RAM may show more performance improvement on your system than upgrading the processor chip.

4

Even though the processing performance of computers has increased considerably in the last several years, input/output (I/O) devices have not kept up with this trend. While processor speed gets roughly eight times faster every ten years, main memory access speed increases by only one third in the same time period. As you realize, this widens the gap between I/O and processing times. So our ability to efficiently use very fast computers depends on our ability to feed the processor with data sufficiently fast. This is called the parallel I/O bottleneck. *The bad news is that this problem is expected to get worse.*

From "Parallel Machines and Their Algorithms" by Takis Metaxas

Read-Only Memory (ROM)

Read-only memory is not *volatile*. Unlike RAM, when you turn off the power to a ROM chip, it will not forget, or lose its memory. ROM is typically used in computers to hold the small BIOS program that initially boots up the computer, and it is used in printers to hold built-in fonts. Programmable ROMs (called EPROMs) allow changes to be made that are not forgotten. A new and inexpensive technology, optical read-only memory (OROM), is provided in proprietary data cards using patented holographic storage. Like the CD recorders described later in the chapter, the cards are write-once. Typically, OROMs offer 128MB of storage, have no moving parts, and use only about 200 milliwatts of power, making them ideal for handheld, battery-operated devices.

Floppy and Hard Disks

Adequate storage space for your production environment can be provided by large-capacity hard disks; a server-mounted disk on a network; Zip, Jaz, or Syquest removable cartridges; optical media; CD-R (compact disc-recordable) discs; tape; floppy disks; banks of special memory devices; or any combination of the above.

Removable media (floppy disks, compact or optical discs, and cartridges) typically fit into a letter-sized mailer for overnight courier service. One or many disks or discs may be required for storage and archiving each project, and you should plan for backups kept off-site.

Floppy disks and hard disks are mass-storage devices for binary data—data that can be easily read by a computer. Hard disks can contain much more information than floppy disks and can operate at far greater data transfer rates. In the scale of things, floppies are, however, no longer "mass-storage" devices.

A floppy disk is made of flexible mylar plastic coated with a very thin layer of special magnetic material. A hard disk is actually a stack of hard metal platters coated with magnetically sensitive material, with a series of recording heads or sensors that hover a hairbreadth above the fast-spinning surface, magnetizing or demagnetizing spots along formatted tracks using technology similar to that used by floppy disks and audio and video tape recording. Hard disks are the most common mass-storage device used on computers, and for making multimedia, you will need one or more large-capacity hard disk drives (see "Vaughan's Law of Capacity" earlier in the chapter).

As multimedia has reached consumer desktops, makers of hard disks have been challenged to build smaller-profile, larger-capacity, faster, and less-expensive hard disks. In 1994, hard disk manufacturers sold nearly 70 million units; in 1995, more than 80 million units. And prices have dropped a full order of magnitude in a matter of months. By 1998, street prices for 4GB drives (IDE) were less than $200. By 2001, 20GB drives cost less than $100. As network and Internet servers drive the demand for centralized data storage requiring terabytes (1 trillion bytes), hard disks will be configured into fail-proof redundant arrays offering built-in protection against crashes.

Zip, Jaz, Syquest, and Optical Storage Devices

For years Syquest's 44MB removable cartridges have been the most widely used portable medium among multimedia developers and professionals, but Iomega's inexpensive Zip drives with their likewise inexpensive 100MB cartridges have significantly penetrated Syquest's market share for removable media. Iomega's Jaz cartridges provide a gigabyte of removable storage media and have fast enough transfer rates for audio and video development. Pinnacle

Micro, Yamaha, Sony, Philips, and others offer CD-R "burners" for making write-once compact discs, and some double as quad-speed players. As blank CD-R discs become available for less than a dollar each, this write-once media competes as a distribution vehicle. CD-R is described in greater detail a little later in the chapter.

Magneto-optical (MO) drives use a high-power laser to heat tiny spots on the metal oxide coating of the disk. While the spot is hot, a magnet aligns the oxides to provide a 0 or 1 (on or off) orientation. Like Syquests and other Winchester hard disks, this is rewritable technology, because the spots can be repeatedly heated and aligned. Moreover, this media is normally not affected by stray magnetism (it needs both heat and magnetism to make changes), so these disks are particularly suitable for archiving data. The data transfer rate is, however, slow compared to Zip, Jaz, and Syquest technologies. One of the most popular formats uses a 128MB-capacity disk—about the size of a 3.5-inch floppy. Larger-format magneto-optical drives with 5.25-inch cartridges offering 650MB to 1.3GB of storage are also available.

Digital Versatile Disc (DVD)

In December 1995, nine major electronics companies (Toshiba, Matsushita, Sony, Philips, Time Warner, Pioneer, JVC, Hitachi, and Mitsubishi Electric) agreed to promote a new optical disc technology for distribution of multimedia and feature-length movies called DVD (see Table 4-1).

With this new medium capable not only of gigabyte storage capacity but also full-motion video (MPEG2) and high-quality audio in surround sound, the bar has again risen for multimedia developers. Commercial multimedia projects will become more expensive to produce as consumers' performance expectations rise. There are two types of DVD—DVD-Video and DVD-ROM; these reflect marketing channels, not the technology.

DVD can provide 720 pixels per horizontal line, whereas current televisions (NTSC) provide 240—television pictures will be sharper and more detailed. With Dolby AC-3 Digital Surround Sound as part of the specification, six discrete audio channels can be programmed for digital surround sound, and with a separate subwoofer channel, developers can program the low-frequency doom and gloom music popular with Hollywood. DVD also supports Dolby Pro-Logic Surround Sound, standard stereo, and mono audio. Users can randomly access any section of the disc and use the slow-motion and freeze-frame features during movies. Audio tracks can be programmed for as many as 8 different languages, with graphic subtitles in 32 languages. Some manufacturers such as Toshiba are already providing parental control features in their players. (Users select lockout ratings from G to NC-17.)

DVD Feature	DVD Specification
Disc diameter	120 mm (5 inches)
Disc thickness	1.2 mm (0.6 mm thick disc × 2)
Memory capacity	4.7 gigabytes/single side
Track pitch	0.74 micrometer
Wave length of laser diode	650 nanometer/635 nanometer
Numerical aperture (NA)	0.6
Error correction	RS-PC (Reed Solomon Product Code)
Signal modulation	8-16
Data transfer rate	Variable speed data transfer at an average rate of 4.69 megabits/second for image and sound
Image compression	MPEG2 digital image compression
Audio	Dolby AC-3 (5.1 ch), LPCM for NTSC and MPEG Audio, LPCM for PAL/SECAM (a maximum of 8 audio channels and 32 subtitle channels can be stored)
Running time (movies)	133 minutes a side (at an average data rate of 4.69 megabits/second for image and sound, including three audio channels and four subtitle channels)
File management structure	Micro UDF and ISO-9660

TABLE 4-1   *DVD Main Specifications* ■

DVD, like compact disc, will not boom from day one. Commercial audio and video encoding systems for MPEG2 will be available this summer, and consumer DVD-Video players will be available in Japan and the U.S. by the end of the year, beginning of next year. So the real market will only pick up next year. In the longer term, we expect that PC software makers will welcome the increased capacity offered by DVD-ROM. Special applications for mapping and digital scanning may lead the way, but new interactive multimedia titles and games are also hungry for space. We believe that the DVD-ROM market will develop faster than DVD-Video. There are several reasons for this. The OEM price of a DVD-ROM drive will be much lower than a complete DVD-Video player. We think a volume OEM price of approximately $200 for a DVD-ROM drive in 1997 is entirely possible. And as I already stated, the need in the PC world for more capacity and better-quality moving video is also much higher than in the consumer market... Around the year 2000, approximately 10 percent of all the 250 million drives sold will be based on DVD. And of this 10 percent, the majority will probably be DVD-ROM.

From the opening speech at CeBIT, Hanover, Germany, March 13, 1996, by Jan Oosterveld, President, Philips Key Modules

CD-ROM Players

Compact disc read-only memory (CD-ROM) players have become an integral part of the multimedia development workstation and are an important delivery vehicle for large, mass-produced projects. A wide variety of developer utilities, graphic backgrounds, stock photography and sounds, applications, games, reference texts, and educational software are available only on this medium.

CD-ROM players have typically been very slow to access and transmit data (150K per second, which is the speed required of consumer Red Book Audio CDs), but developments led to double-, triple-, quadruple-speed, 24x, 48x, and 56x drives designed specifically for computer (not Red Book Audio) use. These faster drives spool up like washing machines on the spin cycle and can be somewhat noisy, especially if the inserted compact disc is not evenly balanced. See Chapter 19 for more details about CD-ROMs.

4

CD Recorders

With a compact disc recorder, you can make your own CDs using special CD-recordable (CD-R) blank optical discs to create a CD in most formats of CD-ROM and CD-Audio (see Chapter 19). Software, such as Adaptec's Toast for Macintosh or Easy CD Creator for Windows, lets you organize files on your hard disk(s) into a "virtual" structure, then writes them to the CD in that order. CD-R discs are made differently than normal CDs but can play in any CD-Audio or CD-ROM player. These write-once CDs make excellent high-capacity file archives and are used extensively by multimedia developers for premastering and testing CD-ROM projects and titles. Because they have become very inexpensive, they are also used for short-run distribution of finished multimedia projects.

Input Devices

A great variety of input devices—from the familiar keyboard and handy mouse to touchscreens and voice recognition setups—can be used for development and delivery of a multimedia project. If you are designing your project for a public kiosk, use a touchscreen. If your project is for a lecturing professor who likes to wander about the classroom, use a remote handheld mouse. If you create a great deal of original computer-rendered art, consider a pressure-sensitive stylus and a drawing tablet.

Keyboards

A keyboard is the most common method of interaction with a computer. Keyboards provide various tactile responses (from firm to mushy) and have various layouts depending upon your computer system and keyboard model. Keyboards are typically rated for at least 50 million cycles (the number of times a key can be pressed before it might suffer breakdown).

The most common keyboard for PCs is the 101 style (which provides 101 keys), although many styles are available with more or fewer special keys, LEDs, and other features, such as a plastic membrane cover for industrial or food-service applications or flexible "ergonomic" styles. Macintosh keyboards connect to the Apple Desktop Bus (ADB), which manages all forms of user input—from digitizing tablets to mice.

Mice

A mouse is the standard tool for interacting with a graphical user interface (GUI). All Macintosh computers require a mouse; on PCs, mice are not required but recommended. Even though the Windows environment accepts keyboard entry in lieu of mouse point-and-click actions, your multimedia projects should typically be designed with the mouse or touchscreen in mind. The buttons on the mouse provide additional user input, such as pointing and double-clicking to open a document, or the click-and-drag operation, in which the mouse button is pressed and held down to drag (move) an object, or to move to and select an item on a pull-down menu, or to access context-sensitive help. The Apple mouse has one button; PC mice may have as many as three.

Trackballs

Trackballs are similar to mice, except that the cursor is moved by using one or more fingers to roll across the top of the ball. The trackball does not need the flat space required by a mouse; this is important in small confined environments and for portable laptop computers. Trackballs have at least two buttons: one for the user to click or double-click, and the other to provide the press-and-hold condition necessary for selecting from menus and dragging objects.

Touchscreens

Touchscreens are monitors that usually have a textured coating across the glass face. This coating is sensitive to pressure and registers the location of the user's finger when it touches the screen. The TouchMate system, which has no coating, actually measures the pitch, roll, and yaw rotation of the monitor when pressed by a finger, and determines how much force was exerted and the location where the force was applied. Other touchscreens use invisible beams of infrared light that crisscross the front of the monitor to calculate where a finger was pressed. Pressing twice on the screen in quick succession simulates the double-click action of a mouse. Touching the screen and dragging the finger, without lifting it, to another location simulates a mouse click-and-drag. A keyboard is sometimes simulated using an on-screen representation so users can input names, numbers, and other text by pressing "keys."

Touchscreens are not recommended for day-to-day computer work, but are excellent for multimedia applications in a kiosk, at a trade show, or in a museum delivery system—anything involving public input and simple tasks. When your project is designed to use a touchscreen, the monitor is the only input device required, so you can secure all other system hardware behind locked doors to prevent theft or tampering.

4

First Person

One of the more seductive rewards for working on the steep and slippery learning curves of multimedia is an occasional overwhelming introduction to a new idea or invention, the kind of encounter characterized by a neck-wrenching flash of wonderment as you stop in your tracks for a double-take. "How does that work?"

The TouchMate from Visage is just such an invention. It's about two inches high, sits under your monitor, and requires only a 12-volt power supply and a cable to the RS-232 serial port of your PC. There are no electrical or data connections between the device and the monitor, no occluding membranes glued to glass, and no LEDs buried in a protruding bezel.

So how does TouchMate work if it's not connected to the screen?

It translates tiny three-dimensional changes in monitor position caused by pressure on the screen into screen coordinates. This is the same sort of awesome black-box science that enables inertial navigation systems to guide a 747 from New York to Paris, hands free. TouchMate combines well-understood sensor hardware with the mathematics of force vectors.

The top of TouchMate, where the monitor sits, is mounted on three-dimensional springs, allowing it to move with equal freedom in all directions relative to the base. Internal sensors constantly measure the distance between the top and the base. Each sensor consists of two parallel plates that form a capacitor, one attached to the top of TouchMate and one attached to the base. Two sets of these sensor plates are located in each corner, mounted at a 45-degree angle, providing a total of eight sensors.

When the monitor (sitting on the TouchMate) is touched, the force of the touch causes a slight change in the distance between TouchMate's top and base, typically on the order of a thousandth of an inch. This causes the distance between each set of sensor plates to change slightly, changing the capacitance across the plates. TouchMate uses the change in capacitance across each sensor to determine the amount the top plate moved in the x, y, and z directions and the amount it rotated in each direction (roll, pitch, and yaw). Firmware then calculates what level of force was exerted to cause this movement and the location where the force was applied.

Magnetic Card Encoders and Readers

Magnetic (mag) card setups are useful when you need an interface for a database application or multimedia project that tracks users. You need both a card encoder and a card reader for this type of interface. The encoder connects to the computer at a serial port and transfers information to a magnetic strip of tape on the back of the card. The card reader then reads the information encoded on the card. A visitor to a museum, for example, could slide an encoded card through a reader at any exhibit station and be rewarded with a personalized or customized response from an intelligent database or presentation system. French-speaking visitors to a Norwegian museum, for instance, could hear an exhibit described in French.

---

tip *When you design a project to use mag cards or pen scanners, always provide immediate feedback to an action by the user, such as a beep response or a displayed message.*

Graphics Tablets

Flat-surface input devices are attached to the computer in the same way as a mouse or trackball. A special pen is used against the pressure-sensitive surface of the tablet to move the cursor. Graphics tablets provide substantial control for editing finely detailed graphic elements, a feature very useful to graphic artists and interface designers. Tablets can also be used as input devices for end users: you can design a printed graphic, place it on the surface of the tablet, and let users work with a pen directly on the input surface. On a floor plan, for instance, visitors might draw a track through the hallways and rooms they wish to see and then receive a printed list of things to note along the route. Some tablets are pressure sensitive and are good for drawing: the harder you press the stylus, for example, the wider or darker the line you draw. Graphic artists who try these usually fall prey to Vaughan's One-Way Rule and never return to drawing with a mouse.

Flat-Bed Scanners

A scanner may be the most useful piece of equipment you will use in the course of producing a multimedia project—there are flat-bed and handheld scanners. Most commonly available are gray-scale and color flat-bed scanners that provide a resolution of 300 or 600 dots per inch (dpi). Professional graphics houses may use even higher resolution units. Handheld scanners can be useful for scanning small images and columns of text, but they may prove inadequate for your multimedia development.

Be aware that scanned images, particularly those at high resolution and in color, demand an extremely large amount of storage space on your hard disk, no matter what instrument is used to do the scanning. Also remember that the final monitor display resolution for your multimedia project will probably be just 72 or 95 dpi—leave the very expensive ultra-high-resolution scanners for the desktop publishers. Most inexpensive flat-bed scanners offer at least 300 dpi resolution, and most allow you to set the scanning resolution.

Scans let you make clear electronic images of existing artwork such as photos, ads, pen drawings, and cartoons, and can save many hours when you are incorporating proprietary art into your application. Scans also can give you a starting point for your own creative diversions.

4

Optical Character Recognition (OCR) Devices

Scanners enable you to use optical character recognition (OCR) software, such as OmniPage from Caere (see Figure 4-4) or Perceive from Ocron, to convert printed matter to ASCII text files in your computer. With OCR software and a scanner, you can convert paper documents into a word processing document on your computer without retyping, or *rekeying*.

Barcode readers are probably the most familiar optical character recognition devices in use today—mostly at markets, shops, and other point-of-purchase locations. Using photo cells and laser beams, barcode readers recognize the numeric characters of the Universal Product Code that are printed in a pattern of parallel black bars on merchandise labels. With OCR, or *barcoding*, retailers can efficiently process goods in and out of their stores and maintain better inventory control.

An OCR terminal can be of use to a multimedia developer because it recognizes not only printed characters but also handwriting. This facility may be beneficial at a kiosk or in a general education environment where user friendliness is a goal—there is growing demand for a more personal and less technical interface to data and information.

Infrared Remotes

An infrared remote unit lets a user interact with your project while he or she is freely moving about. Remotes work like mice and trackballs, except they use infrared light to direct the cursor and require no cables to communicate. Remote mice work well for a lecture or other presentation in an auditorium or similar environment, when the speaker needs to move around the room.

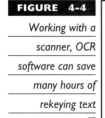

FIGURE 4-4

Working with a
scanner, OCR
software can save
many hours of
rekeying text

Voice Recognition Systems

Voice recognition systems facilitate hands-free interaction with your project. These systems usually provide a unidirectional cardioid, noise-canceling microphone that automatically filters out background noise. Most voice recognition systems currently available can trigger common menu events such as Save, Open, Quit, and Print, and you can teach the system to recognize other commands that are more specific to your application. Systems available for the Macintosh and Windows environments typically must be taught to recognize individual voices and then be programmed with the appropriate responses to the recognized word or phrase. The Macintosh AV and Power Macintosh computers include voice recognition capability, and add-on sound boards such as the Sound Blaster or Diamond Sonic Sound and others provide this feature for PCs.

Digital Cameras

Digital cameras use the same CCD technology as video cameras, described in Chapter 12. They capture still images of a given number of pixels (resolution), and the images are stored in the camera's memory to be uploaded later to a computer. A digital camera that captures an image at a resolution of 1280x1024 pixels captures color information about a total of 1,300,000 pixels (1.3 Megapixels). The higher the Megapixel rating, the higher the resolution of the camera. Images are uploaded from the camera's memory using a serial, parallel, or USB cable, or the camera's memory card is inserted into a PCMCIA reader connected to the computer.

4

Output Hardware

Presentation of the audio and visual components of your multimedia project requires hardware that may or may not be included with the computer itself—speakers, amplifiers, monitors, motion video devices, and capable storage systems. The better the equipment, of course, the better the presentation. There is no greater test of the benefits of good output hardware than to feed the audio output of your computer into an external amplifier system: suddenly the bass sounds become deeper and richer, and even music sampled at low quality may sound acceptable.

Audio Devices

All Macintoshes are equipped with an internal speaker and a dedicated sound chip, and they are capable of audio output without additional hardware and/or software. To take advantage of built-in stereo sound, external speakers are required.

Digitizing sound on your Macintosh requires an external microphone and sound editing/recording software such as SoundEdit16 from Macromedia, SoundForge, or SoundDesigner from DigiDesign. The sound capabilities of both platforms and digitizing software are discussed in detail in Chapter 9.

---

tip *Design your project to use many shorter-duration audio files rather than one long file. This simplifies the reaction of your project within your authoring system, and it may also improve performance because you will load shorter segments of sound into RAM at any one time.*

tip   *The quality of your audio recordings is greatly affected by the caliber of your microphone and cables. A unidirectional microphone helps filter out external noise, and good cables help reduce noise emitted from surrounding electronic equipment.*

Amplifiers and Speakers

Often the speakers you use during a project's development will not be adequate for its presentation. Speakers with built-in amplifiers or attached to an external amplifier are important when your project will be presented to a large audience or in a noisy setting. Altec Lansing's three-piece amplified speaker system, for example, is designed for multimedia presentations and is small and portable. It includes its own digital signal processing (DSP) circuitry for concert hall effects; it has a mixer for two input sources (the computer's digital output and the CD-ROM player's audio output can be blended); and it uses a subwoofer sensitive to 35 Hz.

warning   *Always use magnetically shielded speakers to prevent color distortion or damage to nearby monitors.*

Monitors

The monitor you need for development of multimedia projects depends on the type of multimedia application you are creating, as well as what computer you're using. A wide variety of monitors is available for both Macintoshes and PCs. High-end, large-screen graphics monitors and LCD panels are available for both, and they are expensive.

Serious multimedia developers will often attach more than one monitor to their computers, using add-on graphics boards. This is because many authoring systems allow you to work with several open windows at a time, so you can dedicate one monitor to viewing the work you are creating or designing, and you can perform various editing tasks in windows on other monitors that do not block the view of your work. Figure 4-5 illustrates editing windows that overlap a work view when developing with Macromedia's authoring environment, Director, on one monitor. Developing in Director is best with at least two monitors, one to view your work, the other to view the Score. A third monitor is often added by Director developers to display the Cast. See Chapter 7 for more about Director. For years, one of the advantages of the Macintosh for making multimedia was that it is very easy to attach multiple monitors for development work. With Windows 98, PCs can be configured for more than one monitor.

FIGURE   4-5

Without a second monitor, you will have difficulty editing your project and viewing it at the same time

First Person

A bunch of us worked on a guided tour project destined for Sun SPARCstations. SPARCstations have large monitors with a screen resolution of 1024x768 pixels, but, because we were most proficient with Macintosh graphics tools, we created most of the bitmapped artwork on Macintosh 13-inch, 640x480-pixel RGB monitors. Though the Macintosh software deftly managed the big image sizes, the process was very tiresome to the artists, because the 640x480 monitors provided only a window onto the larger bitmap. We had to scroll the window back and forth over the larger image to see what we were doing. Dragging and dropping was a horror show.

Finally, we installed a 19-inch monitor and set up a Macintosh with a high-resolution video card. It was better, but there were not enough of them to go around. In the end, about 75 percent of the artwork was done in scrolling windows on the Macintosh, and it turned out great.

Large monitors do not necessarily increase the real estate available to you for your graphics and information display: 35-inch monitors, or even the 50-foot projection displays common to auditoriums, may still provide just 640x480 pixels of resolution. The large monitors that do effectively increase the real estate also require higher-resolution boards in Macintosh or PC expansion slots. Again, these are expensive.

Always develop your project using the screen resolution of the destination platform.

Video Devices

No other contemporary message medium has the visual impact of video. With a video digitizing board installed in your computer, you can display a television picture on your monitor. Some boards include a frame-grabber feature for capturing the image and turning it into a color bitmap, which can be saved as a PICT or TIFF file and then used as part of a graphic or a background in your project.

Display of video on any computer platform requires manipulation of an enormous amount of data. When used in conjunction with videodisc players, which give you precise control over the images being viewed, video cards let you place an image into a window on the computer monitor; a second television screen dedicated to video is not required. And video cards typically come with excellent special effects software.

There are many video cards available today. Most of these support various video-in-a-window sizes, identification of source video, setup of play sequences or segments, special effects, frame grabbing, digital moviemaking; and some have built-in television tuners so you can watch your favorite programs in a window while working on other things. Good video greatly enhances your project; poor video will ruin it.

Projectors

When you need to show your material to more viewers than can huddle around a computer monitor, you will need to project it onto a large screen or even a white-painted wall. Cathode-ray tube (CRT) projectors, liquid crystal display (LCD) panels attached to an overhead projector, stand-alone LCD projectors, and light-valve projectors are available to splash your work onto big-screen surfaces.

CRT projectors have been around for quite a while—they are the original "big-screen" televisions. They use three separate projection tubes and lenses (red, green, and blue), and the three color channels of light must "converge" accurately on the screen. Setup, focusing, and aligning is important to getting a clear and crisp picture. CRT projectors are compatible with the output of most computers as well as televisions.

LCD panels are portable devices that fit in a briefcase. The panel is placed on the glass surface of a standard overhead projector available in most schools, conference rooms, and meeting halls. While the overhead projector does the projection work, the panel is connected to the computer and provides the image, in thousands of colors and, with active-matrix technology, at speeds that allow full-motion video and animation. Because LCD panels are small, they are popular for on-the-road presentations, often connected to a laptop computer and using a locally available overhead projector.

More complete LCD projection panels contain a projection lamp and lenses and do not require a separate overhead projector. They typically produce an image brighter and sharper than the simple panel model, but they are somewhat larger and cannot travel in a briefcase.

Light-valves compete with high-end CRT projectors and use a liquid crystal technology in which a low-intensity color image modulates a high-intensity light beam. These units are expensive, but the image from a light-valve projector is very bright and color saturated and can be projected onto screens as wide as ten meters.

4

Printers

With the advent of reasonably priced color printers, hard-copy output has entered the multimedia scene. From storyboards to presentations to production of collateral marketing material, color printers have become an important part of the multimedia development environment. Color helps clarify concepts, improve understanding and retention of information, and organize complex data. As multimedia designers already know (see Chapter 17), intelligent use of color is critical to the success of a project. Xerox offers both solid ink and laser options, and their Phaser 560 will print more than 10,000 pages at a rate of 5 color pages or 14 monochrome pages per minute before requiring new toner. Epson provides lower-cost and lower-performance solutions for home and small business users; Hewlett Packard's Color LaserJet line competes with both. Most printer manufacturers offer a color model—just as all computers once used monochrome monitors but are now color, all printers will become color printers. Table 4-2 shows a comparison of a selection of color printers.

	Xerox Phaser 350 (solid ink)	Xerox Phaser 560 (laser)	HP Color LaserJet 5M (laser)	Lexmark Optra C (laser)	IBM Network Color Printer (laser)
Initial purchase cost	$3,995	$4,995	$5,199	$4,999	$4,999
Cost per page (black & white)	1.5c	2.4c	2.6c	5.5c	5.6c

TABLE 4-2 *Costs and Performance of Various Color Printers in 1998 (data courtesy of Tektronix)* ∎

	Xerox Phaser 350 (solid ink)	Xerox Phaser 560 (laser)	HP Color LaserJet 5M (laser)	Lexmark Optra C (laser)	IBM Network Color Printer (laser)
Cost per page (color)	4c	7c	6c	10c	10c
Approx. time to print a full-color newsletter cover (8.5MB file)	2:00 min	2:20 min	4:40 min	16:00 min	2:00 min

TABLE 4-2 *Costs and Performance of Various Color Printers in 1998 (data courtesy of Tektronix) (continued)* ■

Communication Devices

Many multimedia applications are developed in workgroups comprising instructional designers, writers, graphic artists, programmers, and musicians located in the same office space or building. The workgroup members' computers typically are connected on a local area network (LAN). The client's computers, however, may be thousands of miles distant, requiring other methods for good communication.

Communication among workgroup members and with the client is essential to the efficient and accurate completion of your project. Normal U.S. Postal Service mail delivery is too slow to keep pace with most projects; overnight express services are better. And when you need it immediately, an Internet connection is required. If your client and you are both connected to the Internet, a combination of communication by e-mail and by FTP (File Transfer Protocol) may be the most cost-effective and efficient solution for both creative development and project management.

In the workplace, use quality equipment and software for your communications setup. The cost—in both time and money—of stable and fast networking will be returned to you.

Modems

Modems can be connected to your computer externally at the serial port or internally as a separate board. Internal modems often include fax capability.

Be sure your modem is *Hayes compatible*. The Hayes AT standard command set (named for the ATTENTION command that precedes all other commands) allows you to work with most software communications packages.

Modem speed, measured in baud, is the most important consideration. Because the multimedia files that contain the graphics, audio resources, video samples, and progressive versions of your project are usually large, you need to move as much data as possible in as short a time as possible. Today's standards dictate at least a V.90 56Kbps modem. Compression saves significant transmission time and money, especially over long distance. Today, tens of millions of people use a V.90 modem to connect to the Internet.

According to the laws of physics, copper telephone lines and the switching equipment at the phone companies' central offices can handle modulated analog signals up to about 28,000 bps on "clean" lines, so 56K V.90 depends on hardware-based compression algorithms to crunch the data before sending it, decompressing it upon arrival at the receiving end. If you have already compressed your data into a .sit, .sea, .arc, or .zip file, you may not reap added benefit from the compression because it is difficult to compress an already-compressed file.

First° Person

*A*round midnight, I got a phone call from a client in Europe. His investors were meeting later that day, and he needed the project now, not in two days by DHL courier. Compressed, the code was less than a megabyte. So I went to my office and cranked up the modem, dialed the overseas phone number, and connected. The modem software estimated a total transmission time of 73 minutes, and we started the XMODEM protocols. While the little packets of data were humming out across the continent and an ocean, I made a peanut butter sandwich and kept an eye on the Bytes Remaining counter as it worked its way down in ratchets of 1,024. It was hypnotic.

Annoying spikes and glitches in the phone system had always plagued my modem calls with intermittent transmission failures that required starting over. With about four minutes to go, I began suffering hot flashes and a pounding heart, and found myself riveted to the monitor with head in hands, cheering the system on. "Don't crash now! Just a little more... Pretty please with icing! Nice baby!" All the possible scenarios of disaster paraded in front of me: a shipping calamity in the English channel would cause the transatlantic cable to break at 30 fathoms; a street cleaning truck would take out the electric power pole on the street outside; mice would chew through the antenna leads of a lonely microwave station high in the Colorado Rockies... It all seemed suddenly so fragile. But it made it!

ISDN

For higher transmission speeds, you will need to use Integrated Services Digital Network (ISDN), Switched-56, T1, T3, DSL, ATM, or another of the telephone companies' Digital Switched Network services. Connection options are discussed in greater detail in Chapter 13.

ISDN lines are popular because of their fast 128 Kbps data transfer rate—four to five times faster than the more common 28.8 Kbps analog modem. ISDN lines (and the required ISDN hardware, often misnamed "ISDN modems" even though no modulation/demodulation of the analog signal occurs) are important for Internet access, networking, and audio and video conferencing. They are more expensive than conventional analog or POTS (plain old telephone service) lines, so analyze your costs and benefits carefully before upgrading to ISDN. Newer and faster Digital Subscriber Line (DSL) technology using copper lines and promoted by the telephone companies may overtake ISDN in popularity by the year 2002.

Cable Modems

In November 1995, a consortium of cable television industry leaders announced an agreement with key equipment manufacturers to specify some of the technical ways cable networks and data equipment talk with one another. 3COM, AT&T, COM21, General Instrument, Hewlett Packard, Hughes, Hybrid, IBM, Intel, LANCity, MicroUnity, Motorola, Nortel, Panasonic, Scientific Atlanta, Terrayon, Toshiba, and Zenith currently supply cable modem products. While the cable television networks cross 97 percent of property lines in North America, each local cable operator may use different equipment, wires, and software, and cable modems still remain somewhat experimental. This was a call for interoperability standards.

This international specification will take the World Wide Web a step further, bringing broadband interconnections into homes worldwide. In the next generation of modems, we look for more commonality in cable so that vendors may enjoy mass-market sales and cable customers can be assured that their devices work on TCI systems or Time Warner cable systems or any cable systems in the world.

John C. Malone, President and CEO, Tele-Communications, Inc.

Cable modems operate at speeds 100 to 1,000 times as fast as a telephone modem, receiving data at up to 10 Mbps and sending data at speeds between 2 Mbps and 10 Mbps. They can provide not only high-bandwidth Internet access but also streaming audio and video for television viewing. Most will connect to computers with 10baseT Ethernet connectors.

Cable modems usually send and receive data asymmetrically—they receive more (faster) than they send (slower). In the downstream direction from provider to user, the data is modulated and placed on a common 6 MHz television carrier, somewhere between 42 MHz and 750 MHz. The upstream channel, or *reverse path,* from the user back to the provider is more difficult to engineer because cable is a noisy environment—with interference from HAM radio, CB radio, home appliances, loose connectors, and poor home installation. All this noise accumulates, and the overall noise increases as the signal travels upstream in the local cable network's branching tree structure, where signals from one home become mixed with the signals of hundreds, then thousands of other homes.

4

Multi

> The equipment required for developing your multimedia project will depend on the content of the project, as well as its design.

Among the many devices —

communicate

media

chapter

5

Basic Software Tools

-there are enough wires and connections to resemble the intensive care ward of a hospital.

T H E basic tool set for building multimedia projects contains one or more authoring systems and various editing applications for text, images, sounds, and motion video. A few additional applications are also useful for capturing images from the screen, translating file formats, and moving files among computers when you are part of a team—these are tools for the housekeeping tasks that make your creative and production life easier. Special tools for delivering multimedia to the Internet and World Wide Web are discussed in Chapter 14.

The software in your multimedia toolkit and your skill at using it determine what kind of multimedia work you can do and how fine and fancy you can render it. Making good multimedia means picking a successful route through the software swamp. Alligators and learning curves can rise up out of this swamp to nip you in the knees.

Keep your tools sharp by upgrading them when new software and features become available, by thoroughly studying and learning each tool, by reading tips and tricks in the computer magazines and trade press, by keeping an eye on the conversations and FAQs (Frequently Asked Questions) files online and in Internet newsgroups, and by observing the practices and products of other multimedia developers. Remember, each new tool has a learning curve.

t i p *Always fill out the registration card for your new software and return it to the vendor. Or register online. If the vendor pays attention to product marketing, you will receive upgrade offers and often special newsletters and e-mails with helpful information.*

The tools used for creating and editing multimedia elements on both Windows and Macintosh platforms support the authoring systems described in Chapter 7. They do paint and image processing, image editing, drawing and illustration, 3-D and CAD, OCR and text editing, sound recording and editing, video and moviemaking, and various utilitarian housekeeping tasks.

Text Editing and Word Processing Tools

A word processor is usually the first software tool computer users learn. From letters, invoices, and storyboards to project content, your word processor may also be your most often used tool, as you design and build a multimedia project. The better your *keyboarding* or typing skills, the easier and more efficient will be your multimedia day-to-day life.

Typically, an office or workgroup will choose a single word processor to share documents in a standard format. And most often, that word processor comes bundled in an "Office Suite" that might include spreadsheet, database, e-mail, Web browser, and presentation applications.

Word processors such as Microsoft Word and WordPerfect are powerful applications that include spell checkers, table formatters, thesauruses, and prebuilt templates for letters, resumes, purchase orders, and other common documents. In many word processors, you can actually embed multimedia elements such as sounds, images, and video. Luckily, the population of single-finger typists is decreasing over time as children are taught keyboarding skills in conjunction with computer lab programs in their schools.

OCR Software

Often you will have printed matter and other text to incorporate into your project, but no electronic text file. With optical character recognition (OCR) software, a flat-bed scanner, and your computer, you can save many hours of rekeying printed words, and get the job done faster and more accurately than a roomful of typists.

OCR software turns bitmapped characters into electronically recognizable ASCII text. A scanner is typically used to create the bitmap. Then the software breaks the bitmap into chunks according to whether it contains text or graphics, by examining the texture and density of areas of the bitmap and by detecting edges. The text areas of the image are then converted to ASCII characters using probability and expert system algorithms. Most OCR applications claim about 99 percent accuracy when reading 8- to 36-point printed characters at 300 dpi and can reach processing speeds of about 150 characters per second. These programs do, however, have difficulty recognizing poor copies of originals where the edges of characters have bled; these and poorly received faxes in small print may yield more recognition errors than it is worthwhile to correct after the attempted recognition.

Figure 5-1 shows a document in the process of bitmap-to-character conversion by OmniPage Pro from Caere. Notice the small box that displays an image of the actual section of the 300 dpi bitmap currently being analyzed. With this software, the formatting and layout of the original document can be recognized and imported into Microsoft Word with styles that maintain bolding and font size.

Painting and Drawing Tools

Painting and drawing tools, as well as 3-D modelers, are perhaps the most important items in your toolkit because, of all the multimedia elements, the graphical impact of your project will likely have the greatest influence on the end user. If your artwork is amateurish, or flat and uninteresting, both you and your users will be disappointed. Look in Chapters 15 and 17 for tips on designing effective graphical screens and in Chapter 10 for more about computer graphics.

Painting software, such as Photoshop, Fireworks, and Painter, is dedicated to producing crafted bitmap images. Drawing software, such as CorelDraw, FreeHand, Illustrator, Designer, and Canvas, is dedicated to producing vector-based line art easily printed to paper at high resolution.

Some software applications combine drawing and painting capabilities, but many authoring systems can import only bitmapped images. The differences between painting and drawing (that is, between bitmapped and drawn images) are described in Chapter 10. Typically, bitmapped images provide the greatest choice and power to the artist for rendering fine detail and effects, and today bitmaps are used in multimedia more often than drawn objects. Some vector-based packages such as Macromedia's Flash are aimed at reducing file download times on the Web, and may contain both bitmaps and drawn art. The anti-aliased character shown in the bitmap of Color Plate 5 is an example of the fine touches that improve the look of an image.

Look for these features in a drawing or painting package:

- An intuitive graphical user interface with pull-down menus, status bars, palette control, and dialog boxes for quick, logical selection

- Scalable dimensions, so you can resize, stretch, and distort both large and small bitmaps

- Paint tools to create geometric shapes, from squares to circles and from curves to complex polygons

- Ability to pour a color, pattern, or gradient into any area

- Ability to paint with patterns and clip art

- Customizable pen and brush shapes and sizes

- Eyedropper tool that samples colors

- Autotrace tool that turns bitmap shapes into vector-based outlines

- Support for scalable text fonts and drop shadows

- Multiple undo capabilities, to let you try again

- Painting features such as smoothing coarse-edged objects into the background with anti-aliasing (see Color Plate 5); airbrushing in variable sizes, shapes, densities, and patterns; washing colors in gradients; blending; and masking

- Support for third-party special effect plug-ins

- Object and layering capabilities that allow you to treat separate elements independently

- Zooming, for magnified pixel editing

- All common color depths: 1-, 4-, 8-, and 16-, 24-, or 32-bit color, and gray-scale

- Good color management and dithering capability among color depths using various color models such as RGB, HSB, and CMYK

- Good palette management when in 8-bit mode

- Good file importing and exporting capability for image formats such as PIC, GIF, TGA, TIF, WMF, JPG, PCX, EPS, PTN, and BMP

If you are new to multimedia and to these tools, you should take time to examine more than one graphics software package. Find someone who is already familiar with graphics applications. You will spend many days learning to use your painting and drawing software, and if it does not fit you and your needs, you will be unhappy. Many artists learn to use a single, powerful tool well.

3-D Modeling and Animation Tools

3-D modeling software has increasingly entered the mainstream of graphic design as its ease of use improves. As a result, the graphic production values and expectations for multimedia projects have risen. With 3-D modeling software, objects rendered in perspective appear more realistic; you can create stunning scenes and wander through them, choosing just the right lighting and perspective for your final rendered image. Powerful modeling packages such as AutoDesk's Discreet, StrataVision's 3D, Specular's LogoMotion and Infini-D, Alias' Wavefront, Avid's SoftImage, and Caligari's trueSpace are also bundled with assortments of prerendered 3-D clip art objects such as people, furniture, buildings, cars, airplanes, trees, and plants. Specialized applications for creating and animating 3-D text are discussed in Chapter 8. Important for multimedia developers, many 3-D modeling applications also include export features enabling you to save a moving view or journey through your scene as a QuickTime or AVI animation file. Figure 5-2 shows a simple architectural floor plan rendered to 3-D perspective by VectorWorks.

Each rendered 3-D image takes from a few seconds to a few hours to complete, depending upon the complexity of the drawing and the number of drawn objects included in it (see Chapter 11 for more about rendering). If you are making a complex walk-through or flyby, plan to set aside many hours of rendering time on your computer.

FIGURE 5-2

VectorWorks and other CAD applications can translate 2-D floor plans into 3-D perspective drawings with lighting and shadows

■

tip *If there are small errors or things you would like to change in a rendered movie sequence, it may take less time to edit each frame of the affected sequence by hand, using an image-editing program, than to rerender the corrected original.*

A good 3-D modeling tool should include the following features:

■ Multiple windows that allow you to view your model in each dimension, from the camera's perspective, and in a rendered preview

■ Ability to drag and drop primitive shapes into a scene

■ Ability to create and sculpt organic objects from scratch with Bezier spline drawing tools

■ Lathe and extrude features

■ Color and texture mapping

- Ability to add realistic effects such as transparency, shadowing, and fog

- Ability to add spot, local, and global lights, to place them anywhere, and manipulate them for special lighting effects

- Unlimited cameras with focal length control

- Ability to draw spline-based paths for animation

---

warning   *3-D imaging programs require speedy computers with lots of memory, and the learning curve is steep when you enter this world of nurbs, splines, and bump maps.*

Image-Editing Tools

Image-editing applications are specialized and powerful tools for enhancing and retouching existing bitmapped images. These applications also provide many of the features and tools of painting and drawing programs and can be used to create images from scratch as well as images digitized from scanners, video frame-grabbers, digital cameras, clip art files, or original artwork files created with a painting or drawing package.

---

tip   *If you want to print an image to a 300 dpi printer for collateral reports and attractive print-matter icons, work with the image in the image-editing application at 300 dpi (every pixel will be a very fine laser printer dot). Then save your work as a PICT, TIFF, or BMP file and import it into your word processor. The printed result is a finely detailed image at a high resolution.*

Here are some features typical of image-editing applications and of interest to multimedia developers:

- Multiple windows that provide views of more than one image at a time

- Conversion of major image-data types and industry-standard file formats

- Direct inputs of images from scanner and video sources

- Employment of a virtual memory scheme that uses hard disk space as RAM for images that require large amounts of memory

- Capable selection tools, such as rectangles, lassos, and magic wands, to select portions of a bitmap

- Image and balance controls for brightness, contrast, and color balance

- Good masking features

- Multiple undo and restore features

- Anti-aliasing capability, and sharpening and smoothing controls

- Color-mapping controls for precise adjustment of color balance

- Tools for retouching, blurring, sharpening, lightening, darkening, smudging, and tinting

- Geometric transformations such as flip, skew, rotate, and distort, and perspective changes

- Ability to resample and resize an image

- 24-bit color, 8- or 4-bit indexed color, 8-bit gray-scale, black-and-white, and customizable color palettes

- Ability to create images from scratch, using line, rectangle, square, circle, ellipse, polygon, airbrush, paintbrush, pencil, and eraser tools, with customizable brush shapes and user-definable bucket and gradient fills

- Multiple typefaces, styles, and sizes, and type manipulation and masking routines

- Filters for special effects, such as crystallize, dry brush, emboss, facet, fresco, graphic pen, mosaic, pixelize, poster, ripple, smooth, splatter, stucco, twirl, watercolor, wave, and wind

- Support for third-party special effect plug-ins

- Ability to design in layers that can be combined, hidden, and reordered

Plug-Ins

Image-editing programs usually support powerful plug-in modules available from third-party developers that allow you to warp, twist, shadow, cut, diffuse, and otherwise "filter" your images for special visual effects. Vertigo's HotTEXT lets you turn text into 3-D objects (see Figure 8-11 in Chapter 8). EyeCandy from AlienSkin Software offers a comprehensive set of filters (Figure 5-3a shows the Cutout filter in action). Kai's Power Tools from

Corel (see Figure 5-3*b*) offers special effects and has powerful built-in algorithms for making fractal images. The PhotoTools suite from Extensis lets you quickly add drop shadows, bevels, glows, and embossing effects (see Figure 5-3*c*). The special effects available in these plug-ins make image editing fun!

Sound Editing Tools

Sound editing tools for both digitized and MIDI sound let you see music as well as hear it. By drawing a representation of a sound in fine increments, whether a score or a waveform, you can cut, copy, paste, and otherwise edit segments of it with great precision—something impossible to do in real-time (that is, with the music playing). The basics of computerized sound for both the Macintosh and Windows environments are discussed in Chapter 9.

System sounds are shipped with both Macintosh and Windows systems (see Figure 9-1 in Chapter 9), and they are available as soon as you install the operating system. System sounds are the beeps used to indicate an error, warning, or special user activity. Using sound editing software, you can make your own sound effects and install them as system beeps, to the delight (or perhaps dismay) of colleagues and neighbors.

For digital waveform sounds, Windows ships with the Sound Recorder program, which provides some rudimentary features for sound editing. Neither does the Macintosh ship with more than a rudimentary sound editor. You will need to install software for editing digital sounds. Although you can usually incorporate MIDI sound files into your multimedia project without learning any special skills, using editing tools to make your own MIDI files requires that you understand the way music is sequenced, scored, and published; see Chapter 9 for details. You need to know about tempos, clefs, notations, keys, and instruments. And you will need a MIDI synthesizer or device connected to your computer. Many MIDI applications provide both sequencing and notation capabilities, and some let you edit both digital audio and MIDI within the same application. For more about sound recording, editing, and playback see Chapter 9.

Animation, Video, and Digital Movie Tools

Animations and digital video movies are sequences of bitmapped graphic scenes (*frames*), rapidly played back. But animations can also be made

FIGURE 5-3

*Cutouts, shadows,
special brush effects,
and a myriad of
interesting visual
changes are easy to
do with plug-in filters*
■

a.

b.

c.

within the authoring system by rapidly changing the location of *objects* or *sprites* to generate an appearance of motion. Most authoring tools adopt either a frame- or object-oriented approach to animation, but rarely both (see Chapter 11 for more about animation).

Moviemaking tools typically take advantage of QuickTime for Macintosh and Windows and Microsoft Video for Windows (also known as AVI, or Audio Video Interleaved) technology and let you create, edit, and present digitized motion video segments, usually in a small window in your project.

To make movies from video, you need special hardware to convert the analog video signal to digital data (see Chapter 12). Moviemaking tools such as Premiere, VideoShop, and MediaStudio Pro let you edit and assemble video clips captured from camera, tape, other digitized movie segments, animations, scanned images, and from digitized audio or MIDI files. The completed clip, often with added transition and visual effects, can then be played back—either stand-alone or windowed within your project.

Video Formats

Formats and systems for storing and playing digitized video to and from disk files are available with QuickTime and AVI. Both systems depend on special algorithms that control the amount of information per video frame that is sent to the screen, as well as the rate at which new frames are displayed. Both provide a methodology for *interleaving* or blending audio data with video and other data so that sound remains synchronized with the video. And both technologies allow data to stream from disk into memory in a buffered and organized manner. DVD (Digital Versatile Disc) is a *hardware* format defining a very dense, two-layered disc that uses laser light and, in the case of recordable discs, heat to store and read digital information. The digital information or *software* on a DVD is typically *multiplexed* audio, image, text, and video data optimized for motion picture display using MPEG encoding (see Chapter 4 for more detail about DVD).

QuickTime is an organizer of time-related data in many forms. Classic videotape involves a video track with two tracks of (stereo) audio; QuickTime is a multitrack recorder in which you can have an almost unlimited range of tracks. Digitized video, digitized sound, computer animations, MIDI data, external devices such as CD-ROM players and hard disks, and even the potential for interactive command systems are all supported by the QuickTime format. With QuickTime, you can have a movie with five different available languages, titles, MIDI cue tracks, or the potential for interactive commands.

QuickTime for Windows and Macintosh

The heart of QuickTime is a software-based *architecture* for seamlessly integrating sound, text, animation, and video (data that changes over time) on Macintosh and Windows platforms. QuickTime is also used to deliver multimedia to the World Wide Web as a plug-in for Netscape and Internet Explorer. On the Web, QuickTime can deliver 3-D animation, real-time special effects, virtual reality, and streaming video and audio. QuickTime is discussed in this chapter about software tools because, while it is not an "authoring tool," nor a video, image, sound, or text editor, its role as a powerful cross-platform integrator of multimedia objects and formats makes it a tool upon which multimedia developers depend.

QuickTime Building Blocks

Three elements make up QuickTime:

- QuickTime movie file format
- QuickTime Media Abstraction Layer
- QuickTime media services

The movie file format is a container that provides a standard method for storing video, audio, and even text descriptions about a media composition. The Media Abstraction Layer describes how your computer should access the media that is included in the QuickTime movie. The media services part of QuickTime not only has built-in support for over 35 media file formats, including most major video, still image, audio, animation, and MIDI formats, but also allows developers to plug in their own new or custom media formats. Remember, QuickTime is an architecture, a system for multimedia delivery, and is extensible.

QuickTime Pro is a necessary upgrade to the free QuickTime package so you can do more than simply play back movies. The upgrade contains two applications. Movie Player (see Figure 5-4) lets you import and combine over 30 different file formats. You can compress them into deliverable multimedia projects using the Sorenson Video and QDesign audio compressors so they will stream from any Internet-ready Web server. With built-in filters in Movie Player, you can adjust colors, contrast, and brightness, and you can apply special effects to your composition, such as film noise and edge detection. The Picture Viewer application is used for viewing and converting still

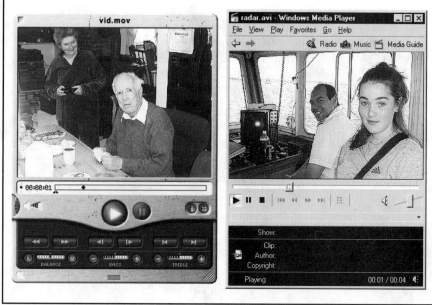

FIGURE 5-4

QuickTime's Movie Player and the Windows Media Player can play back video clips ■

images among many standard image-file formats, including Photoshop's native format.

QuickTime includes built-in support for ten different media types (video, audio, text, timecode, music/MIDI, sprite/animation, tween, MPEG, VR, 3-D) and offers a comprehensive set of "services," such as:

- Timing and synchronization
- Audio and image data compression and decompression
- Image blitting, format conversion, scaling, composition, and transcoding
- Audio mixing, sample rate conversion, and format conversion
- Audio and video effects and transitions
- Synchronized storage read and write
- Media capture
- Media import and export
- Standard user interface elements, such as movie controllers, media previewers, and media capture dialogs

QuickTime Embedded Commands for HTML

When delivering QuickTime projects on the World Wide Web, you can embed powerful commands into your HTML documents that control and fine-tune the display of your QuickTime file:

- AUTOPLAY starts a movie playing automatically.
- BGCOLOR sets a background color for the movie display.
- CACHE indicates whether the movie should be cached (Netscape Navigator 3.0 or later).
- CONTROLLER specifies whether to display the QuickTime movie controller bar.
- HEIGHT and WIDTH specify size of the movie in Web pages.
- HIDDEN allows sound-only movies to play in the background without affecting the look of a Web page.
- HREF indicates which URL to link to when the movie is clicked.
- LOOP loops movie playback automatically.
- SCALE scales the movie display automatically.
- TARGET provides a frame target for the URL specified in an HREF tag.
- VOLUME sets the default playback volume.

In addition, QuickTime has the following VR commands:

- CORRECTION specifies an image correction mode.
- FOV sets the initial field-of-view angle.
- NODE sets the initial node.
- PAN sets the initial pan angle.
- TILT sets the initial tilt angle.

Microsoft Video for Windows

Audio Video Interleaved (AVI) is a Microsoft-developed format for playing full-motion interleaved video and audio sequences in Windows, without specialized hardware. Video data is interleaved with audio data within the file that contains the motion sequence, so the audio portion of the movie remains synchronized to the video portion.

The AVI file format is not an extensible, "open" environment and lacks features needed for serious video editing environments. To improve this situation, a group of interested companies recently created the OpenDML file format to make AVI more useful for the professional market. But because QuickTime works with OpenDML files and delivers on both Macintosh and Windows platforms and across the Web, look for a growing number of neat multimedia projects housed in a QuickTime container.

Like Apple's QuickTime, AVI provides the following features:

- Playback from hard disk or CD-ROM

- Playback on computers with limited memory; data is streamed from the hard disk or CD-ROM player without using great amounts of memory

- Quick loading and playing, because only a few frames of video and a portion of audio are accessed at a time

- Video compression to boost the quality of your video sequences and reduce their size

Movie Editors

With the invention of QuickTime and Video for Windows, desktop video publishing (DVP) on Macintoshes and PCs became a digital process (see Chapter 12 for a discussion of the analog process). Improved compression and decompression techniques allow quarter-, half-, and full-screen/full-motion movies instead of the small, 160×120-pixel-sized movies characteristic of earlier digital video experiments.

With desktop editing software and an appropriate video digitizing board, you can digitize video clips, edit the clip offline, add special effects and titles, mix sound tracks, and save the finished product as a digital file on magnetic or optical media.

Video digitizing boards for making Macintosh QuickTime movies from videotape are available from RasterOps, Radius, Fast, and others. The Targa board from TrueVision, VideoBlaster from Creative Labs, Super VideoWindows SL from New Media Graphics, and other boards are available for making AVI movies for Windows.

Specialized video editors have been designed around this technology for both the Macintosh and PC environments—for example, AVID's

VideoShop, Media100, Fast's VideoMachine, Adobe's Premiere, and Ulead's Media-Studio Pro (see Chapter 12). These applications let you mix video clips, audio recordings, animation, still images, and graphics to create QuickTime or AVI movies. You arrange your clips linearly, cutting and pasting and layering them into transitions with special effects such as dissolves, page turns, spins, tinting, distorting, and replicating. A familiar push-button control panel is used for stop, rewind, play, fast-forward, record and single-stop, and these applications display time references, frame counts, and audio and transparency levels.

Figure 5-5 shows a movie being edited in Premiere, with visual effects and sounds. Adobe's After Effects is a powerful addition to the video editing suite, with sophisticated tools for combining digital video, audio, and images into fully controlled time-based projects. Special video plug-ins for After Effects that will make your movies look truly professional are available from AlienSkin.

---

warning *Digital video editing and playback requires an immense amount of free disk space, even when the video files are compressed.*

---

tip *Because digital movie data must stream rapidly and without interruption from your disk drive, be sure that you defragment and optimize your disk with a utility such as Norton's Speed Disk before recording and playing back your movie files. If your movie file is fragmented, the read head of the disk drive may need to pause sending data while it physically moves to wildly different locations on the disk; a defragmented file lets the head read sequentially from one adjoining sector to the next.*

Compressing Movie Files

Image compression algorithms are critical to the delivery of motion video and audio on both the Macintosh and PC platforms. Without compression, there is simply not enough bandwidth on the Macintosh or PC to transfer the massive amounts of data involved in displaying a new screen image every 1/30 of a second.

To understand compression, consider these three basic concepts:

- *Compression ratio*: The compression ratio represents the size of the original image divided by the size of the compressed image—that is, how much the data is actually compressed. Some compression schemes yield ratios that are dependent on the image content: a busy image of a field of multicolored tulips may yield a very small compression ratio, and an image of blue ocean and sky may yield a very high

FIGURE 5-5

Premiere from Adobe being used to edit a QuickTime movie

5

compression ratio. Video compression typically manages only the part of an image that changes from image to image (the *delta*).

- *Image quality:* Compression is either lossy or lossless. *Lossy* schemes ignore picture information the viewer may not miss, but that means the picture information is in fact lost—even after decompression. And as more and more information is removed during compression, image quality decreases. *Lossless* schemes preserve the original data precisely—an important consideration in medical imaging, for example. The compression ratio typically affects picture quality because, usually, the higher the compression ratio, the lower the quality of the decompressed image.

- *Compression/decompression speed:* You will prefer a fast compression time while developing your project. Users, on the other hand, will appreciate a fast decompression time to increase display performance.

For compressing video frames, the MPEG format used for DVD employs three types of encoding: I-Frames (Intra), P-Frames (Predicted), and B-Frames (Bidirectional Predicted). Each type crams more or less information into the tiniest possible storage space. For example, B- and P-Frames only contain information that has changed from one frame to the next, so a sequence from a "talking head" interview might only contain data for the movement of lips (as long as the rest of the subject is still). B- and P-Frames cannot be played on their own, then, because they contain only the information about the lips that changed; the complete image is based on the data stored in the I-Frame. Sequences of these frame types are compiled into a GOP (Group of Pictures), and all the GOPs are stitched into a stream of images. The result is an MPEG video file.

Helpful Accessories

No multimedia toolkit is complete without a few indispensable utilities to perform some odd, but oft-repeated, tasks. These are the comfortable and well-worn accessories that make your computer life easier.

On both the Macintosh and in Windows, a screen-grabber is essential. Because bitmapped images are so common in multimedia, it is important to have a tool for grabbing all or part of the screen display so you can import it into your authoring system or copy it into an image-editing application. Screen-grabbing to the Clipboard, for example, lets you move a bitmapped image from one application to another without the cumbersome steps of first exporting the image to a file and then importing it back into the destination application. In Windows, press the Print Screen key to place the contents of your screen onto the Clipboard. On the Macintosh, press the Command key, Control key, Shift key and the number 4 all at the same time; then drag a rectangle across the screen. What is in the rectangle is placed on the Clipboard, ready for pasting into an image editing application.

Format converters are another indispensable tool for projects in which your source material may originate on Macintoshes, PCs, Unix workstations, or even mainframes. This is an issue particularly with image files, because there are many formats and many compression schemes. Figure 5-6 illustrates deBabelizer, an image converter and editor from Equilibrium Technologies that also automates batch processing.

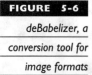

FIGURE 5-6

deBabelizer, a

conversion tool for

image formats

5

Multi

[
Keep your software tools
sharp by upgrading them when
new features become available.
]

The software in your multimedia
toolkit, and your skill at using it...

test and review

media

chapter

6

Making Instant
Multimedia

...determine what kind of multimedia work you can do and how fine and fancy you can render it.

T HERE is no reason to buy a dedicated multimedia authoring package if your current software (or an inexpensive upgrade) can do the job. Indeed, not only can you save money by doing multimedia with tools that are familiar and already at hand, but you also save the time spent on arduous and sometimes lengthy learning curves involved in mastering many dedicated authoring systems. Common desktop presentation tools have become multimedia powerful, while dedicated multimedia authoring systems are offering simplified, easy-to-use versions (see Chapter 7).

Most personal computers sold today are able to produce at least the sound and animation elements of multimedia. Manufacturers of popular software for word processing, spreadsheets, database management, graphing, drawing, and presentation have added capabilities for sound, image, and animation to their products. You can call a voice annotation, picture, or QuickTime or AVI movie from most word processing applications. You can click a cell in a spreadsheet to enhance its content with graphic images, sounds, and animations. Your database can include pictures, audio clips, and movies. Your presentation software can easily generate interesting titles, visual effects, and animated illustrations for your product demo. With these multimedia-enhanced software packages, you get many more ways to effectively convey your message than just a slide show.

To enliven your material and provide interesting illustrations, you can add multimedia elements to familiar tools such as word-processed documents, spreadsheets, presentation aids, and even HTML documents. But where do you get these elements? You can either make your images, sounds, and animations from scratch, or you can import them from collections of clip media. You can also license rights to use resources or content, such as pictures, songs and music, and video, from their owners. Importing from stock material limits you somewhat, but it may be all you need, and these collections can yield quick and simple multimedia productions. If you make your multimedia elements from scratch or edit existing material, you'll need to have special software and hardware tools to customize the images, sounds, and animations, but the results are more spectacular and dramatic.

---

warning   *You need special multimedia tools for digitizing your sounds and creating animations and movies before you can attach these objects to your word, data, or presentation documents. These tools are discussed in Chapter 5.*

Some multimedia projects may be so simple that you can cram all the organizing, planning, rendering, and testing stages into a single effort, making "instant" multimedia.

Here is an example: The topic at your weekly sales meeting is sales force performance. You want to display your usual spreadsheet so the group can see real names and numbers for each member of the team; then you want to show a multicolored 3-D bar graph for visual impact. Preparing for your meeting, you annotate the cell containing the name of the most productive salesperson for the week, using sounds of applause taken from a public domain CD-ROM, or a recording of your CEO saying "Good job!" or a colleague's "Wait till next week, Pete!" At the appropriate time during the meeting, you click that cell and play the annotation. And that's it—you have just made and used instant multimedia.

The following overviews do not include all products in each category of software tools, but they will give you a good sense of how multimedia might be applied in your everyday life working with computers. You will also find some tips and advice on using them in your multimedia projects.

Linking Multimedia Objects

The elements of multimedia (and other digitized information) are often treated as discrete *objects* that have particular characteristics or *properties*. With objects described in a common format using object-oriented programming systems (OOPs), text, bitmapped images, sounds, and video clips can be dynamically linked among applications and documents or even embedded in them. This object-oriented approach to information management is supported on both Macintosh and Windows platforms and is utilized at the core of some multimedia authoring systems (see Chapter 7).

When an object such as an image or drawing is *embedded* in a *destination* file it becomes part of that file, and the original or *source* file can be edited and changed without changing the embedded object. When an object is *linked*, however, only the location of the source file and a *representation* of its data are kept in the destination file—the actual data for the object is still stored in the source file. For large objects such as a 30MB video clip or a long sound track, linking is preferable to embedding, and embedding often is not even permitted.

AppleEvents

On the Macintosh, AppleEvents lets applications communicate with each other, sharing data and commands. InterApplication Communication (IAC) works with AppleEvents to automatically update documents that are linked with the "publish-and-subscribe" features of AppleEvents.

When you *publish* an application and then edit the data in it, the changes you make are copied to all of the *subscribers* to that data, even across a network. Publish-and-subscribe uses a transition file called the *edition file*.

You can *subscribe* to a spreadsheet table in a word processing document, for example, and when you change the spreadsheet, the word processing document gets changed automatically. Or you can embed a PICT image or QuickTime file in one application and change it in another, and the changes will appear in both applications—the two applications talk directly to each other.

To use publish-and-subscribe, follow these steps:

1. Select data that you want to place into another application or document.

2. From the Edit menu, choose Create Publisher. This brings up a dialog box asking you to name the edition file that will connect the publisher to the other documents subscribing to the data.

3. After you have created the edition file, go to the document or application where you want to use the data and select Subscribe To... from the Edit menu.

Now you have placed a *live* copy of the data in your document; whenever you modify the original publisher data, the subscriber is automatically updated, too.

DDE and OLE

Dynamic Data Exchange (DDE) and *Object Linking and Embedding* (OLE, pronounced "olay") are two methods for linking data objects among Windows applications. For example, let's say you want to advertise your new mousetrap design with a flashy graphic—an illustration showing your mousetrap compared to other mousetraps on the market—and some text describing its extraordinary features. First, you make a colorful picture in a graphics application such as Micrografx Designer, then you create a bar chart comparing the number of mice in a spreadsheet program such as Excel, and finally, you paste all your elements into a word processor such as Microsoft Word.

---

cross platform   *QuickTime for Windows supports OLE, so QuickTime movies made on the Macintosh can be integrated into Windows applications that support OLE.*

When two applications share data through DDE, they are in a *conversation.* DDE allows data to be transmitted between a *client* (the application that initiates the conversation) and a *server* (the application responding to the client). Data can be transmitted as a *hot link* so that modifications in the server application are also updated in the client application, or as a *cold link* so that data in the client application remains independent of the server after it has been imported.

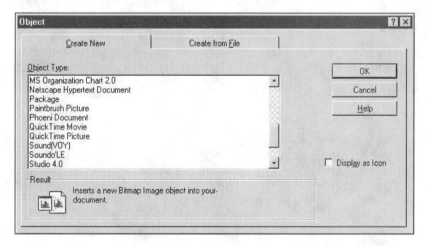

OLE lets you embed or link data objects created in different Windows or Macintosh applications. An *embedded* object becomes a part of the file into which it is pasted, independent of the original application where it was created. A *linked* object, on the other hand, is changed automatically in a *container* file that *points* to the original file when the original file is updated. Linking is a useful feature for data that may be modified after it has been placed into other files.

---

warning   *Using OLE, make sure that your linked files aren't moved to other directories, or the links may be broken. Although recent versions have improved the ability to track links between containers and objects, the best way to ensure that your object isn't "lost" is to embed it in a file.*

Office Suites

Office suites integrate into a single package the various productivity tools essential to running a business. Suites offer the convenience of a common interface with similar menus, commands, and toolbars, and they also allow you to share data among the applications in that suite using OLE and DDE. Suites also provide compatibility across the Macintosh and Windows platforms. Microsoft Office, for example, contains Word for word processing; Excel, a spreadsheet program; PowerPoint for creating presentations; and for Windows, a database manager (Access) and a scheduler. Each program is a stand-alone application, but all are interlinked through OLE and DDE. Claris's ClarisWorks for Macintosh and Windows provides a word processor, spreadsheet program, database manager, presentation tool, drawing/painting tool, and communications software in one application. Works offers seamless cross-platform file sharing between Macintosh and Windows platforms.

Word Processors

Many word-processed documents are ultimately printed to paper, but many are also delivered on a server or floppy disk, to an electronic mailbox, or as HTML documents on the World Wide Web. If others will be viewing your document on a computer, consider attaching multimedia voice notes, pictures, or animated illustrations to emphasize your point or to clarify something that is difficult to express in words. The "First Person" in this chapter illustrates the use of multimedia elements (in this case, QuickTime graphics) embedded into the working draft of a manuscript. The manuscript is shown, as are the graphics, along with a note to the editor.

First Person

Working draft of Chapter 4, revision 2, reads:

My father said that Mommy was still in a coma and my little brother was sleeping. We should go home now. So we went out the back way to the physician's parking lot: down the elevator and past the noisy kitchen with its racks of trays, white-uniformed cooks, piles of canned goods, and the steamy smells of institutional stew. The green screen door slammed indelibly into my five-year-old memory, and the attendant waved to my dad; he probably didn't know we were there on family business. It was all pretty serious.

We found Mommy's car behind the police station. I stayed in my seat while my father got out and walked very slowly around the twisted metal. He was calculating the impact forces, visualizing the accident in slow-motion freeze frames, and at one point, he leaned in through the broken glass and ran his hand across the dent in the steel glove compartment where my brother had smashed his face. He went around only the one time, then got back in. "She must have been doing about forty when she hit the pole," he offered as if I were an adult, and we drove out the narrow circular drive alongside the station house. It was a crisp, clear, football-and-pumpkins Saturday afternoon in October.

Editorial note to Sally: Per your comment last week, pick a good illustration from the file of images that I have attached. One of them should fit the bill... Thanks! See you next week.

Word

Microsoft's Word for Macintosh and Windows provides essentially the same user interface on both platforms and offers special multimedia features. You can make and import various image formats, including PICT, TIFF, BMP, and EPS, to place them in your document. You can add QuickTime movies to your document (see Figure 6-1); control the movie's playback characteristics (forward, backward, start, and stop); and perform simple editing with cut, copy, and paste commands. In the Windows version, AVI movies can also be played within your

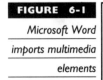

FIGURE 6-1

Microsoft Word

imports multimedia

elements

■

Word document. You can import digitized sounds, and you can record voice comments from an internal microphone, saving the recording (with a portion of the text or an icon as an identifier) for playback. Annotations can be searched for sound effects and content, edited, and even saved as separate files in any of four formats. With Word for Windows, you can also create links to other programs using OLE. Figure 6-2 demonstrates graphic chart information derived from an Excel spreadsheet linked to a Word document.

WordPerfect

In Corel's WordPerfect's Macintosh version, a tool palette and drawing commands allow you to create and edit graphics with the standard Macintosh drawing tools, as well as create Bezier curves and polygons; there's also a free rotation tool. A color editor lets you blend, rainbow, and complement colors. You can edit, size, scale, and crop graphic images, and then click and drag them anywhere in your document while text automatically reformats around them.

WordPerfect for Macintosh offers a QuickTime movie-playing facility (see Figure 6-3). The movie is represented by its poster, usually the first frame of the movie. You can represent your movie as a character, anchor it to a page or paragraph, move it, add a caption, or put a frame around it, just as you can with graphics. There is a movie controller that gives you many options, such as custom playback or changing the poster.

FIGURE 6-2

An Excel chart

linked into a Word

document

FIGURE 6-3

WordPerfect for

Macintosh provides

a QuickTime player

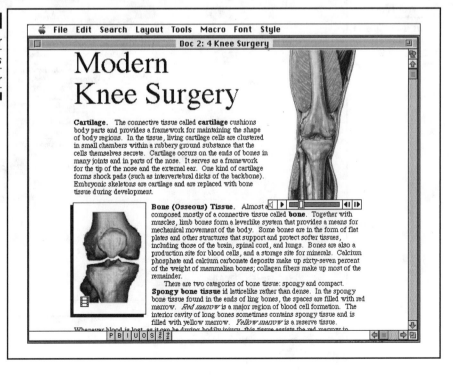

tip *For voice annotation in WordPerfect, you can put sounds and voice into the audio track of a QuickTime movie, and they will play back just fine.*

Using DDE, WordPerfect for Windows can share data with other DDE-compatible programs that use DDE links. If the data changes in a linked program, it is automatically updated in the WordPerfect document. A figure editor makes it easy to add graphics to your documents. You can view, retrieve, create, modify, and size figures, and save or import them into your document. WordPerfect for Windows works with the common graphic formats for DOS, as well as Windows metafiles and bitmaps.

Word Pro

With its Windows DDE and OLE capabilities, Lotus Word Pro can link to other applications and embedded objects, such as sounds and AVI movies. Using DDE, you can paste a link in Windows bitmap or metafile format into an empty selected frame. You can even create a macro to control another application through DDE. With OLE, you can link or embed objects into a frame in a Word Pro document (see Figure 6-4).

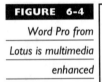

FIGURE 6-4

Word Pro from Lotus is multimedia enhanced

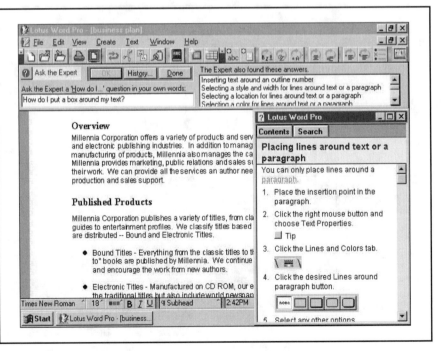

Spreadsheets

Spreadsheets have become the backbone of many users' information management systems. A spreadsheet organizes its data in columns and rows. Calculations are made based on user-defined formulas for, say, analyzing the survival rates of seedlings, or the production of glass bottles in Russia, or a household's consumption of energy in ergs per capita. Spreadsheets can answer what-if questions, build complex graphs and charts, and calculate a bottom line. From Alaska to Zimbabwe, spreadsheets have become a ubiquitous computer tool.

Most spreadsheet applications provide excellent chart-making routines; some allow you to build a series of several charts into an animation or movie, so you can dramatically show change over time or under varying conditions. Full-color curves that demonstrate changing annual sales, robbery and assault statistics, or birth rates may have a far greater effect on an audience than will a column of numbers.

The latest spreadsheets let you attach special notes and drawings, including full multimedia display of sounds, pictures, animations, and video clips.

6

Lotus 1-2-3

Lotus 1-2-3 lets you rearrange graph elements by clicking and dragging and using a menu to access data objects from the outside world. You can place bitmapped pictures and other objects such as QuickTime movies anywhere in your spreadsheet. There is a complete color drawing package for placing lines, circles, arrows, and special text on top of the spreadsheet to help illustrate its content (see Figure 6-5).

Excel

You can embed objects from many applications into Excel, too. Figure 6-6 shows an Excel document embedded with a Windows WAV sound, an image from Photoshop, a second WAV sound from Sound Forge, and a video movie. The Insert menu shown in Figure 6-6 will be used to add a picture into the spreadsheet directly from a digital camera.

FIGURE 6-5

Lotus 1-2-3

spreadsheets can

contain images and

movies

■

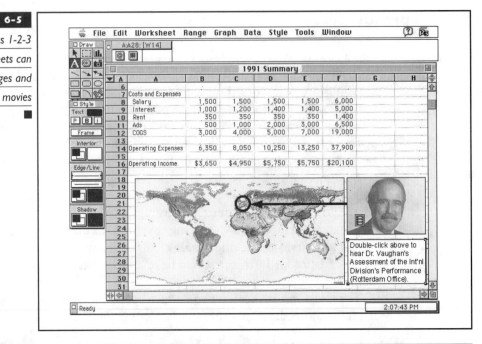

FIGURE 6-6

Microsoft Excel can

include embedded

objects made with

other applications

■

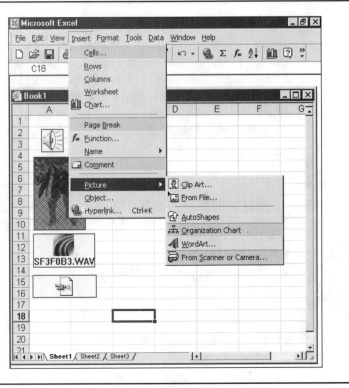

Databases

A database program can store, sort, retrieve, and organize many types of information. Like spreadsheets, databases can exist in a digital environment without ever needing to be printed to paper. Images, sounds, and movies are treated as objects and can be stored, retrieved, and played by many databases.

During the coming years, it is likely that multimedia databases will become a primary method by which corporate users interact with multimedia elements.

FileMaker Pro

FileMaker Pro, a relational database, rates high in ease of use and cross-platform capability with both Windows and Macintosh versions (see Figure 6-7). It also provides an easy method for publishing a FileMaker database as Web pages. FileMaker Pro has a relatively simple interface, yet it is powerful enough to handle moderately complex operations through scripting capabilities. You can use the built-in graphics tools and record sound within the application, or you can import images, sounds, and QuickTime movies from other applications. Although you can design layouts from scratch, there are 40 customizable templates from which to choose for business, education, or home use. FileMaker Pro supports AppleEvents in the Macintosh version and OLE/DDE in the Windows version.

FIGURE 6-7

A FileMaker Pro employee database can include image and sound resources

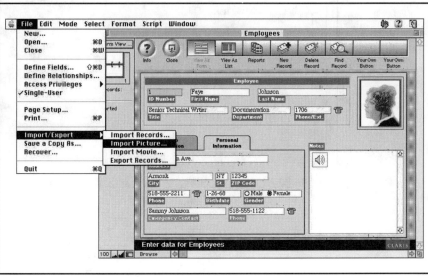

Access

Microsoft Access (Windows only; see Figure 6-8) is a relational database application available on its own or as part of the Microsoft Office Professional bundle of products. With a relational database, you input and store data only once, but you can view data in various ways. With Access, you can view the data in tables that show data from many records at once, forms that show data from each individual record, and reports from which to summarize and print data. The Database Wizard automatically builds tables, queries, forms, and reports with common business and personal database templates, including ones for asset management, order entry, and music collection tracking. It even adds sample data to help you get started. Or, if you already have a flat-file list or spreadsheet, use the Table Analyzer Wizard to import the data into an Access database. Access supports OLE objects and allows you to import images into forms and reports.

FIGURE 6-8

Microsoft Access handles images and other multimedia objects

Presentation Tools

Presentation software was originally developed to computerize the creation and delivery of presentations to audiences and conferences—as printed output that could be distributed on paper or shown on large screens by overhead projector, or digitally produced as 35 mm color slides. As direct connections from computer monitor outputs to projectors became commonplace, these same tools became useful for live computer-driven (interactive) presentations with or without printed handouts.

A cloudy area is emerging between presentation tools and multimedia authoring systems, as software publishers develop methods to accommodate the needs of computer-based presenters and as large-scale video and LCD panel projection systems become more affordable. Presentation software might, indeed, be considered multimedia authoring software, because the publishers of these tools have made their products multimedia capable. On the other hand, the features of dedicated presentation software are being incorporated into the three core office products—word processor, spreadsheet, and database—so many developers of these specialized tools have gone out of business.

The line between multimedia authoring and desktop presentation software is already a wide gray area. As system tools make multimedia easier to understand and implement, it will become more common in mainstream applications. The same thing happened in desktop publishing. Initially, people were buying PageMaker to dress up office memos. Now, virtually all word processors have basic page layout capabilities, and the dedicated "publishing" products are targeted at professionals. Multimedia authoring is headed the same way.

Karl Seppala, Macintosh Product Line Manager, Gold Disk, Inc.

Magicians use live props that often run across the stage or fly out of hats, as well as other attention-grabbing effects, to direct viewers' attention away from tricks and sleight of hand. In contrast, multimedia presenters use the same delivery techniques (the smoke and mirrors of computerized visual effects) to focus their viewers' attention on presentation content, so that the content will be remembered even when it's competing with a heavy lunch or a dimly lit conference room.

Presentation tools add synchronized audio, self-running animations, and video to the slide show presentation armamentarium.

PowerPoint

PowerPoint from Microsoft, for both Macintosh and Windows, offers a complete drawing and text package with an automatic or manual slide show feature. You can embed graphics and data from other applications into PowerPoint, and you can embed bitmapped images, slides, and presentations from PowerPoint into other applications. As shown in Figure 6-9, you can build live links between PowerPoint and other applications, and you can link and embed data and objects such as Flash and Shockwave files (.swf), movies or desktop video files (.avi, .mov, .qt, .mpg, and .mpeg), and animated GIF files. If they are larger than 100KB, sounds are automatically linked to a PowerPoint file, rather than embedded in it. Remember, like fonts, when your project uses linked files, these linked files must travel with you if you are going to be presenting on another computer!

FIGURE 6-9

Microsoft PowerPoint provides multimedia linking and embedding features

Multi

[
Common desktop presentation
tools are becoming more
multimedia powerful ...
]

sound and animation

media

In another few years,

most personal computers sold will be able to
produce at least the sound and animation elements of multimedia.

chapter

7

Multimedia
Authoring Tools

M ULTIMEDIA authoring tools provide the important framework you need for organizing and editing the elements of your multimedia project, including graphics, sounds, animations, and video clips. Authoring tools are used for designing interactivity and the user interface, for presenting your project on screen, and for assembling multimedia elements into a single, cohesive project.

Authoring software provides an integrated environment for binding together the content and functions of your project. Authoring systems typically include the ability to create, edit, and import specific types of data; assemble raw data into a playback sequence or cue sheet; and provide a structured method or language for responding to user input. With multimedia authoring software, you can make

- Video productions

- Animations

- Games

- Interactive Web sites

- Demo disks and guided tours

- Presentations

- Kiosk applications

- Interactive training

- Simulations, prototypes, and technical visualizations

Types of Authoring Tools

This chapter arranges the various authoring tools into groups based on the metaphor used for sequencing or organizing multimedia elements and events:

- Card- or page-based tools
- Icon-based, event-driven tools
- Time-based and presentation tools

Card- or page-based tools: In these authoring systems, elements are organized as pages of a book or a stack of cards. Thousands of pages or cards may be available in the book or stack. These tools are best used when the bulk of your content consists of elements that can be viewed individually, like the pages of a book or cards in a card file. The authoring system lets you link these pages or cards into organized sequences. You can jump, on command, to any page you wish in the structured navigation pattern. Card- or page-based authoring systems allow you to play sound elements and launch animations and digital video.

Icon-based, event-driven tools: In these authoring systems, multimedia elements and interaction cues (events) are organized as objects in a structural framework or process. Icon-based, event-driven tools simplify the organization of your project and typically display flow diagrams of activities along branching paths. In complicated navigational structures, this charting is particularly useful during development.

Time-based tools: In these authoring systems, elements and events are organized along a timeline, with resolutions as high or higher than 1/30 second. Time-based tools are best to use when you have a message with a beginning and an end. Sequentially organized graphic frames are played back at a speed that you can set. Other elements (such as audio events) are triggered at a given time or location in the sequence of events. The more powerful time-based tools let you program jumps to any location in a sequence, thereby adding navigation and interactive control.

In multimedia authoring systems, multimedia elements and events are often treated as *objects* that live in a hierarchical order of parent and child relationships. Messages passed among these objects order them to *do* things according to the *properties* or *modifiers* assigned to them. In this way, for example, Suzie (a teenager object) may be programmed to take out the trash every Friday evening, and does so when she gets a message from Dad. Spot, the puppy, may bark and jump up and down when the postman arrives. Spot is defined by barking and jumping modifiers; Suzie by hauling-trash modifiers or child objects (groan, sit up, stand up, saunter slowly, get bag, carry bag, slam door, etc.). Objects typically take care of themselves. Send them a message and they do their thing without external procedures and programming. Objects are particularly useful for games, which contain many components with many "personalities," and for simulating real-life situations, events, and their constituent properties.

The Right Tool for the Job

Each multimedia project you undertake will have its own underlying structure and purpose and will require different features and functions. In the best case, you must be prepared to choose the tool that best fits the job; in the worst case, you must know which tools will at least "get the job done." Authoring tools are constantly being improved by their makers, who add new features and increase performance with upgrade development cycles of six months to a year. It is important that you study the software product reviews in computer trade journals, as well as talk with current users of these systems, before deciding on the best ones for your needs.

---

w a r n i n g   *Because multimedia authoring systems are constantly being updated, make sure you purchase and use the latest version of software.*

Editing Features

The elements of multimedia—images, animations, text, digital audio and MIDI music, and video clips—need to be created, edited, and converted to standard file formats, and the specialized applications described in Chapters 5, 8, 9, 10, 11, and 12 provide these capabilities. Also, editing tools for these elements, particularly text and still images, are often included in your authoring system. The more editors your authoring system has, the fewer specialized tools you will need. In many cases, however, the editors that come with an authoring system will offer only a subset of the substantial features found in dedicated tools. According to Vaughan's Law of Multimedia Minimums (see Chapter 9), these features may very well be sufficient for what you need to do; on the other hand, if editors you need are missing from your authoring system, or if you require more power, it's best to use one of the specialized, single-purpose tools.

Organizing Features

The organization, design, and production process for multimedia (described in Chapters 16 and 17) involves storyboarding and flowcharting. Some authoring tools provide a visual flowcharting system or overview facility for illustrating your project's structure at a macro level. Storyboards or navigation diagrams, too, can help organize a project. Because designing the interactivity and navigation flow of your project often requires a great deal of planning and programming effort, your storyboard should describe not just the graphics of each screen, but the interactive elements as well. Features that help organize your material, such as those provided by SuperEdit, Authorware, IconAuthor, and other authoring systems, are a plus.

7

Programming Features

Multimedia authoring systems offer one or more of the following approaches, which are explained in the paragraphs that follow.

- Visual programming with cues, icons, and objects
- Programming with a scripting language
- Programming with traditional languages, such as Basic or C
- Document development tools

Visual programming with icons or objects is perhaps the simplest and easiest authoring process. If you want to play a sound or put a picture into your project, just drag the element's icon into the playlist. Or drag it away to delete it. Visual authoring tools such as Authorware and IconAuthor are particularly useful for slide shows and presentations.

Authoring tools that offer a very high level language (VHLL) or interpreted scripting environment for navigation control and for enabling user inputs—such as Macromedia Director, Macromedia Flash, HyperCard, MetaCard, and ToolBook—are more powerful. The more commands and functions provided in the scripting language, the more powerful the authoring system. Once you learn a scripting language, you will be able to learn other scripting languages relatively quickly; the principles are the same, regardless of the command syntax and keywords used. Many scripting languages on both platforms are similar to HyperTalk, a pioneering VHLL developed at Apple in 1987 as the underlying scripting language for HyperCard.

A scripted handler to generate a system beep may be very similar, regardless of platform. In HyperTalk, MetaTalk and Lingo, a script that makes the computer beep one time reads

```
on mouseUp
  beep
end mouseUp
```

In OpenScript, used by ToolBook, a similar script reads

```
to handle buttonUp
  beep 1
end buttonUp
```

As with traditional programming tools, look for an authoring package with good debugging facilities, robust text editing, and online syntax reference. Other scripting augmentation facilities are advantages, as well. In complex projects, you may need to program custom extensions of the scripting language for direct access to the computer's operating system. On the Macintosh, this means being able to use external commands and functions (XCMDs and XFCNs) written in C. In Windows, you will need to call Dynamic Link Libraries (DLLs).

A powerful document reference and delivery system is a key component of some projects. Some authoring tools offer direct importing of preformatted text, indexing facilities, complex text search mechanisms, and hypertext linkage tools. These authoring systems are useful for development of CD-ROM information products, online documentation and help systems, and sophisticated multimedia-enhanced publications.

With scripts, you can perform computational tasks; sense and respond to user input; create character, icon, and motion animations; launch other applications; and control external multimedia devices.

Interactivity Features

Interactivity empowers the end users of your project by letting them control the content and flow of information. Authoring tools should provide one or more levels of interactivity:

- *Simple branching,* which offers the ability to go to another section of the multimedia production (via an activity such as a keypress, mouse click, or expiration of a timer)

- *Conditional branching,* which supports a go-to based on the results of IF-THEN decisions or events

- A *structured language* that supports complex programming logic, such as nested IF-THENs, subroutines, event tracking, and message passing among objects and elements

Performance Tuning Features

Complex multimedia projects require exact synchronization of events—for example, the animation of an exploding balloon with its accompanying sound effect. Accomplishing synchronization is difficult because performance varies widely among the different computers used for multimedia development and delivery. Some authoring tools allow you to lock a production's playback speed to a specified computer platform, but others provide no ability whatsoever to control performance on various systems. In many cases, you will need to use the authoring tool's own scripting language or custom programming facility to specify timing and sequence on systems with different (faster or slower) processors. Be sure your authoring system allows precise timing of events.

Playback Features

As you build your multimedia project, you will be continually assembling elements and testing to see how the assembly looks and performs. Your authoring system should let you build a segment or part of your project and then quickly test it as if the user were actually using it. You will spend a great deal of time going back and forth between building and testing as you refine and smooth the content and timing of the project.

Delivery Features

Delivering your project may require building a run-time version of the project using the multimedia authoring software. A *run-time* version allows your project to play back without requiring the full authoring software and all its tools and editors. Often, the run-time version does not allow users to access or change the content, structure, and programming of the project. If you are going to distribute your project widely, you should distribute it in the run-time version. Make sure your authored project can be easily distributed. Chapter 19 discusses delivery of multimedia projects in more detail.

Cross-Platform Features

It is also increasingly important to use tools that make transfer across platforms easy. For many developers, the Macintosh remains the multimedia authoring platform of choice, but 80 percent of that developer's target market may be Windows platforms. If you develop on a Macintosh, look for tools that provide a compatible authoring system for Windows or offer a run-time player for the other platform.

Internet Playability

Because the Web has become a significant delivery medium for multimedia, authoring systems typically provide a means to convert their output so that it can be delivered within the context of HTML or DHTML, either with special plug-ins or by embedding Java, JavaScript, or other code structures in the HTML document. Chapters 14 and 15 discuss design and delivery of multimedia on the Web.

Card- and Page-Based Authoring Tools

Card- and page-based authoring systems provide a simple and easily understood metaphor for organizing multimedia elements. Because graphic images typically form the backbone of a project, both as navigation menus and as content, many developers first arrange their images into logical sequences or groupings similar to the chapters and pages of a book, or cards in a card catalog. Navigation routines become, then, simply directives to go to a page or card that contains appropriate images and text, and associated sounds, animations, and video clips.

Page-based authoring systems contain media objects: the objects are the buttons, text fields, graphic objects, backgrounds, pages or cards, and even the project itself. The characteristics of objects are defined by properties (highlighted, bold, red, hidden, active, locked, etc.). Each object may contain programming script, usually a property of that object, that is activated when an event (such as a mouse click) related to that object occurs. Events cause messages to pass along the hierarchy of objects in your project; for example, a mouse-click message can be sent from a button to the background, to the page, and then to the project itself. As the message travels, it looks for handlers in the script of each object; if it finds a matching handler, the authoring system then executes the task specified by that handler.

Most page-based authoring systems provide a facility for linking objects to pages or cards (by automatically programming branching go-to statements for navigating by mouse clicks), but learning to write your own scripts and understanding the message-passing nature of these authoring tools is essential to making them perform well. Following are some typical messages that might be passed along the object hierarchy of the HyperCard, MetaCard, and ToolBook authoring systems:

HyperCard and MetaCard	ToolBook Message
closeCard	leavePage
closeStack	leaveBook
idle	idle
mouseDown	buttonDown
mouseStillDown	buttonStillDown
mouseUp	buttonUp
newBackground	newBackground
openCard	enterPage
openStack	enterBook

Now let's look at specific examples. To go to the next card or page when a button is clicked, you would place a message handler into the script of that button. (In the languages demonstrated below, handlers begin with "on" or "to handle.") Here is an example in HyperTalk and MetaTalk:

```
on mouseUp
  go next card
end mouseUp
```

Here is an example in OpenScript (ToolBook):

```
to handle buttonUp
  go next page
end buttonUp
```

The handler, if placed in the script of the card or page, will execute its commands upon receiving a "mouseUp" or "buttonUp" event message occurring at any location on the card or page—not just while the cursor is within the bounds of a button.

Most card- or page-based authoring systems require a special intermediate file that also receives scripted message handlers and acts as a repository for special routines and resources that are available to all projects being executed by the application. In HyperCard, this file is called Home; in ToolBook, you may have one or more System Books.

Card- and page-based systems typically provide two separate layers on each card: a background layer that may be shared among many cards, and a foreground layer that is specific to a single card. Figure 7-1 demonstrates use of foreground and background layering by design: when the gray cover on the foreground layer is wiped away with an "eraser," the graphic image on the background layer is revealed. In this figure, an animated earth is made up of 18 characters and rotates underneath a marker to point out the habitat of the monkey species that is hidden below the cover. When enough of the cover is erased so the user can recognize the monkeys, the user releases the mouse button and chooses a name from a menu. If the name is incorrect, a sound plays and a cat appears and wags its tail (the cat is a button icon), and the user can continue. If the user selects the correct monkey, an encyclopedia of information about that species is presented, and a pull-down menu (see Figure 7-2) provides access to a sound bite or video clip before going on. There are 25 monkeys, and the program keeps score.

http://www.metacard.com
http://www.asymetrix.com

Card- and page-based authoring tools

FIGURE 7-1

The gray cover in the foreground layer of a card is erased to reveal the image on the background layer beneath ∎

FIGURE 7-2

Sound, animation, and video can be played in card- and page-based systems ∎

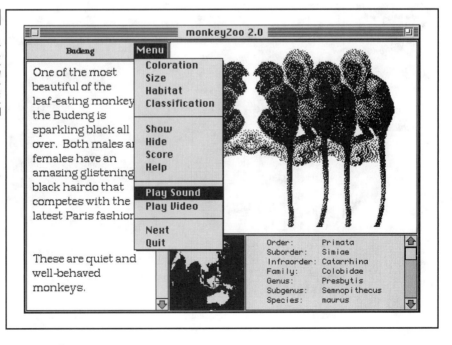

Icon-Based Authoring Tools

Icon-based, event-driven tools provide a visual programming approach to organizing and presenting multimedia. First you build a structure or flowchart of events, tasks, and decisions, by dragging appropriate icons from a library. These icons can include menu choices, graphic images, sounds, and computations. The flowchart graphically depicts the project's logic. When the structure is built, you can add your content: text, graphics, animation, sounds, and video movies. Then, to refine your project, you edit your logical structure by rearranging and fine-tuning the icons and their properties.

With icon-based authoring tools, nontechnical multimedia authors can build sophisticated applications without scripting. By placing icons on a flow line, you can quickly sequence events and activities, including decisions and user interactions. These tools are useful for storyboarding, as you can change sequences, add options, and restructure interactions by simply dragging and dropping icons. You can print out your navigation map or flowchart, an annotated project index with or without associated icons, design and presentation windows, and a cross-reference table of variables.

Figure 7-3 shows the layout of an online magazine published on CD-ROM using Authorware as the authoring system. Note that Interaction icons branch to other topics.

FIGURE 7-3

Authorware provides a structural and navigational overview of your entire project, using icons

http://www.macromedia.com/software/authorware/
http://www.mentergy.com/products/authoring_design/quest/

More about icon-based authoring tools

Time-Based Authoring Tools

Time-based systems are popular multimedia authoring tools. Each uses its own distinctive approach and user interface for managing events over time. Many use a visual timeline for sequencing the events of a multimedia presentation, often displaying layers of various media elements or events alongside the scale in increments as precise as one second. Others arrange long sequences of graphic frames and add the time component by adjusting each frame's duration of play.

Director

Macromedia's Director is a powerful and complex multimedia authoring tool from Macromedia with a broad set of features to create multimedia presentations, animations, and interactive multimedia applications. It requires a significant learning curve, but once mastered, it is among the most powerful of multimedia development tools. In Director, you assemble and sequence the elements of your project using a Cast and a Score. A demo version of Director is available on the Macromedia CD-ROM, found inside the back cover of this book.

Director movies are generally good for cross-platform delivery. To make run-time "projectors" for both platforms, however, you need to use a Mac version to make the Mac projector and a Windows version to make a Windows projector. This can be costly because you need a copy of Director on each platform. If you make a Shockwave projector, however, it will launch from both Mac and Windows platforms using the Shockwave Player.

Cast

The Cast is a multimedia database containing still images, sound files, text, palettes, QuickDraw shapes, programming scripts, QuickTime movies, Flash movies, and even other Director files. As shown in Figure 7-4, not only can you import a wide range of data types and multimedia element formats directly into this Cast, but you can also create multimedia elements from scratch using Director's own tools and editors.

FIGURE 7-4

Director's Cast

feature contains

all the multimedia

elements of your

project ■

A full-featured painting tool lets you create bitmapped artwork in any color depth. You can create gradients, tile patterns, and animated transformations (such as rotations and skews) of artwork. Other tools edit and create QuickDraw shapes, text, QuickTime movies, palettes, and scripts.

Score

Once you have imported or created the multimedia elements for your project and placed them into your Cast, you tie these Cast members together using the Score facility. Score is a sequencer for displaying, animating, and playing Cast members, and it is made up of frames that contain Cast members, tempo, a palette, timing, and sound information. Each frame is played back on a "stage" at a rate specified in the tempo channel. The Score provides elaborate and complex visual effects and transitions, adjustments of color palettes, and tempo control. In Figure 7-5, which shows a screen from the draft of an interactive multimedia novel, the frames are the vertical bands, and the channels are the numbered horizontal bands.

Animations, for example, are made by placing a graphic or *sprite* onto the stage and changing its location slightly over several or more frames. When the frames are played back at tempo, the sprite moves. You can synchronize

FIGURE 7-5

Director's Score

features sequences

and sets the tempo

for playback

■

7

animations with sound effects by highlighting a range of frames and selecting the appropriate sound from your Cast.

Lingo

Director utilizes Lingo, a full-featured object-oriented scripting language, to enable interactivity and programmed control. A built-in script editor offers Lingo debugging facilities. Because you can attach scripts to individual elements of the Cast, you can copy and paste complete interactive sequences. Lingo also uses Xtras, which are special code segments used to control external sound and video devices. Several Xtras and extensive examples of their use are shipped with Macromedia Director. With Lingo, you can also control operations on the Internet such as sending mail, reading documents and images, and building Web pages on the fly.

Using Lingo scripts, you can chain together separate Director documents and call other files as subroutines. You can also import elements into your Cast using pointers to a file. This allows you to share the same elements among many Casts; when your Score calls for that element, it is loaded into RAM from the file. Chaining and sharing let you create Director projects as large or complex as your storage medium will accommodate.

http://www.macromedia.com/software/director/
http://www.mcli.dist.maricopa.edu/director/

There are many Web sites containing a wealth of up-to-date Director tips and resources

Cross-Platform Authoring Notes

You face two major hurdles when you move multimedia projects across platforms; these hurdles have to do with the different schemes Macintosh and Windows computers use to manage text and colors.

If your project uses only bitmapped images and sounds, the text issue is moot. But if you use text in fields or require user entry of text, you will face size and shape issues (see Chapter 8). The Macintosh and Windows environments each use different fonts (even when the fonts have the same name), so you may wish to experiment with your fonts before designing or converting a project.

Each platform also uses its own character set; some special characters may appear as different characters on the other platform. The following Macintosh characters do not map across platforms, and you will have to use a substitute character:

Macintosh Character	Suggested Substitute
• (bullet)	* (asterisk)
" " (smart quotes)	" (normal quote)
≠ (does not equal)	<>
≤ (less than or equal to)	<=
≥ (greater than or equal to)	>=
…(ellipsis)	... (three periods)

Here are some important tips for working with text in cross-platform applications:

- For text in boxes, center the text, leaving plenty of space or margin to avoid possible word-wrap on the other platform.

- Avoid outline and shadow styles on the Macintosh. They are not currently supported in Windows and may default to boldface.

- When the look of a larger-size font is extremely important, turn it into a bitmap by screen capturing before you convert.

- If you use TrueType fonts or Adobe ATM, the fonts must be installed and available on both platforms, or must be embedded in the playback application.

Colors can also be difficult to manage in cross-platform projects, because both computer platforms employ different palette-mapping systems. The colors you use on the Macintosh, for example, may not appear the same on the PC. When you convert a Macintosh 256-color graphics file to Windows, all colors are mapped to their nearest equivalents, so the results you get will depend on the color palettes used on each platform. Color palettes are discussed in detail in Chapter 10.

---

t i p   *Rather than dithering a 256-color bitmap to 16 colors with unattractive results, try using gray-scale images instead.*

7

Multi

> Today's poets and songwriters concentrate text by distilling prose into a very few words heavy with meaning.

6,000 years ago..............................

words have
meaning

media

SUMERIA

MESOPOTAMIA

Babylonia

part

3

Multimedia
Building Blocks

...........................meaningful marks were scraped onto mud tablets and left to harden in the sun.

EGYPT

Multi

Words and symbols in any form, spoken or written, are the most common system of communication.

6,000 years ago..............................

words have
meaning

media

SUMERIA

MESOPOTAMIA

Babylonia

chapter

8

Text

............................meaningful marks were scraped onto mud tablets and left to harden in the sun.

EGYPT

U SING text and symbols for communication is a very recent human development that began about 6,000 years ago in the Mediterranean Fertile Crescent—in Mesopotamia, Egypt, Sumeria, and Babylonia—when the first meaningful marks were scraped onto mud tablets and left to harden in the sun. Only members of the ruling classes and the priesthood were allowed to read and write the pictographic signs and cuneiforms.

The earliest messages delivered in written words typically contained information vital to the management of people, politics, and taxes. Because this new medium did not require rote memorization by frail human gray matter, written messages became popular among the elite. Unlike their human counterparts, these new messages were less likely to perish due to dysentery, acts of God, or amnesia. Even if a message were intercepted by foes or competitors, it would still be indecipherable except by those few who had acquired reading skills.

In fact, because those who could read probably attended the same private school together, reading, writing, and power politics in those days were naturally intertwined. In some former eras it was a capital offense to read unless you belonged to the proper social class or possessed a patent granted by your rulers.

Today, text and the ability to read it are doorways to power and knowledge. Reading and writing are expected and necessary skills within most modern cultures. Now, depending upon your proficiency with words, you may be awarded a doctorate instead of the death penalty. And, as has been the case throughout history, text still delivers information that can have potent meaning.

In the 15th century, when the Church was a strong power throughout Europe, Johann Gensfleisch zum Gutenberg, a trained goldsmith from Mainz, Germany, invented moveable type for printing presses. And he began producing religious literature, indulgence slips, and the Holy Bible. In the case of the Bible, he sold his copies to people who could read Latin and pay the equivalent of three years of a clerk's wage to own a personal copy of this Great Work. Other printers, including the Estienne family in France and Aldus Manutius in Italy, soon entered the publishing marketplace to compete, and they changed the fabric of society. The mass production of identical copies of text enabled an information-based paradigm shift that changed the human universe in a substantial way. Lots of scribes and the illuminators were put out of business.

By way of pointing out that some elements of the human equation may be constant throughout history, I would remark that Gutenberg, like many adventurers surfing the waves of today's revolution, took on a financial investor, Johann Fust. Gutenberg, who was a visionary craftsman perhaps better suited to lab and shop work, defaulted on a payment to Fust in 1455, was sued, and lost his press and all its profits. Toward the end of his life, it is said that he was granted a place as courtier to the archbishop of Mainz, a position perhaps better remunerating than the diminishing social security plan rewarding today's surfer who wipes out while hanging ten at the leading edge of the business world.

—From a speech by Tay Vaughan to the jointly held World Conference on Educational Multimedia and Hypermedia and World Conference on Educational Telecommunications, Freiburg, Germany, June 1998.

With the recent explosion of the Internet and the World Wide Web, text has become more important than ever. Indeed, the native language of the Web is HTML (Hypertext Markup Language), originally designed to display simple text documents on computer screens, with occasional graphic images thrown in as illustrations (see Chapter 13 for more history about the Internet). Academic papers, magazine articles, complex instruction manuals, and even the contents of entire books are now available for reading with a Web browser. Add a built-in function that links, with a click of the mouse, selected words and phrases to other related and perhaps more-detailed material (the "hypertext" part of HTML discussed later in this chapter), and you can surf the Net in a medium much richer than the paper pages of a book.

The social impact of this text-biased medium on the way people access and use information will be profound as the Web matures. In contrast to today's television medium, which consists of sound and images with a few text headlines "dumbed down" to a perceived lowest common denominator of a passive audience, the Web offers an active experience laden with enough choices to challenge even bright people who can read. More than television, with its 5 or 50 or even 500 channels, the Web offers an explorer's paradise of millions of HTML documents. As bandwidth improves and more multimedia elements are successfully embedded within these documents, developers of content will not escape the difficult design issues discussed in Chapter 17. Who is the audience? What words should I use?

With its penchant for interactivity, multimedia too often ignores the power of narrative, of stories. There's really something to be said for documents with a beginning, middle, and end.

Steven Levy, author of Hackers, Artificial Life, Insanely Great, Unicorn's Secret, and Crypto; Senior Editor and chief technology writer for *Newsweek*

The Power of Meaning

Even a single word may be cloaked in many meanings, so as you begin working with any medium it is important to cultivate accuracy and conciseness in the specific words you choose. In multimedia, these are the words that will appear in your titles, menus, and navigation aids.

Today's poets and songwriters concentrate text by distilling lengthy prose into few words heavy with meaning. Advertising wordsmiths render the meaning of entire product lines into an evocative single word, logo, or tag line. Multimedia authors weave words, symbols, sounds, and images, and then blend text into the mix to create integrated tools and interfaces for acquiring, displaying, and disseminating messages and data, using computers.

"Barbie," "green," and "lite" may each easily trigger a rush of different meanings. A piercing cry in the night, the sight of fire engines leaving your street as you steer your car into your neighborhood, the scent of drying kelp along the seashore, the feel of rough pine bark against your chest as you climb, fingernails on a chalkboard—all these raw sensory messages are important only because of what they mean to you. Indeed, you alone know the words that will stop you dead in your tracks with anger, or, better, soothe you seductively over a quiet dinner for two. These words have meaning.

All of these examples demonstrate the following multimedia principle: it's important to design labels for title screens, menus, and buttons using words that have the most precise and powerful meanings to express what you need to say. Understand the subtle shadings. GO BACK! is more powerful than *Previous*; Quit is more powerful than *Close*. TERRIFIC! may work better than *That Answer Was Correct*.

Experiment with the words you plan to use by letting others try them. If you have the budget, set up a focus group to have potential users experience your words. Watch them work. See if users flinch, balk, or click the Help button in confusion. See if they can even find Help.

Words and symbols in any form, spoken or written, are the most common system of communication. They deliver the most widely understood meaning to the greatest number of people—accurately and in detail. Because of this, they are vital elements of multimedia menus, navigation systems, and content. You will reward yourself and your users if you take the time to use excellent words. Let your poet loose!

---

tip *Browse through a thesaurus. You will be surprised at the number of synonyms and related words that are closely associated to the word you start with, and you will certainly find the one word that most perfectly fits your need. The majority of today's popular word processors ship with a bundled electronic thesaurus.*

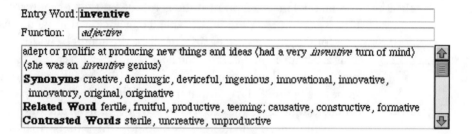

If you are reading this book in English, you might consider yourself lucky. A recent study by the British Council concluded that 1 billion people will speak English by the year 2000 as a first, second, or "foreign" language. English is the official or joint official language of more than 75 countries, and Algeria recently dumped French in favor of English as the second language in schools, irritating a great many Parisian intellectuals. More than two thirds of the world's scientists read English, and three quarters of the world's mail is written in English. Eighty percent of the world's information that is stored on computers is written in English.

When we have a technical meeting with engineers coming from Germany, France, Spain, Sweden, Japan, and other countries, people say "Hello!" when they walk into the room; English is clearly the international common language of business and commerce and science. Sometimes the etiquette of polite speech is even more fascinating: when you have a room with a group of Germans talking to each other in German and suddenly a foreign visitor comes in, from one sentence to the other, they seamlessly switch to English.

Dipl.-Ing. Roland Cuny, webwasher.com, Paderborn, Germany

About Fonts and Faces

A *typeface* is a family of graphic characters that usually includes many type sizes and styles. A *font* is a collection of characters of a single size and style belonging to a particular typeface family. Typical font *styles* are boldface and italic. Other style attributes, such as underlining and outlining of characters, may be added by your computer software. Type sizes are usually expressed in points; one *point* is .0138 inches or about 1/72 of an inch. The font's size is the distance from the top of the capital letters to the bottom of the descenders in letters such as *g* and *y*. Helvetica, Times, and Courier are typefaces; Times 12-point italic is a font. In the computer world, the term font is commonly used when typeface or face would be more correct.

A font's size does not exactly describe the height or width of its characters. This is because the *x-height* (the height of the lowercase letter *x*) of two fonts may vary, while the height of the capital letters of those fonts may be the same (see Figure 8-1). Computer fonts automatically add space below the descender (and sometimes above) to provide appropriate line spacing, or *leading* (pronounced "ledding," named for the thin strips of lead inserted between the lines by traditional typesetters). There can be significant variation among fonts.

Leading can be adjusted in most programs on both the Macintosh and in Windows. Typically you will find this fine-tuning adjustment in the Text menu of image-editing programs or the Paragraph menu of word processing programs, though this is not an official standard. No matter where your application has placed the controls for leading, you will need to experiment with them to achieve the best result for your font. With a font editing program like Fontographer from Macromedia (you'll see an example of it later in the chapter), adjustments can also be made along the horizontal axis of text: the character metrics of each character and the kerning of character pairs can be altered. *Character metrics* are the general measurements applied

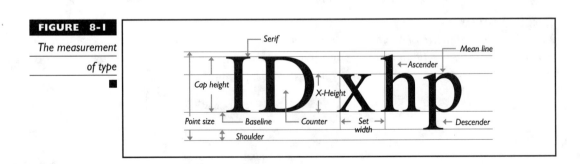

FIGURE 8-1

The measurement of type

to individual characters; *kerning* is the spacing between character pairs. Working with PostScript, TrueType, and Master fonts, but not bitmapped fonts (see "Computers and Text" later in this chapter), the metrics of a font can be altered to create interesting effects. For example, you can adjust the body width of each character from *regular* to *condensed* to *expanded*, displayed in the Sabon font used in this book:

Regular
Condensed
Expanded

Or you can adjust the spacing between characters (*tracking*) and the kerning between pairs of characters:

Tighter Track
Looser Track

Av Av

Kerned   Unkerned

   When it draws or *rasterizes* the letter A on the screen or in printed output, the computer must know how to represent the letter using tiny square pixels or dots. It does this according to the hardware available and according to your specification from a choice of available typefaces and fonts. High-resolution monitors and printers can make more attractive-looking and varied characters. And today's broad selection of software fonts makes it easier to find the right typeface and font for your need. Here are some examples of the same letter displayed using different fonts:

A A A A A A A A A

8

Cases

In centuries when type was set by hand, the type for a single font was always stored in two trays, or *cases*; the upper tray held capital letters, and the lower tray held the small letters. Today a capital letter is called *uppercase,* and a small letter is called *lowercase.*

tip *Studies have shown that words and sentences with mixed upper- and lowercase letters are easier to read than words or sentences in all caps.*

In some situations, such as for passwords, a computer is *case sensitive*. But nowadays, in most situations requiring keyboard input—on the Macintosh or in Windows—the computer recognizes both the upper- and lowercase forms of a character to be the same. In that manner, the computer is said to be *case insensitive*.

warning *The directory and file names used in Uniform Resource Locator (URL) addresses on the Internet are case sensitive! Thus, http://www.timestream.com/ info/people/biotay/biotay1.html points to a different directory and file than http://www.timestream.com/info/people/bioTay/biotay1.html. On the other hand, the record type (HTTP) and the domain name (www.timestream.com), and e-mail addresses (tay@timestream.com) as well, are usually case insensitive. Read more about addresses on the Internet in Chapter 13.*

Recently, company and product names such as EveryWare, AirWorks, PhotoDisc, PageMaker, LogoMotion, FileMaker, and WebStar have become popular. Placing an uppercase letter in the middle of a word, called an *intercap*, is a trend that emerged from the computer programming community where coders discovered they could better see the words they used for variables and commands.

Serif Versus Sans Serif

Typefaces can be described in many ways, just as a home advertised by a realtor, a wine described by a food critic, or a political candidate's platform can all be described in many ways. Type has been characterized as feminine, masculine, delicate, formal, capricious, witty, comic, happy, technical, newsy—you name it. But one approach for categorizing typefaces is universally understood, and it has less to do with the reader's response to the type than it does with the type's mechanical and historical properties. This approach uses the terms *serif* and *sans serif*.

Serif versus sans serif is the simplest way to categorize a typeface; the type either has a serif or it doesn't (*sans* is French for "without"). The serif is the little decoration at the end of a letter stroke. Times, New Century Schoolbook, Bookman, and Palatino are examples of serif fonts. Helvetica, Arial, Optima, and Avant Garde are sans serif. Notice the difference between serif and sans serif in the following illustration:

On the printed page, serif fonts are traditionally used for body text because the serifs are said to help guide the reader's eye along the line of text. Sans serif fonts, on the other hand, are used for headlines and bold statements. But the computer world of standard, 72 dpi monitor resolution is not the same as the print world, and it can be argued that sans serif fonts are far more legible and attractive when used in the small sizes of a text field on a screen. Indeed, careful selection of a sans serif font designed to be legible in the small sizes (such as Geneva on the Macintosh or Small Fonts in Windows) makes more sense when you are presenting a substantial amount of text on the screen. The Times font at 9-point size may look too busy and actually be difficult and tiring to read. And a large, bold serif font for a title or headline can deliver a message of elegance and character in your graphic layout. Use what is right for your delivery system, which may not necessarily be the same as what is right when you print the material to paper—WYSIWYG (What You See Is What You Get) when printing out what you create on a computer monitor is more of a goal than absolute fact.

Using Text in Multimedia

Imagine designing a project that used no text at all. Its content could not be at all complex, and you would need to use many pictures and symbols to train your audience how to navigate through the project. Certainly voice and sound could guide the audience, but users would quickly tire of this—greater effort is required to pay attention to spoken words than to browse text.

A single item of menu text accompanied by a single action (a mouse click, keystroke, or finger pressed to the monitor) requires little training and is clean and immediate. Use text for titles and headlines (what it's all about), for menus (where to go), for navigation (how to get there), and for content (what you see when you get there).

---

tip   *In designing your navigation system, bring the user to a particular destination with as few actions and as short a wait as possible. If the user never needs the Help button to get there, you are doing everything right!*

Designing with Text

Computer screens provide a very small workspace for developing complex ideas. At some time or another, you will need to deliver high-impact or very concise text messages on the computer screen in as condensed a form as possible. From a design perspective, your choice of font size and the number of headlines you place on a particular screen must be related both to the complexity of your message and to its venue.

If your messages are part of an interactive project or Web site where you know the user is seeking information, you can pack a great deal of text information onto the screen before it becomes overwhelmingly busy. Seekers want dense material, and while they travel along your navigational pathways, they will scroll through relevant text and study the details. Here is where you must strike a balance, however. Too little text on a screen requires annoying page turns and unnecessary mouse clicks and waits; too much text can make the screen seem overcrowded and unpleasant.

On the other hand, if you are providing public-speaking support, the text will be keyed to a live presentation where the text accents the main message. In this case, use large fonts and few words with lots of white space. Let the audience focus on the speaker at the podium, rather than spend their time reading fine points and subpoints projected on a screen.

---

tip *A lengthy text document read by a Web browser may scroll for hundreds of lines without annoying the user; it's expected. As a rule of thumb, however, try to make your Web pages no longer than one-and-a-half to two screenfuls of text. Many "standard" pages are 600 pixels in height (about one and a half screens on a VGA monitor). For pages intended to get people's attention, make your page about 400 pixels high so there will be no scrolling at all. For printing text documents, provide a separate link to a complete document in either text, word processor, or Adobe PDF format instead of relying on a browser's print facilities. It is often more convenient to print and read a document than to scroll through many pages of text on a monitor.*

Choosing Text Fonts

Picking the fonts to use in your multimedia presentation may be somewhat difficult from a design standpoint. Here again, you must be a poet, an advertising psychologist, and also a graphic designer. Try to sense the potential reaction of the user to what is on the screen. Here are a few design suggestions that may help:

- For small type, use the most legible font available. Decorative fonts that cannot be read are useless:

    Can you read me?

    𝕮𝖆𝖓 𝖞𝖔𝖚 𝖗𝖊𝖆𝖉 𝖒𝖊?

- Use as few different faces as possible in the same work, but vary the weight and size of your typeface using italic and bold styles where they look good. Using too many fonts on the same page is called ransom-note typography.

- In text blocks, adjust the leading for the most pleasing line spacing. Lines too tightly packed are difficult to read.

- Vary the size of a font in proportion to the importance of the message you are delivering.

- In large-size headlines, adjust the spacing between letters (kerning) so that the spacing feels right. Big gaps between large letters can turn your title into a toothless waif. You may need to kern by hand, using a bitmapped version of your text.

- To make your type stand out or be more legible, explore the effects of different colors and of placing the text on various backgrounds. Try reverse type for a stark, white-on-black message.

- Use anti-aliased text where you want a gentle and blended look for titles and headlines. This can give a more professional appearance. *Anti-aliasing* blends the colors along the edges of the letters (called *dithering*) to create a soft transition between the letter and its background. Color Plate 6 shows an example of anti-aliased type.

- Try drop caps (like this "T") and initial caps to accent your words. Most word processors and text editors will let you create drop caps and SMALL CAPS in your text. Adobe and others make initial caps (such as the one shown below from Adobe, called "Gothic"). The letters are actually carefully drawn artwork and are available in special libraries as encapsulated PostScript files (EPSF).

- If you are using centered type in a text block, keep the number of lines to a minimum.

- For attention-grabbing results, try graphically altering and distorting the text. Wrap your word onto a sphere, bend it into a wave, or splash it with rainbow colors. Font editing tools such as ResEdit, Fontographer, FontMonger, and FontChameleon are discussed later in this chapter. Also, paint and drawing packages for customizing text and bitmaps are discussed in Chapter 5.

- Experiment with drop shadows. Place a copy of the word on top of the original and offset the original up and over a few pixels. Then color the original gray (or any other color). The word may become more legible and provide much greater impact. At Web sites, shadowed text and graphics on a plain white background add depth to a page. See Chapter 10 for tips on making shadows.

- Surround headlines with plenty of white space. *White space* is a designer's term for roomy blank areas; programmers call the invisible character made by a space (ASCII 32) or a tab (ASCII 9) white space.

- Pick the fonts that seem right to you for getting your message across; then double-check your choice against other opinions. Learn to accept criticism.

- Use meaningful words or phrases for links and menu items.

- Text links (*anchors*) on Web pages can accent your message: they stand out by color and underlining. Use link colors consistently throughout a site, and avoid iridescent green on red or purple on puce.

- Bold or emphasize text to highlight ideas or concepts, but do not make text look like a link or a button when it is not.

- On a Web page, put vital text elements and menus in the top 320 pixels. Studies of surfer habits have discovered that only 10 percent to 15 percent of surfers *ever* scroll *any* page.

---

cross platform *Characters identified in a particular font (say, Courier 12 point) do not look the same on a Macintosh as they do on Windows display monitors. Typically, what is called 12 point on a Macintosh will be a 10- or 9-point size in Windows. And the actual shape of the characters will be different (see Figure 8-2).*

FIGURE 8-2

Examples
of Courier typeface
on the Macintosh
and PC

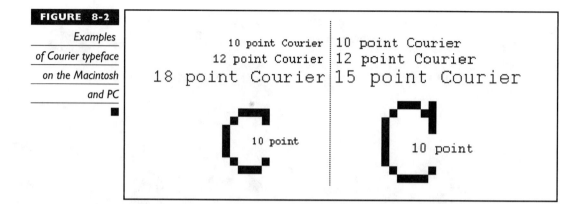

Menus for Navigation

An interactive multimedia project or Web site typically consists of a body of information or *content* through which a user navigates by pressing a key, clicking a mouse, or pressing a touchscreen. The simplest menus consist of text lists of topics. Users choose a topic, click it, and go there. As multimedia and graphical user interfaces become pervasive in the computer community, certain intuitive actions are being widely learned.

For example, if there are three words on a computer screen, the typical response from the user, without prompting, is to click one of these words to evoke activity. Sometimes menu items are surrounded by boxes or made to look like push buttons. Or, to conserve space, text such as Throw Tomatoes, Play Video, and Press to Quit is often shortened to Tomatoes, Video, and Quit. Regardless, the intention remains clear to the user.

Text is helpful to users to provide perpetual cues about their location within the body of content. When users must click up and down through many layers of menus to reach their goal, they may not get lost, but they may feel transported to the winding and narrow streets of a medieval city where only the locals know the way. This is especially true if the user moves slowly from screen to screen en route to that goal. If Throw Tomatoes leads to Red or Green, then to California or Massachusetts, then to President or Vice President, then to Forehead or Chest, then to Arrested or Got Away, and so on, the user can end up tangled in the branches of a navigation tree without cues or a map. However, if an interactive textual or symbolic list of the branches taken (all the way from the beginning) is continuously displayed,

8

the user can at any time skip intervening steps in a nonlinear manner or easily return to one of the previous locations in the list.

Tomatoes

Red

Massachusetts

President

Chest

Arrested

The more locations included in the menu list, the more options available for navigation. On the Web, designers typically place on every page at least a Main Menu of links that offers the user a handhold and mechanism for returning to the beginning. Navigation methodologies and navigation maps are discussed in greater detail in Chapter 17 and, in the case of surfing the Web, in Chapter 15.

---

tip *Avoid using more than a few levels of GO BACKs or RETURNs if you do not provide a map. Too much tunneling in and out with repetitive mouse clicks will frustrate users and discourage exploration. Display a perpetual menu of interactive text or symbolic cues, so users can always extricate themselves from any place in the tunnel. In a Web browser, this is handled by a Back button containing a history of places visited.*

Buttons for Interaction

In most modern cultures a doorbell is recognized by its context (next to the door itself, possibly lit); but if you grew up in a high-rise apartment, you may have seen 50 or more buttons at the entrance. Unless you knew that yours was the third from the top on the left, you could find your button only by reading the printed or scrawled name beside it. And certainly your Aunt Barbara needed this text cue to avoid having to push the Help button, which in this case rang in the building superintendent's apartment.

In multimedia, *buttons* are the objects, such as blocks of text, a pretty blue triangle, or a photograph, that make things happen when they are clicked. They were invented for the sole purpose of being pushed or prodded with cursor, mouse, key, or finger—and to manifest properties such as highlighting or other visual or sound effects to indicate that you hit the target. On the

Web, text and graphic art may be buttons. Buttons and the art of button design and human interaction are discussed in detail in Chapter 17. For now, remember that the rules for proper selection of text and fonts in your projects apply to buttons as well as headlines, bullet items, and blocks of text.

::::::::::::::::::::::::::::::::

When I was four years old, a button was the little plastic knob mounted in brass next to the front door. When I pushed it, a muffled ringing sound worked its way through the house from the kitchen. Sometimes I would push the button a lot and somebody would always come to the door. As an adult, I'm still pushing buttons to make things happen.

::::::::::::::::::::::::::::::::

Ann Stewart, Cyx•D, Smyrna, Tennessee

The automatic button-making tools supplied with multimedia and HTML page authoring systems are useful, but in creating the text for you, they offer little opportunity to fine-tune the look of the text. Character- and word-wrap, highlighting, and inverting are automatically applied to your buttons, as needed, by the authoring system. These default buttons and styles may seem overused or trite, but by using common button styles, shapes, borders, and highlights, you increase the probability that users will know what to do with them—especially when they are also labeled.

warning *The text that labels your predesigned buttons is typically generated by the same routines that draw text into fields. So make sure that the fonts you select for your buttons are available in the environments in which you will run your software. Your button fonts will need to travel with your project. See Table 8-1 for a list of fonts typical in Windows and Macintosh installations. These are perhaps safest for button labeling and for page design on the Web; you can expect them to be available on most personal computers.*

Windows	Macintosh
Arial	Charcoal
Book Antiqua	Chicago
Bookman Old Style	Courier
Bookshelf Symbol	Geneva
Century Gothic	Helvetica

TABLE 8-1 *Faces Included in Typical Windows and Macintosh System Installations* ■

Windows	Macintosh
Comic Sans MS	Monaco
Courier New	New York
Garamond	Palatino
Haettenschweiler	Symbol
Impact	Times
Lucida Console	
Marlett	
Monotype Corsiva	
Monotype Sorts	
MS Outlook	
MS Sans Serif	
MS Serif	
Small Fonts	
Symbol	
Tahoma	
Times New Roman	
Trebuchet MS	
Verdana	
Webdings	
WingDings	

TABLE 8-1 *Faces Included in Typical Windows and Macintosh System Installations* (continued) ■

Before you can use a font, it must be recognized by the computer's operating system. If you want to use fonts other than those installed with your operating system, you will need to install them. TrueType fonts delivered as core fonts for Windows are installed in four weights and styles. With Macintosh systems come the TrueType fonts Charcoal, Chicago, Courier, Geneva, Helvetica, Monaco, Palatino, Symbol, Times, and ZapfDingbats. When you install applications, other fonts are often added to your collection.

Pick a font for buttons that is, above all, legible; then adjust the text size of the labels to provide adequate space between the button's rim and the text. You can choose from many styles of buttons and several standard methodologies for highlighting. You will want to experiment to get the right combinations of font, spacing, and colors for just the right look.

In HTML, the <font> tag can be used to specify a font to be displayed (if the font is present on the system). In a list of choices, you can include the names of both Windows and Macintosh fonts; if the font is not found on the local computer, the browser's default font will be displayed:

<font face="Verdana, Arial, Helvetica">

---

warning   *Although in HTML 4 you can specify a base font size, color, and face for displaying text on a Web page, you have no guarantee that that font is installed in the user's system. If it is missing, a browser will attempt to substitute a similar font, but the look is not guaranteed to be the same as the one you have designed. Provide a way to download the font to the end user's computer if the right look is important to you.*

In most authoring platforms, it is easy to make your own buttons from bitmaps or drawn objects. In a message-passing authoring system, where you can script activity when the mouse button is up or down over an object, you can quickly replace one bitmap with another highlighted or colored version of the bitmap to show that the button has been "pushed" or that the mouse is over it. Making your own buttons from bitmaps or drawn objects gives you greater design power and creative freedom and also insures against the missing font problem. On the other hand, this custom work may require a good deal more time. Interesting text and graphic buttons for the Web can be created as GIF or JPG bitmaps that, when clicked, link to other pages. There is no easy provision in HTML for highlighting or animating these graphic images, but typically the destination address (URL) is displayed in the status window of the browser when the mouse is over a linked image or text element. So users know first if the mouse is over an active button and second, where that button will take them if they click. If you take a short step beyond vanilla HTML, with a few lines of JavaScript you *can* program your button image to switch with another when the mouse is over it or "pushing down" (see Chapter 15 for sample code to do this).

Whether default or custom, treat the design and labeling of your buttons as an industrial art project: buttons are the part of your project the user touches.

8

Fields for Reading

You are already working uphill when you design text to be read on the screen. Experiments have shown that reading text on a computer screen is slower and more difficult than reading the same text in hard copy or book form. Indeed, many users, it seems, would rather print out their reports and e-mail messages and read them on paper than page through screens of text. Reading hard copy is still more comfortable.

---

w a r n i n g   *Research has shown that when people read text on a computer screen they blink only 3 to 5 times per minute, but they blink 20 to 25 times per minute when reading text on paper. This reduced eye movement may cause dryness, fatigue, and possibly damage to the eyes. Research also suggests that monitors should be placed lower than eye level.*

Unless the very purpose of your multimedia project or Web site is to display large blocks of text, try to present to the user only a few paragraphs of text per page. Use a font that is easy to read rather than a prettier font that is illegible. Try to display whole paragraphs on the screen, and avoid breaks where users must go back and forth between pages to read the entire paragraph.

Portrait Versus Landscape

Traditional hard copy and printed documents in the taller-than-wide orientation are simply not readable on a typical monitor with a wider-than-tall aspect ratio. The taller-than-wide orientation used for printed documents is called *portrait*; this is the 8.5-by-11-inch size unique to the United States or the internationally designated standard A4 size, 8.27 by 11.69 inches. The wider-than-tall orientation normal to monitors is called *landscape*. Shrinking an 11-inch-tall portrait page of text into your available monitor height usually yields illegible chicken tracks. There are four possible solutions if you are working with a block of text that is taller than what will fit:

- Put the text into a scrolling field. This is the solution used by Web browsers.

- Put the text into a single field or graphic image in a project window and let the user move the whole window up or down upon command. This is most appropriate when you need to present text with page breaks and formatting identical to the printed document. This is used by Adobe's popular Acrobat Reader for displaying PDF files.

- Break the text into fields that fit on monitor-sized pages, and design control buttons to flip through these pages.

- Design your multimedia project for a special monitor that is taller than it is wide (portrait). Such "page view" monitors are expensive; they are used for commercial print-based typesetting and layout.

HTML Documents

The standard document format used for pages on the Web is called Hypertext Markup Language (HTML). In an HTML document you can specify typefaces, sizes, colors, and other properties by "marking up" the text in the document with *tags*. The process of marking up documents is simple: Where you want text to be bold, surround it with the tags <B> and </B>; the text between the tags will then be displayed by your browser application in bold type. Where you have a header, surround it with <H1> and </H1>; for an ordered list of things (1, 2, 3, ... or a, b, c, ..., etc.), surround your list with <OL> and </OL>. There are many tags you can use to lay out a page. How HTML works is discussed in greater detail in Chapters 14 and 15. There are also many good HTML learning guides and references available on the Web.

....

http://www.w3.org/TR/html4/
http://www.w3.org/MarkUp/Guide/
http://www.ncsa.uiuc.edu/General/Internet/WWW/HTMLPrimer.html

Check out these Web sites for more information about HTML

8

The remarkable growth of the Web is straining the "old" designs for displaying text on computers. Indeed, while marked-up text files (HTML documents) remain at the foundation of Web activity, when you visit a well-designed Web site, you often discover graphic images, animations, and interactive work-arounds contrived to *avoid* displaying text. The neat paragraphs, indented lists, and formats for text documents for which HTML was originally intended are evolving into multimedia documents, not text documents, and the HTML method and standard is consequently suffering great stress.

As features and tags and plug-ins and special scripts are tacked onto or embedded into HTML to satisfy the demand for multimedia interfaces, at some point HTML will need to be redesigned from the ground up—as a multimedia delivery tool, not just a text display tool with assorted attachments. Indeed, this redesign is currently under way in the form of Dynamic HTML (DHTML).

HTML doesn't provide you with much flexibility to make pretty text elements, but you may be able to lay out pleasing documents using block-quote indents, tables, frames, and horizontal rules. Pretty text in HTML documents is typically done as graphical bitmaps that are placed within the HTML document's layout with image tags, <IMG >. Indeed, using plain HTML, you do not know what font a reader will use to view your document—the default display font is a preference that can be set in the browser and is one known to be available on the viewer's machine. So some viewers may read your words in serif Times Roman, others in sans serif Helvetica or Arial. Dynamic HTML, however, uses *cascading style sheets* (CSS) to define choices ranging from line height to margin width to font face. A font face, if not found, is degraded to the next best match. Indeed, using CSS, you can define the following text properties: font-weight, font-family, font-size, font-size-adjust, font-variant, font-style, font-stretch, text-decoration, text-transform, text-shadow, letter-spacing, word-spacing, line-height, vertical-align, text-indent, text-align, and direction. Designing documents for the Web is discussed in Chapter 15.

Symbols and Icons

Symbols are concentrated text in the form of stand-alone graphic constructs. Symbols convey meaningful messages. The Macintosh trash can symbol, for instance, tells you where to throw away old files; the Windows hourglass cursor tells you to wait while the computer is processing. Though you may think of symbols as belonging strictly to the realm of graphic art, in multimedia you should treat them as text—or visual words—because they carry meaning. Symbols such as the familiar trash can and hourglass are more properly called *icons*; these are symbolic representations of objects and processes common to the graphical user interfaces of many computer operating systems.

Certainly text is more efficient than imagery and pictures for delivering a precise message to users. On the other hand, pictures, icons, moving images, and sounds are most easily recalled and remembered by viewers. With multimedia, you have the power to blend both text and icons (as well as colors, sounds, images, and motion video) to enhance the overall impact and value of your message.

Word meanings are shared by millions of people, but the special symbols you design for a multimedia project are not; these symbols must be learned before they can be useful message carriers. Some symbols are more widely used and understood than others, but readers of even these common symbols had to grow accustomed to their meanings. Learning a system of symbols can be as difficult as lessons in any foreign language.

warning *Do not be seduced into creating your own language of symbols and icons.*

Here are some symbols you may already know:

And here are some astronomer's symbols from the days of Kepler and Galileo that you may not have learned—still in heavy use by astrologers, they represent the 12 constellations of the zodiac:

♀ ♈ ♉ ♊ ♋ ♌ ♍ ♎ ♏ ♐ ♑ ♒ ♓

But why are there 13 icons in the illustration above? Or did you notice? Find the sign for the planet Venus among the constellations. Not easy if you are unfamiliar with the meaning of these symbols.

When HyperCard was first introduced in 1987, there was a flurry of creative attempts by graphic artists to create interesting navigational symbols to alleviate the need for text. The screens were pure graphic art and power—all lines and angles and stunning shadows. But many users were frustrated because they could not get to the data right away and had to first wade through help and guidance material to learn the symbols. In this context it is clearly safer, from a product design point of view, to combine symbols with text cues. This ensures the graphic impact of the symbols but allows prompting the user on their meaning. The Macintosh trash can icon, incidentally, also has a text label, "Trash," just in case people don't get the idea from the symbol.

Nonetheless, a few symbols have emerged in the interactive multimedia world as an accepted lexicon of navigation cues that do not need text. These symbols are by no means universal, but Figure 8-3 shows some that have roots from the days of teletypewriters, others from early HyperCard and videodisc development, and yet others from the consumer electronics world. Even for these common symbols, text labels are often added to the graphic icons to avoid uncertainty.

Animating Text

There are plenty of ways to retain a viewer's attention when displaying text. For example, you can animate bulleted text and have it "fly" onto the screen. You can "grow" a headline a character at a time. For speakers, simply

Some symbols are easily recognized but may still require text titles; "smiley" symbols, or emoticons, used in Internet conversation to express mood, are made up entirely of text and punctuation characters

plain old smile	**:-)**	Go Back a Chapter	Play	
smile with a wink	**;-)**	Go Back	Stop	
indifferent	**:-|**	Go to Previous Menu	Eject	
heavy sarcasm	**:->**	Go Forward	Go to Next	
frown	**:-(**	Go to Next Chapter	Previous	
with spectacles	**8-)**		Fast Forward	
surprise	**:-D**		Fast Backward	
perplexed	**:-/**			

highlighting the important text works well as a pointing device. When there are several points to be made, you can stack keywords and flash them past the viewer in a timed automated sequence (as in the roadside Burma Shave ads—signs placed every half mile or so along the highway, each offering the motorist just a few more words toward a complete slogan). You might fly in some keywords, dissolve others, rotate or spin others, and so forth, until you have a dynamic bulleted list of words that is interesting to watch. But be careful—don't overdo the special effects, or they will become boring.

Powerful but inexpensive applications such as Xaos Tools' TypeCaster (see "Making Pretty Text") let you create 3-D text using both TrueType and Type 1 Adobe fonts. You can also use Illustrator or FreeHand EPS (Encapsulated PostScript) outline files to create still images in 3-D and then animate the results to create QuickTime movies with broadcast-quality rendering.

Computers and Text

Very early in the development of the Macintosh computer's monitor hardware, Apple chose to use a resolution of 72 picture elements (*pixels*) per inch. This matches the standard measurement of the printing industry (72 *points* per inch) and allows desktop publishers and designers to see on the monitor what their printed output will look like (called "What You See Is What You

Get," or WYSIWYG). In addition, Apple made each pixel square shaped, providing even measurements in all directions. Until the Macintosh was invented, and the VGA video standard set for the PC (at 96 pixels per inch), pixels were typically taller than they were wide. The aspect ratio for older EGA monitors, for example, is 1.33:1, taller than wide. VGA monitor resolutions for both Macintosh and Windows display 640 pixels across the screen and 480 pixels down the screen (called 640×480 resolution), and the pixels themselves have an aspect ratio of 1:1 (square).

The Font Wars

In 1985, the desktop publishing revolution was spearheaded by Apple and the Macintosh computer, in combination with word processing and page layout software products that enabled a high-resolution 300 dpi laser printer using special software to "draw" the shapes of characters as a cluster of tiny square pixels computed from the geometry of the character. This special software was Adobe's PostScript page description and outline font language. It was licensed by Apple and included in the firmware of Apple's LaserWriter laser printer.

PostScript is really a method of describing an image in terms of mathematical constructs (Bezier curves), so it is used not only to describe the individual characters of a font but also to describe entire illustrations and whole pages of text. Because each PostScript character is a mathematical formula, it can be easily scaled bigger or smaller so it looks right whether drawn at 24 points or 96 points, whether the printer is a 300 dpi LaserWriter or a high-resolution 1200, 2400, or even 3600 dpi image setter suitable for the finest print jobs. And the PostScript characters can be drawn much faster than in the old-fashioned way. Before PostScript, the printing software looked up the character's shape in a bitmap table containing a representation of the pixels of every character in every size. PostScript quickly became the de facto industry font and printing standard for desktop publishing and played a significant role in the early success of Apple's Macintosh computer.

There are two kinds of PostScript fonts: Type 3 and Type 1. Type 3 font technology is *older* than Type 1 and was developed for output to printers; it is rarely used by multimedia developers. There are currently over 6,000 different Type 1 typefaces available. Type 1 fonts also contain *hints*, which are special instructions for grid-fitting to help improve resolution. Hints can apply to a font in general or to specific characters at a particular resolution. For displaying PostScript fonts on both Macintosh and Windows monitors, Adobe developed Adobe Type Manager (ATM, described in the next section). Type 3 fonts do not work with ATM.

8

Other companies followed Adobe into the desktop publishing arena with their own proprietary and competitive systems for scalable outline fonts. In May 1989, Apple and Microsoft announced a joint effort to develop a "better and faster" quadratic curves outline font methodology, called TrueType. In addition to printing smooth characters on printers, TrueType would draw characters to a low-resolution (72 dpi or 96 dpi) monitor. Furthermore, Apple and Microsoft would no longer need to license the Post-Script technology from Adobe for their operating systems. Today, TrueType fonts ship with the Windows and Macintosh computers. Microsoft licensed a set of fonts from Monotype, a font "foundry," which became the fonts that ship with Windows.

---

tip *On the Macintosh, if you have installed multiple bitmapped, TrueType, and PostScript versions of the same font, the system will attempt first to use the bitmaps, then the TrueType version, then a PostScript Type 1 version. If the selected font is not available, the system will use a default font.*

Though the PostScript-versus-TrueType war continues to reverberate through the computer and publishing industries, multimedia developers really only need to be concerned about how these scaled fonts look on monitors, not about how they are printed to paper—unless, of course, you are printing perfect proposals, bids, storyboards, reports, and above all, invoices :-). TrueType and PostScript (with ATM) outline fonts allow text to be drawn at any size on your computer screen without *jaggies*:

The Jaggies

Jaggies are avoided by anti-aliasing the edges of the text characters, making them seem smoother to the eye. See Color Plate 6 for an example of anti-aliased text.

Adobe Type Manager

Adobe Type Manager (ATM) is required to display Type 1 PostScript fonts at all sizes without jaggies. This software is available for both the Macintosh and Windows. Once it's installed, ATM works automatically with word processing, page layout, spreadsheet, and graphics applications, including multimedia authoring systems.

In Windows, the ATM software requires about 450K of disk space, and each Type 1 PostScript outline font will take up another 40K. Using the ATM Control Panel (see Figure 8-4), you can add to and take away from your list of installed fonts. PostScript fonts typically are placed in a directory called PSFONTS in the root of your hard disk. TrueType fonts are stored in the C:\Windows\Fonts directory. Adding and deleting fonts is a simple procedure using the special options in the pull-down File menu of this directory. Neither TrueType nor PostScript fonts require bitmap representations in Windows.

On the Macintosh, fonts are stored in *suitcases* (see Figure 8-5). For PostScript fonts, the suitcase must contain at least one bitmap representation of the font, while the outline font, sometimes called the *printer font*, is stored outside of the suitcase in the Fonts folder. For TrueType fonts, the suitcase contains the outline font and optional bitmapped representations. Three-dimensional and drawing applications will use the outline font, not the bitmap information in the font suitcase, to make letters. To make PostScript fonts display without jaggies when there is no bitmap available for the size you desire, you need to install Adobe's ATM desk accessory into your Control Panel folder in the System folder.

Small Typefaces

In the early days of both Macintosh and Windows, a bitmap for the font and size was always required in the system in order to display text without jaggies. A collection of special, memory-hungry bitmaps was required to display fonts outside the normal range installed on the computer. TrueType and PostScript/ATM, using mathematical formulas, allow you to display smooth-edged type of any size and style on your monitor without requiring a collection of bitmap files.

8

FIGURE 8-4

Adobe Type Manager (ATM) Control Panel

FIGURE 8-5

Macintosh and Windows manage fonts differently, but both handle TrueType and PostScript
■

Macintosh PostScript Font
The suitcase and printer font reside in the Fonts folder. Bitmapped fonts reside in the suitcase.

Carta   Carta 10   Carta 12

Carta

Macintosh TrueType Font
The outline and optional bitmapped fonts reside in the suitcase

Times   Times   Times 9   Times 10   Times 12

Windows Fonts
TrueType and bitmapped fonts reside in the \WINDOWS\FONTS directory PostScript fonts are in \PSFONTS in the root.

Courier 10,12,15   Courier New   Cob___.pfb

Bitmap   TrueType   PostScript

Unfortunately, this helpful innovation does not come without a penalty. The smaller fonts (12 points and less) are not as legible on your monitor when drawn by mathematical formula as they are when drawn from bitmaps. TrueType and PostScript/ATM do their best to render the small sizes, but they are hard pressed to compete with the clarity of font bitmaps. These were carefully hand-tweaked by type designers to provide optimum legibility at monitor resolutions. Moving a single pixel in a small letter can make a subtle but critical difference.

warning   *Bitmapped, TrueType, and PostScript fonts do not display (or print) exactly the same, even though they may share the same name and size. The three technologies use different formulas. This means that word-wrapping in a text field may change. Text fields created under ATM, for example, will look different after ATM is disabled. So if you build a field or a button that precisely fits text displayed with PostScript, be aware that if you then display it with the same font in TrueType, the text may be truncated or wrapped, wrecking your layout.*

Font Foundries

Collections of fonts are available through retail channels or directly from their manufacturers. Typefaces are created in a *foundry*, a term much like *case*, that has carried over from times when lead was poured into molds to make letter faces. There is also a special interest group (SIG) at America Online (go to

Computing:Software Libraries:Desktop & Web Publishing Forum:Fonts) where people who enjoy designing and making interesting fonts post them for others to download—hundreds and hundreds of them with names like Evil of Frankenstein, CocaCola, Kerouac, LED, PonchoVia (sic), Spaghetti, TreeFrog, and Sassy. When you purchase some applications, such as Corel Draw, Adobe Illustrator, or Micrografx Publisher, many extra fonts are included for free.

---

http://www.typequarry.com/
http://www.adobe.com
http://www.esselte.com
http://www.bitstream.com
http://www.monotype.com
http://www.YandY.com
http://www.dol.com
http://www.cs.purdue.edu/homes/gwp/dtp/fonts.html
http://www.will-harris.com/type.htm

Commercial type foundries and font sites. These gateways lead to a discussion of fonts and where to find them. With *Esperfonto*, Will Harris provides an interesting tool for making font decisions: Casual or Formal, Body or Display, Friendly or Serious, Cool or Warm, Modern or Traditional.

8

warning   *It is easy to spend hours and hours downloading neat and interesting fonts; they are like the midnight snack table on a Mediterranean cruise liner—ice carvings and delectable goodies laid out as far as the eye can see.*

Managing Your Fonts

Never assume that the fonts you have installed on your computer will also be installed on a user's computer. Choose a system of type management and stick with it so that you will never face the nightmare of your carefully picked fonts being replaced by an ill-suited default font (see the next "First Person"). If your work is being distributed to sites that may not have the fonts you are using, or if you do not license these fonts for distribution with your work, be sure to bitmap the special font text you use for titles, headlines, buttons, and so forth. For text to be entered by users, it is safest to stay with the installed Windows or Macintosh fonts, because you know they are universally available on that platform. In Windows, use the TrueType fonts installed during the Setup procedure.

First Person

We had a short break between sessions to install the software for a panel discussion about multimedia. Four of us brought media with discussion material. Our moderator installed her presentation first, and we heard her wail, "Something's wrong with my fonts!" We all looked at her ugly 48-point Geneva and felt sorry for her; we knew her mistake. The beautiful fonts she had installed on her home system were not installed in the system of the Macintosh used for the big-screen projector, and she had failed to bring the fonts along, separately or in the resource fork of her project. By then, it was too late, anyway.

 You won't be able to print with Helvetica or stroke its characters because the font's outline file is missing or ATM is turned off.

[OK]

tip *Always be sure your fonts travel with your application when you are delivering software to run on a hardware platform other than the one you used to create the application. To avoid many font display problems, particularly for menus and headlines, you may wish to snap a picture of your text with a screen capture utility and use this image, or bitmap, instead of text that you type into a text field. (Chapter 10 describes bitmaps and how to capture and edit images.) This will ensure that the screen always looks right, regardless of what hardware platform you use or what fonts are installed.*

Character Sets and Alphabets

Knowing that there is a wide selection of characters available to you on your computer and understanding how you can create and use special and custom-made characters will broaden your creative range when you design and build multimedia projects.

The ASCII Character Set

The American Standard Code for Information Interchange (ASCII) is the 7-bit character coding system most commonly used by computer systems in the United States and abroad. ASCII assigns a number or value to 128 characters, including both lower- and uppercase letters, punctuation marks, Arabic numbers, and math symbols. Also included are 32 control characters used for device control messages, such as carriage return, line feed, tab, and form feed.

ASCII code numbers always represent a letter or symbol of the English alphabet, so that a computer or printer can work with the number that represents the letter, regardless of what the letter might actually look like on the screen or printout. To a computer working with the ASCII character set, the number 65, for example, always represents an uppercase letter A. Later, when displayed on a monitor or printed, the number is turned into a typeface.

ASCII was invented and standardized for analog teletype communication early in the age of bits and bytes. The capabilities of the technology have now moved far beyond the original intent of the standard, but because millions of installed computers and printers use ASCII, it is difficult to set any new standards for text without the expense and effort of replacing existing hardware. At least, for these 128 characters, most computers and printers share the same values.

On the Macintosh, use KeyCaps, a desk accessory delivered with the system and found in the Apple menu to examine the fonts and characters available to your Macintosh system. In Windows, use the Character Map accessory (Charmap.exe) to view and access characters, especially those "un-Roman" fonts not on the keyboard, such as Carta or Symbol, as illustrated in Figure 8-6.

---

tip   *The Charmap application (Charmap.exe) is part of Windows, but is not always automatically installed with the system software. Look in Start | Programs | Accessories; if it's not there, look in your Windows folder for Charmap.exe. To install Charmap.exe from your Windows CD, go to Start | Settings | Control Panel. Select Add/Remove Programs. Then click on the Windows Setup tab. Double-click on Accessories, and checkmark the box next to Character Map. Click OK, and Windows will install Charmap.exe from the installer CD into your Windows folder.*

The Extended Character Set

A byte, which consists of 8 bits, is the most commonly used building block for computer processing. ASCII uses only 7 bits to code its 128 characters; the 8th bit of the byte is unused. This extra bit allows another 128 characters to be encoded before the byte is used up, and computer systems today use these extra 128 values for an extended character set. The extended character set is most commonly filled with ANSI (American National Standards Institute) standard characters, including often-used symbols, such as ¢ or ∞, and international diacritics or alphabet characters, such as ä or ñ. This fuller set of 255 characters is also known as the ISO-Latin-1 character set; it is used when programming the text of HTML Web pages.

FIGURE 8-6

KeyCaps on the

Macintosh and

Charmap.exe

in Windows let

you see which

key to press on

the keyboard to

print a character in

a font face ∎

cross platform *The rules for encoding extended characters are not standardized. Thus ASCII value 165, for example, may be a bullet (●) character on the Macintosh; the character for Japanese yen (¥) in Windows (ANSI); or a capital N with tilde (Ñ) in DOS.*

Unicode

As the computer market has become more international in the past ten years, one of the resulting problems has been handling the various international language alphabets. It was at best difficult, and at times impossible, to translate the text portions of programs from one script to another. For example, the differences between the Roman script used by western European writers and the kanji script used by Japanese writers made it particularly challenging to transfer innovative programs from one market to another.

http://www.unicode.org

The Unicode organization supports standards for managing the characters of all known languages in the world

Since 1989, a concerted effort on the part of linguists, engineers, and information professionals from many well-known computer companies has been focused on a 16-bit architecture for multilingual text and character encoding. Called *Unicode*, the original standard accommodated up to about 65,000 characters to include the characters from all known languages and alphabets in the world.

While 65,000 characters are sufficient for encoding most of the many thousands of characters used in major languages of the world, the Unicode standard and ISO/IEC 10646 now support three encoding forms that use a common repertoire of characters but allow for encoding as many as a million more characters. This is sufficient for all known character encoding requirements, including full coverage of all historic scripts of the world, as well as common notational systems.

The Unicode® Standard: A Technical Introduction
(http://www.unicode.org/unicode/standard/principles.html)

8

Where several languages share a set of symbols that have a historically related derivation, the shared symbols of each language are unified into collections of symbols (called *scripts*). A single script can work for tens or even hundreds of languages (for example, the Latin script used for English and most European languages). Sometimes, however, only one script will work for a language (such as the Korean Hangul). Here are the 25 supported scripts of Version 2.0 of the Unicode standard:

Arabic	Gujarati	Latin
Armenian	Gurmkhi	Lao
Bengali	Han	Malayalam
Bopomofo	Hangul	Oriya
Cyrillic	Hebrew	Phonetic
Devanagari	Hiragana	Tamil
Georgian	Kannada	Telugu
Greek	Katakana	Thai
		Tibetan

Unicode also contains collections of symbols and special characters in secondary scripts:

Numbers	General diacritics	General punctuation
General symbols	Mathematical symbols	Technical symbols
Dingbats	Arrows, blocks, box drawing forms, and geometric shapes	Miscellaneous symbols
		Presentation forms

The Unicode standard includes more than 18,000 Han characters (ideographs for Japanese, Chinese, and Korean), and future releases will include obsolete alphabets such as cuneiform, hieroglyphs, and ancient Han characters. In addition, character space will be reserved for users and publishers to create their own scripts, designed especially for their own applications. For example, a carpenter might develop a script that included a character meaning "half-inch Sheetrock," another character meaning "three-quarter-inch plywood," and so forth. HTML 4.0 allows access to the Unicode characters by numeric reference. Thus 水 (in hexadecimal) represents the Chinese character for "water."

Microsoft, Apple, Sun, Netscape, IBM, Xerox, and Novell (among others) are participating in the development of this standard, and both Microsoft and Apple have incorporated Unicode into their operating systems.

Mapping Text Across Platforms

If you build your multimedia project on a Windows platform and play it back on a Macintosh platform (or vice versa), there will be subtle (and sometimes not-so-subtle) differences. Fonts are perhaps the greatest cross-platform concern, because they must be *mapped* to the other machine. If a specified font doesn't exist on the target machine, a substitute must be provided that does exist on the target. This is *font substitution*. Windows and Macintosh provide default fonts for this substitution.

In many cross-platform-savvy applications, you can explicitly define the mapping of your fonts. In Macromedia's Director, for example, you can control font mapping behavior by altering the FONTMAP.TXT file; Director remaps those fonts that the target system cannot provide. Table 8-2 shows some typical mappings used by Director when crossing platforms.

It is not just fonts that are problematic; characters, too, must be mapped across platforms. Character mapping allows bullets, accented characters, and other curious characters that are part of the extended character set on one

Mac→Win	Win→Mac
Mac:Chicago→Win:System	Win:Arial→Mac:Helvetica
Mac:Courier→Win:Courier New	Win:Courier→Mac:Courier
Mac:Geneva→Win:MS Sans Serif	Win:Courier New→Mac:Courier
Mac:Helvetica→Win:Arial	Win:MS Serif→Mac:New York
Mac:Monaco→Win:Terminal	Win:MS Sans Serif→Mac:Geneva
Mac:New York→Win:MS Serif	Win:Symbol→Mac:Symbol Map None
Mac:Symbol→Win:Symbol Map None	Win:System→Mac:Chicago
Mac:Times→Win:Times New Roman (sizes: 14→12, 18→14, 24→18, 30→24	Win:Terminal→Mac:Monaco
Mac:Palatino => Win:"Times New Roman"	Win:Times New Roman→Mac:Times (sizes: 12→14, 14→18, 18→24, 24→30)

TABLE 8-2   *Typical Mappings for Standard Macintosh and Windows Fonts Used by Macromedia's Director* ■

platform to appear correctly when text is moved to the other platform. Curly quotation marks, for example, rarely, if ever, map successfully across platforms.

To solve font and character uncertainties when working across platforms, many multimedia developers convert the text of their projects into bitmaps. These bitmaps may also be converted to 1-bit images that do not require great memory for storage in a project. Once converted to bitmaps, however, text cannot be easily edited or reworked.

First Person

While we were in the early phases of producing my CD-ROM, Multimedia: Working It Out!, I sold the rights to distribute it into Korea and Mainland China. Nobody on the production team had ever seen a computer that typed short-form Mandarin, and we knew that even when the English was localized, we would be hard pressed to recognize any of the text, much less edit or alter it in its new form.

So we devised a structured system of labels and names for Multimedia: Working It Out! and converted all the text in the project (about 600 "pages" of about a paragraph each) into 1-bit bitmaps in a Director movie. Donna Booher edited and formatted the text in Microsoft Word, Dan Hilgert bitmapped and screen-captured each page with Capture and Photoshop, and Peter Wolf imported the PICT files into Director (by the hundreds) as cast members. Each cast member had a unique (but systematic) name associated with a Director movie, a heading, and various icons. It took a while.

First Person continued

The localizers across the Pacific, then, would simply translate a page or a series of pages using their own native-language word processor, capture their own bitmaps, and we would substitute the new bitmaps for the old using the unique identification labels. No language skills required!

When we started, Terry Thompson devised a color-coded master filing system and database so that all the word-processed text and the screen-captured bitmaps would remain neatly side by side and concurrent. This is called version control. By the time this project shipped, Donna's computer was crashing four or five times a day and we had lost files, Dan had gone back to school, Peter and I were slapping miscellaneous text elements into the project without tracking where they came from, and we were changing labels and moving cast members around as we streamlined performance, debugged, and staggered toward a golden master and the Federal Express drop-off. We had converted Terry's neatly organized system into chaos.

After the CD-ROMs were pressed, and there wasn't anything anybody could change anymore anyway, we did a tricky thing with Lingo programming, DeBabelizer, and OmniPage Pro to convert the final project's bitmapped text back into word processor text.

First we collected all the bitmapped text into a single Director movie (we weren't interested in pretty pictures, QuickTime, sounds, or other types of cast members, just text). Then we placed each page of bitmapped text into a movie frame (Cast to Time), neatly labeled that frame at the top with the identifying code of the image using a Lingo handler, and saved all of the frames as PICT images (an automatic command in Director's Export menu). With DeBabelizer, we batch-converted these hundreds of PICT images from 72 dpi (screen capture resolution) to 300 dpi (printer resolution) and saved each as a 1-bit TIFF image. The process was automatic.

OmniPage Pro is a powerful optical character recognition (OCR) program that usually reads documents on a flatbed scanner and turns them into nicely formatted word processing documents. OmniPage (ah ha!) allows batch processing of TIFF (and more recently, PICT) images at 300 dpi, so we ran all of these TIFFs (automatically) through OmniPage, and bingo!, they came out as archival word processing files. Then we sent the word files to Guido Mozzi in Italy so his team of translators could begin localizing there.

Some efforts are cyclical, we have discovered. The trick is to learn something and improve the process each time the task comes around!

Languages in the World of Computers

In modern Western languages, words are made up of symbols or letters strung together, representing as a whole the sounds of a spoken word. This is not so for Eastern languages such as Chinese, Japanese, and Korean (and the ancient languages of Sumeria, Egypt, and Mesopotamia). In these languages, an entire concept might be represented by a single word symbol that is unrelated to a specific phonetic sound.

The letters or symbols of a language are its alphabet. In English, the alphabet consists of 26 Roman or Latin letters; in Japanese, the kanji alphabet comprises more than 3,000 kanas, or whole words. The Russian alphabet, made up of Cyrillic characters based on the ancient Greek alphabet, has about the same number of letters as a Roman alphabet. All languages, from Navajo to Hebrew, have their own unique alphabets.

The written Japanese language consists of three different types of character sets, namely: kanji, katakana, and hiragana. Kanji was originally taken from the Chinese language and is essentially a pictographic representation of the spoken word. Each kanji has two different readings, "on-yomi" and "kun-yomi," respectively, the "Chinese rendering" and the "Japanese rendering." Both are used depending on the conjugation of the kanji with other kanji. Due to certain incompatibilities between the Japanese spoken word and kanji, two sets of kana or phonetic syllabary (alphabet) were developed. Katakana is the "square" kana and is used today for writing only foreign words or onomatopoeic expressions. Hiragana is the "cursive" kana and can be used alone to represent a certain word or combined with kanji to form other words and sentences. Romaji, a more recent addition to the alphabets of Japan, allows for the phonetic spelling of the Japanese language using the Roman characters familiar to the Western world.

Ross Uchimura, Executive Vice-President, GC3 Ltd., a cross-cultural expert

Most modern alphabets share one very important attribute: the graphic shapes and method for writing the Arabic numbers 0 1 2 3 4 5 6 7 8 9. This is a simple system for representing decimal numbers, which lends itself to easy reading, writing, manipulation, and calculation. Expressing and performing

$$16 + 32 = 48$$

is much easier in Arabic numbers than in Roman or Greek numerals:

$$XVI + XXXII = XLVIII$$

$$ι\varsigma + \lambda\beta = \mu\eta$$

Use of Arabic notation has gradually spread across the world to supplant other systems, although Roman numerals are still used today in Western languages in certain forms and contexts.

Translating or designing multimedia (or any computer-based material) into a language other than the one in which it was originally written is called *localization*. This process deals with everything from the month/day/year order for expressing dates to providing special alphabetical characters on keyboards and printers. Even the many Western languages that share the Roman alphabet have their own peculiarities and often require special characters to represent special sounds. For example, German has its umlaut (ä); French its various accents (é), the cedilla (ç), and other diacritics; and Spanish its tilde (ñ). These characters are typically available in the extended character set of a font.

Special Characters in HTML   In HTML, *character entities* based upon the ISO-Latin-1 standard make up the alphabet that is recognized by browser software on the World Wide Web. All of the usual characters of an English keyboard are included (the 7-bit ASCII set is built in), but for the extended character set that includes tildes, umlauts, accents, and special symbols, you must use an escape sequence to represent them in an HTML document. A character entity is represented either by a number or by a word and is always prefixed by an ampersand (escape) and followed by a semicolon. For example, the name for the copyright symbol is "copy" and its number is 169; it may be inserted into a document either as © or as ©—either way, the character © is generated by the browser. The list of character entities allowed in standard HTML is growing and will soon include mathematical symbols and even icons to represent things like trash cans, clocks, and disk drives. Word processors for languages other than English automatically insert the necessary character entities when a document is saved in HTML format.

First Person

When I was in Germany some years ago, I read a curious report in the Frankfurter Allgemeine about a fellow who was suing the local electric utility for not correcting the spelling of his name to its proper form in the German alphabet. His name had an umlaut in it (Wörm), but his bill always read Woerm. In German, the letter ö sounds different from the letter o, so I can't say I blamed him. At first he didn't pay his bill, claiming that he wasn't that person; then the courts told him to pay anyway. So he initiated a civil suit to protect his name.

It seems the utility was using a legacy IBM system with a high-speed chain printer to produce the monthly bills, and none of the umlaut characters were available on the ASCII-based chain. By long-standing convention, when you are limited to the English alphabet, the letter e immediately follows any umlautless vowel, to indicate that the umlaut should be there but isn't. Today, with high-speed laser printers and special fonts, the problem has probably gone away.

More recently, there are reports that the California Department of Motor Vehicles cannot handle blank spaces in the name fields of its massive database, so Rip Van Winkle's name was changed to Rip VanWinkle without his permission. Expect a lawsuit.

http://www.w3.org/TR/REC-html40/sgml/entities.html

An encyclopedic discussion and reference for HTML character entity references

Multilanguage Web Pages   When building a project in more than one language for the Web, consider translating the languages that use Roman fonts and displaying them as text in the browser in the normal way. Languages other than English may have many escaped characters, as you can see in Figure 8-7. If Chinese or Japanese or Arabic is desired, translate the Roman text onto a computer running an operating system using that native language. For the Web page, the translator can then capture a screen image of the translated text, and you can embed that image into your Web page. This process takes precise coordination among the designers, the content providers, and the translators, but it can be done smoothly with careful labeling of the bits and pieces.

FIGURE 8-7

Portion of a five-language Web site using normal HTML code for the Roman languages and screen-captured graphic images to display the Chinese and Japanese translations

```
<p>
What can this integrated network solution offer your business? Lower costs, in-
creased flexibility, and greater reliability by supporting all voice and data require-
ments, including:</p>
<p>
O que esta solu&ccedil;&atilde;o de rede integrada pode oferecer a sua empresa?
Menores custos, elevada flexibilidade, e maior confiabilidade, pelo suporte a todos
os requisitos de voz e dados, incluindo:</p>
<p>
Qu&eacute; puede ofrecerle a su negocio esta soluci&oacute;n integrada de redes?
Menores costos, mayor flexibilidad y mayor fiabilidad mediante la compatibilidad
con todos los requisitos para voz y datos, incluso:</p>
<p>
<img src="images/chinese/story1-1.gif">
```

這種綜合性的網路產品能為您的公司企業帶來哪些好處呢？它能降低成本，提昇
服務的靈活性，以及具有更大的可靠性，因為它能支持各種話音與數據傳輸的要
求，包括：

```
</p>
<p>
<img src="images/japanese/story1-1.gif">
```

この統合的ネットワークソリューションは，以下を含む音声・データ要件のすべてに対応し，費用
節減，フレキシビリティや信頼性の向上を実現させます。

求，包括：

```
</p>
```

8

Font Editing and Design Tools

Special font editing tools can be used to make your own type, so you can communicate an idea or graphic feeling exactly. With these tools, professional typographers create distinct text and display faces. Graphic designers, publishers, and ad agencies can design instant variations of existing typefaces.

Typeface designs fall into the category of industrial design and have been determined by the courts in some cases to be protectable by patent. For example, design patents have been issued for Bigelow & Holmes' Lucida, ITC Stone, and for Adobe's Minion.

---

warning *If your commercial project includes special fonts, be sure that your license agreement with the font supplier allows you to distribute them with your project.*

Occasionally in your projects you may require special characters. With the tools described in the paragraphs that follow, you can easily substitute characters of your own design for any unused characters in the extended character set. You can even include several custom versions of your client's company logo or other special symbols relevant to your content or subject right in your text font.

• •

http://www.fontfoundry.com
http://www.larabiefonts.com/

There are hundreds of sites for downloading free and shareware fonts drawn by others. For starters, try these two

ResEdit

ResEdit is a resource editor available from Apple that is useful for creating and changing graphic resources such as cursors, icons, dialog boxes, patterns, keyboard maps, and bitmapped fonts on the Macintosh. It can be used to edit or create new FONT resources for storing the bitmaps of screen fonts. If you need to make small adjustments to a screen font or create special characters, as illustrated in Figure 8-8, try ResEdit.

Fontographer

Fontographer, supplied by Macromedia, is a specialized graphics editor for both Macintosh and Windows platforms. You can use it to develop PostScript,

FIGURE 8-8

ResEdit can edit

bitmapped fonts on

the Macintosh

∎

FIGURE 8-8

ResEdit can edit bitmapped fonts on the Macintosh ∎

TrueType, and bitmapped fonts for Macintosh, Windows, DOS, NeXT, and Sun workstations. Designers can also modify existing typefaces, incorporate PostScript artwork, automatically trace scanned images, and create designs from scratch. A sample Fontographer screen is shown in Figure 8-9, and a working version is included on the Macromedia Showcase CD-ROM included with this book.

Fontographer's features include a freehand drawing tool to create professional and precise inline and outline drawings of calligraphic and script characters, using either the mouse or alternative input methods (such as Wacom pressure-sensitive pen systems, Kurta digitizing tablets, and CalComp DrawingBoard). Fontographer allows the creation of multiple font designs from two existing typefaces, and you can design lighter or heavier fonts by modifying the weight of an entire typeface.

Fontographer for Windows opens any PostScript Type 1 or TrueType font for the PC and lets you create condensed, expanded, and oblique versions of the same font or modify any of those fonts to suit your design needs. One character, several characters, or entire fonts can be scaled, rotated, and skewed to create new and unique typefaces. A metric window provides complete control over character width, spacing, offset, and kerning. The current Windows version of Fontographer does not make Multiple Master fonts

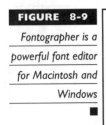

FIGURE 8-9

Fontographer is a powerful font editor for Macintosh and Windows ∎

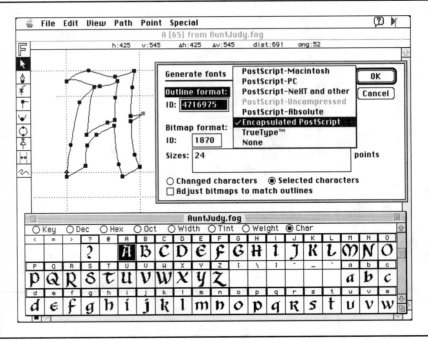

(PostScript fonts that allow you to adjust a range of certain characteristics for a set of characters, such as serif to sans serif or condensed to extended) or Type 3 PostScript fonts, and it does not have an Option-Copy, Paste feature for bringing drawings through the Clipboard from FreeHand or Illustrator. Nor can the current version read a Macintosh Fontographer database; font transfer is accomplished through Type 1 PostScript.

Making Pretty Text

To make your text look pretty, you need a toolbox full of fonts and special graphics applications that can stretch, shade, shadow, color, and anti-alias your words into real artwork. Pretty text is typically found in bitmapped drawings where characters have been tweaked, manipulated, and blended into a graphic image. Simply choosing the font is the first step. Most designers find it easier to make pretty type starting with ready-made fonts, but some will create their own custom fonts using font-editing and design tools such as Fontographer, described above.

With the proper tools and a creative mind, you can create endless variations on plain-old type, and you not only choose but also customize the styles that will fit with your design needs.

When they first invented typesetting there were variants cut of each character so text would look as if it had been handwritten by a monk! Desktop designers have been fighting so hard to get their setting to look like it's come from a Berthold system, that most of the new potential of desktop typography has been overlooked.

David Collier, Author of *Collier's Rules for Desktop Design and Typography*

Most image-editing and painting applications let you make text using the fonts available in your system. You can colorize the text, stretch, squeeze, and rotate it, and you can filter it through various "plug-ins" to generate wild graphic results.

Figure 8-10 is an image with text created in Photoshop. The rose was scanned from a photograph, separated from its background (1), and placed onto black (2). A 200-point word, "Rose," was typed in bold black Peignot Light onto a white background without anti-aliasing (3). Then a rainbow of hues was "stolen" from the little strip on Photoshop's color wheel by screen-capturing, and the strip was duplicated horizontally until it would be large enough to cover the entire word (4). Selecting and dragging the rainbow of colors on top of the word, the rainbow was laid onto the black letters by removing white from the underlying image using Photoshop's Composite Controls—note the lower slider is moved one value to the left, from 255 to 254 (5). The characters of the word were then selected along their edges by

8

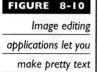

FIGURE 8-10

Image editing applications let you make pretty text

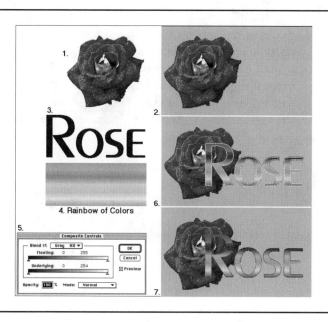

selecting all the white background with the Magic Wand tool, then inverting that selection (Invert in the Select menu). The rainbow word was dragged on top of the red rose (6), and a two-pixel border around it was selected (Border in the Select menu). Then the word was finally anti-aliased onto the background using the Blur filter, blurring just the border of the word (7).

Three-dimensional modeling programs allow you to create a character, add depth to it or extrude it, shade and light it, and manipulate it into other shapes. The character here was generated in just this way and, when animated using Macromedia's Director, spins in place:

AAAAAAAAIII

Inexpensive applications such as Brøderbund's TypeStyler, RayDream's addDepth 2, COOL 3D from U-Lead, and plug-ins for Photoshop from Xaos Tools (TypeCaster) and Vertigo (HotTEXT) are designed to manipulate typefaces in a graphical way. Figure 8-11 shows text being drawn and manipulated using COOL 3D and HotTEXT. The custom-tortured characters can be captured as a bitmap and incorporated into your project. Figure 8-12 shows TypeCaster's easy-to-use interface working in Photoshop with drag-and-drop textures. These 3-D programs let you put together interesting still and animated titles and headlines for Web pages, documents, presentations, reports, videos, and multimedia titles. You can rotate the text, adjust style, color, texture, camera angle and background, and even map images onto the surface. There are many sources of support for GIF animations with transparency and interlacing. Working in 3-D space takes some practice until you become intuitively comfortable with the notion of roll, pitch, and yaw and familiar with the application's controls for adjusting lights, textures, and views.

FIGURE 8-11

COOL 3D and HotTEXT let you extrude, warp, twist, and rotate characters and adjust lighting and texture effects for high-impact 3-D titles

■

Hypermedia and Hypertext

Multimedia—the combination of text, graphic, and audio elements into a single collection or presentation—becomes *interactive multimedia* when you give the user some control over what information is viewed and when it is viewed. Interactive multimedia becomes *hypermedia* when its designer provides a structure of linked elements through which a user can navigate and interact.

When a hypermedia project includes large amounts of text or symbolic content, this content can be indexed and its elements then linked together to afford rapid electronic retrieval of the associated information. When words are keyed or indexed to other words, you have a *hypertext system*; the "text" part of this term represents the project's content and meaning, rather than the graphical presentation of the text. Hypertext is what the World Wide Web is all about.

When text lives in a computer instead of on printed pages, the computer's powerful processing capabilities can be applied to make the text more accessible and meaningful. The text can then be called *hypertext*; because the words, sections, and thoughts are linked, the user can navigate through text in a nonlinear way, quickly and intuitively.

Using hypertext systems, you can electronically search through all the text of a computer-resident book, locate references to a certain word, and then immediately view the page where the word was found. Or you can create complicated Boolean searches (using terms such as AND, OR, NOT, and BOTH) to locate the occurrences of several related words, such as "Elwood," "Gloria," "mortgage," and "happiness," in a paragraph or on a page. Whole documents can be linked to other documents.

A word can be made *hot*, as can a button, thus leading the user from one reference to another. Click on the word "Elwood," and you may find yourself reading a biography or resume; click on "mortgage," and a calculator pops up. Some authoring systems (see Chapter 7) incorporate a hypertext facility that allows you to identify words in a text field using a bold or colored style, then link them to other words, pages, or activities, such as playing a sound or video clip related to that hot word. You cannot do this kind of nonlinear and associative navigation in a sequentially organized book. But on a CD-ROM, where you might have more than 100,000 pages of text to investigate, search, and browse, hypertext is invaluable.

Because hypertext is the organized cross-linking of words not only to other words but also to associated images, video clips, sounds, and other exhibits, hypertext often becomes simply an additional feature within an overall multimedia design. The term "hyper" (from the Greek word υπερ—"over") has come to imply that user interaction is a critical part of the design, whether for text browsing or for the multimedia project as a whole. When interaction and cross-linking is then added to multimedia, and the navigation system is nonlinear, multimedia becomes hypermedia.

In 1945, Vannevar Bush wrote a seminal eight-page article, "As We May Think," for the *Atlantic Monthly* (http://www.theatlantic.com/unbound/flashbks/computer/bushf.htm). This short treatise, in which he discusses the need for new methodologies for accessing information, has become the historic cornerstone of hypertext experimentation. Doug Englebart (inventor of the mouse) and Ted Nelson (who coined the term "hypertext" in 1965) have actively championed the research and innovations required of computer technology for implementing useful hypertext systems, and they have worked to combat the historic inertia of linear thought. Nelson would claim that the very structure of thought is neither sequential nor linear and that computer-based hypertext systems will fundamentally alter the way humans approach literature and the expression of ideas during the coming decades.

The argument against this theory of associative thought is that people are, indeed, more comfortable with linear thinking and are easily overwhelmed by too much freedom, becoming quickly lost in the chaos of nonlinear gigabytes.

As a practical reminder, it is important always to provide location markers, either text-and-symbol menus or illustrative maps, for users who travel the threads of nonlinear systems.

....

[Vannevar] Bush identified the problem—and the need to provide new ways to access information—but was he right about how the mind works? I suspect a purely associative model of human memory and mental processes is too simplistic.

....

Philip Murray, *From Ventura to Hypertext,* Knowledge Management Associates, Danvers, MA, 1991

The Power of Hypertext

In a fully indexed hypertext system, all words can be found immediately. Suppose you search a large database for "boats," and you come up with a whopping 1,623 references or *hits*—among them, Noah's Ark (open boat in water), television situation comedies (*The Love Boat*), political criticisms of cabinet members who challenged the status quo (rocked the boat), cabinet members who were stupid (missed the boat), and Christmas dinner trimmings (Grandmother's gravy boat). So you narrow your search and look for "boats" and "water" when both words are mentioned on the same page; this time you get 286 hits. "Boats," "water," and "storms" gets you 37; "boats," "water," "storms," and "San Francisco," a single hit. With over a thousand hits, you are lost. With one hit, you have something! But you still may not find what you are looking for, as you can see in this fictional example:

> The *storm* had come and gone quickly across the Colorado plains, but *water* was still puddled at the foot of the house-high bank of mud that had slid into town when the dam burst. In front of the general store, which had remained standing, four strong men carefully lifted a tiny *boat* onto the large dray wagon borrowed from the wood-cutters. On a layer of blankets in the bilge of the *boat*, the undertaker had carefully laid out the remains of both the mayor and his paramour. The mayor had not drowned in the flood, but died of a heart attack in the midst of the panic. Children covered the *boat* with freshly cut pine boughs while horses were quickly harnessed to the wagon, and a strange procession began to move slowly down *San Francisco* Street toward the new cemetery...

The power of such search-and-retrieval systems provided by a computer for large volumes of data is immense, but clearly this power must be channeled in meaningful ways. Links among words or clusters of information need to be designed so that they make sense. Judgments must be made about relationships and the way information content is organized and made available to users. The lenses through which vast amounts of data are viewed must necessarily be ground and shaped by those who design the access system.

The hype about hypertext may be justified. It can provide a computer-supported information environment which can add to our appreciation of the text, can go some way towards aping the mental agility of the human mind, can allow navigation along patterns of association, can provide a nonlinear information environment. But the problems of constructing nonlinear documents are not few and can prove to be very complex.

Patricia Baird, Editor of *Hypermedia,* a scientific journal published in the United Kingdom

The issue of who designs the lenses and how the designers maintain impartial focus is troubling to many scientists, archivists, and students of cognitive thinking. The scientists would remain "hermeneutically" neutral, they would balance freedom against authority and warn against the epistemological unknowns of this new intellectual technology. They are aware of the forces that allow advertising and marketing craftspeople to intuitively twist meanings and spin events to their own purposes, with actions that can affect the knowledge and views of many millions of people and thus history itself. But these forces remain poorly understood, are not easily controlled by authority, and will express themselves with immeasurably far-reaching, long-term impact on the shape of human culture.

Hypermedia on its own simply functions as a reference tool. But when it is integrated within a goal-based activity, it becomes a powerful learning resource.

Brigid Sealy & Paul Phelan, INESC, Porto, Portugal(conclusions from research funded by the European Commission's Human Capital and Mobility Program)

The multimedia designer controls the filtering mechanisms and places the lenses within the multimedia project. A manufacturer, for instance, that presents its products using interactive multimedia can bring abundant information and selling power within reach of the user, including background information, collateral marketing material, pricing statistics, and technical data. The project design will be, of course, biased—to sell more of the manufacturer's products and generate more profit; but this bias is assumed and understood in these circumstances. When the assumptions and understandings of inherent bias in any information base break down, when fiction or incomplete data is presented as full fact, that is when the powerful forces of multimedia and hypermedia can have their greatest deleterious effect.

warning *Bad multimedia projects will not alter the collective view of history; really bad projects might.*

Using Hypertext

Special programs for information management and hypertext have been designed to present electronic text, images, and other elements in a database fashion. Commercial systems have been used for large and complicated mixtures of text and images—for example, a detailed repair manual for a Boeing 747 aircraft, a parts catalog for Pratt & Whitney jet turbine engines, an instant reference to hazardous chemicals, and electronic reference libraries used in legal and library environments. Such searchable database engines are widely used on the Web, where software *robots* visit millions of Web pages and index entire Web sites. Hypertext databases rely upon proprietary indexing systems that carefully scan the entire body of text and create very fast cross-referencing indexes that point to the location of specific words, documents, and images. Indeed, a hypertext index by itself can be as large as 50 percent to 100 percent the size of the original document. Indexes are essential for speedy performance. Google's search engine produces about 9,730,000 hits in less than a tenth of a second!

Commercial hypertext systems were developed historically to retrofit gigantic bodies of information. Licenses for use and distribution of these commercial systems are expensive, and the hypertext-based projects typically require the large mass-storage capability of one or many CD-ROMs and/or dedicated gigabyte hard disks. Simpler but effective hypertext indexing tools are available for both Macintosh and Windows, and they offer fairly elaborate features designed to work in concert with many multimedia authoring systems. Server-based hypertext and database engines designed for the Web are now widely available and competitively priced.

---

tip *Rather than designing an elaborate, fully cross-referenced hypertext system for your multimedia project, you can "hardwire" the links between the most salient words (highlight them in your text) so that a mouse click leads to a topic menu specific to the chosen word. Though this constrains the user's movement through the text, the user will not perceive it as such, and you can thus maintain strict control over your navigation pathways and design.*

Searching for Words

Although the designer of a hypermedia database makes assumptions, he or she also presents users with tools and a meaningful interface to exercise the assumptions. Employing this interface, users can tailor word searches to find very specific combinations. Following are typical methods for word searching in hypermedia systems:

- Categorical: Selecting or limiting the documents, pages, or fields of text within which to search for a word or words.

- Word relationship: Searching for words according to their general proximity and order. For example, you might search for "party" and "beer" only when they occur on the same page or in the same paragraph.

- Adjacency: Searching for words occurring next to one another, usually in phrases and proper names. For instance, find "widow" only when "black" is the preceding adjacent word.

- Alternates: Applying an OR criterion to search for two or more words, such as "bacon" or "eggs."

- Association: Applying an AND criterion to search for two or more words, such as "skiff," "tender," "dinghy," and "rowboat."

- Negation: Applying a NOT criterion to search exclusively for references to a word that are not associated with the word. For example, find all occurrences of "paste" when "library" is not present in the same sentence.

- Truncation: Searching for a word with any of its possible suffixes. For example, to find all occurrences of "girl" and "girls," you may need to specify something like **girl#**. Multiple character suffixes can be managed with another specifier, so **geo*** might yield "geo," "geology," and "geometry," as well as "George."

8

- Intermediate words: Searching for words that occur between what might normally be adjacent words, such as a middle name or initial in a proper name.

- Frequency: Searching for words based on how often they appear: the more times a term is mentioned in a document, the more relevant the document is to this term.

Hypermedia Structures

Two buzzwords used often in hypertext systems are link and node. *Links* are connections between the conceptual elements, that is, the *nodes* containing text, graphics, sounds, or related information in the knowledge base. Links connect Caesar Augustus with Rome, for example, and grapes with wine, and love with hate. The art of hypermedia design lies in the visualization of these nodes and their links so that they make sense, not nonsense, and can form the backbone of a knowledge access system. More recently, with the popularization of HTML for the World Wide Web, the term *anchor* is used for the reference from one document to another document, image, sound, or file on the Web (see Chapter 15).

Links are the navigation pathways and menus; nodes are accessible topics, documents, messages, and content elements. A *link anchor* is where you come from; a *link end* is the destination node linked to the anchor. Some hypertext systems provide unidirectional navigation and offer no return pathway; others are bidirectional.

The simplest way to navigate hypermedia structures is via buttons that let you access linked information (text, graphics, and sounds) that is contained at the nodes. When you've finished examining the information, you return to your starting location. A typical navigation structure might look like the following:

Pages of text with hot words linked to InfoBites only

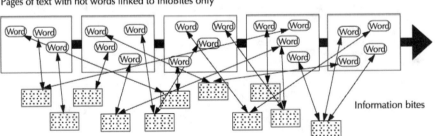

Information bites

Navigation becomes more complicated when you add associative links that connect elements not directly in the hierarchy or sequence. These are the paths where users can begin to get lost if you do not provide location markers. A link can lead to a node that provides further links, as shown here:

Pages of text with hot words linked to InfoBites linked to pages and to other InfoBites

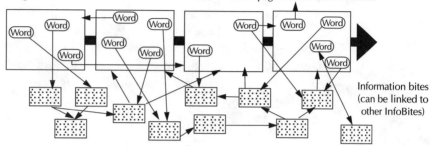

Information bites (can be linked to other InfoBites)

When you offer full-text search through an information base, there may be links between any number of items at your current node and any number of other nodes with items that meet your relationship criteria. When users are browsing freely through this system, and one page does not follow the next (as expected in the linear metaphor of books and literature), users can get lost in the associative maze of the designer's content:

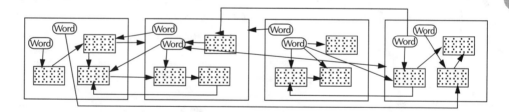

One publisher of hypermedia products claims that becoming lost in "hyperspace" may not be all that bad. The struggle to find your way back can be valuable in itself, and certainly a learning experience.

Hypertext Tools

Two functions are common to most hypermedia text management systems, and they are often provided as separate applications: building (or authoring) and reading. The builder creates the links, identifies nodes, and generates the all-important index of words. The index methodology and the search algorithms used to find and group words according to user search criteria are typically proprietary, and they represent an area where computers are carefully optimized for performance—finding search words among a list of many tens of thousands of words requires speed-demon programming.

Hypertext systems are currently used for electronic publishing and reference works, technical documentation, educational courseware, interactive kiosks, electronic catalogs, interactive fiction, and text and image databases. Today these tools are used extensively with information organized in a linear fashion; it still may be many years before the majority of multimedia project users become comfortable with fully nonlinear hypertext and hypermedia systems. When (and perhaps if) they do, the methodology of human thought and conceptual management—indeed, the way we think—will be forever changed.

Hypermedia can take advantage of powerful capabilities that are becoming clearer as the new multimedia medium matures—a greater choice in exploration, if not in outright plot definition, for example. From my experiences with "Playa Sirenas," the real challenge facing storytellers in this new medium is allowing readers appropriate choices (some authorship of the story, really) while they navigate through the hypermedia experience, without destroying the successful and basic patterns that have been part of storytelling since people first gathered around campfires. There is something organic about these time-proven storytelling patterns. As an author in the new medium, you must first design the DNA or template of your story, then allow (and promote) mutation along evolutionary lines that you, as the author, have created as part of the template...

Hermann Steffen, Hypermedia Novelist, San Jose, Costa Rica

Multi

> [How you use the power of sound
> can make the difference between an
> ordinary multimedia presentation
> and a professionally spectacular one.]

the
power
of sound

media

chapter

9

Sound

These waves spread like the ripples from a pebble tossed into a still pool and when they reach your eardrums, you experience the changes of pressure, or vibrations, as sound.

S OUND is perhaps the most sensuous element of multimedia. It is meaningful "speech" in any language, from a whisper to a scream. It can provide the listening pleasure of music, the startling accent of special effects, or the ambience of a mood-setting background. Some feel-good music powerfully fills the heart, generating emotions of love or otherwise elevating listeners closer to Heaven. How you use the power of sound can make the difference between an ordinary multimedia presentation and a professionally spectacular one. Misuse of sound, however, can wreck your project.

The Power of Sound

When something vibrates in the air by moving back and forth (such as the cone of a loudspeaker), it creates waves of pressure. These waves spread like the ripples from a pebble tossed into a still pool, and when they reach your eardrums, you experience the changes of pressure, or vibrations, as sound. In air, the ripples propagate at about 750 miles per hour, or Mach 1 at sea level. Sound waves vary in sound pressure level (amplitude) and in frequency or pitch. Many sound waves mixed together form an audio sea of symphonic music, speech, or just plain noise.

Acoustics is the branch of physics that studies sound. Sound pressure levels (loudness or volume) are measured in decibels (dB); a decibel measurement is actually the ratio between a chosen reference point on a logarithmic scale and the level that is actually experienced. When you quadruple the sound output power, there is only a 6 dB increase; when you make the sound 100 times more intense, the increase in dB is not hundredfold, but only 20 dB. This scale makes sense because humans perceive sound pressure levels over an extraordinarily broad dynamic range. The decibel scale, with some examples, is shown in Table 9-1; notice the relationship between power (measured in watts) and dB.

dB	Watts	Example
195	25–40 million	Saturn rocket
170	100,000	Jet engine with afterburner
160	10,000	Turbojet engine at 7,000-pounds thrust
150	1,000	ALSETEX splinterless stun grenade
140	100	2 JBL2226 speakers pulling 2400 watts inside an automobile
130	10	75-piece orchestra, at fortissimo
120	1	Large chipping hammer
110	0.1	Riveting machine
100	0.01	Automobile on highway
90	0.001	Subway train; a shouting voice
80	0.0001	Inside a 1952 Corvette at 60 mph
70	0.00001	Voice conversation; freight train 100 feet away
60	0.000001	Large department store
50	0.0000001	Average residence or small business office
40	0.00000001	Residential areas of Chicago at night
30	0.000000001	Very soft whisper
20	0.0000000001	Sound studio

TABLE 9-1 *Typical Sound Levels in Decibels (dB) and Watts* ■

9

Sound is energy, like the waves breaking on a sandy beach, and too much volume can permanently damage the delicate receiving mechanisms behind your eardrums, typically dulling your hearing in the 6 kHz range. In terms of volume, what you hear subjectively is not what you hear objectively. The perception of loudness is dependent upon the frequency or pitch of the sound: at low frequencies, more power is required to deliver the same perceived loudness as for a sound at the middle or higher frequency ranges. You may feel the sound more than hear it. For instance, when the ambient noise level is above 90 dB in the workplace, people are likely to make increased numbers of errors in susceptible tasks—especially when there is a high-frequency component to the noise. When the level is above 80 dB, it is quite impossible to use a telephone. Experiments by researchers in residential areas have shown that a sound generator at 45 dB produces no reaction from neighbors; at 45 to 55 dB, sporadic complaints; at 50 to 60 dB, widespread complaints; at 55 to 65 dB, threats of community action; and at more than 65 dB, vigorous community action. This research from the 1950s continues to provide helpful guidelines for practicing rock musicians and multimedia developers today.

There is a great deal more to acoustics than just volume and pitch. If you are interested, there are many texts that discuss why middle C on a cello does not sound like middle C on a bassoon; or why a five-year-old can hear a 1,000 Hz tone played at 20 dB while an older adult with presbycusis (loss of hearing sensitivity due to age) cannot. Your use of sound in multimedia projects will not likely require highly specialized knowledge of harmonics, intervals, sine waves, notation, octaves, or the physics of acoustics and vibration, but you do need to know the following:

- How to make sounds
- How to record and edit sounds on your computer
- How to incorporate sounds into your multimedia work

Multimedia System Sounds

You can use sound right off the bat on both the Macintosh and on a multimedia PC running Windows because beeps and warning sounds are available as soon as you install the operating system. On the Macintosh, you can choose one of several sounds for the system alert: ChuToy, Glass, Indigo, Laugh, Logjam, Pong2003, Purr, Simple Beep, Sosumi, Submarine, Temple, Uh oh, and Voltage. Open the Sounds Control Panel to listen to these and set your sound; or make a new, custom sound (see Figure 9-1).

In Windows, system sounds are WAV files, and they reside in the Windows\Media subdirectory. Available system event sounds include start.wav, chimes.wav, chord.wav, ding.wav, logoff.wav, notify.wav, recycle.wav, tada.wav, and the Microsoft sound.wav that typically plays when Windows starts up. If you have installed Microsoft Office 2000, you will have more choices: applause.wav, camera.wav, carbrake.wav, cashreg.wav, chimes.wav, clap.wav, driveby.wav, drumroll.wav, explode.wav, glass.wav, gunshot.wav, laser.wav, projctor.wav, ricochet.wav, type.wav, and whoosh.wav.

As Figure 9-1 shows, you can assign these sounds to system events such as Windows startup, warnings from other applications, or clicks outside of an open dialog box (which causes the default beep in Windows). And you can create *schemes* of sounds and select a particular scheme according to your mood. You can add your own sound files and install them so they play when

FIGURE 9-1

Sound Control

Panels for Windows

and Macintosh

system events occur: place the WAV sound files in your Windows\Media directory and use the Sound Control Panel to select them.

If you are new to either platform (Mac or Windows), your first multimedia sound experience might be simply finding one of these system sounds in the Sound Control Panel and testing it.

Using Macintosh models with a connected microphone, you can record and label new system sounds. This recording software is built into the system: just click on the Sound Control Panel's New button. In Windows, click the Start Menu button and select Programs | Accessories | Entertainment to find the Sound Recorder application that is installed by Windows:

MIDI Versus Digital Audio

MIDI (Musical Instrument Digital Interface) is a communications standard developed in the early 1980s for electronic musical instruments and computers. It allows music and sound synthesizers from different manufacturers to communicate with each other by sending messages along cables connected to the devices. MIDI provides a protocol for passing detailed descriptions of a musical score, such as the notes, sequences of notes, and what instrument will play these notes. But MIDI data is not digitized sound; it is a shorthand representation of music stored in numeric form. Digital audio is a recording, MIDI is a score—the first depends on the capabilities of your sound system, the other on the quality of your musical instruments *and* the capabilities of your sound system.

A MIDI file is a list of time-stamped commands that are recordings of musical actions (the pressing down of a piano key or a sustain pedal, for example, or the movement of a control wheel or slider) that, when sent to a MIDI playback device, results in sound. A concise MIDI message can cause a complex sound or sequence of sounds to play on an instrument or synthesizer; so MIDI files tend to be significantly smaller (per second of sound delivered to the user) than equivalent digitized waveform files.

In contrast to MIDI data, *digital audio* data is the actual representation of a sound, stored in the form of thousands of individual numbers (called *samples*). The digital data represents the instantaneous amplitude (or *loudness*) of a sound at discrete slices of time. Because it is not device dependent, digital audio sounds the same every time it is played. But that consistency comes at a price: large data storage files. Digital sound is used for music CDs.

MIDI data is to digital audio data what vector or drawn graphics are to bitmapped graphics. That is, MIDI data is device dependent; digital data is not. Just as the appearance of vector graphics differs depending on the printer device or display screen, the sounds produced by MIDI music files depend on the particular MIDI device used for playback. Similarly, a roll of perforated player-piano score played on a concert grand would sound different than if played on a honky-tonk piano. Digital data, on the other hand, produces sounds that are more or less identical regardless of the playback system. The MIDI standard is like PostScript, letting instruments communicate in a well-understood language.

MIDI has several advantages over digital audio and two huge disadvantages. First, the advantages:

- MIDI files are much more compact than digital audio files, and the size of a MIDI file is completely independent of playback quality. In general, MIDI files will be 200 to 1,000 times smaller than CD-quality digital audio files. Because MIDI files are small, they don't take up as much RAM, disk space, and CPU resources.

- Because they are small, MIDI files embedded in Web pages load and play more quickly than their digital equivalents.

- In some cases, MIDI files may sound better than digital audio files if the MIDI sound source you are using is of high quality.

- You can change the length of a MIDI file (by varying its tempo) without changing the pitch of the music or degrading the audio quality. MIDI data is completely editable—right down to the level of an individual note. You can manipulate the smallest detail of a MIDI composition (often with submillisecond accuracy) in ways that are impossible with digital audio.

Now for the disadvantages:

- Because MIDI data does not represent sound but musical instruments, you can be certain that playback will be accurate only if the MIDI playback device is identical to the device used for production. Imagine the emotional humming chorus from *Madame Butterfly* sung by a chorus of Budweiser frogs—same score, wrong instrument. Even with the General MIDI standard (see the General MIDI table of instrument sounds in Table 9-3), the sound of a MIDI instrument varies according to the electronics of the playback device and the sound generation method it uses.

- Also, MIDI cannot easily be used to play back spoken dialog, although expensive and technically tricky digital samplers are available.

In general, the most important advantage of digital audio is its consistent playback quality, but this is where MIDI is the least reliable! With digital audio you can be more confident that the audio track for your multimedia project will sound as good in the end as it did in the beginning when you created it. For this reason, it's no surprise that digital audio is used far more frequently than MIDI data for multimedia sound tracks.

There are two additional and often more compelling reasons to work with digital audio:

- A wider selection of application software and system support for digital audio is available for both the Macintosh and Windows platforms.

- The preparation and programming required for creating digital audio do not demand a knowledge of music theory; working with MIDI data usually does require a modicum of familiarity with musical scores, keyboards, and notation as well as audio production.

9

Choosing Between MIDI and Digital Audio

In general, use MIDI data in the following circumstances:

- Digital audio won't work because you don't have enough RAM, hard disk space, CPU processing power, or bandwidth.
- You have a high-quality MIDI sound source.
- You have complete control over the playback hardware.
- You don't need spoken dialog.

In general, use digital audio in the following circumstances:

- You don't have control over the playback hardware.
- You have the computing resources and bandwidth to handle digital files.
- You need spoken dialog.

Digital Audio

You can digitize sound from a microphone, a synthesizer, existing tape recordings, live radio and television broadcasts, popular CDs, and your favorite long-playing records. In fact, you can digitize sounds from any source, natural or prerecorded. The hardware and software requirements for digitizing sound are discussed in Chapter 4.

Digitized sound is *sampled sound*. Every *n*th fraction of a second, a sample of sound is taken and stored as digital information in bits and bytes. How often the samples are taken is the *sampling rate*, and the amount of information stored about each sample is the *sample size*. The more often you take a sample and the more data you store about that sample, the finer the resolution and quality of the captured sound when it is played back.

The three sampling frequencies most often used in multimedia are CD-quality 44.1 kHz (kilohertz), 22.05 kHz, and 11.025 kHz. Sample sizes are either 8 bits or 16 bits. The larger the sample size, the better the data describes the recorded sound. An 8-bit sample size provides 256 equal units to describe the dynamic range or amplitude—the level of sound at that time—of the slice of sound captured. A 16-bit sample size, on the other hand, provides a staggering 65,536 equal units to describe the dynamic range. As you can see in Figure 9-2, slices of analog waveforms are sampled at various frequencies, and each discrete sample is then stored either as 8 bits or 16 bits of data.

FIGURE 9-2

It is impossible to reconstruct the original waveform if the sampling frequency is too low ■

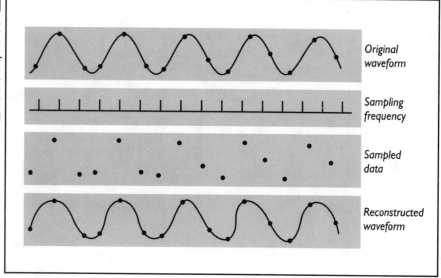

Original waveform

Sampling frequency

Sampled data

Reconstructed waveform

The value of each sample is rounded off to the nearest integer (*quantization*), and if the amplitude is greater than the intervals available, clipping of the top and bottom of the wave occurs (see Figure 9-3). Quantization can produce an unwanted background hissing noise, and clipping may severely distort the sound.

Preparing Digital Audio Files

Preparing digital audio files is fairly straightforward. If you have analog source materials—music or sound effects that you have recorded on analog media such as cassette tapes—the first step is to digitize the analog material by recording it onto computer-readable digital media. In most cases, this just means playing sound from one device (such as a tape recorder) right into your computer, using appropriate audio digitizing software.

You want to focus on two crucial aspects of preparing digital audio files:

■ Balancing the need for sound quality with your available RAM and hard disk resources

■ Setting proper recording levels to get a good, clean recording

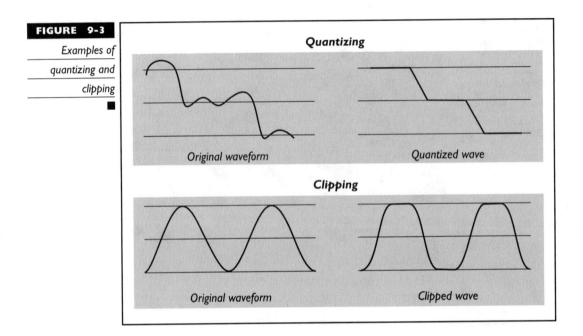

FIGURE 9-3

*Examples of
quantizing and
clipping*

Quantizing

Original waveform

Quantized wave

Clipping

Original waveform

Clipped wave

File Size Versus Quality

Remember that the sampling rate determines the frequency makeup of the recording. Sampling at higher rates more accurately captures the high-frequency content of your sound. *Audio resolution* determines the accuracy with which a sound can be digitized. Using more bits for the sample size yields a recording that sounds more like its original.

---

warning *The higher the sound quality, the larger your file will be.*

Stereo recordings are more lifelike and realistic because human beings have two ears. Mono recordings are fine, but tend to sound a bit "flat" and uninteresting when compared with stereo recordings. Logically, stereo sound files require twice as much storage space as mono files for the same length of play time.

Table 9-2 provides some commonly used sampling rates and resolutions, with resulting file sizes.

Sampling Rate	Resolution	Stereo or Mono	Bytes Needed for 1 Minute	Comments
44.1 kHz	16-bit	Stereo	10.5MB	CD-quality recording; the recognized standard of audio quality.
44.1 kHz	16-bit	Mono	5.25MB	A good trade-off for high-quality recordings of mono sources such as voice-overs.
44.1 kHz	8-bit	Stereo	5.25MB	Achieves highest playback quality on low-end devices such as most of the sound cards in Windows PCs.
44.1 kHz	8-bit	Mono	2.6MB	An appropriate trade-off for recording a mono source.
22.05 kHz	16-bit	Stereo	5.25MB	Darker sounding than CD-quality recording because of the lower sampling rate, but still full and "present" because of high bit resolution and stereo. Preferred for CD-ROM projects.
22.05 kHz	16-bit	Mono	2.5MB	Not a bad choice for speech, but better to trade some fidelity for a lot of disk space by dropping down to 8-bit.
22.05 kHz	8-bit	Stereo	2.6MB	A popular choice for reasonable stereo recording where full bandwidth playback is not possible.
22.05 kHz	8-bit	Mono	1.3MB	A thinner sound than the choice just above, but very usable. Any Macintosh or any MPC can play back this type of file. About as good as listening to your TV set.
11 kHz	8-bit	Stereo	1.3MB	At this low a sampling rate, there are few advantages to using stereo.
11 kHz	8-bit	Mono	650K	In practice, probably as low as you can go and still get usable results; very dark and muffled.
5.5 kHz	8-bit	Stereo	650K	Stereo not effective.
5.5 kHz	8-bit	Mono	325K	About as good as a bad telephone connection.

TABLE 9-2 *One-Minute Digital Audio Recordings at Common Sampling Rates and Resolutions* ■

Here are the formulas for determining the size (in bytes) of a digital recording. For a monophonic recording:

sampling rate * duration of recording in seconds * (bit resolution / 8) * 1

For a stereo recording:

sampling rate * duration of recording in seconds * (bit resolution / 8) * 2

Thus the formula for a 10-second recording at 22.05 kHz, 8-bit resolution would be

22050 * 10 * 8 / 8 * 1

which equals 220,500 bytes. Sampling rate is measured in kHz, or thousand samples per second, while resolution is measured in bits per sample (remember, there are 8 bits in a byte). A 10-second stereo recording at 44.1 kHz, 16-bit resolution (meeting the CD-quality Red Book Audio standards—an international recording standard discussed later in this chapter) would be

44100 * 10 * 16 / 8 * 2

which equals 1,764,000 bytes. A 40-second mono recording at 11 kHz, 8-bit resolution would be

11000 * 40 * 8 / 8 * 1

which equals 440,000 bytes.

....

I have a 20-second sample of a song which I play to my class at 8K, 22K, 44K, and 48K, and I have the students listen and compare quality. They comment that 8K does not sound all that bad until *they hear the 44K and 48K. They also see (hear) very little difference between 44K and 48K.*

....

Dennis Woytek, Assistant Professor of Multimedia Technology, Duquesne University

Consumer-grade audio compact discs are recorded in stereo at a sampling rate of 44.1 kHz and a 16-bit resolution. Fortunately, for hard disk storage requirements at least, user expectations of audio quality are somewhat lower for computer-based multimedia presentations than they are for Grammy Award–winning recordings. (See Vaughan's Law of Multimedia Minimums in the "Production Tips" section of this chapter.) Particularly on the Macintosh, 8-bit, 22 kHz recordings are typical. Even lower rates are used for sound effects in many games.

---

tip *The only reason to digitize audio at a higher specification than can be used by the target playback device is for archiving it. As playback technologies and bandwidth improve over time, you may wish (someday) for higher-quality original files when you upgrade a product.*

Setting Proper Recording Levels

A distorted recording sounds terrible. If the signal you feed into your computer is too "hot" to handle, the result will be an unpleasant crackling or background ripping noise. Conversely, recordings that are made at too low a level are often unusable because the amount of sound recorded does not sufficiently exceed the residual noise levels of the recording process itself. The trick is to set the right levels when you record.

Any good piece of digital audio recording and editing software will display digital meters to let you know how loud your sound is. Watch the meters closely during recording, and you'll never have a problem. Unlike analog meters that usually have a 0 setting somewhere in the middle and extend up into ranges like +5, +8, or even higher, digital meters peak out. To avoid distortion, do not cross over this limit. If this happens, lower your volume (either by lowering the input level of the recording device or the output level of your source) and try again. Try to keep peak levels between -3 and -10. Any time you go over the peak, whether you can hear it or not, you introduce distortion into the recording.

Editing Digital Recordings

Once a recording has been made, it will almost certainly need to be edited. Apple's QuickTime Player Pro, shown in Figure 9-4, provides a basic look at a sound file's structure and allows for primitive playback and editing. A more serious sound editor is Sonic Foundry's Sound Forge for Windows,

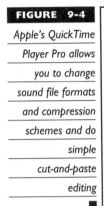

FIGURE 9-4

Apple's QuickTime

Player Pro allows

you to change

sound file formats

and compression

schemes and do

simple

cut-and-paste

editing

shown in Figure 9-5 with its special effects menu. With this tool you can create professional sound tracks and digital mixes. The basic sound editing operations that most multimedia producers need are described in the paragraphs that follow.

Trimming Removing "dead air" or blank space from the front of a recording and any unnecessary extra time off the end is your first sound editing task. Trimming even a few seconds here and there might make a big difference in your file size. Trimming is typically accomplished by dragging the mouse cursor over a graphic representation of your recording and choosing a menu command such as Cut, Clear, Erase, or Silence.

Splicing and Assembly Using the same tools mentioned for trimming, you will probably want to remove the extraneous noises that inevitably creep into a recording. Even the most controlled studio voice-overs require touch-up. Also, you may need to assemble longer recordings by cutting and pasting

FIGURE 9-5

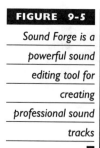

Sound Forge is a

powerful sound

editing tool for

creating

professional sound

tracks

together many shorter ones. In the old days, this was done by splicing and assembling actual pieces of magnetic tape.

Volume Adjustments   If you are trying to assemble ten different recordings into a single sound track, there is little chance that all the segments will have the same volume. To provide a consistent volume level, select all the data in the file, and raise or lower the overall volume by a certain amount. Don't increase the volume too much, or you may distort the file. Best is to use a sound editor to *normalize* the assembled audio file to a particular level, say 80 percent to 90 percent of maximum (without clipping), or about –16 dB. Without normalizing to this rule-of-thumb level, your final sound track might play too softly or too loudly. Even pros can leave out this important step. Sometimes an audio CD just doesn't seem to have the same loudness as the last one you played, or it is too loud and you can hear clipping. Figure 9-6 shows the normalizing process at work in Sound Forge.

Format Conversion   In some cases, your digital audio editing software might read a format different from that read by your presentation or authoring program. Most Macintosh sound editing software will save files in SND and AIF formats, and most authoring systems will read these formats. In Windows, most editing software writes WAV files.

9

FIGURE 9-6

Normalizing evens

out the sound level

in an audio file

■

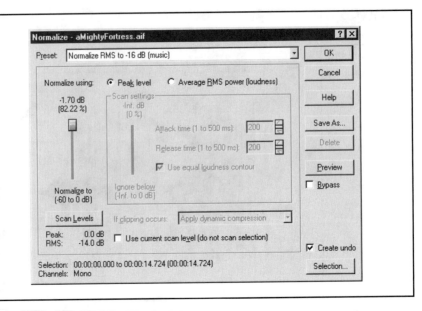

Resampling or Downsampling   If you have recorded and edited your sounds at 16-bit sampling rates but are using lower rates and resolutions in your project, you must resample or downsample the file. This process will save considerable disk space.

Fade-ins and Fade-outs   Most programs offer enveloping capability, useful for long sections that you wish to fade in or fade out gradually. This enveloping is important to smooth out the very beginning and the very end of a sound file.

Equalization   Some programs offer digital equalization (EQ) capabilities that allow you to modify a recording's frequency content to sound brighter or darker.

Time Stretching   More advanced programs let you alter the length (in time) of a sound file without changing its pitch. This feature can be very useful, but watch out: most time-stretching algorithms will severely degrade the audio quality of the file if the length is altered more than a few percent in either direction.

Digital Signal Processing (DSP)   Some programs allow you to process the signal with reverberation, multitap delay, chorus, flange, and other special effects.

Being able to process a sound source with effects can greatly add to a project. To create an environment by placing the sound inside a room, hall, or even a cathedral can bring depth and dimension to a project. But a little can go a long way—do not overdo the sound effects! Once a sound effect is processed and mixed onto a track, it cannot be further edited; so always save the original so you can tweak it again if you are not happy.

Reversing Sounds   Another simple manipulation is to reverse all or a portion of a digital audio recording. Sounds, particularly spoken dialog, can produce a surreal, otherworldly effect when played backward.

Making MIDI Audio

Composing your own original score can be one of the most creative and rewarding aspects of building a multimedia project, and MIDI is the quickest, easiest, and most flexible tool for this task. Yet creating an original MIDI score is hard work. Knowing something about music, being able to play the piano, and having a lot of good ideas are just the prerequisites to building a good score; beyond that, it takes time and musical skill to work with MIDI.

Happily, you can always hire someone to do the job for you. In addition to the talented MIDI composers who charge substantial rates for their services, many young composers are also available who want to get into multimedia. With a little research, you can often find a MIDI musician to work for limited compensation. Remember, however, that you often get what you pay for.

To make MIDI scores, you will need sequencer software (such as illustrated in Figure 9-7) and a sound synthesizer (typically built into the sound

FIGURE 9-7

Sequencing software allows you to record, edit, and save music generated from a MIDI keyboard or instrument

board on PCs, but an add-on board or peripheral for the Macintosh). A MIDI keyboard is also useful to simplify the creation of musical scores. The MIDI keyboard is not, however, necessary for playback unless the keyboard has its own built-in synthesizer (most do) that you wish to specify for play-back. Sequencer software lets you record and edit MIDI data and quantizes your score to adjust for timing inconsistencies (a great feature for those who can't keep the beat). The sequencer software records your actions on the MIDI keyboard (or another MIDI device) in real-time, and will play back ex-actly the notes you played on the keyboard; the software may also print a neatly penned copy of your score to paper. Sound boards and other hard-ware components of MIDI are discussed in Chapter 4.

Instruments that you can synthesize are identified by a General MIDI numbering system that ranges from 0 to 127 (see Table 9-3). Until this sys-tem came along, there was always a risk that a MIDI file originally composed with, say, piano, electric guitar, and bass, might be played back with piccolo, tambourine, and glockenspiel if the ID numbers were not precisely mapped to match your original hardware setup. This was usually the case when you played a MIDI file on a MIDI configuration different from the one that re-corded the file.

ID	Sound	ID	Sound
0	Acoustic grand piano	4	Rhodes piano
1	Bright acoustic piano	5	Chorused piano
2	Electric grand piano	6	Harpsichord
3	Honky-tonk piano	7	Clarinet

TABLE 9-3 *General MIDI Instrument Sounds* ■

ID	Sound	ID	Sound
8	Celesta	23	Tango accordion
9	Glockenspiel	24	Acoustic guitar (nylon)
10	Music box	25	Acoustic guitar (steel)
11	Vibraphone	26	Electric guitar (jazz)
12	Marimba	27	Electric guitar (clean)
13	Xylophone	28	Electric guitar (muted)
14	Tubular bells	29	Overdriven guitar
15	Dulcimer	30	Distortion guitar
16	Hammond organ	31	Guitar harmonics
17	Percussive organ	32	Acoustic bass
18	Rock organ	33	Electric bass (finger)
19	Church organ	34	Electric bass (pick)
20	Reed organ	35	Fretless bass
21	Accordion	36	Slap bass 1
22	Harmonica	37	Slap bass 2

TABLE 9-3   *General MIDI Instrument Sounds* (continued) ■

ID	Sound	ID	Sound
38	Synth bass 1	53	Voice oohs
39	Synth bass 2	54	Synth voice
40	Violin	55	Orchestra hit
41	Viola	56	Trumpet
42	Cello	57	Trombone
43	Contrabass	58	Tuba
44	Tremolo strings	59	Muted trumpet
45	Pizzicato strings	60	French horn
46	Orchestral harp	61	Brass section
47	Timpani	62	Synth brass 1
48	String ensemble 1	63	Synth brass 2
49	String ensemble 2	64	Soprano saxophone
50	SynthStrings 1	65	Alto saxophone
51	SynthStrings 2	66	Tenor saxophone
52	Choir aahs	67	Baritone saxophone

TABLE 9-3   *General MIDI Instrument Sounds* (continued) ∎

ID	Sound	ID	Sound
68	Oboe	83	Lead 4 (Chiff lead)
69	English horn	84	Lead 5 (Charang)
70	Bassoon	85	Lead 6 (Voice)
71	Clarinet	86	Lead 7 (Fifths)
72	Piccolo	87	Lead 8 (Bass + lead)
73	Flute	88	Pad 1 (New Age)
74	Recorder	89	Pad 2 (Warm)
75	Pan flute	90	Pad 3 (Polysynth)
76	Bottle blow	91	Pad 4 (Choir)
77	Shakuhachi	92	Pad 5 (Bowed)
78	Whistle	93	Pad 6 (Metallic)
79	Ocarina	94	Pad 7 (Halo)
80	Lead 1 (Square)	95	Pad 8 (Sweep)
81	Lead 2 (Sawtooth)	96	FX 1 (Rain)
82	Lead 3 (Calliope lead)	97	FX 2 (Soundtrack)

TABLE 9-3 *General MIDI Instrument Sounds* (continued) ∎

9

ID	Sound	ID	Sound
98	FX 3 (Crystal)	113	Agogo
99	FX 4 (Atmosphere)	114	Steel drums
100	FX 5 (Brightness)	115	Wood block
101	FX 6 (Goblins)	116	Taiko drum
102	FX 7 (Echoes)	117	Melodic Tom
103	FX 8 (Sci-Fi)	118	Synth drum
104	Sitar	119	Reverse cymbal
105	Banjo	120	Guitar fret noise
106	Shamisen	121	Breath noise
107	Koto	122	Seashore
108	Kalimba	123	Bird tweet
109	Bagpipe	124	Telephone ring
110	Fiddle	125	Helicopter
111	Shanai	126	Applause
112	Tinkle bell	127	Gunshot

TABLE 9-3 *General MIDI Instrument Sounds (continued)* ■

ID	Sound	ID	Sound
Percussion Keys		49	Crash cymbal 1
35	Acoustic bass drum	50	High tom
36	Bass drum 1	51	Ride cymbal 1
37	Side stick	52	Chinese cymbal
38	Acoustic snare	53	Ride bell
39	Hand clap	54	Tambourine
40	Electric snare	55	Splash cymbal
41	Low-floor tom	56	Cowbell
42	Closed high-hat	57	Crash cymbal 2
43	High-floor tom	58	Vibraslap
44	Pedal high-hat	59	Ride cymbal 2
45	Low tom	60	High bongo
46	Open high-hat	61	Low bongo
47	Low-mid tom	62	Mute high conga
48	High-mid tom	63	Open high conga

9

TABLE 9-3 *General MIDI Instrument Sounds* (continued) ■

ID	Sound	ID	Sound
64	Low conga	73	Short guiro
65	High timbale	74	Long guiro
66	Low timbale	75	Claves
67	High agogo	76	High wood block
68	Low agogo	77	Low wood block
69	Cabasa	78	Mute cuica
70	Maracas	79	Open cuica
71	Short whistle	80	Mute triangle
72	Long whistle	81	Open triangle

TABLE 9-3   *General MIDI Instrument Sounds* (continued) ■

tip   *Making MIDI files is as complex as recording good sampled files; so it often pays to find someone already set up with the equipment and skills to create your score, rather than investing in both the hardware and learning curve.*

Once you have gathered your audio material, you will need to edit it to precisely fit your multimedia project. As you edit, you will continue to make creative decisions. Because it is so easy to edit MIDI data, you can make many fine adjustments to your music.

MIDI's true place in multimedia work may be as a production tool rather than a delivery medium. MIDI is by far the best way to create original music for multimedia projects, so use MIDI to get the flexibility and creative control you want. Then, once the music is completed and fits your project, lock it down for delivery by turning it into digital audio data, as discussed below.

t i p *Test your MIDI files thoroughly by playing them back on a variety of hardware devices before you incorporate them into your multimedia project.*

Many MIDI sequencing applications let you print your MIDI score as sheet music. SmartScore software from Musitek is not only a sequencer, it can be used to go the other way, too: using a scanner, it will recognize notation and convert sheet music to multitrack MIDI files in your computer (see Figure 9-8).

FIGURE 9-8

SmartScore from Musitek converts sheet music to multitrack MIDI files

http://www.musitek.com

Scanner software reads sheet music and turns it into MIDI files

Audio File Formats

When you create multimedia, it is likely that you will deal with file formats and translators for text, sounds, images, animations, or digital video clips. A sound file's format is simply a recognized methodology for organizing the digitized sound's data bits and bytes into a data file. The structure of the file must be known, of course, before the data can be saved or later loaded into a computer to be edited and/or played as sound. Table 9-4 shows some of the common sound formats used for multimedia.

On the Macintosh, digitized sounds may be stored as data files (for example, AIF or SDII), or they may be stored as resources in the resource fork of the system or application as SNDs. The Macintosh uses a unique dual-fork file structure, and you will need to know whether the file resides in a resource fork or as a stand-alone file.

In Windows, digitized sounds are most commonly stored as WAV files. For the Internet, new formats are emerging as companies develop solutions for streaming and playing sound on the Web. These solutions are discussed in detail in Chapter 13.

There are many ways to store the bits and bytes that describe a sampled waveform sound. The method used for Red Book Audio data files on consumer-grade music CDs is Linear Pulse Code Modulation. An audio CD can provide up to 80 minutes of playing time, which is enough for a slow-tempo rendition of Beethoven's Ninth Symphony. Incidentally, being able to contain Beethoven's Ninth is reported to be Philips's and Sony's actual size criterion during early research and development for determining the length of the sectors and ultimately the physical size of the compact disc format itself. The CD-ROM/XA (extended architecture) format for reading and writing CDs was developed later so you could put several recording sessions onto a single CD-R (recordable) disc.

The AIFF sound format (or AIFC when supporting MACE compression schemes of 3:1 and 6:1) is preferred for Macintosh sound files, where all the sound data resides in the data fork. The wave format (WAV) was introduced by Microsoft and IBM with the introduction of Windows.

Both Macintosh and Windows can make use of MIDI files. A MIDI interface is built into many sound boards on the PC. On the Macintosh, a MIDI adapter is required for MIDI instrument input and output. On both platforms, MIDI sounds are typically stored in files with the .mid extension.

Sound for the World Wide Web

In the early days of the Internet, when connected machines typically ran in a Unix environment, the common file format for sounds (.au) was the international telephone format (CCITT G711) of *uLaw* (also known as *Mu-law* or *μ-law*, nicknamed the "TalkRadio" or "Geek of the Week" format and pronounced "mew-law"). It provided meager 8 kHz sampling rates at 8-bit mono, but produced very small file sizes. Today, the uLaw format supports 8 kHz at 16 bits in 2:1 compression. *aLaw* is the European equivalent of uLaw. Many more sound file types are now commonly found on the Web (see Table 9-4).

Purpose	Extension	MIME Type
669 MOD Music	.669	
AIFF Audio	.aifc	audio/aiff
AIFF Audio	.aiff	audio/aiff
AIFF Sound	.aiff	audio/x-aiff
AIFF Sound Compressed	.aife	audio/x-aiff
AIFF Sound	.aif	audio/x-aiff
aLAW Sound	.al	
Amiga 8-bit sound	.8svx	
Amiga IFF Sound	.svx	
Amiga MED Sound	.med	
Amiga OctaMed music	.8med	
AU Audio	.snd	audio/basic
AU Audio	.ulw	audio/basic
Beatnik	.rmf	audio/rmf
Beatnik	.rmf	audio/x-rmf
MIDI	.kar	audio/mid

TABLE 9-4 *Common File Types Used for Digitized Sounds (Internet MIME Types)* ∎

Purpose	Extension	MIME Type
MIDI	.kar	audio/midi
MIDI	.kar	audio/x-midi
MIDI	.mid	audio/mid
MIDI	.mid	audio/midi
MIDI	.mid	audio/x-midi
MIDI	.midi	audio/mid
MIDI	.midi	audio/midi
MIDI	.midi	audio/x-midi
MIDI	.smf	audio/mid
MIDI	.smf	audio/midi
MIDI	.smf	audio/x-midi
μLaw Sound	.au	audio/basic
μLaw Sound	.ul	audio/basic
MP3 Audio	.mp3	audio/mpeg
MP3 Audio	.mp3	audio/x-mpeg
MPEG audio stream	.mla	audio/mpeg
MPEG audio stream	.mls	audio/mpeg
MPEG audio stream	.mls	audio/x-mpeg
MPEG audio stream	.mp2	audio/x-mpeg
MPEG audio stream	.mpa	audio/mpeg
MPEG audio stream	.mpeg	audio/x-mpeg
MPEG audio stream	.mpg	audio/mpeg
MPEG audio stream	.mpg	audio/x-mpeg
MPEG audio stream	.mpm	audio/mpeg
MPEG audio stream	.mpm	audio/x-mpeg
MPEG audio stream	.mpv	video/mpeg
MPEG-1 Audio Movie	.mp2	audio/x-mpeg

TABLE 9-4 *Common File Types Used for Digitized Sounds (Internet MIME Types)* (continued) ■

Purpose	Extension	MIME Type
MPEG-1 Audio Movie	.mpa	audio/x-mpeg
MPEG-1 Audio Movie	.m15	
MPEG-1 Audio Movie	.m1a	audio/x-mpeg
MPEG-1 Audio Movie	.m75	
MPEG-1 Layer 3	.mp3	
QCP Audio	.qcp	audio/vnd.qcelp
Real Time Streaming Protocol	.rtsp	application/x-rtsp
RealAudio	.ra	audio/x-pn-realaudio
RealAudio	.ra	audio/vnd.rn-realaudio
RealAudio	.ram	audio/x-pn-realaudio
RealAudio	.rm	audio/x-pn-realaudio
Sound Designer 2 File	.sd2	
Sound of various types	.snd	
SoundEdit Sound ex SOX	.hcom	
VOC Sound	.voc	
WAV Audio	.wav	audio/wav

TABLE 9-4   *Common File Types Used for Digitized Sounds (Internet MIME Types)* (continued) ∎

There are two methods for playing either digital or MIDI sound on the Web. First, you can wait for the entire sound file to download to your computer, then play it back with a helper application. Second, you can begin to play a downloading sound file as soon as enough of the sound is cached in your computer's *buffer* and the downloading continues to fill the buffer faster than you empty it by playing the sound file: the sound file *streams* into your computer in the background, keeping ahead of what has already been played so the playback doesn't pause or break up. Streaming files are dependent upon connection speed: you must wait longer (*streaming latency*) before the streamed sound begins to play when using a 28.8 Kbps modem (low bandwidth) than using a high-speed T1 connection (high bandwidth).

Macromedia's Flash allows you to integrate the sound tracks that you have made using a sound editor into a Web-based multimedia presentation, including both event sounds like button clicks and streaming sounds like background music. Able to read and save .mp3 files, Flash offers Web designers serious and powerful options for solving the quality conundrum of high-quality (big) files and slow downloads versus low-quality (small) files and speedy delivery—with nice results. Figure 9-9 shows Flash being used to assemble a music and graphic project. Check out Chapter 14, which discusses the browser plug-ins and techniques used to deliver sound and motion video for the Web.

I used to make two-measure loops and fight file size constraints. Now, with MP3 technology, particularly in such Web applications as Flash5 from Macromedia, audio file size has been drastically reduced while retaining relatively good sound quality. This gives the sound designer much more room to work creatively and affords a much richer product for Web delivery.

Chip Harris, Composer and Musician, Chip Harris Music+Sound Design/charrismusic.com

FIGURE 9-9

Flash can be used to integrate many audio files and deliver them to the Web

Adding Sound to Your Multimedia Project

The original 128K Macintosh, released in January 1984, was technically a multimedia-capable machine. It displayed bitmapped graphics (albeit in black and white) and, more significantly, boasted 8-bit digital audio capability right on the motherboard. In fact, the very first Macintosh actually introduced itself by voice when it was unveiled by Steve Jobs. (See Chapter 4 to read what it said.)

Here's a little history: In order to use the Apple moniker, the original founders of Apple Computer, Inc., worked out an arrangement with the Beatles (yes, *those* Beatles). One part of that agreement stipulated that Apple Computer, Inc., would never venture into the music business. To Steve Jobs and Steve Wozniak, working out of their garage in the late 1970s on a machine that could barely manage a convincing system beep, that clause probably seemed a harmless one. Little did they know that less than ten years later their computer would become the most popular music computer in the world.

Over the years, many people have speculated that the agreement with the Beatles has kept Apple out of the music business and delayed development of system software for audio applications. Although Apple would doubtless deny this, the company did finally pay representatives of the Beatles about $30 million to settle the issue once and for all.

Apple then broke new ground, outpacing Microsoft's Audio/Video Interleaved technology, with the release of QuickTime. QuickTime has become a standard file format for displaying digitized motion video from hard disk or CD-ROM without special hardware. Digital audio data is interleaved with video information in the file, and when it is played back, the audio stays synchronized to the motion picture. You can use QuickTime just to play stereo sounds and MIDI; the video part of QuickTime is not required. QuickTime will display many graphic image formats as well.

Whether you're working on a Macintosh or in Windows, you will need to follow certain steps to bring an audio recording into your multimedia project. Here is a brief overview of the process:

9

1. Decide what kind of sound is needed (such as background music, special sound effects, and spoken dialog). Decide where these audio events will occur in the flow of your project. Fit the sound cues into your storyboard, or make up a cue sheet.

2. Decide where and when you want to use either digital audio or MIDI data.

3. Acquire source material by creating it from scratch or purchasing it.

4. Edit the sounds to fit your project.

5. Test the sounds to be sure they are timed properly with the project's images. This may involve repeating steps 1 through 4 until everything is in sync.

When it's time to import your compiled and edited sounds into your project, you'll need to know how your particular multimedia software environment handles sound data. Each program handles it a bit differently, but the process is usually fairly straightforward: just tell your software which file you want to play and when to play it. This is usually handled by an importing or "linking" process during which you identify the files. Multimedia authoring tools and environments are discussed in Chapter 7. Presentation, word processing, and spreadsheet applications that allow you to import sounds are discussed in Chapter 6.

Scripting languages such as OpenScript (ToolBook), Lingo (Director), and ActionScript (Flash) provide a greater level of control over audio playback, but you'll need to know about the programming language and environment. In authoring environments, it is usually a simple matter to play a sound when the user clicks a button, but this may not be enough. If the user changes screens while a long file is playing, for example, you may need to program the sound to stop before leaving the current screen. If the file to be played cannot be found on the hard disk, you may need to code an entire section for error handling and file location. Sample code is generally provided in both printed and online documentation for software that includes sound playback.

First Person

In April 1992, Microsoft rolled out its new version of Windows 3.1 with speeches and a live MIDI performance at the Spring COMDEX/Windows World Trade Show in Chicago.

Tracy Hurst played the piano and Steve Peha worked the electronic interface. As Tracy played "Striving for Glory: The Windows 3.1 Theme" on his Roland HP-5700, the music was instantaneously transcribed by Midisoft Studio, and the notes ran real-time across the 50-foot big screen, like sing-along bouncing balls. The show worked perfectly, and Windows magazine later called it a tour de force for Windows multimedia. It was slick.

But I knew these people who looked so professional and confident. I knew about the late nights, the crashed disk drives, the long drive from Boston, and the hurried runs to the nearest Radio Shack. This performance was not just about MIDI; it was about multimedia development in general. Hard work and technology are the substantial invisible part of the iceberg supporting multimedia's visible leading edge.

Toward Professional Sound: The Red Book Standard

The method for digitally encoding the high-quality stereo of the consumer CD music market is an international standard, ISO 10149. This is also known as the Red Book standard (derived simply from the color of the standard's book jacket). Developers of this standard claim that the digital audio sample size and sampling rate of Red Book Audio (16 bits at 44.1 kHz) allow accurate reproduction of all sounds that humans can hear. Until recently, dedicated professional sound-studio equipment was used for this high-fidelity recording; today high-end sound boards are available that will record and play 16-bit sampled sound at 44.1 kHz and at 48 kHz. These boards are available for both Macintosh and PC platforms. Software such as Toast and CD-Creator from Adaptec can translate the digital files of Red Book Audio found on consumer compact discs directly into a digital sound editing file or decompress .mp3 files into CD-Audio.

Space Considerations

The substantial amount of digital sound information required for high-quality sound takes up a lot of disk storage space, especially when the quantity is doubled for two-channel stereo. It takes about 1.94MB to store 11 seconds of uncompressed Red Book stereo sound.

If monaural sound is adequate for your project, you can cut your storage space requirement in half or get double the play time in the same memory space. With compression techniques, you might be able to store the sound in one-eighth the space, but you will lose some fidelity due to the rounding-off effects of quantization. Further, to conserve space you can try downsampling, or reducing the number of sample slices you take in a second. Many multimedia developers use 8-bit sample sizes at 22.05 kHz sampling rates because they consider the sound to be good enough (about the quality of AM radio), and they save immense amounts of digital real estate by not using the Red Book standard.

The following formula will help you estimate your storage needs. If you are using two channels for stereo, double the result.

(sampling rate * bits per sample) / 8 = bytes per second

You face important trade-offs when deciding how to manage digitized sound in your multimedia project. How much sound quality can you sacrifice in order to reduce storage? What compression techniques make sense? Will compressed sound work in your authoring platform? What is good

9

enough but not amateurish? Can you get away with 8 bits at 11.025 kHz for voice mail, product testimonials, and voice-overs and then switch to higher sampling rates for music?

::::::::::::::::::::::::::::::::::::::

With the collaboration of composer Dave Soldier, Komar & Melamid's Most Wanted Painting project (http://www.diacenter.org/km/index.html) was extended into the realm of music. A poll, written by Dave Soldier, was conducted on Dia's Web site (http://www.diacenter.org) in Spring 1996. Approximately 500 visitors took the survey. Dave Soldier and Nina Mankin used the survey results to write music and lyrics for the Most Wanted and Most Unwanted songs.

A note from the composer:

This survey confirms the hypothesis that today's popular music indeed provides an accurate estimate of the wishes of the vox populi. The most favored ensemble, determined from a rating by participants of their favorite instruments in combination, comprises a moderately sized group (three to ten instruments) consisting of guitar, piano, saxophone, bass, drums, violin, cello, synthesizer, with low male and female vocals singing in rock/r&b style. The favorite lyrics narrate a love story, and the favorite listening circumstance is at home. The only feature in lyric subjects that occurs in both most wanted and unwanted categories is "intellectual stimulation." Most participants desire music of moderate duration (approximately 5 minutes), moderate pitch range, moderate tempo, and moderate to loud volume, and display a profound dislike of the alternatives. If the survey provides an accurate analysis of these factors for the population, and assuming that the preference for each factor follows a Gaussian (bell-curve) distribution, the combination of these qualities, even to the point of sensory overload and stylistic discohesion, will result in a musical work that will be unavoidably and uncontrollably "liked" by 72 plus or minus 12 percent (standard deviation; Kolmogorov-Smirnov statistic) of listeners. The most unwanted music is over 25 minutes long, veers wildly between loud and quiet sections, between fast and slow tempos, and features timbres of extremely high and low pitch, with each dichotomy presented in abrupt transition. The most unwanted orchestra was determined to be large and features the accordion and bagpipe (which tie at 13 percent as the most unwanted instrument), banjo, flute, tuba, harp, organ, synthesizer (the only instrument that appears in both the most wanted and most unwanted ensembles). An operatic soprano raps and sings atonal music, advertising jingles, political slogans, and "elevator" music, and a children's choir sings jingles and holiday songs. The most unwanted subjects for lyrics are cowboys and holidays, and the most unwanted listening circumstances are involuntary exposure to commercials and elevator music. Therefore, it can be shown that if there is no covariance—someone who dislikes bagpipes is as likely to hate elevator music as someone who despises the organ, for example— fewer than 200 individuals of the world's total population would enjoy this piece.

::::::::::::::::::::::::::::::::

Dave Soldier, Composer and Musician, who provides
The Most Wanted Song and The Most Unwanted Song on a CD
at http://www.diacenter.org/km/musiccd.html

Production Tips

A classic physical anthropology law (Leibig's Law of the Minimums) proposes that the evolution of eyesight, locomotor speed, sense of smell, or any other species trait will cease when that trait becomes sufficiently adequate to meet the survival requirements of the competitive environment. If the trait is good enough, the organism expends no more effort improving it. Thus, if consumer-grade electronics and a handheld microphone are good enough for making your sound, and if you, your client, and your audience are all satisfied with the results, conserve your energy and money and avoid any more expenditure. And keep this Law of Minimums in mind when you make all your trade-off decisions involving other areas of high technology and multimedia, too.

Vaughan's Law of Multimedia Minimums

There is an acceptable minimum level of adequacy that will satisfy the audience, even when that level may not be the best that technology, money, or time and effort can buy.

9

Audio Recording

You can record your sound material to cassette tapes as the first step in the digitizing process. With tape, you can do many takes of the same sound or voice, listen to all the takes, and pick the best one to digitize. By recording on inexpensive media rather than directly to disk, you avoid filling up your hard disk with throw-away stuff. If your project requires CD-quality digitized sound at 44.1 kHz and 16 bits, you should hire a sound studio. High-fidelity sound recording is a specialized craft, a skill learned in great part by trial and error, much like photography. If you do decide to do it yourself at CD-quality levels, be prepared to invest in an acoustically treated room, high-end amplifiers and recording equipment, and expensive microphones.

As already stated, there are many trade-offs involved in making multimedia. For example, if you are satisfied with 22.05 kHz in your project or are constrained to this rate by storage considerations, any consumer-grade tape recorder of reasonable quality will do fine. This, of course, also applies to conversations recorded from the telephone, where a sampling rate of 11.025 kHz is adequate. Noise reduction circuits and metal tapes are helpful to remove hiss, but at a sampling rate of 22.05 kHz you are only going to be digitizing audio frequencies as high as about 11 kHz, anyway. Both the high and low ends of the audio hearing spectrum are therefore less important to you, and that is OK, because those areas are precisely the add-value focus of very elaborate and expensive consumer equipment.

Video cassette recorders (VCRs) usually have excellent stereo audio circuits, and many good multimedia sounds were first recorded and digitized using the audio tracks of videotape.

Digital audio tape (DAT) systems have now entered the consumer marketplace. They provide a tape-based 44.1 kHz, 16-bit record and playback capability. You may, however, find that DAT is high-fidelity overkill for your needs, because the recordings are too accurate, precisely recording glitches, background noises, microphone pops, and coughs from the next room. A good editor can help reduce the impact of these noises, but at the cost of your time and money.

Keeping Track of Your Sounds

If you use a tape deck or recorder, be sure it has a good counter built into it, so that you can mark and log the locations of various takes and events on the tape and quickly find them later. Get into the habit of jotting down the counter position and tape content whenever you record sounds.

In an elaborate project with many sounds, maintain a good database, keeping a physical track of your original material—just in case you need to revert to it when your disk drive crashes. This database is particularly important because you may need to give your sound files such unhelpful names as SND0094A.WAV or CHAPT1-3.WAV; these names won't contain many cues about the files' actual content, and you will need at hand a more descriptive cross-reference. You don't want to have to load and play all the sound files from SND0080.WAV through SND0097.WAV just to find the one you need.

See Chapter 16 for suggestions about the management of such multimedia project resources.

Testing and Evaluation

Putting everything together can be tough, but testing and evaluating what you've done can be even tougher—especially if your project involves a complicated live presentation, or if you're shipping a commercial multimedia application. Unless you plan ahead, problems will not emerge until you begin testing.

Both digital audio and MIDI are time-based events, but most animation and computer-based video will play only as fast as the CPU can handle it. A 60-second digital audio or MIDI file will play for the same length of time on both slow and fast computers. On the other hand, an animation on a fast machine may run five to ten times faster than on a slow one. If you time your music to animations running on a slow machine, and then play your project back on a faster machine, you may find that the music plays on after the speedier animation sequences are done. Since you can't make a slow machine run faster, the usual solution is to make a fast machine run slower. Chapter 4 discusses the need for determining minimum platform specifications early in the development of any project.

---

tip   *During editing and authoring, regularly test the sound-and-image synchronization of your project on the slowest platform as well as the fastest. If you are delivering your sound on the Web, test it with different browsers and different connection speeds.*

Don't forget to evaluate your sound storage medium. How much RAM does your project need to run effectively? Some authoring and delivery packages will stream sound directly off the hard disk or CD-ROM; others require the sound to be loaded into memory from the hard disk before they play. Sometimes you will need to break a sound or a music file into smaller parts. Some 8-bit audio cards may choke on a 16-bit file. And MIDI files that sound terrific on an expensive General MIDI sound card during development will not have the same quality on a low-end FM-synthesis device at the end user's site.

In the world of professional film and video production, sound is incorporated during postproduction, or a *post* session, after all the film and video footage has been assembled. Just so with multimedia—and don't give it short shrift because of time or budget constraints. The sound track can make or break your project!

Copyright Issues

Ownership rights are significant issues for multimedia producers who would love to use a few bars of Madonna's latest hit or a nostalgic background of

Bach suites played by Pablo Casals. Producers may rightfully fret about copyrights and permissions. Most developers play it safe by always making their own custom music from scratch in a sound studio, or with synthesizers, or by using sounds that have a clear and paid-for ownership and permission trail. Others simply take a risk and break the law.

---

warning *You are breaking the law if you record and use copyrighted material without first securing the rights from the owner or publisher of the material.*

Over the coming years, as more and more multimedia is produced by more and more developers hungry for sound content, the copyright of sounds and images will become a major issue—not so much about who owns something, but how much of it they own. Because it is so easy to manipulate and edit a sound, just how much of someone's original work do you have to change before it then becomes your own? Copyright issues and methods of securing permission for use (equally relevant for sounds, still images, and motion video) are discussed in more detail in Chapter 18.

A number of software vendors have entered the multimedia marketplace by selling digitized clip sounds with an unlimited-use, royalty-free license. Some of these products include musical clips, and some just include sound effects (doors closing, dogs barking, and water dripping). Other products have a mixture of both. But beware of public domain sources downloaded from online sites that offer "Phaser" and "Beam-Me-Up" clips from such favorites as *Star Trek*, or one-liners from Humphrey Bogart movies; these sounds have likely been used without permission.

We needed some digital sound effects for the Dr. J and Larry Bird basketball game we were making. So we bought some Warriors tickets and took a tape recorder to the Oakland Coliseum and just recorded the sounds while we watched the game. It was a great tax deduction, and we got to go to the game for nothing!

Trip Hawkins, Chairman, Electronics Arts

Multi

At the beginning of a project,
the screen is a blank canvas,
ready for you, the multimedia
designer, to express your craft.

visual
connection

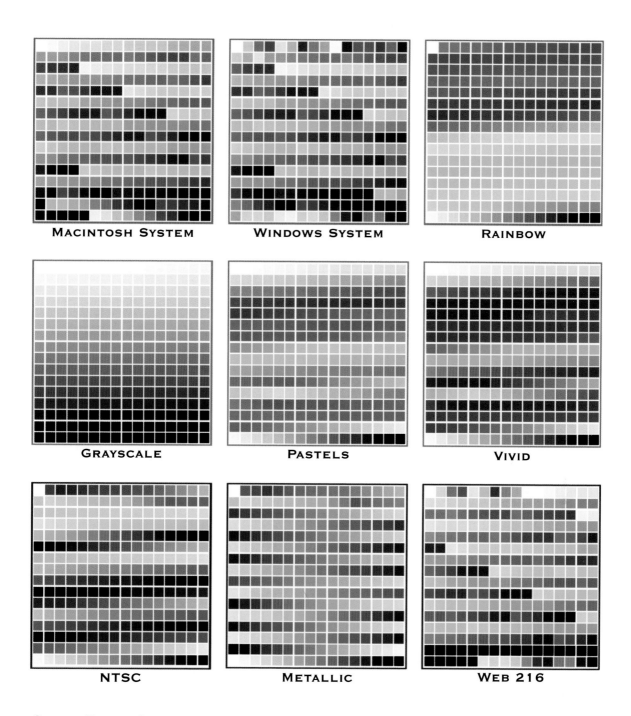

MACINTOSH SYSTEM

WINDOWS SYSTEM

RAINBOW

GRAYSCALE

PASTELS

VIVID

NTSC

METALLIC

WEB 216

COLOR PLATE 1:
These palettes of 256 colors (8-bit color depth) are provided in Macromedia's Director. Images saved in the popular GIF format for use on the Web cannot contain more than 256 colors. See Chapter 10 for more about color depth and palettes.

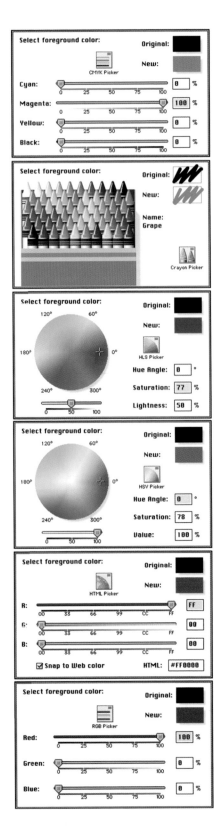

Color Plate 2:

Color pickers allow you to select a color using one or more different models of color space. See Chapter 10.

COLOR PLATE 3:

The images at the top were saved in the JPEG format, which compresses image data and trades image quality for small file size. The resulting compressed images show the "lossy" nature of JPEGs. For the Web, use the JPEG format for photo-realistic images that are busy with color; use the GIF format for line art and drawings where there are large areas of the same color. The photo at top left is 71K in size when saved as a GIF and only 27K as a JPEG (bottom left). The drawing at top right is 17K when saved as a GIF and 46K as a JPEG.

1

7

COLOR PLATE 4:

These pictures illustrate color depth. Image 1 is 24 bits deep (millions of colors); Image 2 is dithered to 8 bits using an adaptive palette (the best 256 colors to represent the image); Image 3 is also dithered to 8-bits, but uses the Macintosh system palette (an optimized standard mix of 256 colors); Image 4 is dithered to 4 bits (any 16 colors); Image 5 is dithered to 8 bit gray-scale (256 shades of gray); Image 6 is dithered to 4 bit gray-scale (16 shades of gray); and Image 7 is dithered to 1 bit (2 colors–in this case, black and white). Note that Images 4 and 6 require the same memory (same file size), but the gray-scale image is superior.

2

6

3

4

5

COLOR PLATE 5:

These images were dithered in Photoshop to best fit the 8-bit palettes of GIF files (Adaptive, System, or Custom 216 Netscape). Also shown are JPEG files compressed with highest and lowest quality and their actual file sizes. The files were then displayed using Netscape Navigator at 16-bit and then 8-bit color depth. Note the subtle differences among palettes and systems, especially in the gradient blue background. Gradients do not usually dither well into 8-bit palettes. Chapters 10 and 15 provide more detail about making images for the Web.

COLOR PLATE 6:

Anti-aliasing text and graphics creates "smooth" boundaries between colors. The top row of letters is not anti-aliased; the bottom row is. Note the improved look of the anti-aliased letters. Taking an image that was anti-aliased onto a light background and pasting it onto a darker background can be problematic: the blending pixels along the edge will show as a halo and may have to be edited one by one.

COLOR PLATE 7:

This SMPTE color bar pattern can be used for calibration at the beginning of a videotape. The RGB values of each bar are included so you can make your own screen using an image-editing application. See Chapter 12.

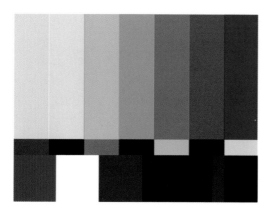

R: 204 G: 204 B: 204	R: 255 G: 255 B: 0	R: 0 G: 255 B: 255	R: 0 G: 255 B: 0	R: 255 G: 0 B: 255	R: 255 G: 0 B: 0	R: 0 G: 0 B: 255
R: 0 G: 0 B: 255	R: 19 G: 19 B: 19	R: 255 G: 0 B: 255	R: 19 G: 19 B: 19	R: 0 G: 255 B: 255	R: 19 G: 19 B: 19	R: 204 G: 204 B: 204

| R: 8
G: 62
B: 89 | R: 255
G: 255
B: 255 | R: 58
G: 0
B: 126 | R: 19
G: 19
B: 19 | 0
0
0 | 19
19
19 | 38
38
38 | R: 19
G: 19
B: 19 |

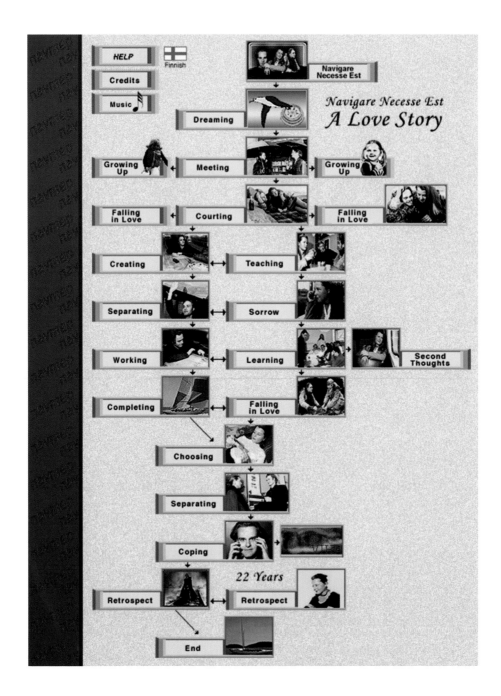

COLOR PLATE 8:

A simplified navigation map not only provides an overview of a multimedia project but also contains active links to documents using "hot" areas of the graphic. (Chapter 15 explains ISMAPs and USEMAPs in Web documents.) This is the navMap page from Navigare Necesse Est, a student-built love story found at http://www.hkkk.fi/mmedia/. Clearly, the linking of information in such easy-to-make GUIs demonstrates the power of multimedia.

COLOR PLATE 9:

There are many design approaches for buttons and interactive hot spots. Screen 1 is a collection of Web pages that combine graphic and text buttons (see Chapter 17); screens 2a, 2b, 2c, and 2d show a typical hierarchical menu system from Multimedia: Working It Out, the CD-ROM version of this book; screen 3 is from an Osborne/McGraw-Hill CD-ROM catalog; screen 4 shows the author and a few friends–click on any face for small-town secrets.

COLOR PLATE 10:

Commercial Web site designers tend to prefer white or light-colored backgrounds with shadowed graphic elements and screens that are not too cluttered or busy. Buttons that change as the mouse rolls over them, sound elements, and animations are common multimedia additions. Tips for creating and delivering multimedia on the Web can be found in Chapters 14 and 15.

COLOR PLATE 11:

Morphing software was used to seamlessly transform the images of 16 kindergartners. When a sound track of music and voices was added to the four-minute piece, it made a compelling QuickTime video about how similar children are to each other.

media

Many multimedia designers are known to experience a mild shiver when they pull down the New... menu and draw their first colors onto a fresh screen.

chapter

10

Images

W HAT you see on a multimedia computer screen at any given time is a composite of elements: text, symbols, photograph-like bitmaps, vector-drawn graphics, three-dimensional renderings, distinctive buttons to click, and windows of motion video. Some parts of this image may even twitch or move so that the screen never seems still and tempts your eye. It may be a very colorful screen with gentle pastel washes of mauve and puce, or it may be brutally primary with splashes of Crayola red and blue and yellow and green. It might be stark black and white, full of sharp angles, or softened with gray-scale blends and anti-aliasing. It may be elegant or, by design, not. The computer screen is where the action is: it contains much more than your message; it is also the viewer's primary connection to all of your project's content.

This chapter will help you understand the visual elements that make up a multimedia screen. Graphic elements can usually be scaled to different sizes, colorized or patterned or made transparent, placed in front of or behind other objects, or be made visible or invisible on command. How you blend these elements, how you choose your colors and fonts, what tricks you use that catch the eye, how adept you are at using your tools—these are the hallmarks of your skill, talent, knowledge, and creativity coalesced into the all-important visual connection to your viewers.

Before You Start to Create

At the beginning of a project, the screen is a blank canvas, ready for you, the multimedia designer, to express your craft. The screen will change again and again during the course of your project as you experiment, as you stretch and reshape elements, draw new objects and throw out old ones, and test various colors and effects—creating the vehicle for your message. Indeed, many multimedia designers are known to experience a mild shiver when they pull down the New... menu and draw their first colors onto a fresh screen. Just so; this screen represents a powerful and seductive avenue for channeling creativity.

---

warning *Multimedia designers are regularly lured into agonizingly steep learning curves, long nights of cerebral problem solving, and the pursuit of performance perfection. If you are fundamentally creative, multimedia may become a calling, not a profession.*

Plan Your Approach

Whether you use templates and ready-made screens provided by your authoring system; whether you use clip art or objects crafted by others; even if you simply clone the look and feel of another project—there will always be a starting point where your page is "clean." But even before reaching this starting point, be sure you have given your project a good deal of thought and planning. Work out your graphic approach either in your head or during creative sessions with your client or colleagues. There are strong arguments against drawing on a fresh screen without such foresight and preparation. To get a handle on any multimedia project, you start with pencil, eraser, and paper. Outline your project and your graphic ideas first: make a flow chart; storyboard the project using stick figures; use three-by-five index cards and shuffle them until you get it right.

The organizing and creative process begins with drawings in pen or pencil on paper. Too many times we are enthused about the color and the computer graphics tools, but they can overwhelm the creative design process.

Dennis Woytek, Assistant Professor, Duquesne University

10

Organize Your Tools

Most authoring systems provide the tools with which you can create the graphic objects of multimedia (text, buttons, vector-drawn objects, and bitmaps) directly on your screen. If one of these tools is not included, the authoring system usually offers a mechanism for importing the object you need from another application. When you are working with animated objects or motion video, most authoring systems include a feature for activating these elements, such as a programming language or special functions. You'll also usually have a library of special effects—zooms, wipes, and dissolves, for instance. Many multimedia designers do not limit their toolkits to the features of a single authoring platform, but employ a variety of applications and tools to accomplish many specialized tasks.

I like "do-overs," where you make quick and dirty buttons now, or live text now, but go back later and replace those placeholders with more refined images or pretty bitmapped text. This do-over approach lets you work two ends against the middle—you can get right into designing navigation and animation, but know that you will put in the "good" images later.

Sherry Hutson, Lecturer, University of Illinois at Springfield

Multiple Monitors

When developing multimedia, it is helpful to have more than one monitor, or a single high-resolution monitor with lots of screen *real estate*, hooked up to your computer. In this way, you can display the full-screen working area of your project or presentation and still have space to put your tools and other menus. This is particularly important in an authoring system such as Macromedia Director, where the edits and changes you make in one window are immediately visible in the presentation window—provided the presentation window is not obscured by your editing tool! During development there is a lot of cutting and pasting among windows and among various applications, and with an extra monitor, you can open many windows at once and spread them out. Both Macintosh and Windows systems support this extra hardware.

A few weeks of having to repeatedly bring windows to the front and then hide them again to see the results of your editing will probably convince you to invest in a second or larger monitor.

Making Still Images

Still images may be small or large, or even full screen. They may be colored, placed at random on the screen, evenly geometric or oddly shaped. Still images may be a single tree on a wintry hillside; stacked boxes of text against a gray, tartan, or Italian marble background; an engineering drawing; a snapshot of your department manager's new BMW. Whatever their form, still images are generated by the computer in two ways: as *bitmaps* (or paint graphics) and as *vector-drawn* (or just plain drawn) graphics.

Bitmaps are used for photo-realistic images and for complex drawings requiring fine detail. Vector-drawn objects are used for lines, boxes, circles, polygons, and other graphic shapes that can be mathematically expressed in angles, coordinates, and distances. A drawn object can be filled with color and patterns, and you can select it as a single object. The appearance of both types of images depends on the display resolution and capabilities of your computer's graphics hardware and monitor. Both types of images are stored in various file formats and can be translated from one application to another or from one computer platform to another. Typically, image files are compressed to save memory and disk space; many image formats already use compression within the file itself—for example, GIF, JPEG, and PNG.

Still images may be the most important element of your multimedia project. If you are designing multimedia by yourself, put yourself in the role of graphic artist and layout designer. Take the time necessary to discover all the tricks you can learn about your drawing software. Competent, computer-literate skills in graphic art and design are vital to the success of your project. Remember—more than anything else, the user's judgment of your work will be most heavily influenced by the work's visual impact.

First Person

A few years ago a large corporation asked us and one other multimedia developer to bid on a long-term contract for computer-based training. Though busy with other active projects, we didn't want this possibly lucrative opportunity to slip by, so we spent a few days hastily putting together a demonstration of our technical skills for building nifty databases, designing tricky telecommunications systems, and integrating live video from videodisc into the computer. We even "wire-framed" a bit of a working multimedia database with real data we got from the corporation.

We showed our demo to about a dozen management and training executives, in a fancy boardroom that had a built-in projector and sound system with mixers and light dimmers—a place where we could knock the socks off anybody. But within 30 seconds, the disaster bells started tinkling: most of our presentation was going way over their heads. Afterward, there were one or two vague questions and some thank-you's.

Our competitor's presentation, on the other hand, provided a slick series of finely rendered bitmapped screen images and elegant visuals. It was heavy on pretty menu screens and very light on how-it-is-done technology. We later learned that one of their graphic artists had worked for two solid weeks

on the color bitmaps for that demo. In the follow-up phone call, we were told by our potential clients that the competition's "incredible artwork" had won out over our "excellent technology demonstration."

To cover our disappointment, we mumbled something to ourselves about not wanting to work with computer illiterates, anyway—people who could be taken to the cleaners by fresh paint. But we knew we'd missed a hefty piece of contract work because we hadn't invested serious graphic art talent in our demonstration. We decided that's why the real peas in the can are never the same bright green as the ones on the label. So we learned a marketing lesson.

10

Bitmaps

A *bitmap* is a simple information matrix describing the individual dots that are the smallest elements of resolution on a computer screen or other display or printing device. A one-dimensional matrix is required for monochrome (black and white); greater depth (more bits of information) is required to describe the more than 16 million colors the picture elements may have, as illustrated in Figure 10-1. These picture elements (known as *pels* or, more commonly, *pixels*) can be either on or off, as in the 1-bit bitmap—most often "monochrome" black or white but, depending upon your software, any two colors that represent the on and off states. Or they can represent varying shades of color (4-bit, 16 colors; 8-bit, 256 colors; 15-bit, 32,768 colors; 16-bit, 65,536 colors; 24-bit, 16,772,216 colors). Together, the state of all the pixels on a computer screen (in about 1/60 second, which is about how often the screen is redrawn) make up the image seen by the viewer, whether in combinations of black and white or colored pixels in a line of text, a photograph-like picture, or a simple background pattern.

....

Is there a colour scheme that will appear coloured or at least solid black for the colour-impaired?

If you're gathering empirical evidence, I have something called red-green colour blindness (it is quite common in males). It doesn't mean that you don't know which traffic light is showing! What it means mainly is that the tone of red-type colours doesn't seem so different to the tone of greens—the obvious case is a poppy field. I can see the poppies as red OK if I look carefully or they are pointed out to me, but other people see them kind of exploding out of the green...

For people like me, a vibrant yellow always works. I read somewhere that black on yellow is a reliable "strong" combination. Certainly it is used by one of the motoring organisations in the UK for special diversion notices and the like.

....

Graham Samuel, Educational Software Developer, The Living Fossil Co., London

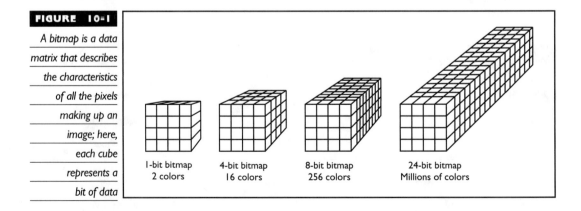

FIGURE 10-1
A bitmap is a data matrix that describes the characteristics of all the pixels making up an image; here, each cube represents a bit of data

1-bit bitmap
2 colors

4-bit bitmap
16 colors

8-bit bitmap
256 colors

24-bit bitmap
Millions of colors

Where do bitmaps come from? How are they made? You can

- Make a bitmap from scratch with a paint or drawing program.

- Grab a bitmap from an active computer screen with a screen capture program, and then paste it into a paint program or your application.

- Capture a bitmap from a photo, artwork, or a television image using a scanner or video capture device that digitizes the image.

Once made, a bitmap can be copied, altered, e-mailed, and otherwise used in many creative ways.

Clip Art

If you do not want to make your own, you can get bitmaps from suppliers of clip art, and from photograph suppliers who have already digitized the images for you. Clip art is available on CD-ROMs and through online services. Many graphics applications are shipped with clip art and useful graphics, or the company will send you a collection when you register the product. A clip art collection may contain a random assortment of images, or it may contain a series of graphics, photographs, sound, and video related to a single topic. For example, Corel, Micrografx, and Fractal Design bundle extensive clip art collections with their image-editing software. Some 3-D modeling programs incorporate libraries of premade 3-D models into the application, allowing you to drag and drop common objects into a scene.

Figure 10-2 shows a page of thumbnails from a commercially available resource called PhotoDisc. Each CD-ROM contains about 400 full-color, high-resolution bitmaps with a license for "unlimited use." But you should note that "unlimited use" often contains caveats: in many cases there is an upper limit to the number of "units" of your own product that you may distribute without paying more, so you need to read the fine print. These fees are usually reasonable, however, and affect only commercial multimedia publishers. In the case of ClipPix from PhotoDisc, for example, 10,000 units is the break point. Figure 10-3 shows portions of text from that license agreement (reproduced here with the permission of PhotoDisc, Inc.).

You can also download a bitmap from a Web site: On a Macintosh, click and hold on the image to see a menu of options; in Windows, right-click on an image to see a menu. Choose "download image to disk." or "Save picture as..."

Once you have a clip art bitmap, you can then manipulate and adjust many of its properties (such as brightness, contrast, color depth, hue, and size). You can also cut and paste among many bitmaps using specialized

10

PhotoDisc™　　　　　　　　　　　**Volume 2: People and Lifestyles**

 001

 002

 003

 004

 005

 006

 007

 008

 009

 010

 011

 012

 013

 014

 015

FIGURE 10-3

Text from the

PhotoDisc license

agreement, typical

of usage rights you

receive when you

purchase a clip art

library

■

END USER LICENSE AGREEMENT

THIS IS A LEGAL AGREEMENT BETWEEN YOU AND PHOTODISC. INC. BY OPENING THIS PACKAGE YOU AGREE TO BE BOUND BY THE TERMS OF THIS AGREEMENT. IF YOU DO NOT AGREE, PROMPTLY RETURN THE UNOPENED CD PACKAGE IN THE ORIGINAL CARTON FOR A FULL REFUND.

GRANT OF LICENSE. PhotoDisc grants you the nonexclusive, nonassignable right to install and use the ClipPix images and any derivatives or copies thereof (collectively, the "Images") and the other software on this disc on one computer and with one user at a time. The Images may be copied, modified, and incorporated in materials in accordance with the following provisions:

(1) Personal Use. You may make copies of the Images in digital or printed form for personal or internal company use.

(2) Advertising and Promotions. You may make copies of the Images, in digital or printed form, for use in advertising or promotional materials for you or your clients.

(3) Products for Sale.

● Copies of the Images, in digital (but not printed form), may be incorporated in up to 10,000 individual product copies made by you (your "Products") and may be distributed as part of your Products.

● You may sublicense the right to use the Images in digital form as part of your Products. You may not sublicense the right to copy the Images or to incorporate the Images into other materials or other products.

● You agree not to distribute or market copies of the Images separately in any manner. You agree not to use the Images in any product which is similar to or competitive with this disc.

● Your Products must include the following language in the Product credits or on the Product packaging: "PhotoDisc ClipPix Images ©1994 PhotoDisc, Inc."

Any use of the Images not explicitly granted by this agreement is prohibited. If you wish to use the Images in television programming, cable programming, motion pictures, or wide area networks, you must first obtain additional licensing from PhotoDisc. Pornographic use of the Images is prohibited. Except as specifically permitted above, you may not copy this disc.

10

image-editing or "darkroom" programs. If the clip art image is high resolution (aimed at 300 dpi printers, not 72 dpi monitors), you may discover that you can grab just a tiny portion of the high-res image—say, a sheep in the far corner of a farmyard or a car in a parking lot—and it will look great when enlarged to monitor resolution.

Bitmap Software

The abilities and features of image-editing programs for both the Macintosh and Windows range from simple to complex. The better editors are available in versions that run and look the same on both platforms, and the graphics files you make can be saved in many formats, readable across platforms.

The Macintosh does not ship with a painting tool, and Windows provides only the rudimentary Paint (see Figure 10-4), so you will need to acquire this very important software separately—often bitmap editing or *painting* programs come as part of a bundle when you purchase your computer, monitor, or scanner. Most multimedia authoring tools offer bitmap editing features. Director (see Figure 10-5) includes a powerful image editor that provides advanced tools such as "onion-skinning" and image filtering using common plug-ins from Photoshop and other third-party designers.

More sophisticated are elaborately featured bitmap painting and editing programs such as Adobe's Photoshop or Macromedia's Fireworks. Fireworks, for both Macintosh and Windows, focuses on creating, editing, and animating Web graphics with bitmap as well as vector tools (more about vector graphics a little later in the chapter). Images can be exported into Dreamweaver and other HTML editors (see Figure 10-6). Buying and learning to use a high-powered image editor is an important investment in your multimedia future.

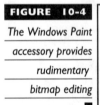

FIGURE 10-4

The Windows Paint accessory provides rudimentary bitmap editing

FIGURE 10-5

Director, like most serious multimedia authoring packages, includes powerful image-editing tools

FIGURE 10-6

Fireworks provides tools for bitmap and vector graphics destined for Web presentations

10

For photo-realism, scan a photograph or use a digital camera, and then edit the image in Photoshop, Fireworks, or another image-editing program. It is virtually impossible to "paint" a realistic-looking photo using a painting program. You can also use your image editor to create original images, such as cartoons, symbols, buttons, bitmapped text, and abstract images that have a refined "graphic" look.

Capturing and Editing Images

The image you see on your monitor is a digital bitmap stored in video memory, updated about every 1/60 second or faster, depending upon your monitor's scan rate (see Chapter 4). As you assemble images for your multimedia project, you may often need to capture and store an image directly from your screen. The simplest way to capture what you see on the screen at any given moment is to press the proper keys on your computer keyboard. This causes a conversion from the screen buffer to a format that you can use.

- On the Macintosh, the keystroke combination COMMAND-SHIFT-3 creates a readable PICT2-format file named Picture and places it in your active disk drive's root directory. You can then import this file's image into your multimedia authoring system or paint program. You can also press COMMAND-CONTROL-SHIFT-4 to drag a rectangle on your screen, capturing what is inside the rectangle and placing it on the Clipboard, ready for pasting.

- Both the Macintosh and Windows environments have a Clipboard—an area of memory where data such as text and images is temporarily stored when you cut or copy them within an application. In Windows, when you press PRINT SCREEN, a copy of your screen's image goes to the Clipboard. From the Clipboard, you can then paste the captured bitmap into an application (such as Paint, which comes with Windows).

- Screen capture utilities for Macintosh and Windows go a step further and are indispensable to multimedia artists. With a keystroke, they let you select an area of the screen and save the selection in various formats (see Figure 10-7). With this facility, you can quickly copy and paste small or large 72 dpi images between applications.

The way to get more creative power when manipulating bitmaps is to use an image-editing program. These are the king-of-the-mountain programs that let you not only retouch the blemishes and details of photo images but also do tricks like placing an image of your own face at the helm of a square-rigger or right at the sideline at last year's Super Bowl. Figure 10-8 shows just such a composite image, made from two photographs. It was

10

created by Russel Brown, one of the designers of Adobe's Photoshop, during a nationally broadcast live television show. While you might recognize his name in the credits every time you launch Photoshop, with Photoshop he deftly and seamlessly placed himself between a better-known couple in order to illustrate to the viewing audience the power of image-editing tools and the potential for misuse of this technology in everyday life.

In addition to letting you enhance and make composite images, image-editing tools allow you to alter and distort images. A color photograph of a red rose can be changed into a purple rose, or blue if you prefer. A small child standing next to her older brother can be "stretched" to tower over him. *Morphing* is another effect that can be used to manipulate still images or to create interesting and often bizarre animated transformations. Morphing allows you to smoothly blend two images so that one image seems to melt into the next, often producing some amusing results. Color Plate 11, created using Morph, a software application by Gryphon, shows an example of a girl morphing into a boy.

Image-editing programs may, indeed, represent the single most significant advance in computer image processing during the late 1980s, bringing truly amazing power to PC desktops. Such tools are indispensable for excellent multimedia production.

cross platform   When you import a color or gray-scale bitmap from the Macintosh to Windows, the colors will seem darker and richer, even though they have precisely the same red, green, and blue (RGB) values. In some cases, this may improve the look of your image, but in other cases you will want to first lighten (increase the brightness and possibly lower the contrast) of the Macintosh bitmap before bringing it into Windows.

We have to keep saturation in mind all the time when doing our Web pages... viewing the graphics on both Macs and PCs before actually using them. For instance, when doing our Halloween pages, we used a very cool pumpkin background that was beautifully saturated on the Mac side. On Windows, though, it was way too dark, and you couldn't read the overlying text. We had to lighten the GIF on the Mac side a few times before using it cross platform.

Rich Santalesa, Editor, *NetGuide* Magazine

Scanning Images

After poring through countless clip art collections, you still haven't found the unusual background you want for a screen about gardening. Sometimes when you search for something too hard, you don't realize that it's right in front of your face. Everyday objects can be scanned and manipulated using image-editing tools, such as those described in the previous section, to create unusual, attention-getting effects. For example, to enliven a screen with a gardening motif, scan a mixture of seeds, some fall foliage, or grass-stained garden gloves. Open the scan in an image-editing program and experiment with different filters, the contrast, and various special effects. Be creative, and don't be afraid to try strange combinations—sometimes mistakes yield the most intriguing results.

Another alternative to computer-generated graphics is to create artwork using traditional methods: watercolors, pastels, and even crayons. You can then scan the image, make necessary alterations, and tweak pixels on the computer. Too many designers have fallen into the trap of trying to draw detailed sketches using a mouse or drawing tablet, when a pencil or pen on paper would have produced better results quicker. In Chapter 17, Figure 17-7 shows a Web page that uses a large image map of a seacoast village for navigation. The picture of the village was drawn on a large sheet of paper by artist Carolyn Brown using a fine pen. Then it was digitized in sections because the original drawing was too large for the scanner top. Four scans were stitched together into a single image using Photoshop layers, and the image was resized to fit the Web page. Finally, it was colorized to look "old" and reduced in color depth to 4 bits so that it would load quickly on the Internet as a GIF.

Vector Drawing

Most multimedia authoring systems provide for use of vector-drawn objects such as lines, rectangles, ovals, polygons, and text.

- Computer-aided design (CAD) programs have traditionally used vector-drawn object systems for creating the highly complex and geometric renderings needed by architects and engineers. (CAD tools are discussed in Chapter 5.)

- Graphic artists designing for print media use vector-drawn objects because the same mathematics that put a rectangle on your screen can also place that rectangle (or the fancy Bezier curves of a good line-art illustration) on paper without jaggies. This requires the higher resolution of the printer, using a page description language such as PostScript.

- Programs for 3-D animation also use vector-drawn graphics. For example, the various changes of position, rotation, and shading of light required to spin the extruded corporate logo shown in Figure 10-9 must be calculated mathematically. (Animation is discussed in Chapter 11.)

How Vector Drawing Works

Vector-drawn objects are described and drawn to the computer screen using a fraction of the memory space required to describe and store the same object in bitmap form. A *vector* is a line that is described by the location of its two endpoints. A simple rectangle, for example, might be defined as follows:

RECT 0,0,200,200

Using Cartesian coordinates, your software will draw this rectangle starting at the upper-left corner of your screen, going 200 pixels horizontally to the right, and 200 pixels downward. This rectangle would be a square, as all sides are identical lengths. For this description

RECT 0,0,200,200,RED,BLUE

your software will draw the same square with a red boundary line and fill the square with the color blue. You can, of course, add other parameters to describe a fill pattern or the width of the boundary line.

FIGURE 10-9 *A few of the many* *still images required* *to "spin" a logo* ■	

Vector-Drawn Objects Versus Bitmaps

The concise description of the vector-drawn colored square described in the previous section contains less than 30 bytes of alphanumeric data (even less when the description is tokenized or compressed). On the other hand, the same square as an uncompressed bitmap image, in black and white (which requires the least memory, at 1-bit color depth per pixel) would take 5,000 bytes to describe (200 × 200 / 8). Furthermore, an image made in 256 colors (8-bit color depth per pixel) would require a whopping 40K as a bitmap (200 × 200 / 8 × 8).

For the Web, pages that use vector graphics in plug-ins such as Flash download faster and, when used for animation, draw faster than bitmaps. It is only when you draw many hundreds of objects on your screen that you may experience a slowdown while you wait for the screen to be re-freshed—the size, location, and other properties for each of the objects must be computed. Thus a single image made up of 500 individual line and rectangle objects, for example, may take longer for the computer to process and place on the screen than an image consisting of just a few drawn circle objects. Vector objects are easily scalable without losing resolution or image quality. A large drawn image can be shrunk to the size of a postage stamp, and, while it may not look good on a computer monitor at 72 dpi, it will likely still look good when printed at 300 dpi to a color printer.

tip *Using a single bitmap for a complicated image may give you faster screen-refresh performance than using a large number of vector-drawn objects to make that same screen.*

Converting Between Bitmaps and Drawn Images

10

Most drawing programs offer several file formats for saving your work, and, if you wish, you can convert a drawing that consists of several vector-drawn objects into a bitmap when you save the drawing. You can also grab a bitmapped screen image of your drawn objects with a capture program.

Converting bitmaps to drawn objects is more difficult. There are, however, programs and utilities that will compute the bounds of a bitmapped image or the shapes of colors within an image and then derive the polygon object that describes the image. This procedure is called *autotracing* and is available in vector drawing applications such as Illustrator or Freehand.

3-D Drawing and Rendering

Drawing in perspective or in 3-D on a two-dimensional surface takes special skill and talent. Dedicated software is available to help you render three-dimensional scenes, complete with directional lighting and special effects, but get ready for another steep learning curve! From making 3-D text to creating detailed walk-throughs of 3-D space, each application will demand study and practice before you are efficient and comfortable with its feature set and power.

The production values of multimedia projects have increased dramatically since the late 1980s, and as the production bar has risen, end users' expectations have also ratcheted upward. The multimedia production bar moves like a high jump or pole vault contest—as each new project improves on the last, competitors must jump to meet the new, higher standard. Flat and colorless 2-D screens are no longer sufficient for a successful commercial multimedia project. 3-D-rendered graphic art and animation has become commonplace, providing more lifelike substance and feel to projects. Luckily, in an arena where only high-powered workstations could supply the raw computing horsepower for effective 3-D designing, inexpensive desktop PCs and excellent software have made 3-D modeling attainable by most multimedia developers.

Today many products—including Ray Dream Designer, Caligari True Space 2, Specular Infini-D, and form*Z—are touted as essential tools for illustration, animation, and multimedia production.

Creating objects in three dimensions on a computer screen can be difficult for designers used to drawing squares, circles, and other x (width) and y (height) geometries on a two-dimensional screen. Be prepared for late nights and steep learning curves as you become familiar with nurbs, deformations, mesh generations, and skinning.

····································

*Form*Z is a state-of-the-art 3-D solid and surface modeler with drafting and rendering, Boolean operations, 3-D form editing and sculpting, terrain modeling, curved splines, and meshes including NURBS, 3-D text, object rounding, symbol instances and libraries, helixes, deformations, metaformz, image-based mesh generation and displacements, skinning, numerous file format translators, and more. RenderZone adds photo-realistic rendering, and RadioZity provides the most accurate simulation of light effects.*

····································

Marketing literature from autodessys, Inc. (www.formz.com)

For 3-D, the depth (z dimension) of cubes and spheres must be calculated and displayed so the perspective of the rendered object seems correct to the eye. As illustrated in Figure 10-10, most 3-D software packages provide adjustable views so you can see your work from the top, bottom, or sides.

A great deal of information is needed to display a 3-D scene. *Scenes* consist of *objects* that in turn contain many small elements such as blocks, cylinders, spheres, or cones (described using mathematical constructs or formulas). The more elements contained in an object, the more complicated its structure will be and, usually, the finer its resolution and smoothness.

Objects and elements in 3-D space carry with them *properties* such as shape, color, texture, shading, and location. A scene contains many different objects. Imagine a scene with a table, chairs, and a background. Zoom into one of the objects—the chair, for example, in Figure 10-11. It has 11 objects made up of various blocks and rectangles. Objects are created by *modeling* them using a 3-D application.

FIGURE 10-10

3-D applications provide x, y, and z axes and adjustable perspective views

10

To model an object that you want to place into your scene, you must start with a *shape*. You can create a shape from scratch, or you can import a premade shape from a library of shapes, typically blocks, cylinders, spheres, and cones. In most 3-D applications, you can create any 2-D shape with a drawing tool or place the outline of a letter, then extrude or lathe it into the third dimension along the z axis (see Figure 10-12). When you *extrude* a plane surface, it extends

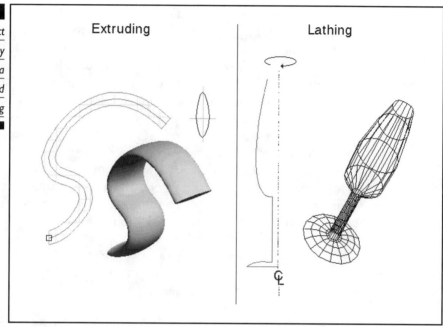

its shape some distance, either *perpendicular* to the shape's outline or along a defined path. When you *lathe* a shape, a profile of the shape is *rotated* around a defined axis (you can set the direction) to create the 3-D object. Other methods for creating 3-D objects differ among the various software packages.

Once you have created a 3-D object, you can apply textures and colors to it to make it seem more realistic—rough and coarse or shiny and smooth. You can also apply a color or pattern or even a bitmapped picture to texture your object. Thus you can build a table, apply an oak finish, then stain it purple or blue or iridescent yellow. You can add coffee cup rings and spilled cheese dip with appropriate coloring and texturing.

To model a scene, you place all of your objects into 3-D space. Some complex scenes may contain hundreds (if not thousands) of elements. In modeling your scene, you will also set up one or more lights that will create diffuse or sharp shade and shadows on your objects and will also reflect, or *flare,* where the light is most intense. Then you will add a background and set a camera view, the location and angle from which you will view the final rendered scene.

10

Shading can usually be applied in several ways. As illustrated in Figure 10-13, flat shading (*b*) is the fastest for the computer to render and is most often used in preview mode. Gouraud shading (*a*), Phong shading (*d*), and ray tracing (*c*) take longer to render but provide photo-realistic images.

When you have completed the modeling of your scene or an object in it, you then must render it for final output. *Rendering* is when the computer finally uses intricate algorithms to apply the effects you have specified on the objects you have created. Figure 10-14 shows a background, an object, and the rendered composite.

Rendering an image requires great computing muscle and often takes many hours for a single image—you will feel the strength (or weakness) of your hardware. Indeed, some multimedia and animation companies dedicate certain computers solely for rendering. The final images for the classic animated movie *Toy Story* were rendered on a "farm" of 87 dual-processor and 30 quad-processor 100 MHz SPARCstation 20s. It took 46 days of continuous processing to render that film's 110,000 frames at a rate of about one frame every one to three hours.

---

note *Farms of many computers hooked together may also be called "clusters of workstations," or COWs. There is occasionally humorous contention regarding proper nomenclature: it seems that developers who live and work in cities tend to prefer the notion of computer farms; developers in rural communities already familiar with farms prefer to call these beasts COWs.*

FIGURE 10-13
A scene rendered
with four different
methods of shading

a

b

c

d

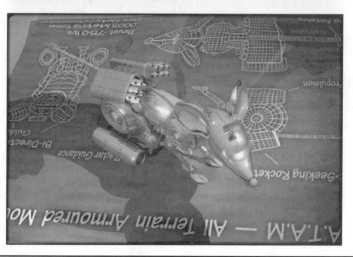

10

Panoramas

QuickTime VR (QTVR) provides a method for viewing a single surrounding image as if you were "inside" the picture and able to look up or down, turn, or zoom in on features. To make this work, you need to stitch together many images taken from different angles around a circle. Software such as ULead360 or Panorama Factory (shareware) works by importing a sequence of photos and letting you adjust them precisely into a single seamless bitmap, where the right edge attaches to the left edge. You should allow some overlap when you take each photo in your 360-degree panorama, and you may need to adjust each photo's contrast, brightness, hue, and saturation while stitching. Most software also allows you to adjust perspective to compensate for different focal lengths or camera heights. When done, you can save this panoramic image to QTVR format or as a flat image.

Color

Color is a vital component of multimedia. The next few sections explain where color comes from and how colors are displayed on a computer monitor. Management of color is both a subjective and a technical exercise. Picking the right colors and combinations of colors for your project can involve many tries until you feel the result is right. But the technical description of a color may be expressed in known physical values (humans, for example, perceive colors with wavelengths ranging from 400 to 600 nanometers on the electromagnetic spectrum), and there are several methods and models to describe color space using mathematics and values (see Color Plate 2).

Understanding Natural Light and Color

Light comes from an atom when an electron passes from a higher to a lower energy level; each atom produces uniquely specific colors. This explanation of light, known as the *quantum theory,* was developed by physicist Max Planck in the late 19th century. Niels Bohr, another physicist, later showed that an excited atom that has absorbed energy and whose electrons have moved into higher orbits will throw off that energy in the form of *quanta,* or *photons,* when it reverts to a stable state. This is where light comes from.

Color is the frequency of a light wave within the narrow band of the electromagnetic spectrum to which the human eye responds. The letters of the mnemonic ROY G. BIV, learned by many of us to remember the colors of the rainbow, are the ascending frequencies of the visible light spectrum: red, orange, yellow, green, blue, indigo, and violet. Light that is infrared, or below the frequency of red light and not perceivable by the human eye, can be created and viewed by electronic diodes and sensors, and it is used for TV and VCR remote controls, for wireless communications among computers, and for night goggles used in the military. Infrared light is radiated heat. Ultraviolet light, on the other hand, is beyond the higher end of the visible spectrum and can be damaging to humans.

The color white is a noisy mixture of all the color frequencies in the visible spectrum. Sunlight and fluorescent tubes produce white light; tungsten lamp filaments produce light with a yellowish cast; sodium vapor lamps, typically used for low-cost outdoor street lighting, produce an orange light characteristic of the sodium atom. These are the most common sources of light in the everyday (or every night) world. The light these sources produce typically reaches your eye as a reflection of that light into the lens of your eye.

The cornea of the eye acts as a lens to focus light rays onto the retina. The light rays stimulate many thousands of specialized nerves called *rods* and *cones* that cover the surface of the retina. Receptors in the cones are sensitive to red, green, and blue light, and all the nerves together transmit the pattern of color information to the brain. The eye can differentiate among millions of colors, or *hues,* consisting of combinations of red, green, and blue.

As color information is sent to the brain, other parts of the mind massage the data en route to its point of cognitive recognition. Human response to color is complicated by cultural and experiential filters that cause otherwise straightforward color frequencies to carry pleasant, unpleasant, soothing, depressing, and many other special meanings. In Western cultures, for example, red is the color of anger and danger; in Eastern cultures, red is the color of happiness. Red is the traditional color for Chinese restaurant motifs, to make them attractive and happy places; Western restaurants are often decorated in quieter pastels and earth tones. White, not black, is the color of funerals in Chinese culture.

Green, blue, yellow, orange, purple, pink, brown, black, gray, and white are the ten most common color-describing words used in all human languages and cultures. Komar and Melamid's interesting Internet study (http://www.diacenter.org/km/index.html) has determined that the favorite color in the world is blue.

10

Computerized Color

Because the eye's receptors are sensitive to red, green, and blue light, by adjusting combinations of these three *additive primary colors,* the eye and brain will interpolate the combinations of colors in between. This is the psychology, not the physics, of color: what you perceive as orange on a computer monitor is a combination of two frequencies of green and red light, not the actual spectral frequency you see when you look at that namesake fruit, an orange, in sunlight. All these factors make computerized color pretty tricky to manage.

The reflected light that reaches your eye from a printed page is made up of tiny halftone dots of a few primary colors (printers use the *subtractive primary colors,* cyan, magenta, and yellow, with black). In contrast, the screen of a computer monitor is, like the sun, a source of light. On the back of the glass face of a monitor are thousands of phosphorescing chemical color dots (red, green, and blue), which are bombarded by electrons that paint the screen at very high speeds. These dots are each about .30 mm or less in diameter (the *dot pitch*) and are positioned very carefully and very close together.

The red, green, and blue dots light up when hit by the electron beam, and the eye sees the combination of red, green, and blue (RGB) light and interpolates it. When one of the primary colors is subtracted from this RGB mix, the subtractive primary color is perceived, as follows:

RGB Combination	Perceived Color
Red only	Red
Green only	Green
Blue only	Blue
Red and green (blue subtracted)	Yellow
Red and blue (green subtracted)	Magenta
Green and blue (red subtracted)	Cyan
Red, green, and blue	White
None	Black

Various color models are illustrated in color in the Color Signature.

Monitors and Color

Multimedia is typically presented on color monitors that display 8 bits of color information per pixel in a matrix of 640 pixels across and 480 pixels down (640×480). With fewer colors than the 256 afforded by 8 bits of depth, there is not enough range to make good photo-realistic images, although gray-scale pictures with as few as 16 shades of gray (4 bits) often come out well. With more colors, your computer must work harder to display the image on the screen, and performance can take a serious hit. While computer systems and monitors may default to 800×600-pixel or even 1024×768-pixel screens and offer millions of colors per pixel, if you wish to reach the widest audience with your multimedia work, including schools and families using older equipment, you should design for this 640×480 VGA standard.

Computer Color Models

The color of a pixel on your computer monitor is typically expressed as an amount of red, green, and blue. It takes more computer memory and processing speed to digitally manage and display the greater combinations of red, green, and blue values that make more shades of color visible to the eye.

Models or methodologies used to specify colors in computer terms are RGB, HSB, HSL, CMYK, CIE, and others. Using the 24-bit RGB (red, green, blue) model, you specify a color by setting each amount of red, green, and blue to a value in a range of 256 choices. 8 bits of memory are required to define 256 possible choices; a total of 24 bits of memory are therefore needed to describe the exact color, which is one of "millions" (256×256×256=16,777,216). When Web browsers were first developed, the software engineers chose to represent the color amounts for each color channel in a hexadecimal pair. Two hexadecimal numbers, written in a scale of "0123456789ABCDEF," represent the required 8 bits (16×16=256) needed to specify the intensity of the red, green, and blue channels. Thus, in HTML, you can specify pure green as #00FF00, where there is no red (first pair is #00), there is maximum green (second pair is #FF), and there is no blue (last pair is #00). The number sign (#) specifies the value as hexadecimal.

Red	Green	Blue	Color
255 (#FF)	255 (#FF)	255 (#FF)	White (#FFFFFF)
255 (#FF)	255 (#FF)	0 (#00)	Yellow (#FFFF00)
255 (#FF)	0 (#00)	255 (#FF)	Magenta (#FF00FF)
0 (#00)	255 (#FF)	255 (#FF)	Cyan (#00FFFF)
255 (#FF)	0 (#00)	0 (#00)	Red (#FF0000)
0 (#00)	255 (#FF)	0 (#00)	Green (#00FF00)
0 (#00)	0 (#00)	255 (#FF)	Blue (#0000FF)
0 (#00)	0 (#00)	0 (#00)	Black (#000000)

In the HSB (hue, saturation, brightness) and HSL (hue, saturation, lightness) models, you specify hue or color as an angle from 0 to 360 degrees on a color wheel, and saturation, brightness, and lightness as percentages. Lightness or brightness is the percentage of black or white that is mixed with a color. A lightness of 100 percent will yield a white color; 0 percent is black; the pure color has a 50 percent lightness. Saturation is the intensity of the color. At 100 percent saturation, the color is pure; at 0 percent saturation, the color is white, black, or gray.

Color	Degrees
Red	0°
Yellow	60°
Green	120°
Cyan	180°
Blue	240°
Magenta	300°

The CMYK color model is less applicable to multimedia production. It is used primarily in the printing trade where cyan, magenta, yellow, and black are used to print process color separations.

Other color models include CIE, YIQ, YUV, and YCC. CIE describes color value in terms of frequency, saturation, and illuminance (blue/yellow or red/green, which in turn corresponds to the color receptors in the cones of the eye). CIE more closely resembles how human beings perceive color, but certain devices such as scanners are unable to replicate the process.

YIQ and YUV were developed for broadcast TV (composite NTSC, as explained in Chapter 12). They are based on luminance and chrominance expressed as the amplitude of a wave and the phase of the wave relative to some reference. Detail is carried by luminance (black and white), so reduction in color does not result in the loss of image definition detail. This analog process can be translated to a number value so that the computer can use a palette or CLUT (color lookup table) to assign a pixel a color.

The Photo YCC model has been developed by Kodak to provide a definition that enables consistent representation of digital color images from negatives, slides, and other high-quality input. YCC is used for PhotoCD images, described in Chapter 18.

Color Palettes

Palettes are mathematical tables that define the color of a pixel displayed on the screen. On the Macintosh, these tables are called *color lookup tables* or CLUTs. In Windows, the term palette is used. The most common palettes are 1, 4, 8, 16, and 24 bits deep:

Color Depth	Colors Available
1-bit	Black and white (or any two colors)
4-bit	16 colors
8-bit	256 colors (good enough for color images)
16-bit	Thousands of colors (excellent for color images)
24-bit	More than 16 million colors (totally photo-realistic)

For 256-color, 8-bit VGA systems, your computer uses a color lookup table or palette to determine which 256 colors out of the millions possible are available to you at any one time. Color Plate 1 shows the default Macintosh and Windows system palettes as well as other combinations of 256 colors. The default system colors were statistically selected by Apple and Microsoft engineers (working independently) to be the colors and shades that are most "popular" in photographic images; the two palettes are, of course, different.

To generate a palette which is best for representing a particular image, we support Heckbert's median cut algorithm. This algorithm first builds a three-dimensional table (a histogram cube) indicating how popular any given colour in the RGB cube is in the image being converted. It then proceeds to subdivide this histogram cube (by dividing boxes in half) until it has created as many boxes as there are palette entries. The decision as to where to divide a box is based on the distribution of colours within the box. This algorithm attempts to create boxes which have approximately equal popularity in the image. Palette entries are then assigned to represent each box. There are other methods of generating a palette from an image, but Heckbert's algorithm is generally regarded as the best trade-off between speed and quality.

Allan Hessenflow of HandMade Software, makers of Image Alchemy,
describing how an 8-bit palette is made

10

Paint programs provide a palette tool for displaying available colors. Most color pickers and selectors (see examples shown in Color Plate 2) also provide a mechanism for specifying a palette color numerically when precision is required. Palette display and color picking tools, however, are not uniform among applications or across platforms.

In 24-bit color systems, your graphics adapter works with three channels of 256 discrete shades of each color (red, green, and blue) represented as the three axes of a cube. This allows a total of 16,777,216 colors (256×256×256). Like the 44.1 kHz sampled-sound standard for CD music on compact discs that is discussed in Chapter 9, the color range offered by 24-bit systems covers what the human eye can sense. Even though millions of colors can be painted on a computer screen in 24-bit mode, only 307,200 (640×480) actual pixels will be available at any one time on a typical Macintosh or Windows display monitor set to 640×480. This is, however, more than sufficient for excellent gradients and photo-realism. A 16-bit system provides a total of 32,768 different colors (32×32×32) that are quite realistic and smooth.

---

note *Macintosh terminology is different from Windows terminology in describing color depth. On the Macintosh, display choices are typically "256, Thousands, or Millions." In Windows, you may choose from "256, High-color, or True-color." Both descriptions represent 8-bit, 16-bit, and 24-bit color depth, respectively.*

About Palette Flashing

When you work with the 256 colors of an 8-bit palette, only one combination of any 256 colors can be displayed on your monitor at any given moment. If you change the colors in the current palette by remapping, there will be an annoying flash of strange colors in your image while the computer remakes its color lookup table and the old colors change to the new. This *palette flashing* is a serious practical problem for multimedia designers. For example, it occurs when you show a series of images (an animation), each with its own optimal palette; when the new image replaces the old one, a flash occurs.

All techniques for handling the palette-flashing problem involve design solutions:

- The simplest solution is to map all images in your project to a single, shared palette. The disadvantage here is that you will trade the best 256 colors that show a single image for an "average" of 256 colors shared among all images. Applications such as Equilibrium's DeBabelizer specialize in creating "super palettes."

- A less simple but more effective technique is to fade each image to white or black before showing the next image. Black and white are usually present in all palettes.

Most image-editing, painting, and authoring applications let you remap, optimize, and customize palettes. When you input an image with a flat-bed color scanner or a video frame-grabber, the resulting image file will likely be three 8-bit channels of color information. Your images will be highly detailed, showing rich and subtle color variations, wood grain, and various lighting conditions. If you dither this image to 8 bits, you must weigh the compromises.

And here are some color techniques to avoid when the destination of your animation is a videotape:

- Avoid using a pattern or mosaic.

- Avoid thin horizontal lines.

- Avoid extremely bright or intense colors that may flare up on a television screen; stick to pastels and earth colors.

- Avoid some reds that may turn brown on television.

Dithering

If you start out with a scanned image that contains millions of colors, it must be dithered to 256 colors. *Dithering* is a process whereby the color value of each pixel is changed to the closest matching color value in the target palette, using a mathematical algorithm. Often the adjacent pixels are also examined, and patterns of different colors are created in the more limited palette to best represent the original colors. Thus any given pixel might not be mapped to its closest palette entry, but instead to the average over some area of the image; this average will be closer to the correct color than a substitute color would be. Depending upon the algorithm used, dithering can render a very good approximation of the original. Color Plate 4 compares the same scanned image dithered from millions of colors to 256 colors, 16 colors, 16 grays, and black and white.

tip *To improve performance on the Web, a common trick is to make two files: a very compact black-and-white dithered image and the full-color image. Use the HTML <lowsrc> attribute for the <img> graphic tag so the black-and-white picture displays fast. Then later, the browser will draw the full-color graphic over the black-and-white one.*

Dithering concepts are important to understand when you are working with bitmaps that are derived from RGB information or are based upon different palettes or CLUTs. The palette for the image of a rose, for example, may contain mostly shades of red with a number of greens thrown in for the stem and leaves. The image of your pretty Delft vase, into which you want to electronically place the rose, may be mostly blues and grays. Your software will use a dithering algorithm to find the 256 color shades that best represent both images, generating a new palette in the process.

....

Multimedia is just another way to transform ambiguity. There were so many ambiguous colors in this scan, I decided to make them unambiguous. How do you like the purple?

....

Lars Hidde, explaining why he dithered a perfectly fine
256-color image into a 16-color default palette

Dithering software is usually built into image-editing programs and is also available in many multimedia authoring systems as part of the application's palette management suite of tools.

---

tip   *Instead of trying to display a photo-realistic image using 16 colors, or if you are not satisfied with the colors of your image, consider dithering your photo to a gray-scale image. It will show extraordinary detail.*

---

warning   *It is very difficult to create outstanding graphics with just 16 colors. Using various two-color dithers will certainly improve your range of perceived colors, but you will need to double your graphics budget—optimizing the look of drawn and painted objects at this color depth is painstaking and time consuming.*

Image File Formats

As mentioned earlier in this chapter, there are many file formats used to store bitmaps and drawings. Developers of paint and draw applications continually create native file formats that allow their programs to load and save files more quickly or more efficiently. Most of these applications, however, offer a Save As option that lets you write files in other common formats. And third-party translators are now widely available, for files generated on the same platform as well as for going cross platform between Macintosh and PC/Windows (and others).

If you are using a specialized application to make bitmaps or drawings, make sure your multimedia authoring package can import the image files you produce, and that your application can export such a file. You need a common format.

First Person

I needed to get about 40 bitmap files from the Macintosh to the Sun SPARCstation. "Piece of cake," I said. "Give me a few minutes." The network hadn't gone down in three days, and we were connected at Ethernet speeds. Well, the files had been saved in native Photoshop format on the Macintosh. So I launched Photoshop, opened each file, and then saved it in PICT format. The translator program I wanted to use to convert Macintosh PICT files to Sun raster files was an MS-DOS application, so I renamed all the Macintosh files to fit the DOS eight-plus-three-character file name convention. Then I cranked up the 486, launched the translator, and batch-processed all of the files into RAS files using the network. The 40 new files were now on the Macintosh, mixed in with the original PICTs. I collected the needed raster files into a single folder on the Macintosh and then sent the whole thing over to the Sun.

A few minutes? The process kept three chairs warm for about two hours.

Macintosh Formats

On the Macintosh, just about every image application can import or export PICT files. PICT is a complicated but versatile format developed by Apple as a common format that is always available to Macintosh users. In a PICT file, both bitmaps and vector-drawn objects can live side by side, and programs such as MetaCard or Canvas make use of this feature, providing editors for both drawn and bitmapped graphics. Many drawing programs for the Macintosh, such as Illustrator or Freehand, will allow you to import a bitmap but offer no facility for editing it. Multimedia authoring programs that can import PICT images may not utilize the drawn objects that are part of the file, but will usually convert them to bitmaps for you.

Windows Formats

Windows uses device-independent bitmaps (DIBs) as its common image file format, usually written as BMP files. DIBs can stand alone, or they can be buried within a Resource Interchange File Format (RIFF) file. A RIFF is actually the preferred file type for all multimedia development in Windows, because this format was designed to contain many types of files, including bitmaps, MIDI scores, and formatted text. In Windows, there is no "standard" provision for managing drawn objects in a common format, as is provided by Macintosh PICT files.

10

The bitmap formats used most often by Windows developers are DIB, BMP, PCX, and TIFF. A BMP file is a Windows bitmap file. PCX files were originally developed for use in Z-Soft MS-DOS paint packages; these files can be opened and saved by almost all MS-DOS paint software and desktop publishing software. TIFF, or Tagged Interchange File Format, was designed to be a universal bitmapped image format and is also used extensively in desktop publishing packages. Often, applications use a proprietary file format to store their images. Adobe creates a PSD file for Photoshop and an AIx file for Illustrator; Corel creates a CDR file; Micrografx Designer and Picture Publisher applications use DSF and PPF files. If you import your artwork into other programs, such as multimedia authoring systems, be sure you save your bitmaps in a format that can be imported by that application.

The following list contains image file formats you might find in the Windows environment:

Format	Extension
Microsoft Windows DIB	.bmp, .dib, .rle
Microsoft RLE DIB	.dib
Microsoft Palette	.pal
Microsoft RIFF DIB	.rdi
Computer Graphics Metafile	.cgm
Micrografx Designer/Draw	.drw
AutoCAD Format 2-D	.dxf
Encapsulated PostScript	.eps
CompuServe GIF	.gif
HP Graphic Language	.hgl
JPEG	.jpg
PC Paintbrush	.pcx
Apple Macintosh PICT	.pic or .pct
Lotus 1-2-3 Graphics	.pic
AutoCAD Import	.plt
Truevision TGA	.tga
TIFF	.tif
Windows Metafile	.wmf
DrawPerfect	.wpg

Cross-Platform Formats

For handling drawn objects across many platforms, there are two common formats: DXF and IGS. DXF was developed by AutoDesk as an ASCII-based drawing interchange file for AutoCAD, but the format is used today by many computer-aided design applications. IGS (or IGES, for Initial Graphics Exchange Standard) was developed by an industry committee as a broader standard for transferring CAD drawings. These formats are also used in 3-D rendering and animation programs. Applications such as DeBabelizer and Image Alchemy provide specialized image format translators.

JPEG and GIF images are the most common bitmap formats used on the Web and may be considered cross platform, as all browsers will display them. These formats are discussed in detail in Chapter 15.

10

Multi

Animation is possible because of
a biological phenomenon known
as persistence of vision

Animation is a button actually moving across the screen...

dynamic action

media

chapter

11

Animation

a spinning globe of our earth;
■ a car driving along a line-art highway;
■ a bug crawling out from under a stack of disks,
■ with a screaming voice from the speaker telling you to "Shoot it, now!"

A NIMATION adds visual impact to your multimedia projects and Web pages. Many multimedia applications for both Macintosh and Windows provide animation tools, but you should first understand the principles of how the eye interprets the changes it sees as motion.

The Power of Motion

You can animate your whole project, or you can animate here and there, accenting and adding spice. For a brief product demonstration with little user interaction, it might make sense to design the entire project as a movie and keep the presentation always in motion. For speaker support, you can animate bulleted text or fly it in, or you can use charts with quantities that grow or dwindle; then, give the speaker control of these eye-catchers. In a parts-assembly training manual, you might show components exploding into an expanded view.

Visual effects such as wipes, fades, zooms, and dissolves are available in most authoring packages, and some of these can be used for primitive animation. For example, you can slide images onto the screen with a wipe, or you can make an object implode with an iris/close effect. Figure 11-1 shows the many transition effects available in Macromedia Director and in Adobe Premiere.

But animation is more than wipes, fades, and zooms. Animation is an object actually moving across or *into* or *out of* the screen; a spinning globe of our earth; a car driving along a line-art highway; a bug crawling out from under a stack of disks, with a screaming voice from the speaker telling you to "Shoot it, now!" Until QuickTime and AVI motion video became more commonplace, animations were the primary source of dynamic action in multimedia presentations.

Tools for designing animated multimedia presentations are discussed in detail in Chapters 6 and 7. Creating and displaying animations for Web pages is discussed in Chapters 14 and 15.

Principles of Animation

Animation is possible because of a biological phenomenon known as *persistence of vision* and a psychological phenomenon called *phi*. An object seen by the human eye remains chemically mapped on the eye's retina for a brief time after viewing. Combined with the human mind's need to conceptually complete a perceived action, this makes it possible for a series of images that are changed very slightly and very rapidly, one after the other, to seemingly blend together into a visual illusion of movement. The following shows a few cells or frames of a rotating logo. When the images are progressively and rapidly changed, the arrow of the compass is perceived to be spinning.

Television video builds 30 entire frames or pictures every second; the speed with which each frame is replaced by the next one makes the images appear to blend smoothly into movement. Movies on film are typically shot at a shutter rate of 24 frames per second, but using projection tricks (the projector's shutter flashes light through each image twice), the flicker rate is increased to 48 times per second, and the human eye thus sees a motion picture. On some projectors each frame is shown 3 times before the pull-down claw moves to the next frame, for a total of 72 flickers per second, which helps to eliminate the flicker effect: the more interruptions per second, the more continuous the beam of light appears. Quickly changing the viewed image is the principle of an animatic, a flip-book, or a zoetrope. To make an object travel across the screen while it changes its shape, just change the shape and also move or *translate* it a few pixels for each frame. Then, when you play the frames back at a faster speed, the changes blend together and you have motion and animation. It's the same magic as when the hand is quicker than the eye, and you don't see the pea moving in the blur of the gypsy's cups.

Animation Techniques

Today, computers have taken a great deal of handwork out of the animation and rendering process, and commercial films such as *Jurassic Park*, *Beauty and the Beast*, *Toy Story*, and *Shrek* have utilized the power of computers. (See Chapter 10 for an account of the historic "computer wall" of 117 Sun SPARCstations used to render the animated feature *Toy Story*.)

When you create an animation, organize its execution into a series of logical steps. First, gather up in your mind all the activities you wish to provide in the animation; if it is complicated, you may wish to create a written script with a list of activities and required objects. Choose the animation tool best suited for the job. Then build and tweak your sequences; experiment with lighting effects. Allow plenty of time for this phase when you are experimenting and testing. Finally, post-process your animation, doing any special renderings and adding sound effects.

Cel Animation

The animation techniques made famous by Disney use a series of progressively different graphics on each frame of movie film (which plays at 24 frames per second). A minute of animation may thus require as many as 1,440 separate frames. The term *cel* derives from the clear celluloid sheets that were used for drawing each frame, which have been replaced today by acetate or plastic. Cels of famous animated cartoons have become sought-after, suitable-for-framing collector's items.

Cel animation artwork begins with *keyframes* (the first and last frame of an action). For example, when an animated figure of a man walks across the screen, he balances the weight of his entire body on one foot and then the other in a series of falls and recoveries, with the opposite foot and leg catching up to support the body. Thus the first keyframe to portray a single step might be the man pitching his body weight forward off the left foot and leg, while his center of gravity shifts forward; the feet are close together and he appears to be falling. The last keyframe might be the right foot and leg catching the body's fall, with the center of gravity now centered between the outstretched stride, and the left and right feet positioned far apart.

The series of frames in between the keyframes are drawn in a process called tweening. *Tweening* an action requires calculating the number of frames between keyframes and the path the action takes, and then actually sketching onto a cel with pencil the series of progressively different outlines. As tweening progresses, the action sequence is checked by flipping through the frames. The penciled frames are assembled and then actually filmed as a pencil test to check smoothness, continuity, and timing.

When the pencil frames are satisfactory, they are permanently inked, and acrylic colors are painted on. In the hands of a master, cel paint applied to the back of acetate can be simply flat and perfectly even, or it can produce beautiful and subtle effects, with feathered edges or smudges.

The cels for each frame of our example of a walking man—which may consist of a text title, a background, a left arm, a right arm, legs, shoes, a body, and facial features—are carefully registered and stacked. It is this composite that becomes the final photographed frame in an animated movie.

11

Computer Animation

Computer animation programs typically employ the same logic and procedural concepts as cel animation, using layer, keyframe, and tweening techniques, and even borrowing from the vocabulary of classic animators. On the computer, paint is most often filled or drawn with tools using features such as gradients and anti-aliasing. The word *inks,* in computer animation terminology, usually means special methods for computing RGB pixel values, providing edge detection, and layering so that images can blend or otherwise mix their colors to produce special transparencies, inversions, and effects.

You can usually set your own frame rates on the computer, but the rate at which changes are computed and screens are actually refreshed will depend on the speed and power of your display platform and hardware. Although your animations will probably never push the limits of your monitor's scan rate (about 60 to 70 frames a second), animation does put raw computing horsepower to task. If you cannot compute all your changes and display them as a new frame on your monitor within, say, 1/15 second, then the animation may appear jerky and slow.

---

tip *The smaller the object, the faster it can move. Bouncing a 10-pixel-diameter tennis ball on your screen provides far snappier motion than bouncing a 150-pixel-diameter beach ball.*

Kinematics Kinematics is the study of the movement and motion of structures that have joints, such as a walking man. Animating a walking step is tricky: you need to calculate the position, rotation, velocity, and acceleration of all the joints and articulated parts involved—knees bend, hips flex, shoulders swing, and the head bobs. Fractal Design's Poser, a 3-D modeling program, provides preassembled adjustable human models (male, female, infant, teenage, and superhero) in many poses, such as "walking" or "thinking." As Figure 11-2 shows, an appendage can be adjusted or a pose quickly configured simply by dragging or rotating the appropriate body part. And surface textures can then be applied to create muscle-bound hulks or smooth chrome androids. Inverse kinematics is the process in which you link objects such as hands to arms and define their relationships and limits (for example, elbows cannot bend backwards), then drag these parts around and let the computer calculate the result.

Fractal Design's Poser understands human motion and inverse kinematics: move an arm, and the shoulders follow

Morphing   Morphing is a popular (if not overused) effect in which one image transforms into another. Morphing applications and other modeling tools that offer this effect can transition not only between still images but often between moving images as well. Some products that offer morphing features are Avid's Elastic Reality, Black Belt's WinImages, Gryphon Software's Morph, Human Software's Squizz, ImageWare's MorphWizard, MetaTools' Digital Morph, North Coast's PhotoMorph, RomeBlack's RomeBlack, Strata's Visual FX, Ulead's MorphStudio, Valis Group's Flo and MetaFlo, and Villa Crespo's MetaMorf. Color Plate 11 illustrates part of a morph where 16 kindergarten children are dissolved one into the other in a continuous compelling motion video.

The morphed images shown here were built at a rate of eight frames per second, with each transition taking a total of four seconds (32 separate images for each transition), and the number of key points was held to a minimum to shorten rendering time. Setting key points (see Figure 11-3) is crucial for smooth transition between two images. The point you set in the start image will move to the corresponding point in the end image—this is important for things like eyes and noses, which you want to end up in about the same place (even if they look different) after the transition. The more key points, the smoother the morph.

Animation File Formats

Some file formats are designed specifically to contain animations, and they can be ported among applications and platforms with the proper translators. Those formats include Director (.dir and .dcr), AnimatorPro (.fli using 320×200 pixel images and .flc), 3D Studio Max (.max), SuperCard and Director (.pics), Windows Audio Video Interleaved Format (.avi), Macintosh Time-Based Data Format (.qt, .mov), Motion Video (.mpeg or .mpg), CompuServe (.gif), and Flash (.swf). Because file size is a critical factor when downloading animations to play on Web pages, file compression is an essential part of preparing animation files for the Web. A Director movie file (.dir), for example, must be preprocessed and compressed into a proprietary Shockwave animation file (.dcr) for the Web. Compression for Director movies is as much as 75 percent or more with this tool, turning 100K files into 25K files and significantly speeding up download/display times on the

FIGURE 11-3

Matching key points in the start and end image guide the morphing transition ∎

Internet. Flash, widely used for Web-based animation, makes extensive use of vector graphics (see Chapter 10) to keep the post-compression file size at absolute minimums. To render these animations within a Web page, special plug-ins or players are required (see Chapter 14).

Making Animations That Work

Animation catches the eye and makes things noticeable. But, like sound, animation quickly becomes trite if it is improperly applied. Unless your project has a backbone of movielike animated imagery, use animation carefully and sparingly to achieve the greatest impact. Your screens will otherwise become busy and "noisy."

Multimedia authoring systems typically provide tools to simplify creating animations within that authoring system. And they often have a mechanism for playing the special animation files created by dedicated animation software. Today, the most widely used tool for creating multimedia animations for Macintosh and Windows environments is Macromedia's Director (see Chapter 7).

The following sections provide examples to demonstrate that computer-generated animations actually consist of many bits and pieces carefully orchestrated to appear as one image, in motion—just like the many layers in classical cel animation.

A Rolling Ball

Billiard-ball spheres can be made quickly using Photoshop and Kai's Power Tools' Spheroid Designer (see Figure 11-4), a set of graphic manipulation plug-ins. First, create a new, blank image file that is 100×100 pixels, and fill it with a sphere:

Create a new layer in Photoshop, and place some white text on this layer at the center of the image:

Sphererize the text using Photoshop's distortion filter, and save the result:

To animate the sphere by rolling it across the screen, you first need to make a number of rotated images of the sphere. Rotate the image in 45-degree increments to create a total of eight images, rotating a full circle of 360 degrees. When displayed sequentially at the same location, the sphere spins:

For a realistic rolling effect, the circumference (calculated at pi times 100, or about 314 pixels) is divided by 8 (yielding about 40 pixels). As each image is successively displayed, the ball is moved 40 pixels along a line. Being where the rubber meets the road, this math applies when you roll any round object in a straight line perpendicular to your line of sight.

A Bouncing Ball

With the simplest tools, you can make a bouncing ball to animate your Web site using GIF89a. (Animating with GIF89a files is discussed in detail in Chapter 15.) Like the rolling ball, you simply need to flash a ball on the computer screen rapidly and in a different place each time to make it bounce up and down. And like the rolling ball, where you should compute the circumference of the ball and divide by the number of images to determine how far it rolls each time it flashes, there are some commonsense computations to consider with a bouncing ball, too. In the formula, *s* equals distance, *g* equals acceleration due to gravity, and *t* equals time:

$$s = 1/2gt^2$$

Gravity makes your bouncing ball accelerate on its downward course and decelerate on its upward course (when it moves slower and slower until it actually stops and then accelerates downward again). As Galileo discovered while dropping feathers and rocks from the leaning tower of Pisa, a beach ball and a golf ball accelerate downward at the same rate until they hit the ground. But the real world of Italy is full of air, so the feather falls gently while the rock pounds dirt. It is in this real world that you should compose your animations, tempering them always with commonsense physics to give them the ring of truth.

Unless your animation requires precision, ignore the hard numbers you learned in high school (like 32 feet per second per second), and simply figure that your ball will uniformly accelerate and decelerate up and down the pixels of your screen by the squares: 1, 4, 9, 16, 25, 36, 49, 64, 81, 100 are the squares of 1, 2, 3, 4, 5, 6, 7, 8, 9, and 10. This is illustrated in Figure 11-5. In the case of a perpetual-motion bouncing ball (even better than silly putty), it goes up the same way it comes down, forever, and this makes the job easy, because the up and down movements are symmetrical. You can use the same images for downward motion as you use for upward—as in frames 11 through 18 in Figure 11-5—by *reversing* them. You might also add a squash frame (not shown in Figure 11-5) when the ball hits the floor. The amount of squash would be determined by the type of ball—a steel ball or a balloon or a very soft rubber ball. The ball would squash when it hits and un-squash as it bounced up again. With a bit of programming, you might allow the user to choose the elasticity of the object, the amount of gravity, and the length of fall.

Open a graphics program and paint a ball about 15 pixels in diameter (if you have an odd-number diameter, there is a middle pixel that can be your center alignment point). If you wish to be fancy, make the ball with a 3-D

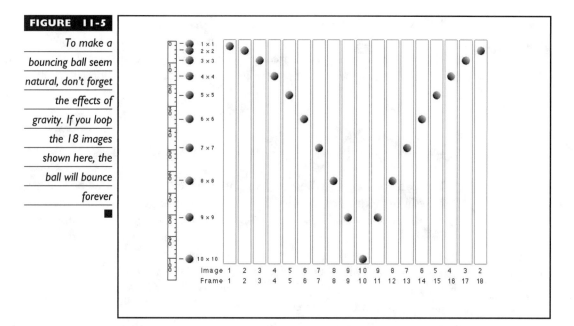

graphics tool that will shade it as a sphere. Then duplicate the ball, placing each copy of it in a vertical line at the ten locations 1, 4, 9, 16, 25, 36, 49, 64, 81, 100. The goal is to create a separate image file for each location of the ball, like the pages of a flip-book. With Photoshop, you can create a single file with ten layers to contain each ball at its proper location, and you can add an eleventh background layer, too. Then save each layer showing against the background as a separate file. (Use numbers in your file names like ball1.gif, ball2.gif, etc., to keep them organized.)

11

This is a construction process also easily managed with Director or Flash, in which you can place the same cast member or object (the ball) where you wish on the presentation stage. In Director, use the score's extended view, because the precise vertical location of your object is reported along the bottom line:

You can also add a background and other art elements, and when you are done, you can export each frame as a graphics file using the export function. You will probably also wish to set the size of your stage to a small area just sufficient for your animation, say 32×120 pixels. The smaller the better if users will be downloading this animated GIF file into their Web browsers.

To turn your collection of images into a GIF89a animation, you need an application like GifBuilder (for Macintosh; see Figure 11-6) or Gif Construction Set (for Windows). These tools organize the sequence of images to be shown, set timing and transparency, and (most importantly) let you save the final GIF file in the proper format. See Chapter 15 for more details about animated GIF files and where to use them.

FIGURE 11-6

GifBuilder lets you organize images into animated GIF files playable by Web browsers

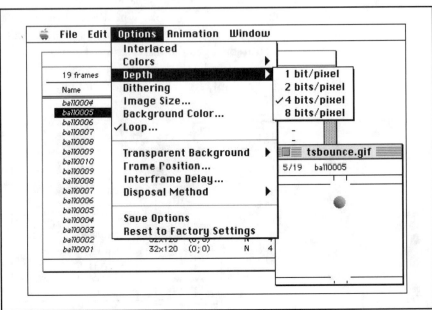

Creating an Animated Scene

The animation example presented here became a small piece of the rollout presentation to developers and the press of Microsoft's Multimedia Extensions for Windows. The event is described in the "First Person" anecdote following.

A creative committee organized a brief storyboard of a gorilla chasing a man. From a CD-ROM containing many unlimited-licensed images, a photograph was chosen of Manhattan's Central Park where a bridge crossed a small river and high-rise apartments lined the horizon. The chase scene would occur across the bridge. To produce frames of the running man, an actor was videotaped running in place against an ultimatte blue background in a studio; a few frames of this were grabbed with a video capture board, and the blue background was removed from each image. The gorilla was difficult to find, so a toy model dinosaur about 25 centimeters tall was used; again, a few frames were captured and the background made transparent. That was all that was required for image resources.

First Person

The animation storyboard called for a photo-realistic monster chasing a running man through a city park amid screams of terror. The man was already in Director, running in great strides across an arched footbridge in a woodsy scene with high-rises in the background; he even looked over his shoulder a few times in panic. We were scouting around for an effective Godzilla when a friend dropped by with a motorized, 12-inch Tyrannosaurus Rex from Toys'R'Us. It was perfect—opening a toothy, gaping mouth every few steps as it lumbered along on C batteries.

I took the dinosaur and a video camera home to the delight and fascination of my three-year-old daughter, who helped rig a white sheet in front of the living room fireplace and a cardboard-box runway where Mr. TRex could strut his stuff before the camera. A couple of lamps gave him a sweaty sheen. We ran about five minutes of VHS tape as my daughter happily retrieved Mr. TRex each time he nosed off the "cliff" at the end of the stage.

Playing the tape on a VCR with a five-head, single-frame advance feature, I grabbed about every fourth frame with an old

ColorSpace digitizing board on the Macintosh and imported the resulting PICT files into Director as cast members. They needed a little cleanup and scaling, but the fellow looked really convincing when he was finally scored to run across the bridge. Next day, I mixed a bunch of sounds—singing birds, running footsteps, screams, roars, sirens, and gunshots—and it was done. We exported it from the Macintosh to Windows as an MMM file.

A few weeks later, in November 1990, Mr. TRex helped introduce Bill Gates to a crowd of 600 at the opening of the first Microsoft Multimedia Developers' Conference.

11

As illustrated in Figure 11-7*a*, the background was carefully cut in half along the edge of the bridge, so the bridge railing could be placed in front of the runners. The running man was organized in a series of six frames that could be repeated many times across the screen to provide the pumping motions of running. The same was done for the dinosaur, to give him a lumbering, bulky look as he chased the little man across the bridge (see Figure 11-7*b*). The result, in Figure 11-7*c*, was simple and quickly achieved.

a

b

c

11

Multi

Carefully planned, well-executed video clips can make a dramatic difference in a multimedia project.

Digital video is the most **engaging** of multimedia venues

compelling

media

pow!

chapter

12

Video

powerful

it is a very **powerful** tool to bring computer users closer to the real world.

S INCE the first silent movie flickered to life, people have been fascinated with "motion" pictures. To this day, motion video is the element of multimedia that can draw gasps from a crowd at a trade show or firmly hold a student's interest in a computer-based learning project. Digital video is the most engaging of multimedia venues, and it is a powerful tool for bringing computer users closer to the real world. It also is an effective method for delivering multimedia to an audience raised on television. With video elements in your project, you can effectively present your messages and reinforce your story, and viewers tend to retain more of what they see. But take care! Video that is not thought out or well produced can degrade your presentation.

Full-motion video on personal computers changes everything. It is like turning a ten-speed bicycle into a Harley-Davidson.

David Bunnell, Editor in Chief, *NewMedia* Magazine

Of all the multimedia elements, video places the highest performance demand on your computer and its memory. Consider that a high-quality color still image on a computer screen could require as much as a megabyte of memory. Multiply this by 30—the number of times per second that the picture is replaced to provide the appearance of motion—and you would need 30 megabytes of memory per second to play your video—or 1.8 gigabytes of memory per minute, or 108 gigabytes per hour. Just moving all this picture data from computer memory to the screen at that rate would challenge the processing capability of a supercomputer. These massive memory storage demands make the Library of Congress look like a magazine rack at your local grocery store. Some of the hottest and most arcane multimedia technologies and research efforts today deal with compressing digital video image data into manageable streams of information.

If you control the delivery platform for your project, you can get the highest video performance by specifying special hardware and software enhancements. Video compression hardware will allow you to work with full-screen, full-motion video. A sophisticated audio board will allow you to use CD-quality sounds. You can install a superfast RAID (Redundant Array of Independent Disks) system that will support high-speed data transfer rates. You can include instructions in your authoring system that will spool video into RAM for rapid playback.

Using Video

Carefully planned, well-executed video clips can make a dramatic difference in a multimedia project. A clip of John F. Kennedy proclaiming, "Ich bin ein Berliner" in video and sound is more compelling than a scrolling text field containing that same speech. Before deciding whether to add video to your project, however, it is essential to have an understanding of the medium, its limitations, and its costs. This chapter provides a basic foundation to help you understand how video works, the different formats and standards for recording and playing video, and the differences between computer and television video. The equipment needed to shoot and edit video, as well as tips for adding video to your project, are also covered.

Since multimedia gives you the ability to present information in a variety of ways, let the content drive the selection of media for each chunk of information to be presented. Use traditional text and graphics where appropriate; add animation when "still life" won't get your message across; add audio when further explanation is required; resort to video only when all other methods pale by comparison.

David A. Ludwig, Interactive Learning Designs

Video standards and formats are still being refined as transport, storage, compression, and display technologies take shape in laboratories and in the marketplace. Working with multimedia video today can be like a Mojave Desert camping trip: you may pitch your tent on comfortable high ground and find that overnight the shifting sands have buried both your approach and your investment. Firm ground tends to shift rapidly in the 100 mph back draft of the many silicon engineers, computer scientists, and startup company salespeople driving in the fast lane of video overlay boards, compression schemes, RAID hard disk towers, and interleaving software.

12

Analog Versus Digital

Digital video has supplanted analog video as the method of choice for making video for multimedia use. While broadcast stations and professional production and post-production houses remain greatly invested in analog video hardware (according to Sony, there are more than 350,000 Betacam SP devices in use today), digital video gear produces excellent finished products at a fraction of the cost of analog. A digital camcorder directly connected to a computer workstation eliminates the image-degrading analog-to-digital conversion step typically performed by expensive video capture cards, and brings the power of nonlinear video editing and production to everyday users.

Obtaining Video Clips

If your project will include video, consider whether you should shoot new footage or acquire preexisting content for your video clips. There are many sources for film and video clips: a friend's home movies may suffice, or you can go to a "stock" footage house or a television station or movie studio. But acquiring footage that you do not own outright can be a nightmare—it is expensive, and licensing rights and permissions may be difficult, if not impossible, to obtain. Each second of video could cost $50 to $100 or more to license. Even a "public domain clip" from the National Archives will cost a minimum of $125 to copy the footage, and the turnaround time can take up to six weeks. Many companies sell royalty-free stock CDs specifically for multimedia productions, but these are lower resolution than broadcast quality and less than full-frame video.

On some projects, you will have no choice but to pay the price for required footage. If it is absolutely essential that your project include a clip of Elvis Presley crooning "You Ain't Nothing but a Hound Dog," and an Elvis impersonator just won't do, you will have to negotiate for rights to use the real thing. If your budget can't cover the cost of licensing a particular video clip, you may want to consider using other alternatives: locating a less expensive archival video source, using a series of still images rather than video, or shooting your own video. If you shoot your own video for a project, make sure you have releases from all persons who appear or speak and permission to use the audio effects and music you weave into it. Licensing, permissions, and legal issues are discussed more fully in Chapter 18.

Before you head out to the field with your camcorder in hand, it is important to understand at least the basics of video recording and editing, as well as the constraints of using video in a multimedia project. The remainder of this chapter will help you to understand how video works and will provide practical guidelines for shooting your own videos.

How Video Works

When light reflected from an object passes through a video camera lens, that light is converted into an electronic signal by a special sensor called a charge-coupled device, or a *CCD*. Top-quality broadcast cameras may have as many as three CCDs (one for each color of red, green, and blue) to enhance the resolution of the camera. The output of the CCD is processed by the camera into a signal containing three channels of color information and synchronization pulses (sync). If each channel of color information is transmitted as a separate signal on its own conductor, the signal output is called *RGB*, which is the preferred method for higher-quality and professional video work. Video output can also be split into two separate chroma channels and a brightness channel, to make *component* video. If all the signals are mixed together and carried on a single cable, it is a *composite* of the three color channels and the sync signal; this system yields less-precise color definition, which cannot be manipulated or color corrected as much as an RGB or component signal.

In analog systems, the video signal from the camera is delivered to the Video In connector(s) of a VCR, where it is recorded on magnetic videotape. (A camcorder may combine both camera and tape recorder in a single device.) One or two channels of sound may also be recorded on the tape (mono or stereo). The video signal is written to tape by a spinning recording head that changes the local magnetic properties of the tape's surface in a series of long diagonal stripes. Because the head follows a helical path, this is called helical scan recording. As illustrated in Figure 12-1, each stripe represents information for one field of a video frame. A single video frame is made up of two fields that are interlaced. Audio is recorded on a separate straight-line track at the top of the videotape, although with some recording systems (notably for 3/4-inch tape and for 1/2-inch tape with high-fidelity audio), sound is recorded helically between the video tracks. At the bottom of the tape is a control track containing the pulses used to regulate speed. *Tracking* is fine adjustment of the tape so that the tracks are properly aligned as the tape moves across the playback head.

Helical scan tape path

Video head

Half-inch videotape

Audio track

Video track

Control track

In digital systems, the video signal from the camera is first digitized as a single frame, and the data is compressed before it is written to the tape in one of several proprietary and competing formats: DV, DVCPRO, or DVCAM (see Figure 12-2).

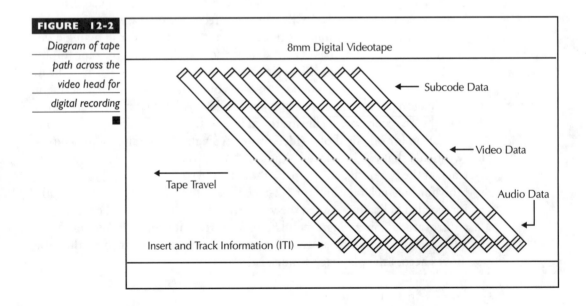

8mm Digital Videotape

Subcode Data

Video Data

Audio Data

Tape Travel

Insert and Track Information (ITI) →

First Person

Surf Alligators live within the cusps of breaking technology waves. They can be snuffed with good knowledge, tools, and a network of colleagues willing to answer arcane questions. Catching these alligators requires the patience of Costa Rican beach children who cast unbaited three-barbed hooks into the incoming waves to yank out their surprised and luckless silver prey.

Years ago, my 19-inch RGB monitor, a Hitachi rebranded by both SuperMac and Silicon Graphics, had BNC inputs for red, green, and blue and required that horizontal sync be superimposed on the green channel. This was supported by SuperMacs and other NuBus video cards at 8-bit color depth. I wanted the Quadra 840AV's internal video support for 19-inch monitors at 16 bits, claimed in Apple's literature. But

no way would my monitor work, and it took four days of calling around to discover why. Sorry, no sync on green from that Quadra, they said. Throw the monitor away. Get one with more BNC inputs.

Apple's User Assistance Center (usually busy and not open at 1:00 a.m.) was of no help. My arcane questions were not in the annoying hierarchy of voice message help, and it took two days to get hold of a real person to tell me the answer wasn't in her data bank. I felt like trolling with those Costa Rican fish hooks across the many rows of phone-answering cubicles at the Assistance Center, and yanking real hard.

Real information was finally forthcoming when I contacted two guys on Apple's Quadra hardware team through e-mail. They had docs that explained all and included the peculiar sensing

codes (pins 4, 7, and 10 of the 15-pin monitor connector) used by the Quadra's built-in video to automatically adjust to most monitors. I felt 100 percent better when I knew the WHY of it, even though I did have to buy a new monitor.

Every time you upgrade your computer hardware, and occasionally when you upgrade your software, you are likely to attract Surf Alligators. These perils aren't like the steep learning curves, where with effort you can incrementally improve your skill; they are brutally mechanical and test you in other ways: either you know it or you don't. If you don't know it, it won't work. Period.

By 2001, small and inexpensive cable adapters were widely available with lots of little dip switches to set the TTL signals Apple uses to declare monitor size and frequency, and for mixing sync onto the green channel.

A video cassette recorder can also add the video and sound signals to a subcarrier and modulate them into a radio frequency in the FM broadcast band. This is the NTSC, PAL, or SECAM signal available at the Antenna Out connector of a VCR. (These signal standards are explained in the next section.) Usually you can choose between Channel 3 or Channel 4 frequencies, and the resulting signal or picture can be viewed on a television. Many television sets provide a separate composite signal connector to avoid the unnecessary step of modulating and demodulating the signal into the broadcast frequency bands.

12

Colored phosphors on the screen glow red, green, or blue when they are energized by the electron beam. Because the intensity of the beam varies as it moves across the screen, some colors glow brighter than others. Finely tuned magnets around the picture tube aim the electrons precisely onto the phosphor screen while the intensity of the beam is varied according to the video signal. This is why you need to keep speakers (which have strong magnets in them) away from the television screen. A strong external magnetic field can skew the electron beam to one area of the screen and sometimes cause a permanent blotch that cannot be fixed by *degaussing*.

All of these electronic activities work in concert to yield a television picture.

Broadcast Video Standards

Four broadcast and video standards and recording formats are commonly in use around the world: NTSC, PAL, SECAM, and HDTV. Because these standards and formats are not easily interchangeable, it is important to know where your multimedia project will be used. A video cassette recorded in the United States will not play on a television set in any European country, even though the recording method and style of the cassette is "VHS." Likewise, tapes recorded in European PAL or SECAM formats will not play back on an NTSC video cassette recorder. Each system is based on a different standard that defines the way information is encoded to produce the electronic signal that ultimately creates a television picture. Multiformat VCRs can play back all three standards but typically cannot dub from one standard to another; dubbing between standards still requires high-end, specialized equipment.

NTSC

The United States, Japan, and many other countries use a system for broadcasting and displaying video that is based upon the specifications set forth by the 1952 National Television Standards Committee. These standards define a method for encoding information into the electronic signal that ultimately creates a television picture. As specified by the NTSC standard, a single frame of video is made up of 525 horizontal scan lines drawn onto the inside face of a phosphor-coated picture tube every 1/30th of a second by a fast-moving electron beam. The drawing occurs so fast that your eye perceives the image as stable. The electron beam actually makes two passes as it draws a single video frame, first laying down all the odd-numbered lines, then all the even-numbered lines. Each of these passes (which happen at a rate of 60 per second, or 60 Hz) paints a field. The process of building a single frame from two fields is called *interlacing*, a technique that helps to prevent flicker on television screens. Remember that computer monitors use *progressive-scan* technology and draw the lines of an entire frame in a single pass, without interlacing them.

Sometimes we define "NTSC" as "Never The Same Color."

Richard Santalesa, R&D Technologies

PAL

The Phase Alternate Line (PAL) system is used in the United Kingdom, Europe, Australia, and South Africa. PAL is an integrated method of adding color to a black-and-white television signal that paints 625 lines at a frame rate of 25 frames per second. Like NTSC, the even and odd lines are interlaced, each field taking 1/50th of a second to draw (50 Hz).

SECAM

The Sequential Color and Memory (SECAM) system is used in France, Russia, and a few other countries. Although SECAM is a 625-line, 50 Hz system, it differs greatly from both the NTSC and the PAL color systems in its basic technology and broadcast method. Often, however, TV sets sold in Europe utilize dual components and can handle both PAL and SECAM systems.

HDTV

There are six video formats in the ATSC DTV standard that are "High Definition Television." They are the 1080-line by 1920-pixel formats at all picture rates (24, 30, and 60 pictures per second) and the 720-line by 1280-pixel formats at these same picture rates. All of these formats have a 16:9 aspect ratio.

High Definition Television (HDTV) provides high resolution in a 16:9 aspect ratio (see Figure 12-3). This aspect ratio allows the viewing of Cinemascope and Panavision movies. There is contention between the broadcast and computer industries about whether to use interlacing or progressive-scan technologies. The broadcast industry has promulgated an ultra-high-resolution, 1920×1080 interlaced format to become the cornerstone of a new generation of high-end entertainment centers, but the computer industry would like to settle on a 1280×720 progressive-scan system

12

for HDTV. While the 1920×1080 format provides more pixels than the 1280×720 standard, the refresh rates are quite different. The higher-resolution interlaced format delivers only half the picture every 1/60 of a second, and because of the interlacing, on highly detailed images there is a great deal of screen flicker at 30 Hz. The computer people argue that the picture quality at 1280×720 is superior and steady. Both formats have been included in the HDTV standard by the Advanced Television Systems Committee (ATSC, http://www.atsc.org).

---

warning *Today's multimedia monitors typically use a screen pixel ratio of 4:3 (640x480), but the new HDTV standard specifies a ratio of 16:9 (1280x720), much wider than tall (see Figure 12-3). There is no easy way to stretch and shrink existing graphics material to fit this new aspect ratio, so new multimedia design and interface principles will need to be developed for HDTV presentations.*

Integrating Computers and Television

There is some confusion of terms when discussing video in computer and television contexts. Bear in mind that current television video is based on analog technology and fixed international standards for the broadcast and display of images. Computer video is based on digital technology and other, more extensible standards for displaying images. In the early 2000s these two technologies—television and computer-based video—are merging, with the introduction of DVD players and HDTV sets.

Video Overlay Systems

The video/computer marriage began when computers were used simply to control analog video images taken from tape decks and videodisc players and displayed on a television. A common computer-based training (CBT) configuration was a dual-monitor workstation, where one monitor showed computer-managed training material, and a television displayed supporting video from a source controlled by the computer's serial port. Trainees using these systems moved their heads in a rhythmic tennis-match tempo set by the application's design metronome. As you might imagine, there was pressure from CBT developers and vendors alike to integrate both the digital and analog images onto a single monitor.

To display analog video (television) images in real-time on a computer monitor, the video signal must first be converted from analog to digital form.

Safe title area
512x384 (4:3)

Monitor 640x480 (4:3)

NTSC television overscan
approx. 648x486 (4:3)   35mm slide / photo
768x512 (3:2)

HDTV
1280x720 (16:9)

A special video digitizing overlay board or hardware on the motherboard must be installed in your computer to take the video signal and convert it to digital information. The analog video signal (converted to digital information) and the computer's own digital graphics are mixed, yielding either a full screen of motion video or a window of video cut into the computer's normal display. Some video overlay hardware simply lets you display video images on your computer screen, usually with several choices of window size. Better and more expensive boards offer visual effects such as freezing, fades, spins, mirrors, and chroma keys. *Chroma keys* allow you to choose a color or range of colors that become transparent, allowing the video image to be seen "through" the computer image. A newscast's weatherman is shot against a blue background that is made invisible when merged with the electronically generated image of the weather map. The weatherman controls the computer part of the display with a small handheld controller.

tip   *Always import video and sound at the highest resolution available. You can reduce the resolution later according to your needs.*

Differences Between Computer and Television Video

Although most computer screens have the same 4:3 aspect ratio as a television screen, a typical computer screen only scans 480 horizontal lines from top to bottom, not the 525 or 625 lines of NTSC or PAL and SECAM television. Also, a computer monitor scans each line progressively, with no interlacing; the scan is full frame at a rate of typically 66.67 Hz or higher, compared to 60 Hz for a television frame that is only half the interlaced picture.

Overscan and the Safe Title Area

As illustrated in Figure 12-3, it is common practice in the television industry to broadcast an image larger than will fit on a standard TV screen so that the "edge" of the image seen by a viewer is always bounded by the TV's physical frame, or bezel. This is called *overscan*. In contrast, computer monitors display a smaller image on the TV's picture tube (*underscan*), leaving a black border inside the bezel. Consequently, when a digitized video image is displayed on an RGB screen, there is a border around the image; and when a computer screen is converted to video, the outer edges of the image will not fit on a TV screen. Only about 360 of the 480 lines of the computer screen will be visible.

---

tip *Avoid using the outer 15 percent of the screen when producing computer-generated graphics and titles for use in television video. The safe title area, where your image will not be affected by overscanning, even in the worst conditions, is illustrated in Figure 12-3.*

Video Color

Color reproduction and display is different between televisions and computer monitors. Because computers use RGB component video (that is, they split colors into red, green, and blue signals), their colors are purer and more accurate than those seen on a television monitor. Consequently, colors used in a graphic image created for computer video may display differently when that image is transformed into NTSC television video.

Indeed, NTSC television uses a limited color palette and restricted luminance (brightness) levels and black levels (the richness of the blacks). Some colors generated by your computer that display fine on an RGB monitor may be "illegal" for display on an NTSC television. These colors are particularly apparent in shades of red, and cause bleeding or noisy shimmering when displayed on a television. Most commercial broadcast facilities and TV studios will refuse to run video programs that include illegal colors. Filters to convert illegal colors to legal colors are available in video and image editing and processing applications.

Captain's Log: We received some excellent design tips from Bernice T. Glenn:

As intermedia applications continue to proliferate, producers and designers need to know how to float between print and color pigment, digital color and RGB as viewed on a monitor, and analog color as viewed on a television screen. Color formulas for multimedia, especially when it is interactive, depend heavily on human factors.

Contrast—the degree of tonal difference between one color and another—is often more important when working with color on a computer screen. A combination of pure yellow with pure violet, or blue and orange, for example, will vibrate when viewed in RGB. On video, disturbing flickers, extraneous colors, and other artifacts usually appear on the borders between pure complementary colors. On top of that, colors that look great on your computer monitor may not even show up when transferred to video.

Important elements can be emphasized by using fully saturated colors against a neutral background, whose color may complement as a grayed-down tint of the color.

When readability is important, contrast in color saturation and value between the type and its background really works, using almost any color combination.

Red or green may need to be avoided as cue colors [for menu buttons and icons] because 8 percent of the population is color blind to some extent and cannot see reds or greens in their true color value.

From "Ask the Captain," a monthly column written by Tay Vaughan for NewMedia Magazine.

When producing a multimedia project, you should consider whether it will be played back on an RGB monitor and/or on a conventional television set. If your work is destined, for example, for a set-top player such as SEGA, Sony PlayStation, or Nintendo, choose your colors to meet the NTSC color specifications. There are many variables in providing perfect colors on a television. End users can control hue and balance (an adjustment not available on most RGB monitors), and it is not likely that many viewers of your project will have perfectly calibrated television sets. So you are fighting an uphill battle from the beginning. It helps to do color corrections and editing on your computer, then view the corrected image on a real television screen, not just the RGB monitor. For this, you need a signal converter card or hardware on the motherboard that can provide NTSC output; video overlay cards usually offer this feature.

12

tip *A useful trick is to grab a standard broadcast color test bar using a video frame grabber, and then save it as a PICT or TIFF image. When viewing the bar in Photoshop, for example, you can check the levels of each color by viewing red, green, and blue one at a time. The gradient of grays in the color bar should be smooth and even for each color channel. See Color Plate 7.*

Interlacing Effects

In television, the electron beam actually makes two passes on the screen as it draws a single video frame, first laying down all the odd-numbered lines, then all the even-numbered lines—they are interlaced. On an RGB monitor, lines are painted one-pixel thick and are not interlaced. Single-pixel lines displayed on an RGB monitor look fine; on a television, these thin lines flicker brightly because they only appear in every other field. To prevent this flicker, make sure your lines are greater than two pixels thick and that you avoid typefaces that are very thin or have elaborate serifs. If you are capturing images from a video signal, you can filter them through a de-interlacing filter provided by image-editing applications such as Photoshop or Fireworks. With typefaces, interlacing flicker can often be avoided by anti-aliasing the type to slightly blur the edges of the characters. The term "interlacing" has a different meaning on the Web, where it describes the progressive display of lines of pixels as image data is downloaded, giving the impression that the image is coming from blurry into focus as increasingly more data arrives (see Chapter 15).

Working with Text and Titles

Titles for video productions can be created with an analog character generator, but your computer can do this digitally using video and image-editing software. Here are some suggestions for creating good titles:

- Fonts for titles should be plain, sans serif, and bold enough to be easily read.

- When you are laying text onto a dark background, use white or a light color for the text.

- Use a drop shadow to help separate the text from the background image.

- Never use black or colored text on a white background.

- Do not kern your letters too tightly.

- If you use underlining or drawn graphics, always make your lines at least two pixels wide. If you use a one-pixel-wide line (or a width measured in an odd number of pixels), the line will flicker when transferred to video due to interlacing.

- Use parallel lines, boxes, and tight concentric circles sparingly. When you use them, draw them large and with thick lines.

- Avoid colors that are too hot.

- Neighboring colors should be markedly different in intensity. For example, use a light blue and a dark red, but not a medium blue and a medium red.

- Keep your graphics and titles within the safe area of the screen. Remember that televisions overscan computer output (see the earlier section, "Differences Between Computer and Television Video").

- Bring titles on slowly, keep them on screen for a sufficient interval, and then fade them out.

- Avoid making busy title screens; use more pages instead.

Shooting and Editing Video

To add full-screen, full-motion video to your multimedia project, you will need to invest in specialized hardware and software or purchase the services of a professional video production studio. In many cases, a professional studio will also provide editing tools and post-production capabilities that you cannot duplicate with your Macintosh or PC.

Expensive professional video equipment and services may not yield proportionately greater benefits than if you used consumer-grade equipment and nonlinear editors. As with audio equipment (see Chapter 9), you need to make balancing decisions using Vaughan's Law of Multimedia Minimums. Most likely, your goal is to expend resources without diminishing returns—to produce multimedia that is adequate and does its job, but doesn't break your bank. If you can, experiment with various combinations of video recording and playback devices hooked to your video digitizing hardware, and test the results using your multimedia authoring platform. You can do a great deal of satisfactory work with consumer-grade video cameras and recording equipment if you understand the limitations of the technology.

12

Video Tips

Listed below are some tips for shooting video for your multimedia project.

Shooting Platform

Never underestimate the value of a steady shooting platform. A classic symbol of amateur home movies is shaky camera work. Using a tripod or even placing the camera on a stable platform, such as a rolled-up sweater on the hood of a car, can improve a shot. With a little care, and careful adjustment of the lockdown screws, a sturdy conventional tripod can do wonders. If you must shoot handheld, try to use a camera with an electronic image stabilization feature for static shots, a "steady-cam" balancing attachment, or use camera moves and a moving subject to mask your lack of steadiness.

Lighting

Perhaps the greatest difference between professional camcorders and consumer camcorders is their ability to perform at low light levels. With proper lighting, however, it may be difficult for uninitiated viewers to differentiate between shots taken with an expensive Betacam SP camcorder and a Hi-8 camcorder. Using a simple floodlight kit, or even just being sure that daylight illuminates the room, can improve your image. Onboard battery lights for camcorders can be useful, but only in conditions where the light acts as a "fill light" to illuminate the details of a subject's face. As in photography, good lighting techniques separate amateurs from professionals in video shoots.

Illustrated in Figure 12-4 is a screen from The Lighting Lab. The standard lighting arrangement of a studio is displayed with fill, key, rim, and background lights. Changing any of these lights can make a dramatic difference in the shot. This Macromedia Director project uses a QuickTime movie containing several hundred single-frame images of the model as she is lighted by every permutation of lamp and intensity; clicking a light switch instantly shows the effect of that combination. If you are not convinced that lighting is critical to the success of a photo or video shoot, it will become immediately clear with this exercise!

Chroma Key or Blue Screen

A useful tool easily implemented in most digital video editing applications is "blue screen," "Ultimatte," or "chroma key" editing. When Captain Picard

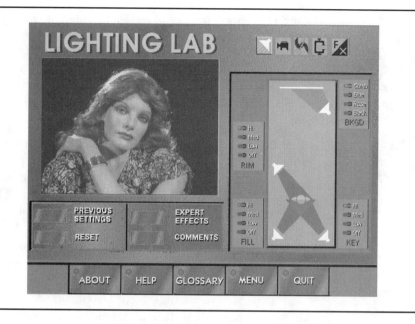

of *Star Trek* fame walks on the surface of the moon, it is likely that he is actually walking on a studio set in front of a screen or wall painted blue. Actually placing Picard on the moon was, no doubt, beyond the budget of the shoot, but it could be faked using blue screen techniques. After shooting the video of Picard's walk against a blue background and shooting another video consisting of the desired background moonscape, the two videos were mixed together: wherever there was blue in the Picard shot, it was replaced by the background image, frame by frame.

Blue screen is a popular technique for making multimedia titles because expensive sets are not required. Incredible backgrounds can be generated using 3-D modeling and graphic software, and one or more actors, vehicles, or other objects can be neatly layered onto that background. Applications such as VideoShop, Premiere, Final Cut Pro, and iMovie provide this capability.

When you are shooting blue screen, be sure that the lighting of the screen is absolutely even; fluctuations in intensity will make this "key" appear choppy or broken. Shooting in daylight, letting the sun illuminate the screen, will mitigate this problem. Also be careful about "color spill." If your actors stand too close to the screen, the colored light reflecting off the screen will spill onto them, and parts of their body will key out. While adjustments in most applications can compensate for this, the adjustments are limited. Beware of fine detail, such as hair or smoke, that wisps over the screen; this does not key well.

12

Figure 12-5 shows frames taken from a video of an actor shot against blue screen on a commercial stage. The blue background was removed from each frame, and the actor himself was turned into a photo-realistic animation that walked, jumped, pointed, and ran from a dinosaur.

Composition

The general rules for shooting quality video for broadcast use apply to multimedia.

Shooting video for playback from CD-ROM or the Web in a small computer window, it is best to avoid wide panoramic shots. The effect of sweeping panoramas is lost in small windows. Use close-ups and medium shots, head-and-shoulders or even tighter. Depending upon the compression algorithm used (see the section on video compression later in the chapter), consider also the amount of motion in the shot: the more a scene changes from frame to frame, the more "delta" information needs to be transferred from the computer's memory to the screen, and the slower the playback speed will be. Keep the camera still instead of panning and zooming; let the subject add the motion to your shot, walking, turning, talking.

FIGURE 12-5

This walking, jumping, and pointing actor was videotaped against a blue screen

Taking Care of Your Tapes

---

warning   *Your original videotapes are irreplaceable, so always make a backup copy of these tapes before you begin editing—tapes can break, be erased, or be eaten up by machinery.*

- Always fast-forward new tapes to the end and then rewind them, a technique known as *packing*, to make sure that tape tension is even from beginning to end. Unequal tape tension can cause timing and editing problems.

- Black-stripe your analog tape by running it through the recorder once with the lens cap on and without audio input. Only black and a uniform control track is recorded. Later, during editing, blank spots in your video program will be a quiet black instead of snowy noise.

- Before you begin editing, always remove the break-off tab on the back of your original video cassettes, to avoid accidental erasure or overwriting.

- Editing videotape requires a lot of shuttling backward and forward, and this can deform the tape. For best results, do not reuse 8 mm video cassettes.

Recording Formats

S-VHS Video

In S-VHS video, color and luminance information are kept on two separate tracks. The result is a definite improvement in picture quality. This standard is also used in Hi-8. Although basically oriented toward consumers, this format is gaining rapid acceptance among lower-end broadcasters. Still, if your ultimate goal is to have your project accepted by broadcast stations, this would not be the best choice.

Component (YUV)

In the early 1980s, Sony began to experiment with a new portable professional video format based on Betamax. Called Betacam, it required speeding the tape up considerably (a 2-hour tape was used up in 20 minutes) and laying the signal on the tape in three channels, one for red, one for blue, and one for luminance information. The resulting format (called "component") produced images that had none of the problems of traditional composite video such as color shift and bleed and crawling edges on graphics. This has evolved into Betacam SP, which features four channels of audio and is superior to 1-inch and even the D-2 digital format in some cases. Though Panasonic has developed their own standard based on a similar technology, called "MII," Betacam SP has become the industry standard for professional video field recording. This format may soon be eclipsed by a new digital version called "Digital Betacam." Featuring four channels of CD-quality audio, its video quality is almost equal to D-1 digital.

Betacam SP is without a doubt *the* choice for the broadcast industry. No format is so widely used and praised. Looking at a typical jerky, one-quarter screen QuickTime movie in a multimedia title, you may think shooting on Betacam SP would be overkill. But you should start thinking to the next wave, when full screen/full motion becomes a reality and the difference between S-VHS or Hi-8 and Betacam becomes apparent.

Component Digital

Around the same time Sony was developing Betacam, they also began research into digital video, where the signal was converted to digital information before it was recorded as bits and bytes. The advantages were many, including better color and image resolution and an ability to make almost unlimited copies without loss of quality. The result of this research was D-1, or "Component Digital." Using a 19 mm (3/4-inch) tape, and recording the signal in a digital version of the component technology developed for Betacam, it quickly proved itself as the format of choice for graphics. Although it is the oldest of digital video formats, D-1 is the standard by which all others are compared. It has most recently spawned DCT (from Ampex), D-5 (from Panasonic), and Digital Betacam (from Sony).

D-1 is at the pinnacle of NTSC video and is the mastering standard of choice among high-end editing facilities. However, this quality comes with an extremely high price tag. (A Quantel Henry editing system costs over $900,000 and can only work with 15 minutes of video.) The result is that this format really only fits super-high-end broadcast projects and not your standard multimedia title.

Composite Digital

Although D-1 was a vastly superior recording format, its steep price scared away broadcasters: recording decks, for example, cost $110,000 or more. To reduce hardware costs, other less expensive formats were developed to record an NTSC composite signal in digital form: D-2 and D-3 (from Panasonic).

Though surpassed in quality by D-1, composite digital may be the most common digital standard for broadcast and editing facilities. Again, this format is more expensive to work with than is justified for multimedia.

Video Hardware Resolutions

Video horizontal resolution is the number of lines of detail a camera is able to reproduce; this aspect is not to be confused with the vertical scan lines on a TV set. The lens used and the number, size, and quality of the CCDs determine this resolution. Poor resolution and image quality when using consumer-grade equipment is usually the result of an inferior lens, cheaper circuit design, and shoddy video record heads.

The following table provides typical resolutions offered by various video recording hardware systems:

Video Type	Resolution
8 mm	230
VHS	240
3/4-SP	330
S-VHS	400
Hi-8	400
Digital	500+
Beta-SP	550
MII	550
Broadcast quality	1000

Consumer-Grade Equipment

Consumer-grade video equipment is designed for mass production and low manufacturing cost. In general, it is easier to use than industrial-grade or broadcast-quality equipment but is not built to suffer wear and tear. The tape transport mechanisms are both fragile and imprecise. VCRs that incorporate special circuits to enhance sharpness provide a superior perceived picture image than do regular VCRs (some less expensive VCRs do not have these circuits). Both Beta- and VHS-type recorders are available with high-fidelity (hi-fi) sound with a dynamic range of up to 90 dB. In analog systems, hi-fi sound is recorded diagonally on the tape between the video scans (but lower on the tape), so video and audio are recorded at the same time.

The High-Band 8 mm (known as Hi-8) and Super VHS (known as S-VHS) formats split the composite video signal into other components to provide a higher-quality signal. Two additional channels are added, one containing luminance or brightness information (Y channel), and one containing chroma or color intensity information (C channel). Cameras and camcorders working in the Hi-8 and S-VHS formats use a four-pin DIN or S connector and produce pictures that are far superior to those of regular VHS and 8 mm systems, especially when viewed on a television or monitor designed for these formats.

Most S-VHS and 3/4-inch industrial equipment have built-in noise reduction circuitry to overcome the poor audio quality inherent in consumer-grade VHS decks. The regular 8 mm tape decks, however, employ a recording method similar to that used for digital audio tape (DAT). Audio is digitized and recorded on a track separate from the video signal, providing a dynamic range of about 88 dB.

Making Tape Copies

When using analog equipment, if you ever plan to copy the tape you make during a production shoot to another tape (say, for a promotion or demo), use at least Super VHS. This will prevent your copies from bleeding colors and being disappointingly fuzzy due to signal loss. Better yet, use Hi-8, which will allow unlimited VHS copies to be made without degradation. If you plan to do video editing on tape (not on the computer), Hi-8 is the consumer-grade option of choice.

Successful copying of video (dubbing) depends upon the format of the tape recording and the quality of equipment used. Copying from Hi-8 to VHS, for example, produces excellent results. Copying from Beta-SP to Super VHS gets good results as long as the Y/C connections are maintained. Dubbing from 1-inch tape to other formats works well, copy after copy. Digital systems do not suffer such dramatic *generation loss* of quality.

When copying from VHS to VHS, color smear and loss of image resolution are very noticeable. The bandwidth of the VHS signal is limited, and during dubbing much information is lost—even in a first generation dub from a Beta-SP edited master to a VHS submaster. A second generation dub (from a VHS master to a first copy) is proportionately worse. Yet another copy of the copy (a third generation) produces a tape that is practically unrecognizable.

Always dub in SP mode, never in LP or SLP, because the faster the video heads write on the tape, the better the recorded image will be. Always use the highest-quality tape to prevent clogging the video heads with loose magnetic particles.

Video Window Size

When you digitize a video image and shrink it to, say, half- or quarter-size, you will notice improvement in the perceived sharpness. This also happens when you switch from watching television on a 19-inch screen to watching a 12-inch screen. The image becomes crisper because the scan lines are physically much tighter. So VHS will work fine in these circumstances. Super VHS and Hi-8 will provide better full-screen images, but your digitizing video board must be able to utilize this resolution; in digitizing the video signal, the board dithers the image on the fly.

Editing with Consumer VCRs

Using two consumer-grade VCRs for editing will cause glitches, picture noise, and rolling, because the VCRs will not be in sync. You may also experience considerable loss in quality when dubbing, and possibly an audio lag. With consumer-grade decks, it is impossible to accurately preroll a tape prior to editing a scene.

To solve this problem, you have to use the tape counter on both the playback deck and the record deck, to reverse both tapes a given distance and then start them playing at exactly the same time. When they are both at speed and have reached the appropriate counter number for your edit, depress the Record button on the recording machine (or release it from Pause mode). If your edit comes in too late, you will have to reverse both machines and try again; if you cut into the scene too soon, you will have to repeat the entire edit of the previous shot and then try again. This can be tedious and time consuming—even if your decks have flying erase heads to avoid edit glitches—and the results may be disappointing.

12

To make fancy transitions, cross-fades, and wipes between scenes, you need two source players feeding into a switcher, all of which are in sync. This is called A/B roll editing. For this you need a time base corrector (TBC) for each VCR. This device corrects timing errors present in all VCRs and replaces the sync with one generated by the TBC.

Two terms are often heard at editing facilities: offline editing and online editing. In offline editing, you spend most of your time making a rough cut—a quick assemblage of everything you decide to use. Then you make an edit decision list (EDL) of all the scenes on your rough cut, the name of the original cassette where the scene is located, and the times of your edit in-points and out-points, using time codes. You take this list and your original footage to an online post-production facility that has expensive equipment to auto assemble your tape according to the EDL, inserting transitions, wipes, graphics, titles, audio, and music segments as required. The result is an edited master.

Editing with two VCRs is less common today in multimedia production than editing with digital editing software designed specifically for use on Macintoshes and PCs, such as Premiere, After Effects, Media 100, or Final Cut. In either case, an edit decision list is useful.

Digital Video

Full integration of motion video on computers eliminates the analog television form of video from the multimedia delivery platform. If a video clip is stored as data on a hard disk, CD-ROM, or other mass-storage device, that clip can be played back on the computer's monitor without overlay boards, videodisc players, or second monitors. This playback of digital video is accomplished using software architectures such as QuickTime or AVI, which are explained in Chapter 5. As a multimedia producer or developer, you may need to convert video source material from its still common analog form (videotape) to a digital form manageable by the end user's computer system. So an understanding of analog video and some special hardware must remain in your multimedia toolbox.

Analog to digital conversion of video can be accomplished using the video overlay hardware described above, or it can be delivered direct to disk using FireWire cables. To repetitively digitize a full-screen color video image every

1/30 second and store it to disk or RAM severely taxes both Macintosh and PC processing capabilities—special hardware, compression firmware, and massive amounts of digital storage space are required.

Video Compression

To digitize and store a 10-second clip of full-motion video in your computer requires transfer of an enormous amount of data in a very short amount of time. Reproducing just one frame of digital video component video at 24 bits requires almost 1MB of computer data; 30 seconds of video will fill a gigabyte hard disk. Full-size, full-motion video requires that the computer deliver data at about 30MB per second. This overwhelming technological bottleneck is overcome using digital video compression schemes or *codecs* (coders/decoders). A codec is the algorithm used to compress a video for delivery and then decode it in real-time for fast playback. Real-time video compression algorithms such as MPEG, P*64, DVI/Indeo, JPEG, Cinepak, Sorenson, ClearVideo, RealVideo, and VDOwave are available to compress digital video information at rates that range from 50:1 to 200:1. JPEG, MPEG, and P*64 compression schemes use Discrete Cosine Transform (DCT), an encoding algorithm that quantifies the human eye's ability to detect color and image distortion. All of these codecs employ lossy compression algorithms.

•••

http://www.icanstream.tv/CodecCentral/index.html

Where detailed information about video codecs can be found

In addition to compressing video data, *streaming* technologies are being implemented to provide reasonable quality low-bandwidth video on the Web. By starting playback of a video as soon as enough data has transferred to the user's computer to sustain this playback, users do not have to wait for an often very large file to download. Microsoft, RealNetworks, VXtreme, VDOnet, Xing, Precept, Cubic, Motorola, Vivo, Vosaic, and Oracle are actively pursuing the commercialization of streaming technology on the Web.

QuickTime, Apple's software-based architecture for seamlessly integrating sound, animation, text, and video (data that changes over time), is often thought of as a compression standard, but it is really much more than that. See Chapter 5 for a detailed discussion about QuickTime.

12

MPEG

The MPEG standard has been developed by the Moving Picture Experts Group (http://www.cselt.it/mpeg/), a working group convened by the International Standards Organization (ISO) and the International Electro-technical Commission (IEC) to create standards for digital representation of moving pictures and associated audio and other data. MPEG1 and MPEG2 are the current standards. Using MPEG1, you can deliver 1.2 Mbps (megabits per second) of video and 250 Kbps (kilobits per second) of two-channel stereo audio using CD-ROM technology. MPEG2, a completely different system from MPEG1, requires higher data rates (3 to 15 Mbps) but delivers higher image resolution, picture quality, interlaced video formats, multiresolution scalability, and multichannel audio features.

MPEG may become the method of choice for encoding motion images because it has become widely accepted for both Internet and DVD-Video (see Chapters 5 and 14). For MPEG1, hardware playback will become common on motherboards and video cards. Software decompression algorithms for MPEG1, while slower than hardware solutions, are incorporated in QuickTime, and Microsoft has licensed a driver from MediaMatics for use with Windows. MPEG2 requires dedicated hardware for playback but looks better than a television screen. Players are widely available for playback of MPEG video on the Web.

MPEG-4 is in development and will provide a new content-based method for assimilating multimedia elements. It will also offer not only indexing, hyperlinking, querying, browsing, uploading, downloading, and deleting functions but also "hybrid natural and synthetic data coding," which will enable harmonious integration of natural and synthetic audiovisual objects. With MPEG-4, multiple views, layers, and multiple soundtracks of a scene, as well as stereoscopic and 3-D views, will be available, making virtual reality workable. MPEG-4 can adjust to varied download speeds, and will become the favored scheme for delivery of video on the Web.

MPEG-7, on the standards horizon, goes a step further by integrating information about the image, sound, or motion video elements being used in a composition—information carried already in the MPEG-4 standard—with *how* these elements are being used. MPEG-7, for example, may include classes for facial expressions, personality characteristics, or any number of content-related variables.

http://www.mpeg.org

All about MPEG

MPEG-4 video aims at providing standardized core technologies allowing efficient storage, transmission, and manipulation of video data in multimedia environments. This is a challenging task given the broad spectrum of requirements and applications in multimedia. In order to achieve this broad goal rather than a solution for a narrow set of applications, functionalities common to clusters of applications are under the scope of consideration. Therefore, video activities in MPEG-4 aim at providing solutions in the form of tools and algorithms enabling functionalities such as efficient compression, object scalability, spatial and temporal scalability, error resilience. The standardized MPEG-4 video will provide a toolbox containing tools and algorithms bringing solutions to the above mentioned functionalities and more.

From Document ISO/IEC JTC1/SC29/WG11 N1410 (Description of MPEG-4)

DVI/Indeo

DVI (also known as "Indeo") is a proprietary, programmable compression/decompression technology based on the Intel i750 chip set. This hardware consists of two VLSI (Very Large Scale Integrated) chips to separate the image processing and display functions.

Two levels of compression and decompression are provided by DVI: Production Level Video (PLV) and Real Time Video (RTV). PLV is a proprietary asymmetrical compression technique for encoding full-motion color video; it requires that compression be performed by Intel at its facilities or at licensed encoding facilities set up by Intel. RTV provides image quality comparable to frame-rate (motion) JPEG and uses a symmetrical, variable-rate compression. PLV and RTV both use variable compression rates.

DVI's algorithms can compress video images at ratios between 80:1 and 160:1. DVI will play back video in full-frame size and in full color at 30 frames per second, whereas JPEG provides only an acceptable image in a small picture window on the computer screen. When tied in with a mainframe computer, DVI playback approaches the quality of broadcast video.

Other Compression Methods

P*64 (pronounced "pee star sixty-four") is a video telephone conferencing standard for compressing audio and motion video images, from the International Telegraph and Telephone Consultative Committee (CCITT). P*64 complies with CCITT's recommendation H.261 and incorporates multiplexing, demultiplexing, framing of data, transmission protocol and bandwidth congruence, and call setup and teardown. Encoder products from telephone service providers such as AT&T and Northern Telecom use

12

P*64 to deliver wide-spectrum telecommunication capabilities incorporating high-speed and very high throughput data transmission over both copper and fiber-optic digital telephone networks.

P*64 encodes real-time motion video and audio for transmission over copper or fiber-optic telephone lines at 30 frames per second, at a bandwidth between 40 Kbps and 4 Mbps.

Other compression systems are being developed by companies including Kodak, Sony, Storm Technology, Iterated Systems, Zing, and C-Cube Micro-systems, and rapid progress is being made in this field.

Optimizing Video Files for CD-ROM

CD-ROMs provide an excellent distribution medium for computer-based video: they are inexpensive to mass produce, and they can store great quantities of information. CD-ROM players offer slow data transfer rates (see Chapter 19), but adequate video transfer can be achieved by taking care to properly prepare your digital video files. QuickTime and AVI video file formats are discussed in Chapter 5, and the multimedia authoring systems for integrating these digital video files into your project are discussed in Chapter 7. Without great care, these digital files may display poorly in low-bandwidth/high-compression environments.

- Limit the amount of synchronization required between the video and audio. With Microsoft's AVI files, the audio and video data are already interleaved, so this is not a necessity, but with QuickTime files, you should "flatten" your movie. *Flattening* means you interleave the audio and video segments together.

- Use regularly spaced key frames, 10 to 15 frames apart, and temporal compression can correct for seek time delays. *Seek time* is how long it takes the CD-ROM player to locate specific data on the CD-ROM disc. Even fast 56x drives must spin up, causing some delay (and occasionally substantial noise).

- The size of the video window and the frame rate you specify dramatically affect performance. In QuickTime, 20 frames per second played in a 160×120-pixel window is equivalent to playing 10 frames per second in a 320×240 window. The more data that has to be decompressed and transferred from the CD-ROM to the screen, the slower the playback.

- Although interleaving CD-quality audio into your video production will theoretically yield the highest-quality sound, the volume of data required may be too great to transfer from the CD-ROM in real-time. Try a lower sampling rate and sample size to reduce the quantity of audio data.

- The software compression algorithm you specify will make a dramatic difference in performance. The Cinepack algorithm, available within both AVI and QuickTime, is optimized for CD-ROM playback. But take care: it can take many hours of computation to compress just a few minutes of digital video.

- Use Norton Speed Disk from Symantec to defragment your files before burning the master.

- If you are working with QuickTime, consider using a specialized application such as Media Cleaner Pro to automatically optimize your digital video file for playback from CD-ROM.

12

During the coming years, most multimedia experiences on the Internet will occur on the World Wide Web.

Predictions claim that more than 35 million

experience

media

4

Multimedia and
the Internet

American households will be connected to the Internet by the year 2000.

network

Multi

Inside the event horizon of the amazing World Wide Web explosion are many uncertainties and unsolved challenges.

Predictions claim that more than 35 million

connections

media

chapter

13

The Internet and How It Works

American households will be connected to the Internet by the year 2000.

network

T H E material covered in this chapter is designed to give you an overview of the Internet while describing particular features that may be useful to you as a developer of multimedia for the World Wide Web. This chapter does *not* provide details about technology for connecting and using the Internet, about setting up servers and hosts, about installing and using applications, or what to do when you are warned of the following:

 This program posts news to thousands of machines throughout the civilized world. Please be sure you know what you are doing.

Embarrassing yourself on the stage of the civilized world can be avoided by easy education. Visit your local bookstore, where, along with the work you are now reading, you may discover as many as a hundred helpful volumes about all the simple and arcane aspects of the Internet. Buy one or two of these and dig in.

If you are already connected to the Internet, much of the documentation you may require can be found by surfing the Net itself. Use a search service such as those listed below. Look particularly for documents called FAQs (Frequently Asked Questions), because they contain answers.

http://www.yahoo.com
http://www.altavista.digital.com
http://www.excite.com
http://www.go.com
http://www.google.com
http://www.hotbot.com
http://www.lycos.com
http://www.mckinley.com
http://www.webcrawler.com

Some search engines on the World Wide Web

History

The Internet began as a research network funded by the Advanced Research Projects Agency (ARPA) of the U.S. Defense Department, when the first node of the ARPANET was installed at the University of California at Los Angeles in September 1969.

By the mid-1970s, the ARPANET "internetwork" embraced more than 30 universities, military sites, and government contractors, and its user base expanded to include the larger computer science research community. By 1983, the network still consisted of but several hundred computers on only a few local area networks.

In 1985, the National Science Foundation (NSF) arranged with ARPA to support a collaboration of supercomputing centers and computer science researchers across the ARPANET. The NSF also funded a program for improving the backbone of the ARPANET, increasing its bandwidth from 56 Kbps to T-1 and then T-3 (see "Connections" a little later in the chapter) and branching out with links to international sites in Europe and the Far East.

In 1989, responsibility and management for the ARPANET was officially passed from military interests to the academically oriented NSF, and research organizations and universities (professors and students alike) became increasingly heavy users of this ever-growing "Internet." Much of the Internet's etiquette and rules for behavior (such as for sending e-mail and posting to newsgroups) was established during this time.

More and more private companies and organizations linked up to the Internet; by the mid-1990s, the Internet included connections to more than 60 countries and more than 2 million host computers with more than 15 million users worldwide. Commercial and business use of the Internet was not permitted until 1992, but businesses have since become its driving force. By

First Person

When I was a kid, I took it for granted that you could see a million stars in the summer sky, and it wasn't until much later that I discovered the truth: only a paltry few thousand stars are actually visible to the naked eye from Earth. While "millions" is a perfect number for a ten-year-old's perception of an infinite universe, the term needs definition. For example, what does "133 million users on the Internet in the year 2000" really mean? The following exercise might help: Start counting to a million, incrementing by one every second: (One) (Two) (Three)... In a minute, you will have counted to 60; in an hour, to 3,600. In 277.77 hours, you will reach a million—that's 11.57 24-hour days of nonstop counting, no pizza, no beer. You could try for the Guinness Book of Records, but you won't stay awake long enough!

13

2001 there were 109,574,429 domain hosts and 407.1 million users of the Internet, representing 6.71 percent of the world's population. And there were 550 billion documents online, and about 7.3 million documents and Web pages were being added every day. Only 1 billion of these documents had been indexed by the search engines.

nternetworking

In its simplest form, a *network* is a cluster of computers, with one computer acting as a server to provide network services such as file transfer, e-mail, and document printing to the client computers of that network. Using gateways and routers, a local area network (LAN) can be connected to other LANs to form a wide area network (WAN). These LANs and WANs can also be connected to the Internet through a server that provides both the necessary software for the Internet and the physical data connection (usually a high-bandwidth telephone line). Individual computers not permanently part of a network (a home computer or a laptop) can dial up to one of these Internet servers and, with proper identification and onboard client software, obtain an IP address on the Internet (see "IP Addresses and Data Packets" later in the chapter).

Internet Addresses

Let's say you get into a taxi at the train station in Trento, Italy, explain in English or Spanish or German or French that you wish to go to the Mozzi Hotel, and half an hour later you are let out of the car in a suburban wood—you have an address problem. You will quickly discover, as you return to the city in the back of a bricklayer's lorry to report your missing luggage, that you also have a serious language problem.

If you know how addresses work and understand the syntax of the Internet, you will likely not get lost and will save much time and expense during your adventures. You will also be able to employ shortcuts and work-arounds.

Top-Level Domains

When the original ARPANET protocols for communicating among computers were remade into the current scheme of TCP/IP (Transmission Control Protocol/Internet Protocol) in 1983, the Domain Name System (DNS) was developed to rationally assign names and addresses to computers linked to the Internet. *Top-level domains* (TLDs) were established as categories to accommodate all users of the Internet:

com	Commercial entities
edu	Four-year degree-granting colleges and universities (schools and two-year colleges register in the country domain)
gov	U.S. federal government agencies (state and local agencies register in the country domain)
int	Organizations established by international treaties and international databases
mil	U.S. military
net	Computers belonging to network providers
org	Miscellaneous and nongovernment organizations
Two-letter country codes	Per the ISO 3166 List of Countries

In late 1998, the Internet Corporation for Assigned Names and Numbers (ICANN) was set up to oversee the technical coordination of the Domain Name System, which allows Internet addresses to be found by easy-to-remember names instead of one of 4.3 billion individual IP numbers. In late 2000, ICANN approved seven additional TLDs:

aero	Air-transport industry
biz	Businesses
coop	Cooperatives
info	Unrestricted use
museum	Museums
name	For registration by individuals
pro	Accountants, lawyers, and physicians

Other TLD names are under discussion and may be added in the future:

web	Entities emphasizing activities related to the Web
arts	Entities emphasizing cultural and entertainment activities
shop	Entities and businesses offering goods to purchase
firm	Online companies and businesses
nom	Personal sites
rec	Entities emphasizing recreation/entertainment activities

13

Companies such as Microsoft, Apple, and IBM have *second-level domain* addresses that read microsoft.com, apple.com, and ibm.com—they are commercial (com) operations. Government (gov) agencies such as the Federal Bureau of Investigation, the Internal Revenue Service (a branch of the U.S. Treasury Department), and the White House have addresses that read fbi.gov, irs.ustreas.gov (a *third-level* address), and whitehouse.gov.

Concerns about "rights" and "ownership" of domains are inappropriate. It is appropriate to be concerned about "responsibilities" and "service" to the community.

J. Postel, from the Network Working Group RFC 1591, March 1994

Many second-level domains contain huge numbers of computers and user accounts representing local, regional, and even international branches as well as various internal business and management functions. So the Internet addressing scheme provides for subdomains that can contain more subdomains. Like a finely carved Russian matryoshka doll, at the epicenter of a cluster of domains live individual workstations.

edu   yale   cis   minerva   ewing

Within the education (edu) domain containing hundreds of universities and colleges, for example, is a second-level domain for Yale University called yale. At that university are many schools and departments (medicine, engineering, law, business, computer science, etc.), and each of these entities in turn has departments and possibly subdepartments and many users. These departments operate one or even several servers to manage traffic to and from the many computers in their group and to the outside world. At Yale, the server for the Computing and Information Systems Department is named cis. It manages about 11,000 departmental accounts—so many accounts that a cluster of subsidiary servers was installed to efficiently deal with the demand. These subsidiary servers are named minerva, morpheus, and mercury. Thus, minerva lives in the cis domain, which lives in the yale domain, which lives in the edu domain. Real people's computers are networked to minerva. Other real people are connected to the morpheus and mercury servers. The computer belonging to the Director of the Science and Engineering Computing Facility, Martin Ewing, is named **martin.ewing@minerva.cis.yale.edu**. To make things easy (exactly what computers are for), the mail system database at Yale maintains a master list of all its people. So as far as the outside world is concerned, the director's e-mail address can be simply **martin.ewing@yale.edu**; the database knows he is really connected to minerva. In e-mail headers, you may see the complete destination address listed as well as names of computers through which your mail may have been routed.

The levels of a domain name are separated by a period (spoken as "dot"); individual computers belonging to people are said to be "at" a domain (written with the @ sign). There are never any blank spaces in an Internet address, and while addresses on the Internet are normally case insensitive, conventional use dictates using all lowercase: the Internet will find **tay@timestream.com**, **TAY@TIMESTREAM.COM**, and **Tay@Timestream.Com** to be at the same address.

The US Domain and Country Codes

The two-letter US domain is based on political boundaries and is used by federal, state, and local government agencies, community colleges, high schools, technical/vocational schools, private schools, elementary schools, libraries, fire and police departments, and regular citizens. Any computer in the United States can be in the US domain. Some fictitious examples might be

statue_liberty.nps.interior.fed.us	Federal agency
senate.fed.us	U.S. Senate
senate.state.pa.us	Pennsylvania state senate
assembly.state.ut.us	Utah state assembly
dmv.state.ca.us	California Department of Motor Vehicles

13

oakland.dmv.state.ca.us	Local office of DMV
police.ci.miami.fl.us	City department
fire.ci.weston.ma.us	City department
sheriff.co.alameda.ca.us	County department
ccsf.cc.ca.us	Public community college
lincoln-high.eh-parish.k12.la.us	Public school
appleton.lib.me.us	Public library
gda.pvt.k12.ma.us	Private school
chevron.richmond.ca.us	Business
lefigaro.portland.or.us	Restaurant
paddys.boston.ma.us	Bar

ftp://rs.internic.net/rfc/rfc1480.txt

The Internet RFC 1480 describes the hierarchical rules for addresses in the US domain

Two-letter country codes, based on the International Standards Organization (ISO) document ISO-3166, are used in the addresses of all computers located outside the United States. Each country has an administrator who is responsible for organizing the naming hierarchy within that country's domain. Some countries use categories similar to com, edu, and org. Others base their naming hierarchies on political boundaries, as in the US country code.

schmidt@cage.rug.ac.be	Professor at University of Gent, Belgium
smythe@fiqus.unl.edu.ar	Student at L.C.S.A, Argentina
smith@iskratel.si	Commercial account, Slovenia
smith@laughs.co.uk	Commercial account, United Kingdom
smithe@idsc.gov.eg	Student at Cairo University, Egypt
smithy@udcf.gla.ac.uk	Researcher at University of Glasgow, Scotland
tsmith@library.usyd.edu.au	Scholar at University of Sydney, Australia

http://www.iana.org/cctld/cctld-whois.htm

List of two-letter country codes

IP Addresses and Data Packets

When a stream of data is sent over the Internet by your computer, it is first broken down into packets by the Transmission Control Protocol. Each packet includes the address of the receiving computer, a sequence number ("this is packet #5"), error correction information, and a small piece of your data. After a packet is created by TCP, the Internet Protocol then takes over and sends the packet to its destination along a route that may include many other computers acting as forwarders. TCP/IP is two key Internet protocols working in concert.

The 32-bit address included in a data packet, the *IP address*, is the "real" Internet address. It is made up of four numbers separated by periods, for example, 140.174.162.10. Some of these numbers are assigned by Internet authorities, and some may be dynamically assigned by an Internet Service Provider (ISP) when a computer logs on from a dial-up account. There are domain name servers throughout the Internet whose sole job is to quickly look up domain name addresses in large distributed databases, convert them into IP addresses, and return them to you for insertion into your data packets. Every time you connect to **http://netscape.com** or send mail to **president@whitehouse.gov**, the domain name server is consulted and the destination address is converted to numbers.

---

tip *IP addresses and domain names can be used interchangeably. Thus, http://luwak.midcoast.com is the same Internet address as **206.26.226.27**. There are occasional problems with the Internet's DNS servers, and with the IP address, you may get connected immediately. With a Ping utility, or using the "whois" function in Unix, you can discover a domain's IP address.*

Connections

If your computer is connected to an existing network at an office or school, it is possible you are already connected to the Internet. Check with your system administrator about procedures for connecting to Internet services such as the World Wide Web; necessary browser software may already be installed on your machine. If you are an individual working from home, you will need a dial-up account to your office network or to an Internet Service Provider or an online service. You will also need a modem (see Chapter 4), an available telephone line, and software.

13

If you are connecting to the Internet through an online service such as America Online (AOL), Microsoft Network (MSN), or Prodigy (see Figure 13-1), you will need special software provided by that service. AOL provides Web, FTP, and Gopher features (see "Internet Services" later in the chapter). MSN software is built into Windows and can be installed during Windows setup.

http://www.aol.com
http://www.msn.com
http://www.prodigy.com
http://www.mediaone.com

Information about online services

For connecting to the Internet through an ISP, software typically consists of the PPP (Point-to-Point Protocol) application for dialing up and TCP/IP software for properly sending and receiving data once you are connected. ISPs usually provide one or more POPs (Points of Presence), which is a local telephone number for connecting to the ISP's server. Figure 13-1 shows the PPP control panel for Macintosh and the Network Control Panel for Windows. Getting connected to the Internet can be a bit daunting, as there are many options to configure. Most ISPs offer detailed instructions and kits to make this job easy.

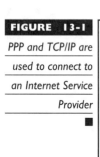

FIGURE   13-1

PPP and TCP/IP are used to connect to an Internet Service Provider

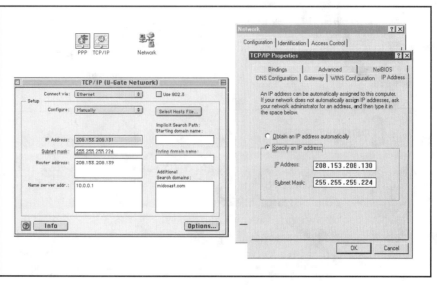

The Bandwidth Bottleneck

Bandwidth is how much data, expressed in bits per second (bps), you can send from one computer to another in a given amount of time. The faster your transmissions (or the greater the bandwidth of your connection), the less time you will spend waiting for text, images, sounds, and animated illustrations to upload or download from computer to computer, and the more satisfaction you will have with your Internet experience. To think in bytes per second, divide the rate by eight. Table 13-1 lists the bandwidth of some common data transfer methods.

Name	Bandwidth (in bits per second) Without Compression	Comment
28.8K Modem	28,800	Maximum analog modem speed for copper wires, data uncompressed.
56K Modem	56,000	Maximum analog modem speed for copper wires, data compressed using V91 standard.
ISDN	56,000 to 128,000	Integrated Services Digital Network basic services (128,000 bps if no voice mixed in).
Frame Relay	56,000 to 45,000,000	Dedicated service offered by long-distance phone companies.
CableModem	300,000 upload; 1,500,000 download	Even though copper coaxial TV cable can be used in a bidirectional fashion, it was originally designed to carry limited signals in one direction.
LocalTalk	230,400	Apple networking hardware and protocol, outdated.
Ethernet-10	10,000,000	Networking hardware and protocol, commonly uses two twisted pairs of copper wire.
T-1	1,544,000	Equal to 24 leased lines at 56 Kbps.
E-1	2,000,000	European equivalent of a T-1 connection.
DSL	1,500,000 to 9,000,000	Digital Subscriber Line service available in various technologies (HDSL, SDSL, ADSL, VDSL, and RDSL) with differing data rates, operating distances, and ratios between downstream and upstream speeds.

TABLE 13-1   *Bandwidth of Typical Internet Connections* ■

Name	Bandwidth (in bits per second) Without Compression	Comment
T-3	45,000,000	Typical backbone speed of major Internet Service Providers in the United States (1996).
Fast SCSI III	80,000,000	Data transfer rate for Fast SCSI III or Ultra SCSI.
Fast Ethernet-100	100,000,000	Networking hardware and protocol, commonly uses two twisted pairs of copper wire.
OC-3	155,000,000	Upgrade for Internet Service Providers in the United States (1997).
OC-48	2,400,000,000 (2.4 gigabits per second)	Typical speed for intercity fiber-optic lines (called SONET or Synchronous Optical Network).
ATM	In steps, from 45,000,000 to 145,000,000 to 2,400,000,000	Asynchronous Transfer Mode—protocol for sending and receiving voice and other data (53-byte cells, each with 5-byte headers and 48-byte content; cell headers waste about 10 percent of available bandwidth). The cell size was a compromise between U.S. and European members of the standards committee, one group wanting 48, the other group, more. The 53-byte compromise was based on the size needed for video without too much packet delay.

TABLE 13-1   *Bandwidth of Typical Internet Connections* (continued) ■

The bottleneck at a typical user's low-bandwidth modem connection is the most serious impediment to sending multimedia across the Internet. At low bandwidth, a page of text (3,000 bytes) can take less than a second to send, but an uncompressed 640×480, 8-bit/256-color image (about 300,000 bytes) can take a few minutes; an uncompressed 640×480, 24-bit/16 million-color image (about 900,000 bytes) can take many minutes to send.

Find bad Web sites 8× faster. Hit the Veeblefester's home page with an analog modem, and it could be days before you get out. But hit it with BitSURFER Pro ISDN modem, and you'll be out long before the first of their 26 vacation pictures starts to appear.

From an advertising campaign by Motorola

To work within the constraints of this challenging bottleneck (until the bottleneck is cleared by the wide use of inexpensive higher-speed cable modems and wireless connections—see Chapter 4), multimedia developers on the Internet have but a few options:

■ Compress data as tightly as possible (into ZIP or SIT files) before transmitting.

■ Require users to download data only once; then store the data in a local hard disk cache (this is automatically managed by most browsers).

■ Design each multimedia element to be efficiently compact—don't use a greater color depth than is absolutely necessary or leave extra space around the edges.

■ Design alternate low-bandwidth and high-bandwidth navigation paths to accommodate all users.

■ Implement streaming methods that allow data to be transferred and displayed incrementally as it comes in (without waiting for the entire data file to arrive).

FTP.ARL.MIL (Army Research Laboratory) Bandwidth Information

This site is connected to the National Science Foundation Network (NSFNET) backbone at both Fix-East in Washington D.C., and Fix-West in San Francisco by a pair of T-3 (45 Mbit/sec, or 5.6 MB/sec) communications lines. The line to Fix-East is a single hop, while the line to Fix-West passes first through Corps of Engineers (Vicksburg, Mississippi), New Mexico, and San Diego.

Regrettably, the full bandwidth of the T-3 line is not available for FTP and Web transfers, as there is a 10 Mbit/sec Ethernet between the T-3 line and the host FTP.ARL.MIL. So you have to suffer with about 8 Mbit/sec (1 MB/sec) actual speed for now. Moving 1MB of data over the T-3 link takes about 1 second, if your end is up to it.

Naturally, no single file transfer ever gets the full bandwidth of these communications lines, as they are a shared resource. This information should help you make a lower-bound estimate on how much time large file transfers might take.

sys-admin@ftp.arl.mil, May 1996

13

By 2001, this bottleneck had been improved to a full OC-12 ATM fiber-optic connection to the ARL-APG campus ATM backbone, providing 622 Mbit/sec of network bandwidth.

Nearly the full bandwidth of our OC-3 external fiber optic is available for off-site FTP and Web transfers. Any loss of performance is most likely to be due to slowdowns at your end, and/or congestion in the Internet itself.

Moving 1 MByte of data over an OC-3 link takes about 0.1 seconds, if your end is up to it.

Moving 1 MByte of data over a T-3 link takes about 1 second, if your end is up to it.

Moving 1 MByte of data over a T-1 link takes about 8 seconds.

Moving 1 MByte of data over a 56 Kbps link takes about 3 minutes.

Moving 1 MByte of data over a 28.8 Kbps modem takes about 5 minutes.

Naturally, no single file transfer ever gets the full bandwidth of these communications lines, as they are a shared resource. These figures should help you make a lower-bound estimate on how much time large file transfers might take. You are free to transfer large files from this site at any time.

http://ftp.arl.army.mil/bandwidth.html.

Internet Services

To many users, the Internet means the World Wide Web. But the Web is only the latest and most popular of services available today on the Internet. E-mail; file transfer; discussion groups and newsgroups; real-time chatting by text, voice, and video; and the ability to log into remote computers are common as well. Internet services include the following:

Service	Purpose
http	For posting and reading documents (from the Hypertext Transfer Protocol used by the World Wide Web)
https	For posting and reading encrypted documents (secure)
pop	For receiving electronic mail (from Post Office Protocol)
ftp	For transferring files between computers; can be anonymous or password protected (from File Transfer Protocol)
gopher	For menus of material available on the Internet
usenet	For participating in discussion groups (from USErs NETwork)
telnet	For logging on and working from remote computers
irc	For real-time text messaging (from Internet Relay Chat)
smtp	For sending mail (Simple Mail Transport Protocol)
mud	For real-time game playing (from MultiUser Dimension)

Each Internet service is implemented on an Internet server by dedicated software known as a *daemon*. (Actually, daemons only exist on Unix/Linux systems—on other systems, such as Windows NT, the services may run as regular applications or background processes.) Daemons are agent programs that run in the background, waiting to act on requests from the outside. In the case of the Internet, daemons support protocols such as the Hypertext Transfer Protocol (HTTP) for the World Wide Web, the Post Office Protocol (POP) for e-mail, or the File Transfer Protocol (FTP) for exchanging files. You have probably noticed that the first few letters of a URL (Uniform Resource Locator)—for example, **http://www.timestream.com/index.html**—notify a server which daemon to bring into play to satisfy a request. In many cases, the daemon for the Web, mail, news, and FTP may run on completely different servers, each isolated by a security fire wall from other servers on a network.

MIME-Types

To work with multimedia on the Internet, you must work within the requirements of the appropriate protocol, using documents and formats that are recognizable. A voice attachment to an e-mail message, for example, must be identified by the Post Office daemon for what it is, then be transmitted with the correct coding to the receiving computer. The receiver must have the proper software (and hardware) for decoding the information and playing it back. To identify the nature of the data transmitted and, by inference, the purpose of that data, the Internet uses a standard list of file name extensions called MIME-types (for Multipurpose Internet Mail Extensions). Most browsers allow you to define MIME-types and map "helper apps" to the type for decoding and playing. For example, with Netscape Navigator you can define Adobe's Acrobat files (PDF files) as a MIME-type and select the Acrobat Reader as the player application.

These are not just used by the e-mail daemon but, by convention, by other Internet daemons, including the Web's HTTP daemon. Perhaps the most widely installed HTTP software for managing Web pages is the open source application called Apache (http://www.apache.org). Table 13-2 shows a list of common MIME-types and their uses. (Note that many come from the Unix world, where the Internet was born.)

http://www1.sympatico.ca/help/Learn/FAQ/mimetypes.html

More information about MIME-types

Extension	Type	Use
ai	application/postscript	PostScript program
aif	audio/x-aiff	Audio
aifc	audio/x-aiff	Audio
AIFF	audio/x-aiff	Audio
aiff	audio/x-aiff	Audio
au	audio/basic	ULAW audio data
avi	video/x-msvideo	Microsoft video
bin	application/octet-stream	Binary executable
cpio	application/x-cpio	Unix CPIO archive
csh	application/x-csh	C shell program
dcr	application/director	Shockwave animation
dvi	application/x-dvi	TeX DVI data
eps	application/postscript	PostScript program
exe	application/octet-stream	Binary executable
fif	application/fractals	Fractal image format
gif	image/gif	CompuServe image format
gtar	application/x-gtar	GNU tape archive
gz	encoding/x-gzip	GNU zip compressed data
hqx	application/mac-binhex40	Macintosh BinHex archive
htm	text/html	Hypertext Markup Language
html	text/html	Hypertext Markup Language
ief	image/ief	Image
jpe	image/jpeg	JPEG image
jpeg	image/jpeg	JPEG image
jpg	image/jpeg	JPEG image
latex	application/x-latex	LaTeX document
man	application/x-troff-man	Unix manual page
me	application/x-troff-me	TROFF document

TABLE 13-2   *Common MIME-Types Used on the Internet* ■

Extension	Type	Use
mov	video/quicktime	QuickTime video
movie	video/x-sgi-movie	SGI video
mpe	video/mpeg	MPEG video
mpeg	video/mpeg	MPEG video
mpg	video/mpeg	MPEG video
ms	application/x-troff-ms	TROFF document
pbm	image/x-portable-bitmap	PBM image
pgm	image/x-portable-graymap	PGM image
pnm	image/x-portable-anymap	PBM image
ppm	image/x-portable-pixmap	PPM image
ps	application/postscript	PostScript program
qt	video/quicktime	QuickTime video
ra	audio/x-pn-realaudio	RealAudio sound
ram	audio/x-pn-realaudio	RealAudio sound
ras	image/x-cmu-raster	CMU raster image
rgb	image/x-rgb	RGB image
roff	application/x-troff	TROFF document
rtf	application/rtf	Rich Text Format
sh	application/x-sh	Bourne shell program
shar	application/x-shar	Unix shell archive
sit	application/x-stuffit	Macintosh archive
snd	audio/basic	ULAW audio data
t	application/x-troff	TROFF document
tar	application/x-tar	Unix tape archive
tcl	application/x-tcl	TCL program
tex	application/x-tex	TeX document
texi	application/x-texinfo	GNU TeXinfo document
texinfo	application/x-texinfo	GNU TeXinfo document

13

TABLE 13-2   *Common MIME-Types Used on the Internet* (continued)   ■

Extension	Type	Use
text	text/plain	Plain text
tif	image/tiff	TIFF image
tiff	image/tiff	TIFF image
tr	application/x-troff	TROFF document
txt	text/plain	Plain text
vox	audio	VoxWare
wav	audio/x-wav	WAV audio
xbm	image/x-xbitmap	X bitmap
xpm	image/x-xpixmap	X pixmap
xwd	image/x-xwindowdump	X Window dump image
Z	encoding/x-compress	Compressed data
zip	application/x-zip-compressed	Zip compressed data

TABLE 13-2 *Common MIME-Types Used on the Internet* (continued) ■

Multimedia elements are typically saved and transmitted on the Internet in the appropriate MIME-type format and are named with the proper extension for that type. For example, Shockwave Flash animation files end in .swf; image files end in .jpg, .jpeg, .gif, or .png; sound files end in .au, .wav, .aif, .mp3, or another conforming format; QuickTime video clips end in .qt or .mov.

warning *Because some MIME-types for multimedia data are new or experimental, all servers may not recognize them. If you have problems with a multimedia file, check with your Internet Service Provider to be sure your server can serve "experimental" MIME-types such as Shockwave. Some ISPs will not install the requisite, and often costly, server software for high-bandwidth streaming MIME-types.*

The World Wide Web and HTML

The World Wide Web (http://www.w3.org) started in 1989 at the European Particle Physics Laboratory (CERN) as a "distributed collaborative hypermedia information system." It was designed by Tim Berners-Lee as a protocol for linking a multiplicity of documents located on computers anywhere within the Internet. This new Hypertext Transfer Protocol (HTTP) provided rules for a simple transaction between two computers on the Internet consisting of (1) establishing a connection, (2) requesting that a document be sent, (3) sending the document, and (4) closing the connection. It also required a simple document format called Hypertext Markup Language (HTML) for presenting structured text mixed with inline images.

An HTML document could contain hyperlinks or anchors (see Chapter 8) that referred to other similar documents. With browser software, users could then click on designated areas of hot text in one document and jump to another, which itself might have more hot text pointing to yet other documents. Users could surf from document to document across the Web, with HTML as the underlying buoyant framework.

First Person

Each year, in the middle of summer, one of my colleagues has a birthday party at the beach. Her friends, a great many of them well-known San Francisco Bay Area multimedia developers and pundits, assemble picnic chests, volleyballs, children, suntan lotion, dogs, and watermelons to gather for an afternoon around a circle of hot and smoky charcoal grills.

During the party of 1994, they carried on about their latest multimedia ventures while turning chicken breasts, salmon, and barbecue meat; the buzz was about getting CD-ROM titles and product into the retail sales channel.

But shadows fell on the CD-ROM marketplace later that year, and the channels grew muddy and expensive—many multimedia developers were badly hurt in the Christmas shake-out.

When those same good developers gathered at the grills in the summer of 1995, the undertow of conversation was about HTML and migration to the growing World Wide Web. This was a new challenge, a new gold rush, and that channel needed multimedia!

Dynamic Web Pages and XML

HTML is fine for building and delivering uncomplicated *static* Web pages. But you will need other tools and programming know-how to deliver *dynamic* pages that are built on the fly from text, graphics, animations, and information that is contained in databases or documents. JavaScript and programs written in Java may be inserted into HTML pages to perform special functions and tasks that go beyond the vanilla abilities of HTML—for mouse rollovers, window control, and custom animations, for example.

Cold Fusion and PHP are applications running side-by-side with a Web server like Apache; they scan an outgoing Web page for special commands

13

and directives, usually imbedded in special *tags*. If they find a special tag in the page, the software will do what the tag tells it to do, like "get today's date and put it into that table cell" or "search this database for all customers with balances greater than $100 and, after alphabetizing, put that list into a table on the Web page being served." Working hand-in-hand with these *application servers*, Oracle, Sybase, and mySQL offer software to manage SQL (Structured Query Language) databases that may contain not only text but also graphics and multimedia resources like sounds and video clips. In concert with HTML, these tools provide the power to do real work and perform real tasks within the context of the World Wide Web.

XML (eXtensible Markup Language) goes beyond HTML; it is the next evolutionary step in the development of the Internet for formatting and delivering Web pages using *styles*. Unlike HTML, you can create your own tags in XML to describe exactly what the data means, and you can get that data from anywhere on the Web. In XML, you can build a set of tags like

    <fruit>

    <type>Tomato</type>

    <source>California</source>

    <price>$.64</price>

    </fruit>

and your XML document, according to your instructions, will find the information to put into the proper place on the Web page in the formatting style you assign. For example, with XML styles, you can declare that all items within the <price> tag will be displayed in boldface Helvetica type.

---

http://www.xml.org
http://www.xml.com

More information about XML

The Web is becoming much more than a static library. Increasingly, users are accessing the Web for "Web pages" that aren't actually on the shelves. Instead, the pages are generated dynamically from information available to the Web server. That information can come from databases on the Web server, from the site owner's enterprise databases, or even from other Web sites.

Charles Goldfarb, who invented SGML
(the parent language of HTML and XML) and coined the term *markup language*.

Multimedia on the Web

During the coming years, most multimedia experiences on the Internet will occur on the World Wide Web, programmed within the constraints of HTML, then stretched by the enhanced capabilities provided by XML, Java, JavaScript, and special plug-ins like Flash and QuickTime to enable browsers to exceed their limits. To design and make effective multimedia for this environment, developers need to understand not only how to create and edit the elements of multimedia, but also how to deliver it for HTML browsers and plug-in/player vehicles. Well-crafted, professionally rendered sites on the Web include text, images, audio, and animation presented in a user-friendly interface that balances the bandwidth deficit against user patience. HTML, the plug-in tools, and players are discussed in Chapter 14. Techniques, tricks, and presentation styles for delivering multimedia on the Web are discussed in Chapter 15.

Inside the event horizon of the amazing World Wide Web explosion are many uncertainties and unsolved challenges. The bandwidth deficit will certainly be met with technology solutions that will be effectively marketed into homes and businesses. But the pressure of more and more users entering the Web will create a terrific need for high-quality, compelling content; multimedia developers and entrepreneurs will fill this creative void.

13

Multi

[
Authoring tools are used
for designing interactivity
and the user interface ...
]

Multimedia authoring tools provide the
important framework for organizing and editing
the elements of your multimedia project ——

interactivity

media

START   STOP

chapter

14

Tools for the World Wide Web

including
graphics,
sounds,
animations,
and
video clips.

T
HIS chapter presents an organized overview of the many Internet tools you may wish to acquire for your multimedia toolbox as you learn to make the Web stand up and dance. URLs and other pointers are included here to lead you to information about how to obtain, install, and use these applications and utilities. Some are demonstrated and applied in the design examples of Chapter 15.

In the late 1990s, multimedia plug-ins and commercial tools aimed at the Web entered the marketplace at a furious pace, each competing for visibility and developer/user mind share in an increasingly noisy venue. In the few years since the birth of the first line-driven HTTP daemon in Switzerland, millions of Web surfers had become hungry for "cool" enhancements to entertaining sites. Web site and page developers needed creative tools to feed the surfers; surfers needed browsers and the plug-ins and players to make these cool multimedia enhancements work. By 2001, Macromedia was leading the pack, claiming that 96 percent of the online audience, or more than 334 million Web users, can view multimedia created with Flash.

A combination of the explosion of tools and user demand for performance is stressing the orderly development of the core HTML standard. Unable to evolve fast enough to satisfy the demand for features (there are committees, international meetings, rational debates, comment periods, and votes in the standards process), the HTML language is constantly being extended de facto by commercial interests (mainly Netscape and Microsoft). These companies regularly release new versions of Web browsers containing *tags* (HTML commands) and features not yet formally approved. By the time (measured in weeks!) millions of users have become dependent upon the features of new browser versions, the more carefully considered official specification has no choice but to incorporate them. By the time features are "official," of course—after more meetings, votes, and understated demonstrations of power—still newer browser versions have been released with yet newer, unofficial features.

What keeps this cycle from being chaotic are the natural selection forces of the marketplace: developers strive toward a successful product that works better and satisfies more users without mutating so far from the core standard that there are no sales and the company collapses. Developers also complain about the contention between Netscape and Microsoft because they must program work-arounds that compensate for the differences between these two benchmark browsers, and they must test the performance of their site on both.

Netscape's Navigator and Microsoft's Internet Explorer contain many unofficial features and extensions to official HTML. Each provides a method for third-party developers to "plug in" special tools that take over certain computational and display activities. Navigator and Explorer also support the Java and JavaScript languages by which programmers can create *applets* or programming code to extend and customize a browser's basic HTML capabilities, especially into the multimedia realm. Thus, while browsers provide the orchestrated foundation of HTML, third-party players and even nonprogrammers can create their own cadenzas to enhance browser performance or perform special tasks. It is often through the plug-ins and applets described in this chapter that multimedia reaches end users. Many of these tools are available as freeware and shareware, while others, particularly servers, are available as expensive engines—most any tool can be downloaded from the Internet in a trial version. Try it. If you like it or use it, buy it.

The stunning growth of the Internet has caused many software developers to redirect their creative efforts toward providing solutions on the Web. This remains a new frontier. No developer wishes to be left behind.

Web Servers

As you learned in Chapter 13, the workings of the Web involve communication between two computers: a server and a client. The server delivers a file when a client asks for it. Because the playback or display performance of your multimedia content—particularly when it is a streaming MIME-type such as RealAudio or Shockwave/Flash or a QuickTime video—depends upon the speed and capabilities of the computer and software serving it (as well as the bandwidth and load factors of the Internet), you should know some basics.

A growing number of software vendors provide Web servers of varying strength and capacity and for a variety of platforms, all of which meet the requirements of the Hypertext Transfer Protocol discussed in Chapter 13. A server is technically not the hardware but the software—you should invest in server software that will stand up to your intended use and be supported by the

14

vendor. Most vendors will also recommend hardware configurations. This combination of software and hardware is critical to your success and happiness if you wish to optimize response time (less than a second), your connections per second (as many as possible), and your throughput (plenty of room before your Internet connection is overwhelmed by traveling packets).

---

warning   *If you do not develop growth predictions based upon sound business practices and install adequate server performance and load balancing, you may discover that those 6,000 hits you received in the hour after you and your brother held up the bedsheet boasting your company's URL during the Super Bowl are being served at 87 bytes per second or refused. At least be sure your choice of server and its connection to the Internet backbone provide a sensible migration path for growth; people don't usually come back to an unsatisfying experience.*

Web Browsers

Your computer's performance is as important as the bandwidth of your connection to the Web. Web browsers are applications that run on a user's personal computer (on the client side on the Internet) to provide the interactive graphical interface for searching, finding, and viewing text documents, sounds, animations, and other multimedia resources on the Web. In 1996, as many as 50 browsers competed for market share, each boasting special or unique features, performance, and cost. Rich Santalesa, editor of *NetGuide* magazine, predicted even then that "the browser wars are over—it's a battle between Microsoft and Netscape, and everyone else is going to dry up and blow away." Indeed, by mid-2001, only two serious competitors remained: Netscape and Microsoft, and Netscape, despite more than 40 million registered users, was beginning a chameleon act. Purchased by AOL, then alloyed by a merger with Time Warner, Netscape was repositioned as a "media hub," not a software company, giving the new Netscape a chance to sell advertising across its many media properties and experiment with subscriptions rather than just free services within the AOL-Time Warner media empire (which includes properties such as *Fortune* and *Time* magazines and the 24-hour cable news network CNN).

The browser is a crown jewel. However, six months from now, you won't consider Netscape to be a browser company.

Jim Bankoff, Netscape President

Despite the legal and financial seriousness of this competition, manifest in very real congressional hearings and complicated multimillion-dollar antimonopoly lawsuits, some of those involved kept their sense of humor. Back in October 1997, late in the night after the gala announcement and rollout of Microsoft's new Explorer 4.0 in San Francisco, a group of Microsoft engineers drove 30 miles south to Netscape's headquarters and placed a truck-sized Explorer logo (the world-circling "e") on the front lawn of the competitor's headquarters, accented with a helium balloon saying "We Love You" and a greeting card with the message, "It's just not fair. Good people shouldn't have to feel bad. Best wishes, the IE team." By mid-morning, Netscape's own engineers had crowned the Explorer logo with a giant dinosaur (their company mascot, named Mozilla) and nailed up a cardboard sign declaring, "Netscape 72, Microsoft 18," (the companies' market share at that time).

The majority of visitors to your Web site will be using Netscape's Navigator or Microsoft's Internet Explorer. In designing a Web site, then, you should be certain that your documents and plug-ins work and look good using those browsers.

Web Page Makers and Site Builders

To deliver multimedia on the Web today, you should know some HTML—you must place the proper tags and references into your documents to launch and control your multimedia. Examples of launching multimedia plug-ins and enablers are found in Chapter 15. Many HTML editors and Web page-making applications offer to shortcut your HTML learning curves and working effort. If you use one of these editors, let it ease your work effort, but do not shy away from learning the syntax and tags of the language. Often these "helpers" generate extremely complicated HTML code (described by some programmers as "garbage") with the idea that if this code is hidden "under the hood," who cares? As you yourself become more informed and better at HTML coding, you might discover that you are the person who cares!

HTML documents are simple ASCII text files saved to disk without any formatting at all—no bolding, underlining, special fonts, margins, or tabs. Professional Web page developers often use only a word processor like BBEdit (see Figure 14-1) rather than a souped-up drag-and-drop HTML editor, and they insert text and tags into their documents manually or with personalized shortcut keys and helper scripts. HTML currently includes about 50 tags, and once you understand their properties and uses, coding, or *marking up*, a document and saving it to your Web site can be a straightforward process.

FIGURE 14-1

BBEdit is a

professional

programmer's text

editor with

dedicated features

for Web page

development

When I was 16, my grandmother loaned me $500 so I could buy my first car. It was a lovely, previously owned, British racing green 1950 MG-TD, happiest doing about 45 miles per hour on tree-lined summer roads in New England. When you hinged up the hood sideways, everything inside was simple and well defined; there was plenty of room to tweak the twin SU carburetors, adjust the distributor, and replace simple parts like the electric fuel pump. I even took the tiny four-cylinder engine entirely out and replaced the shell bearings on the crankshaft. A decade later, with my previously owned 1960 Ford pickup, it was the same—replacing the radiator or changing the starter motor was a piece of cake, and there was plenty of room to work on the engine. But then automobiles got complicated. It started with elaborate emission control systems, then electronic ignitions, then air conditioning, and finally, computers. Opening the hood of a car today, most of us can only stare dumbly at the myriad hoses and wires and color-coded containers for special fluids; and it's so compact a fit, you can't slip a screwdriver between the engine and the fire wall. When the "check engine" light comes on, an expert needs to "pull" the computer codes with a special, expensive reader to see what's wrong.

Writing HTML for the Web today is still simple. But unless you are an expert, you might be staring dumbly at the complex source code created by a new generation of high-powered special Web tools that will deliver mind-boggling multimedia pages built—no muss, no fuss—with simple drag and drop. But like my car today, which is happiest at 70 miles per hour and could cruise at twice that, you won't be doing much under the hood.

HTML translators are built into many word processing programs, so you can export a word-processed document with its text styles and layout converted to HTML tags for headers, bolding, underlining, indenting, and so on. Some are more powerful than others. These work well for simple text documents but tend to choke on powerful HTML features such as tables, forms, frames, and other extensions offered by Navigator, Explorer, or other browsers. Dedicated editors are usually WYSIWYG (What You See Is What You Get) word processors, and they provide more power and more features specifically geared to exploiting HTML. Microsoft Word, for example, automatically opens Web pages in a WYSIWYG view. On the downside, these "helpful" features may cause a page with many embedded graphics to load into the word processor very slowly while it interprets and lays out the page as a browser would, instead of just loading the text of the page's HTML code and letting you change a few tags or lines.

Among the many tools in this emerging marketplace, FrontPage from Microsoft links to Microsoft Office and provides not only WYSIWYG support for many of the latest HTML formatting extensions but also extensive

Web site management support through its FrontPage Explorer application. To use this feature, however, it has to run on a Microsoft server! Pagemaker from Adobe saves pages as HTML documents and as Acrobat PDF files. HoTMetaL Pro from SoftQuad imports and converts files created in Word, WordPerfect, Ami PRO, and other word processors. It has a point-and-click interface for inserting valid HTML tags and elements and provides an enhanced URL editor to manage references and calls to other documents and files. Terry Morse's Myrmidon is a page builder for Macintosh that creates an HTML page from most any document by "printing" it to analyze the content and converting it to HTML. The Netscape Navigator editor offers a one-click interface for inserting images, Live Objects, Java applets, JavaScript scripts, and frames, and it supports inline plug-ins such as Acrobat, Shockwave, Flash, RealAudio, WebFX, and others, so multimedia can be incorporated in your HTML document. Adobe's GoLive! is a WYSIWYG editor that lets you create and edit text pages, import images, and link to other documents. Dreamweaver from Macromedia is a popular Web site design tool with the companion SiteSpring application for managing entire projects.

Managing and maintaining a Web site is a serious undertaking when the site contains many thousands of text documents, images, and other resources. Software and expert system tools for automated Web page development, document management, and site activity analysis are becoming widely available. Combined with page builders and multimedia editors, these applications will evolve into the ubiquitous "word processors" of the new information age, essential to every home and office with outreach to the Web, and able to integrate and present all the elements of multimedia.

Plug-ins and Delivery Vehicles

Plug-ins add the power of multimedia to Web browsers by allowing users to view and interact with new types of documents and images. *Helper applications* or *players* also provide multimedia power by displaying or running files downloaded from the Internet by your browser, but helpers are not seamlessly integrated into the operation of the browser itself. When an unfamiliar embedded MIME-type is called from an HTML document (sounds, movies, unusual text or image files), most browsers will automatically launch a helper application (if it is specified in the browser's preferences) to view or run it, but this helper starts up and runs on your computer separately from the browser.

Many plug-ins are designed to perform special tasks not available without the plug-in installed. If you land on a Web page containing embedded compressed images, for example, and the proper plug-in to decompress those images is not installed, you will not see the images. In their place may be a "broken" plug-in icon:

Designers work around this problem by including in their pages hyperlinks to the site where the missing plug-in may be found. Users must then go there, download and install the required plug-in, and then restart their browser. This is all a bit cumbersome. Until the marketplace determines which plug-ins will become de facto standards for the Web, however, developers have no alternative. Because downloading and installing plug-ins is perceived as a hassle for the end user, many tool developers use the Java and JavaScript capabilities built into today's Web browsers. To offer a plug-in's functionality to visitors at your own Web site, many plug-ins require the addition of MIME-type information to a special setup file on your server. If you do not control or operate your own server, you should let your service provider know what MIME-types you need to have supported. Setting up servers for some of the multimedia plug-ins is not a trivial task, and many Internet Service Providers will not support high-bandwidth data streams for fear of overwhelming their Internet connection by serving your streaming voice or video to the world. Indeed, while a plug-in or a player may be free and readily available to anyone who wishes it, the software to actually build, compress, manipulate, and serve the special data (such as for compressed images, compressed audio, streaming video, animations, and VRML worlds) may be difficult and expensive since the company makes money from the development tool, not the client software.

Text

Text and document plug-ins such as the popular Acrobat Reader get you past the display limitations of HTML and Web browsers, where fonts are unchangeable and page layout is primitive. In file formats provided by Adobe Acrobat, for example, special fonts and graphic images are embedded as data into the file and travel with it, so what you see when you view that file is precisely what the document's maker intended.

14

Images

Most browsers will read only bitmapped JPEG, GIF, and PNG image files. Vector files (see Chapter 10) are a mathematical description of the lines, curves, fills, and patterns needed to draw a picture, and while they typically do not provide the rich detail found in bitmaps, they are smaller and can be scaled without image degradation. Plug-ins to enable viewing of vector formats are useful, particularly when some provide high-octane compression schemes to dramatically shrink file size and shorten the time spent downloading and displaying them. File size and compression sound a recurring theme on the Internet, where data-rich images, movies, and sounds may take many seconds, minutes, or even longer to reach the end user.

Vaughan's Bandwidth Rule

$$\frac{Bandwidth}{File\ Size} = Satisfaction$$

Satisfaction with the Internet is a function of connection speed and the size of the data elements accessed.

Vector graphics are also *device independent*—the image is always displayed at the correct size and with the maximum number of colors supported by the computer. Unlike bitmapped files, a single vector file can be downloaded, cached, and then displayed multiple times at different scaled sizes on the same or a different Web page.

Sound

Sound over the Web is managed in a few different ways. Digitized sound files in various common formats such as WAV, AIF, or AU may be sent to your computer and then played, either as they are being received (streaming playback) or once they are fully downloaded (using a player). MIDI files may also be received and played; as discussed in Chapter 9, these files are more compact, but they depend upon your computer's MIDI setup for quality. Speech files can be specially encoded into a token language and sent at great speed to another computer to be untokenized and played back in a choice of voices. Sound elements may also be embedded into projects made with Director, Authorware, Astound, SuperCard, WebShow, or other applications. And sounds may be embedded into QuickTime, AVI, and MPEG movie files. Some sounds can be multicast (using the multicast IP protocols for the Internet—see RFC 1112), so multiple users can simultaneously listen to the same data streams without duplication of data across the Internet. Web-based telephones also transmit data packets containing sound information.

Animation, Video, and Presentation

The most data-intense multimedia elements to travel the Internet are video streams containing both images and synchronized sound, commonly packaged as Apple's QuickTime, Microsoft's Video for Windows (AVI), and as MPEG files (see Chapters 5 and 12 for more details about these formats). Also data rich are the files for proprietary formats such as Shockwave and Astound, PowerPoint, and other presentation applications. In all cases, the trade-offs between bandwidth and quality are constantly in your face when designing, developing, and delivering animations or motion video for the Web.

Beyond HTML

When an ingot of pure silicon is "pulled" from a furnace, the process begins with a *seed crystal*, around which the ingot forms. HTML is the seed crystal that is shaping and forming the nature of multimedia on the World Wide Web as it extrudes itself onto the Internet's data highway. Within the latticework of HTML servers and browsers, new tags such as <EMBED> and <INSERT> enable text, sound, images, animations, and motion video across the Web. Hooks for powerful platform-independent Java applets and JavaScripts are built into most browsers, so you can design local interaction and activities without a lot of communication between client- and server-based CGI (Common Gateway Interface) programming. CGI is a standard for interfacing external applications with information servers, such as HTTP or Web servers, and CGI programs can be written in C/C++, Fortran, PERL, TCL, a Unix shell, Visual Basic, or even AppleScript, as long as the language is supported by the server platform.

Many software tool companies are developing applications and design environments to work with Java. Aimtech's Cruiser uses a WYSIWYG page layout environment for visually specifying "live" objects (such as animation, graphics, and audio) with drag-and-drop actions. Noware's Java from Down Under provides a Wizard-like Activator and plug-in applets to produce code that can be dropped into a Web page. Symantec's Java Development Kit, Café, provides Java developers with class and project management capabilities within a graphical development environment and also uses

14

software, aptly code-named Caffeine, to add Java development capabilities to the Symantec Project Manager (SPM). HyperWire from Autodesk lets you create 2-D and 3-D animations as Java applets, without writing any code. Microsoft offers ActiveX—small, fast, full-featured components for the Internet and the intranet based on OLE Controls. Mbed Software's mbedlets provide programmed multimedia effects for Web pages, working with a point-and-click interface for collecting and placing multimedia content within Web pages.

Conferencing and collaboration software with strong multimedia components is becoming available on the Internet. BeingThere, for example, is an Internet video phone with chat, file transfer, whiteboarding, and live window sharing. CU-SeeMe from White Pine is a popular desktop video conferencing system for real-time person-to-person or group conferencing on the Internet that offers many features typical of conferencing software:

- Multiplatform compatibility for Windows and Macintosh

- Ability to view up to eight participant windows; unlimited number for audio and talk window

- Message alert box for incoming connections (caller ID)

- Whiteboard for collaboration during conferences; supports multiple users

- Mosaic browser support for direct launch of CU-SeeMe from Web page

- Selectable audio compression algorithms with 100 ms and 50 ms sampling settings:

  —2.4K and 8.5K audio codecs to support 14.4K and 28.8K modem connections

  —16K and 32K codecs for higher bandwidth connections

- Color support for 24-bit true color and 4-bit gray-scale

- Ability to save, add, and edit participant addresses and Reflector sites (Phone Book)

- Video compression at standard and high-resolution settings

- Password, caller ID, and other conference and inbound call security

Netscape's LiveMedia (CoolTalk and CoolView) is a standards-based framework for real-time audio and video in network-based communications and collaborative multimedia applications supported by industry developers, including Progressive Networks, Adobe Systems, Digital Equipment, Macromedia, NetSpeak, OnLive!, Precept, Silicon Graphics, VDOnet, VocalTec, and Xing. The Look@Me plug-in (based on Timbuktu) lets you view another Look@Me user's screen anywhere in the world in real-time, so you can view a remote computer screen and edit documents, collaborate on presentations, review graphics, and provide real-time training and support. Connectix's VideoPhone (including a digital camera) lets you videoconference in or between offices with a shared whiteboard. WebBoard from O'Reilly & Associates is an advanced multithreaded conferencing system for online conferencing to any Windows Web server that fully supports the Windows-CGI interface. Web Crossing from Lundeen & Associates lets you set up a discussion group on a Web site. And for just plain telephoning over the Internet, Voxware's TeleVox lets users make real-time Internet-based "phone calls" to other TeleVox users anywhere in the world, for the price of a local Internet connection.

3-D Worlds

Three-dimensional environments and experiences on the Web are now possible with Intel's Internet 3-D Graphics Software using Macromedia's Director for development and the Shockwave player for delivery. These have supplanted VRML (Virtual Reality Modeling Language) as an independent environment specifically designed to handle high-performance 3-D worlds containing 3-D text and images, textures, animations, morphs, multiple viewpoints, collision detection, gravity, sounds, and all the arcade elements associated with full-bore game action. With claims that well-executed interactive 3-D content can make nearly any Web site more compelling and effective and can better attract, engage, and inform, Intel's algorithms and Macromedia's delivery system allow 3-D content to be automatically scaled and tailored to each user's system and available bandwidth. Spinning off from a foundation of vector graphics (see Chapter 10) and animation (see Chapter 11), 3-D renderings and creative whole worlds present but the latest of multimedia challenges and learning curves for Web developers. As this 3-D technology becomes refined and end-user bandwidth increases during the first decade of the 21st century, the very shape of Web pages will be altered forever.

14

Alias\Wavefront (http://www.aliaswavefront.com/)
Discreet (http://www.discreet.com)
famous3D (http://www.famous3d.com/)
Havok (http://www.havok.com/)
MAXON Computer (http://www.maxon.net/)
NewTek (http://www.newtek.com/)
NVIDIA (http://www.nvidia.com/)
NxView Technologies (http://www.nxview.com/)
Right Hemisphere (http://www.righthemisphere.com/)
Shells Interactive (http://www.shellsinteractive.com/)
SoftImage (http://www.softimage.com/)

For more information about 3-D tools and technology

First Person

When I received a press release from Alternate Realities Corporation, a small startup company spun out of a large research effort in North Carolina, I was intrigued. ARC's president, David Bennett, claimed, "We are redefining Virtual Reality!" He went on to describe "a new generation virtual environment that is a 3-D, immersive, full-color, interactive system enclosed in a 16-foot dome or sphere that can be either portable (inflatable or interlocking) or permanent. The system includes a 360-degree projection system with a 180-degree field of view. Imagine a 16-foot helmet that fits over 15 people at the same time and is nonrestrictive! Larger units (in the 24-foot and up range) are in the early development stage."

I knew I had to have one for my experiments with VRML! The five-meter model, which fits in a 20×20-foot trade-show booth space, was available for $280,000, and the seven-meter model, perfect for my backyard, was only slightly more: $340,000.

Web site and page developers need creative tools; surfers need browsers and the plug-ins and players to make them work.

By 1996, more than 75 percent—

connections

media

chapter

15

Designing for the
World Wide Web

— of all Web site hits were being made by Netscape's Navigator.

L AUNCHED in 1989, the World Wide Web was not originally designed with multimedia in mind, but rather as a simple method for delivering
text documents formatted in HTML, with occasional inline graphic illustrations and figures. By 1995, because it was operational, essentially free, and
good enough to support traffic (see "Vaughan's Law of Multimedia Minimums" in Chapter 9), the Web had become a full-bore information highway
of words and pictures with tens of millions of users cruising along it.

The Doppler backdraft of passing travelers has exposed the gristle of an
overwhelming number of disappointing audio and visual experiences on the
Web: "This is my home page; here is a list of my favorite places; this is me
with my dog..." To fill this vacuum of content and presentation, inventive
multimedia solutions and enhancements now compete for mind share,
stretching the capabilities of HTML, Web browsers, PCs, and the very fabric
of the Internet to bring multimedia power to this environment. You can experience the strong energies of this multimedia rush and the strong forces of
market dynamics and entrepreneurial spirit when you visit any of the plug-in
developers' Web sites listed in Chapter 14. Plain text and pictures are no longer enough for this highway!

Working on the Web

This chapter investigates and illustrates some methods for developing and
presenting the basic elements of multimedia within the constraints of HTML
and the World Wide Web. This chapter is not intended to substitute for a
more complete library of HTML, Web design, and Internet texts, but to present basic examples that will get you started. In 2001, there were more than
2,000 published books with the word "Internet" in their title!

The Workspace

Depending on who your intended audience is, make your Web pages look good on a 640×480-pixel VGA monitor showing 256 colors (8-bit graphics) for home and grade school viewers with older hardware; make them look good on an 800×600 monitor in true color (millions) for investment bankers and highway engineers. It will be a few years, still, before the classic VGA systems are retired, especially in homes. Your working space on a 640×480 monitor is actually about 600 pixels wide by 300 tall because browsers include controls and slider bars (see Figure 15-1). This is where you must place the eye-catchers that will be first loaded and viewed by visitors before they scroll right or down.

15

FIGURE 15-1

Netscape Navigator's viewing area for Web documents on a common Windows VGA (640x480) monitor is 612x306 pixels

Nibbling

The principle you must always keep in mind when designing and making multimedia elements for the Web should be called "nibbling." At a serious metal-working supply store you can buy a power tool called a nibbler—it wantonly devours the edges of sheet metal in an ear-damaging staccato of rapid tiny bites. You must apply this tool to the elegant bitmapped logo you created in Photoshop to trim it from 24- to 8- to 4-bit color depth and resize it from 96 pixels square to 64 pixels square. Nibble the audio clip of your client's theme song from 44.1 kHz to 11 kHz, and see if it's acceptable at 8-bit sample size. Text as HTML is cheap: nibble your page design and throw away the pretty shadowed GIF graphic headers and image maps—re-create your text in HTML headers or emphasized text, and try coloring it. Put on your protective ear muffs—this compromising work is painful—and start nibbling while constantly seeking a balance between quality and the patience of a user who is downloading your material at 28.8 or 56Kbps. Every choice you make should be tempered by bandwidth worry.

---

w a r n i n g   *For every image referenced in an HTML document, a separate Internet HTTP connection must be made between your computer and that image's server before the image itself is downloaded, so using many tiny images (such as graphic images as bullets) may not be efficient.*

HTML and Multimedia

You should have a basic understanding of HTML before you begin developing multimedia for the Web. HTML-coded documents, which are the fundamental vehicles for all types of information delivered on the World Wide Web, are explained in Chapters 8 and 14.

HTML provides tags for inserting media into HTML documents: the <IMG> tag for inline images; the <INSERT> tag for multimedia objects, including audio, video, and programming tools such as Java applets, Microsoft's Component Object Model (COM) objects, OLE Controls, and OLE; the <EMBED> tag for compound document embedding; and Sun's <APP> and <APPLET> tags for code. The <INSERT> tag and some optional attributes to play a QuickTime movie in HTML 3.0 might look something like,

```
<insert data=lizzie.mov type="application/quicktime">
<param name=loop value=infinite>
<img src=soccer.jpeg alt="The Soccer Match">
</insert>
```

where the browser would play the QuickTime movie named "lizzie" if it supported the .mov format and that MIME-type, and it would loop and play forever. If not supported, the browser would show a substituted JPEG image. Using the <IMG> element here provides backward compatibility with older browsers; if the browser has trouble with the JPEG image, it would display an alternate text label, in this case, "The Soccer Match."

The <EMBED> tag first used by Netscape to enable the many multimedia plug-ins described in this chapter and used in the examples may soon be superseded by the more capable <INSERT> tag.

---

tip   *If you develop multimedia for the Internet, budget time and effort for keeping current in this rapidly changing environment—staying at the leading edge takes effort. It will be some years before multimedia delivery tools and techniques for the Web stabilize.*

Text for the Web

Viewers of your Web site may not be displaying the same "preferred" font that you used to design your page because user preferences in the browser may alter the way text in your document looks and flows. To make the best of this uncertainty, many developers design their documents in Times Roman for the proportional font and Courier as the monospaced font. These fonts readily move across platforms and are the default fonts users typically see if they do not set their own preferences. Although you can specify a font and even alternates using the <FONT> tag (for example: <FONT FACE="Verdana, Arial, Helvetica">), browsers can only use a specified font if that font is installed on the end user's computer.

Great efforts are being made to define standard methods for displaying typefaces on the Web, but neither of the two rival camps, TrueDoc (from Bitstream) and OpenType (supported by Adobe, Microsoft, Agfa, and others), seem able to get their technology properly implemented and launched. The font problem will eventually be solved in one of two ways, or in a combination of both: either many more fonts will become readily and cheaply available and will be commonly installed by end users, or a method of embedding a font's character shapes into an HTML document will allow fonts to "ship" with the document. Both OpenType and TrueDoc embed font information in the HTML document, a more reassuring method for developers, but legal issues surround font foundry copyrights. Using an OpenDoc component called WEFT (Web Embedding Font Tool), Microsoft already offers font-embedding capabilities.

If you are looking for some flexibility in font management at your Web site, you can try using cascading style sheets (CSS), available in dynamic HTML (DHTML), for setting text styles across the pages of your Web site.

As with projects built for CD-ROM using a multimedia authoring tool, if you wish to absolutely control the look of text on your Web page, you must use a graphic bitmap rather than text in your HTML document. Embedding graphics into HTML documents is explained later in the chapter.

As you can see in Figure 15-2, you can tag text to be displayed as headers, bolded, italicized, underlined, and in lists, but the viewer's browser determines how these styles are displayed, and, again, you have little control over its final look. Unofficial extensions to Netscape Navigator include tags by which you can control (somewhat) the attributes of displayed text: the COLOR attribute <FONT COLOR="#0080FF"> will set the color of specific

FIGURE 15-2

Web browsers currently offer few methods for making pretty text in an HTML document

This is a First Header

HTML Code: <H1>This is a First Header</H1>

This is a Second Header

HTML Code: <H2>This is a Second Header</H2>

This is a Third Header

HTML Code: <H3>This is a Third Header</H3>

This is a Fourth Header

HTML Code: <H4>This is a Fourth Header</H4>

Text with initial cap oversized.

HTML Code: <font SIZE = +3>T</font>ext with initial cap oversized.

This text is light blue.

HTML Code: <font COLOR="#0080FF">This text is light blue.</font>

ᴛᴛᴛTT**T**TᴛᴛᴛTᴛᴛ

HTML Code for letters that grow:

<font SIZE=-2>T</font>
<font SIZE=-1>T</font>
T
<font SIZE=+1>T</font>
<font SIZE=+2>T</font>
<font SIZE=+3>T</font>
<font SIZE=+4>T</font>
<font SIZE=+3>T</font>
<font SIZE=+2>T</font>
<font SIZE=+1>T</font>
T
<font SIZE=-1>T</font>
<font SIZE=-2>T</font>

characters of text, and the SIZE attribute <FONT SIZE="+2"> increases or decreases the size of the text displayed. You can also set the background color of individual cells in a table by using the BGCOLOR attribute in the cell's data tag <TD BGCOLOR="#0080FF">. This is useful to highlight text information in complicated visual presentations.

Making Columns of Text

The most powerful feature of HTML may be found in the <TABLE> tag. Study this tag and its attributes! Using a table, here is how to organize your text into two columns so it displays more like a newspaper or a magazine (see Figure 15-3):

```
<HTML>
<HEAD>
<TITLE>The Explosion</TITLE>
</HEAD>
<BODY>
<DIV ALIGN="center">
<H2>The Explosion</H2>
</DIV>
<TABLE BORDER=0 CELLSPACING=20>
<TR VALIGN=TOP>
<TD WIDTH=40%>
... text for Column 1 goes here ...
</TD>
<TD WIDTH=40%>
... text for Column 2 goes here ...
</TD>
</TR>
</TABLE>
<HR>
</BODY>
</HTML>
```

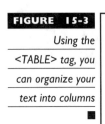

FIGURE 15-3

Using the

<TABLE> tag, you

can organize your

text into columns

Flowing Text Around Images

As you can see in Figure 15-4, it is possible (and easy) to "flow" text around an image using the ALIGN attribute of the <IMG> tag. This is a quick and simple method for mixing text and images in a pleasing layout. Add a <BR CLEAR=left> tag at the end of your text paragraph so that, if there is not enough text to fill the entire vertical height of the image, your next paragraph will begin on a new line, left justified, below the image. To add space around your image so it doesn't butt right up against the text, use the HSPACE and VSPACE attributes of the <IMG> tag.

```
<HTML>
<HEAD>
<TITLE>Sailing</TITLE>
</HEAD>
<BODY>
```

```
<IMG SRC = "gbsky.gif" ALIGN=left HSPACE=15 VSPACE=5>
<H2>Departure</H2>
... text goes here ...
<BR CLEAR=left>
<hr>
</BODY>
</HTML>
```

The following HTML code sets up a more complicated screen with flowing text (see Figure 15-5, available at http://www.hkkk.fi/mmedia/itp96/). It also includes a background image, a portrait image around which the text flows, and an image map that is used for navigation. (Background images and image maps are described later in this chapter.) This document also contains the foreign language special character ä, which is called out in the document using HTML's escape sequence for special characters, in this case, "&aumlaut;". Escape characters begin with an ampersand and end with a semicolon. Also, note the use of a <FONT size="6"> tag to make paragraphs

FIGURE 15-4

You can flow text around an image by using the ALIGN attribute of the <IMG> tag

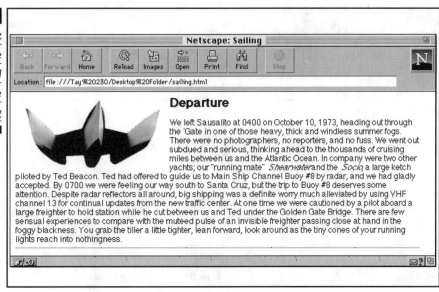

FIGURE 15-5

Images and text can be mixed in an HTML document. Note the use of escape sequences for special characters and the image map for navigation ■

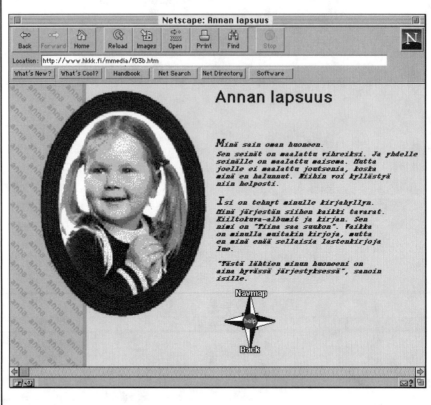

begin with initial caps. A MIDI file is embedded in this page to provide background music.

```
<html>
<head>
<title>Annan lapsuus</title>
</head>
<body background=misc/annataus.gif>
<img src="misc/trans150.gif" width=20 align=left>
<img src="03/i03b.gif" hspace=10 width=264 height=342 align=left>
<h1>Annan lapsuus</h1>
<pre><i><b>
<font size="6">M</font>in&aumlaut; sain oman huoneen.
```

15

```
Sen sein&aumlaut;t on maalattu vihreiksi. Ja yhdelle
sein&aumlaut;lle on maalattu maisema. Mutta
joelle ei maalattu joutsenia, koska
min&aumlaut; en halunnut. Niihin voi kyll&aumlaut;sty&aumlaut;niin helposti.
<font size="6">I</font>si on tehnyt minulle kirjahyllyn.
Min&aumlaut; j&aumlaut;rjest&aumlaut;n siihen kaikki tavarat.
Kiiltokuva-albumit ja kirjan. Sen
nimi on "Tiina saa suukon". Vaikka
on minulla muitakin kirjoja, mutta
en min&aumlaut; en&aumlaut;&aumlaut; sellaisia lastenkirjoja lue.

"T&aumlaut;st&aumlaut; l&aumlaut;htien minun huoneeni on
aina hyv&aumlaut;ss&aumlaut; j&aumlaut;rjestyksess&aumlaut;", sanoin isille.
<img src="misc/komp4a5a.gif" align= left border="0" usemap="#thispagemap">
</pre>
</i></b>

<map name="thispagemap">
<area shape=circle coords="48,48,12" href ="fhelp.htm">
<area shape=polygon coords="50,50,0,0,100,0" href = "fnavmap.htm">
<area shape=polygon coords="50,50,0,100,100,100" href = "f03.htm">
</map>

<EMBED SRC="03/pianobg.mid" width=0 height=2 autostart=true>
</body>
</html>
```

Images for the Web

Theoretically, the Web can support any graphics format the client and server have in common. Practically, even though Web standards do not specify a graphics format you must use, browsers typically recognize two image formats, GIF and JPEG, without resorting to special plug-ins. Both formats use built-in compression algorithms to reduce file size. (Graphic image formats are described in detail in Chapter 10.) For other graphics formats, such as CGM, CMX, DXF, and fractal- and wavelet-compressed images, special proprietary creation software and browser plug-ins may be required (see Chapter 14).

GIF and PNG Images

GIF images (discussed in greater detail in Chapter 10) are limited to 8 bits of color depth (256 colors). This is a commercial image format developed by CompuServe Information Services, an online company once owned by Unisys and presently folded into America Online. In late 1994, Unisys announced a patent fee charge to all software developers who use the GIF format. In an angry industrywide response, a new "open" format called PNG (for Portable Network Graphics Specification, not requiring fees) was developed to re-place GIF. Stay tuned to see if it catches on.

First Person

A few years ago I caught an anecdote from someone who had heard about a quick Web survey: how does the world pronounce .GIF? The results turned out about 50/50 on the hard/soft question, she claimed. Then I spent considerable time using that word (softly) in Europe before realizing everybody was being smirkingly polite about my outlandish pronunciation. In the San Francisco Bay Area, a world center for multimedia development, GIF has the soft "g" of "ginger," "gin," and "gibberish." In New York, where little is soft, and in Europe, .GIF has a more cutting, hard pronunciation, as in "giggling," "gingham," "girdled," "guilty," or "girls." The real question is whether the written word requires a prepended dot.

Color Plate 5 shows images saved in various formats and then displayed from the Web using Netscape Navigator on Windows and Macintosh plat-forms set at 16-bit (thousands of colors) and 8-bit (256 colors) color depths. Note that these photos saved in JPEG format seem to work best in all condi-tions, even dithered to 8 bits on both Windows and Macintosh. The differ-ence between high- and low-quality JPEG compression is hardly noticeable, and the file size savings are great! Also note that dithering to Photoshop's adaptive palette, which optimizes and includes in the 256-color palette as many of the actual colors that are found in that image as possible, is not always displayed well by Navigator or Explorer.

JPEG Images

JPEG images may contain 24 bits of color depth (millions of colors). JPEG uses a powerful but *lossy* compression method that produces files as much as ten times more compressed than GIF.

Use JPEG for photo-realistic images containing many colors, and avoid using it for images already forced into a 256-color palette or for line drawings or 1-bit black-and-white images. GIF compresses drawings and cartoons that have only a few colors in them much better than JPEG, which may introduce visible defects—sharp edges and lines that blur, especially with small-size text. Test the amount of compression acceptable for your JPEG image; stay inside the "threshold of visible error."

---

warning   *Do not edit and reedit files that are in JPEG format. Every time you open a JPEG image and edit it, then recompress and save it as compressed JPEG, the image degrades. After a few editing/saving cycles, you will be very disappointed. Edit and archive your images in a lossless graphic format, then convert to JPEG (if you need to).*

---

tip   *If you download JPEG files from the Internet by FTP using Fetch, be sure to add ".jpg" and ".jpeg" to Fetch's list of binary file types (in the Customize/Suffix Mapping... menu). Otherwise Fetch will retrieve JPEG files in text mode and corrupt the data.*

The JPEG (Joint Photographic Experts Group) compression scheme compresses about 20:1 before visible image degradation occurs. To compress an image with JPEG, the image is divided into 8×8-pixel blocks, and the resulting

64 pixels (called a *search range*) are mathematically described relative to the characteristic of the pixel in the upper-left corner. The binary description of this relationship requires far less than 64 pixels, so more information can be transmitted in less time. JPEG compresses slowly, about one to three seconds for a 1MB image depending upon computer speed, but JPEG can compress images as much as 75:1, with loss. Color Plate 3 shows the "blocky" nature of JPEG compression.

The images in Figure 15-6 are 24-bit (millions of colors), 72 dpi PICT files shown at 3X magnification (so you can see the pixels). The image on the top is uncompressed. The image on the bottom was compressed in Photoshop using the "JPEG - low quality" setting. The uncompressed file is 60K in size,

FIGURE 15-6

Compression schemes save disk space but can degrade an image ■

No compression Not Lossy

Maximum compression JPEG (smallest file size - Lossy)

the compressed file 16K in size. While the compressed image is about one-quarter the size of the uncompressed image, there is a penalty, and it is lossy.

---

ftp://rtfm.mit.edu/pub/usenet/news-answers/jpeg-faq
http://melmac.corp.harris.com/transparent_images.html
http://legendre.ucsd.edu/Research/Fisher/fractal.html
ftp://ftp.uu.net/graphics/jpeg
http://www.isi.edu:80/in-notes/iana/assignments/media-types/image/cgm
http://www.boutell.com/boutell/png/
ftp://ftp.std.com:/ftp/vendors/mmedia/lview/lviewpro.zip
ftp://ftp.coast.net:/SimTel/win3/graphics/winjp276.zip
ftp://ftp.coast.net:/SimTel/win3/graphics/psp311.zip
ftp://mac.archive.umich.edu:/mac/graphics/graphicsutil/
   gifconverter2.37.cpt.hqx
ftp://sumex-aim.stanford.edu:/info-mac/gst/grf/progressify-10.hqx
http://www.timestream.com/mmedia/graphics/depthtst.html

Details and converters for commonly used graphics formats

Using Photoshop

Here are suggestions for using Photoshop to edit and save an image for use on the World Wide Web. If you use a different image-editing application, follow the same logic and use the commands appropriate for that application. Always work in native Photoshop format using PSD files—these images are typically in RGB mode and use the maximum color depth. They are larger, but they contain more information that can be usefully processed when resizing and dithering, and you will get better final results; they also contain layers, a very useful application feature. Use images at 72 pixels per inch resolution. When you convert a 24-bit RGB image to an 8-bit image (change its *mode*), you lose huge amounts of color information that cannot be retrieved—the fine data is gone forever. So do all of your image manipulation (such as resizing, sharpening, and hue adjustments) in RGB mode, and save this source image in RGB mode as a PSD file (not a lossy compression, like JPEG) so you can make changes later.

When you are satisfied with your image and ready to save it as a GIF or JPEG file, archive it as described above. If you make any mistakes while converting modes or saving, you will still have the original, complete with any layers you might have used. To be very safe, duplicate the original file and open the copy before saving to other formats.

Saving as JPEG Files

To save your image as a JPEG file, you do not need to change Photoshop's mode from RGB, but if you are using layers, you will need to *flatten* the image, merging all layers into a single bitmap. Once an image is flattened and you have edited or saved it, its layers cannot be remade without a great deal of difficult cutting and pasting—so again, archive your original file! Photoshop will automatically ask if you wish to flatten when you select JPEG from the Save As... menu. You must name your file with the extension .jpg or .jpeg if you will use it on the Web. Then click on Save, and choose Maximum, High, Medium, or Low-quality compression in the dialog box that appears. Color Plate 5 shows images saved in High- and Low-quality settings; you may wish to examine your saved file to see how it looks. Your file is ready for the Web.

Saving as GIF Files

To save a GIF file using Photoshop, you must first set the mode of your image to Indexed Color, converting it to the best 8-bit palette (256 colors) that will represent the image and be displayed well by Web browsers. Note that the option of saving a Photoshop 24-bit RGB file in GIF format will not be available in Windows, and it will be grayed out on the Macintosh menu until you have converted your image to 8-bit mode: GIF is only for 8-bit images. Only one palette can be active at a time on an 8-bit monitor.

---

t i p *Use GIF files for line art and images that contain large areas of the same color. Use JPEG for photo-realistic images.*

Palettes When you change mode to Indexed Color, you must specify the color depth of the converted image, the color palette to be used, and whether the colors of your image should be dithered (Diffusion or Pattern) or not (None). Figure 15-7 shows the mode changing dialog box from Photoshop, where the custom Netscape Navigator palette for Windows has been selected.

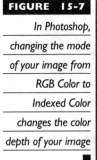

FIGURE 15-7

In Photoshop, changing the mode of your image from RGB Color to Indexed Color changes the color depth of your image

One issue that seriously perplexed me when creating my first Web site was choosing the right palette for photographic or continuous tone images. Because images have to be small, you have to dither them to 8 bits. Well, what 8-bit palette do you dither down to—Macintosh, Windows, Netscape, Mosaic, MacWeb, etc., etc.?

Marlene Sinicki, Designer, San Francisco

Netscape offers only 216 nondithering colors in its palette for the Windows version of Navigator running in 8-bit display mode. (About 20 colors are reserved for the Windows desktop and 20 for Netscape's desktop and animated logo.) Using this custom palette for your GIF image means that viewers using a Windows platform with a 256-color VGA monitor will see an image not further dithered by the Netscape application at run time—the 216 colors that make up the image are exactly those already in Navigator's palette. Running on Macintosh platforms, however, Navigator uses the full 256-color Macintosh system palette. So images saved in Photoshop's system palette will display without dithering on Macintoshes. Images dithered to the Macintosh system palette run the risk of using one or more of the 40 unavailable colors for Windows, which will then be dithered by Navigator on Windows platforms and may cause strange effects. Images saved with the Netscape custom palette will always display the same in Netscape Navigator (and Internet Explorer) on both platforms.

....

http://www.netscape.com/assist/support/client/tn/windows/10117.html
http://the-light.com/netlinks.html
http://www.industrious.com/~industry/consider.html

More about the Netscape palette

....

Interlaced and Progressive Scans   Both GIF and JPEG images can be saved so that when your browser displays the image as it is being downloaded, you can immediately see a chunky approximation of the final image, with resolution improving as more and more data comes in. While in *baseline*, or normal, configuration, image data is stored as a single top-to-bottom scan; in *interlaced* GIF and *progressive* JPEG files, the data is organized in a different sequence within the file. An interlaced GIF file, for example, is arranged into a series of four passes:

Pass 1 : Every 8th row, starting with row 0

Pass 2 : Every 8th row, starting with row 4

Pass 3 : Every 4th row, starting with row 2

Pass 4 : Every 2nd row, starting with row 1

Figure 15-8 shows Photoshop's GIF89a Export tool with its check box to enable saving an image as interlaced, and four increasingly resolved interlaced passes of a GIF image.

Transparency   The GIF89a specification allows for transparency: you can save your file with instructions to a browser to use the color that is in its own background for pixels that are your selected transparency color. In many

15

FIGURE 15-8

Interlacing and transparency settings when exporting a GIF89a file from Photoshop—with interlacing, the image incrementally improves its resolution as it downloads; transparency allows an image to "float" on a document background

cases, such as for company logos and inline illustrations, it is attractive to let an image float on top of the browser's background:

The background of the logo above is white and would (without transparency) be displayed as a rectangle showing white to its edges. To make the white background of the GIF image transparent so that the tree and lettering float on the background, choose white as the transparency index color, and then save the file. Tools that provide a palette from which you can select the transparency index color are available for saving transparent GIF files.

You cannot make a JPEG file transparent.

Backgrounds

Most browsers allow you to specify an image or color to place in the background of your page. Text and images will float on top of this layer.

Background Coloring

You can colorize your documents by choosing background, text, and URL link colors. Color controls are attributes of the <BODY> tag, so you can only set the colors of an *entire* document's background; you cannot change coloring partway through. The BGCOLOR attribute of the <BODY> tag supported by Netscape Navigator lets you change the color of the background without having to specify a graphic image to load. The format Navigator understands is

```
<BODY BGCOLOR="#rrggbb">Document here</BODY>
```

where "#rrggbb" is a hexadecimal red-green-blue triplet used to specify the background color. (See Chapter 10 for an explanation of red-green-blue triplets.)

When you have chosen a background color, you will then want to set the color of your text and establish proper contrasts. Red on green can be shimmery; black on black is invisible. So the four classes of text used in an HTML document are also attributes of Netscape's <BODY> tag.

The <TEXT> tag is used to control the color of all the normal text in a document—text that is not specially colored to indicate a link. The LINK, VLINK, and ALINK tags let you control the coloring of link text. LINK text displays a URL that you have not visited, VLINK text shows a visited link, and ALINK is an active link. The default coloring of these in Netscape Navigator is TEXT = very light gray, LINK = blue, VLINK = purple, and ALINK = red. If you placed these default colors into a <BODY> tag, the tag would read

```
<BODY BGCOLOR="#CDCDCD" TEXT="#000000" LINK="#0000FF"
VLINK="#FF00FF" ALINK="#FF0000">
```

Background Images

You can specify a special background image for your document. Fifty-five textures are publicly available at Netscape's home server and can add polish with little effort. By using background images served directly from Netscape, it is possible that the image will already be in the cache on your hard disk and will load more rapidly. Visit http://www.home.netscape.com/home/bg/backgrounds.html for a menu.

Background images are automatically *tiled*, or repeated, across and down the page, so a randomly distributed "sandy" background image (see Color Plate 8) can easily be made up of a very small source image. None of your document can be displayed until the background image is loaded, so keep your background image small.

Load a background image into a document by specifying its URL in the BACKGROUND attribute of the <BODY> tag, for example:

```
<BODY BACKGROUND="http://home.netscape.com/home/bg/fabric/gray_fabric.gif">
```

> **tip** *It is a good idea, often overlooked, to specify a background color (BGCOLOR="#rrggbb") similar to the prevailing color of the image in the <BODY> tag. If the user viewing your page has Image Loading turned off, or if your background image cannot be loaded for some reason, the page will still look close to the way you designed it. If the background image is not loaded for any reason by Navigator, and a BGCOLOR was not also specified, then any of the foreground controlling attributes (TEXT, LINK, VLINK, and ALINK) will be ignored. Netscape claims that the idea behind this is that if you didn't get your requested background image, setting your requested text colors on top of the default gray background could make your document unreadable. If the image you specify as a background has transparent areas, the BGCOLOR will show through.*

Sidebars

In the navigation map shown in Color Plate 8, a commonly seen graphic layout was used: a vertical bar containing the word "navmap" is displayed at the left of the screen and in the background. When users scroll up or down, this bar remains stationary.

Assuming that most users will have a viewing window about 640 pixels wide, but some may be wider on higher-resolution monitors, make the graphic bar at the left as wide as you wish (say 75 pixels); then set the full width of your image to 1,000 pixels. Fill the space to the right of your bar with plain color or a texture. When this background image tiles, it will repeat itself only when the user widens the viewing window to more than 1,000 pixels; but the image will tile vertically in increments of its height. Here is the basic setup; see Color Plate 8 for a full-page example.

Clickable Buttons

To make a graphic image "clickable" so that it links to another document, simply include the image inside an HTML anchor that points to that document's URL:

```
<A HREF="documentToGoTo.html">
<IMG SRC="imageDisplayed.gif" BORDER=0>
</a>
```

You can also use the <A> tag to provide a link to a larger graphic from the small, thumbnail-sized image, or even to a video clip:

```
<A HREF="bigPicture.jpg"><IMG SRC="thumbnail.gif"></A>
<A HREF="videoClip.mpeg"><IMG SRC="thumbnail.gif"></A>
```

Be sure to include the BORDER=0 attribute in the <IMG> tag if you wish to avoid showing a default border around the button image (usually two blue pixels wide).

Image Maps

Image maps are pictures with defined hot spots that link to other documents when a user clicks on them. Until recently, using image maps at a Web site required a special CGI (Common Gateway Interface) program and a configuration or .map file containing the coordinates of the hot spots to be located on the server. It also required communication between client and server as well as processing time while the CGI program looked up the coordinates in the specified .map file on the server and associated them with a document. Depending upon Internet traffic and delays, performance could be sluggish. And setting up this kind of image map usually required help from a system administrator or the Internet Service Provider who owns the server. In this *server-side* system, the HTML <IMG> tag attribute, ISMAP, tells the server to launch the CGI program, look up the mouse coordinates in the referenced file, and deliver the specified document.

Netscape Navigator and Microsoft Explorer added support for *client-side* image maps so that mouse coordinates and their associated document URLs could be included in the client's own HTML document, thus avoiding the setup and communications hassles of the server-side system. This is managed by the USEMAP attribute of the <IMG> tag.

To make a client-side image map with USEMAP, you need three things: an image, a list of coordinates designating hot spots on the image, and the document URL associated with each hot spot. To program the image map into your HTML document, you use the USEMAP attribute of the <IMG> tag:

```
<IMG src="compas.gif" hspace=5 vspace=50 border="0" usemap="#compass">
<MAP name="compass">
      <AREA shape=circle coords="60,60,10" href="help.htm">
      <AREA shape=polygon coords="60,60,0,0,120,0" href="back.htm">
      <AREA shape=polygon coords="60,60,0,120,120,120" href="forward.htm">
      <AREA shape=polygon coords="60,60,0,0,0,120" href="navmap.htm">
</MAP>
```

In the example above, which is illustrated in Figure 15-9, "compas.gif" is the transparent image, the hspace=5 and vspace=50 attributes provide space between the image and the text around it, and the border=0 attribute makes the image borderless. The usemap="#compass" attribute points to the <map> extension tag that contains the coordinates and URLs. (The pound sign means the <MAP> tag is located in this same document.) A <MAP> segment may be placed anywhere in the body of the HTML document and is related to the correct image by the name="compass" attribute. You can have more than one image map in an HTML document.

Within the <MAP> tag, the <AREA> tag defines the shape of the hot spot (as a circle, polygon, or rectangle) and anchors or links it to a URL. Areas are defined by x,y coordinates of the pixels in your bitmap: a circle by its center location and radius (60,60,10), a polygon by a sequence of x,y locations that

FIGURE 15-9

This enlarged image illustrates the coordinates used to define hot spots for image maps (the ruler is marked in pixels)

close automatically (60,60,0,0,120,0 defines a triangle), or a rectangle (two x,y locations defining top left and bottom right).

Sound for the Web

In the beginning, when the Internet was primarily a collection of Unix machines, sound files were sent from machine to machine in AU format and, when downloaded, were played back using a sound application. Designing and making MIDI and digitized sound files is described in detail in Chapter 9.

As the Web has developed, sound has become more important, and plug-ins currently allow embedding of sounds into documents. Browsers have become sound capable: Microsoft Explorer offers the <BGSOUND> tag to play an AU, WAV, or MIDI sound track in a document background. Netscape and Internet Explorer offer the QuickTime plug-in for playing AIFF, MIDI, WAV, and AU formats. If your browser does not support this sound plug-in, you can still launch an external "viewer" or helper application.

Streaming audio is more useful for the Web, where a sound file can start playing as soon as data begins coming in—streaming is provided by the LiveAudio and QuickTime plug-ins. Plug-ins such as StreamWorks, VocalTec, and RealAudio (see Chapter 14) feature streaming capability and high compression/good fidelity, but they also require special software at the server. The QuickTime plug-in offers a fast-start feature to allow playing before a movie has been completely downloaded: MIDI files and digitized sound embedded in a QuickTime movie will play even without video, text, or image tracks. You can either embed HTML commands in a document to play a QuickTime movie automatically in the background, or you can display a controller providing stop, fast-forward, and rewind for the user.

With the Crescendo MIDI plug-in (which downloads and plays standard MIDI files of MIME-type .mid or .midi), you can automatically launch a background sound when a page opens by using the <EMBED> tag:

```
<EMBED SRC="theme.mid" height=2 width=0 autostart=true>
```

Or you can display a controller on the user's page by specifying a specific height and width in the tag:

```
<embed src="../music/anna.mid" width=200 height=55 autostart=false></embed>
```

Sound will become more fully integrated into the way people use the World Wide Web, and it can be included in Shockwave, PowerPoint, Persuasion, Astound, and other presentation tools that use plug-ins and players. CoolTalk is a real-time audio and information collaboration helper included in Netscape 3.0 to allow full-duplex audio conferencing and textual and graphical data conferencing using a shared whiteboard. Live3D, a VRML viewer and plug-in from Netscape, provides interactive 3-D spaces that include text, images, animation, sound, music, and video.

My eyes glaze over whenever someone rattles off a definition of multimedia. The glaze thickens when they focus on hardware speed or the merits of one platform or a multimedia authoring tool. The key is to become well versed in a tool so you can make it perform whatever your content requires... it's more important to be creative."

Alan Levine, Instructional Technologist, Maricopa Community Colleges, Arizona

Making sound for the Web requires the basic tools and techniques described in Chapter 9. Always nibble at your sound elements and reduce them to the lowest file sizes that will play acceptably. Remember, they will move across the Internet and may be downloaded or played on machines with low-bandwidth connections.

Animation for the Web

HTML makes no provision for animation, by itself delivering only a static page of text and graphics. Boring, many people said, and programmers went to work devising methods to liven up the view. Netscape 1.0 offered the (annoying) <BLINK> tag; Microsoft's Explorer offered the (annoying) <MARQUEE> tag to scroll text horizontally. JavaScript was applied to force (annoying) sliding text into the status bar. Arcane server-push/client-pull programming techniques refreshed images but loaded the network. Things were happening!

GIF89a

With Version 2.0 of Netscape Navigator, Netscape implemented a little-known animation feature of the final 1989 revision "a" of the GIF file format specification. It is possible to make simple animations by putting multiple images, or *frames,* into a single GIF89a file and display them with programmable delays (in 100ths of a second) between them.

When you use the <IMG> tag to embed a GIF89a multiframe image, Netscape Navigator will download the file and store it in the cache folder of your local hard disk. Once fully downloaded, the image will play each frame quickly and smoothly. Limit animated GIFs to small images, and use a more capable plug-in for animations over larger areas.

Plug-ins and Players

When Macromedia introduced Shockwave to allow the animation and interactivity of its flagship tool, Director, to be embedded into pages viewed by Netscape Navigator, real animation and programmable power was available to Web page developers. Later, they added Flash to their animation armory. Players and plug-ins were offered for other multimedia tools with animation capabilities, and the view came alive. Read Chapter 11 to learn the basics of animation. Pick a tool or method and start creating. Visit

http://www.hkkk.fi/mmedia/itp96/f02.htm to see Lokki, the Shockwaved
seagull, created by a beginner in just a few hours:

---

tip   *When embedding a Shockwave, Flash, PowerPoint, Astound, or other plug-in- or
player-supported animation file into a Web page, remember that cross-platform issues
apply: if you use text fields, your fonts must properly map across platforms (see Chapter 8)
unless you convert all text to bitmaps.*

Figure 15-10 shows the QuickTime VR player—when you drag the mouse
across this player's window, the scene tracks and rotates in a 360-degree
panorama. You can see what is going on in the back seat of this car, too, by
panning the image in a circle. QuickTime, VRML browsers, MPEG, and
other streaming technologies for animation, sound, and video still in development will bring the full power of multimedia to the World Wide Web.

FIGURE 15-10

*QuickTime, AVI, and
MPEG tools bring
video to the Web*

Multi

[Plan for the whole process, beginning with your first ideas and ending with completion and delivery of a finished product.]

You must develop an organized outline

experience

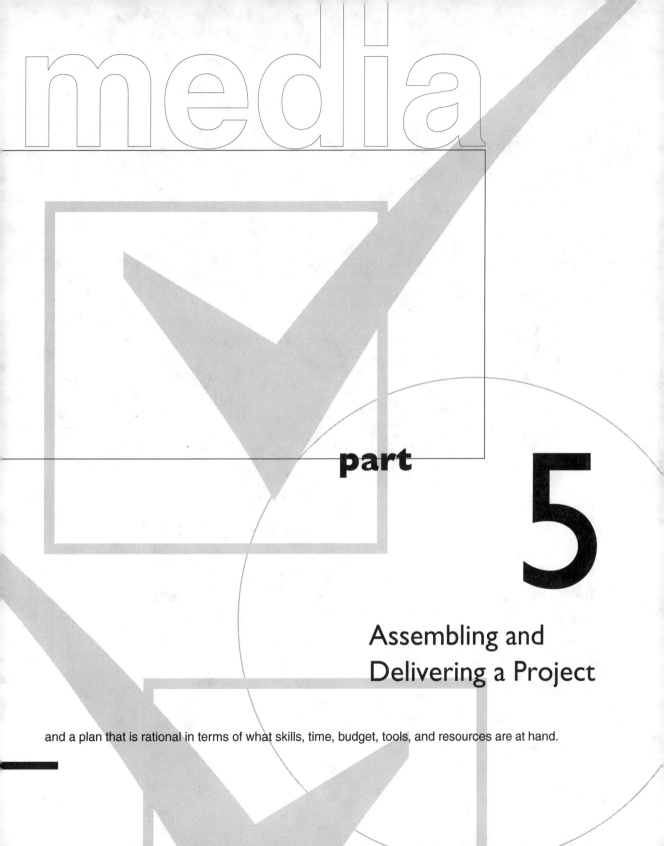

media

part

5

Assembling and Delivering a Project

and a plan that is rational in terms of what skills, time, budget, tools, and resources are at hand.

Multi

Before you begin a multimedia project, you must first develop a sense of its scope and content.

You must develop an organized outline

experience

media

chapter

16

Planning and Costing

and a plan that is rational in terms of what skills, time, budget, tools, and resources are at hand.

B EFORE you begin a multimedia project, you must first develop a sense of its scope and content, letting the project take shape in your head as you think through the various methods available to get your message across to your viewers. Then you must develop an organized outline and a plan that is rational in terms of what skills, time, budget, tools, and resources are at hand. Proper project planning is as important as planning the layout and content. Your plans should be in place before you start to render graphics, sounds, and other components, and you should refer to them throughout the project's execution.

Project Planning

Planning for multimedia projects is like slicing a watermelon at the family picnic: The big picture of your idea is divided into production phases, and these are divided again into smaller and more manageable tasks and items. The resultant pieces are then spread out over a given amount of time to be dealt with one-by-one.

Tasks are the building blocks of project management. Some tasks are prerequisites, and must be completed before others begin, so planning ahead is important. Allocate an estimated amount of time to each task, and place each one along a calendar-based timeline. This is your project plan.

---

tip *The end of each phase is a natural place to set a milestone—that is, a time to deliver work-in-progress, to invoice based upon real work done, to assess or test progress, and/or to solicit and receive constructive feedback. Depending upon the complexity of the project, you may wish to place these milestones at the end of each task as well.*

It is, of course, easiest to plan a project using the experience you have accumulated in similar past projects. Over time, you can maintain and improve your multimedia planning format like a batch of sourdough starter. Just keep adding a little rye and water every time you do a project, and the starter for your next job gets a bit more potent as your estimates become tempered by experience.

Plan for the entire process, beginning with your first ideas and ending with completion and delivery of a finished product. Think in the overview. The stepwise process of making multimedia is illustrated in Figure 16-1. Use this chart to help you get your arms around a new Web site or CD-ROM production! Note the feedback loops for revisions based upon testing and experiment. Note also the constant presence of an "evaluation committee" (who could be simply a project manager) to oversee the whole.

First Person

When I was nine, my father told me about China. He brought the big spinning globe into the kitchen and used a fork to point out where we were and where China was. He explained that if we dug a hole deep enough in the backyard, eventually we would come out in someplace called "Peking." After school the next day, I began, unannounced, trenching a pit into the rocky soil of our New England backyard: the first layer was tough sod, then there was some topsoil and loam, and then a thick stratum of moist pea gravel. I was knee-deep into the next layer—hard-packed clay—when my father discovered the work site at the end of his day. He was pleased I had missed the septic tank by several feet and sternly suggested that more study would be required before I dug any further.

This was my first lesson in project planning, not to mention my first experience with project abandonment. Be sure you analyze the requirements of your multimedia project before you go to the toolshed.

The Process of Making Multimedia

Usually something will click in your mind or in the mind of a client that says, "Hey, wouldn't it be neat if we could…" Your visions of sound and music, flashy images, and perhaps some video will solve a business need, provide an attention-grabbing product demo, or yield a slick front end to an otherwise drab computer database. You might want to spark a little interest or a laugh in an otherwise dull meeting, build an interactive photo album for Christmas greetings to your family, or post your company's annual report in a new set of pages on the Web.

FIGURE 16-1

The process of making multimedia

Idea Analysis

The important thing to keep in mind when you are toying with an idea is balance. As you think through your idea, you must continually weigh your purpose or goal against the feasibility and cost of production and delivery.

We locked eight people in a room with pizza and out popped a design...

Mike Duffy, Chief Technical Officer, Software Toolworks,
describing how the design for the "20th Century Almanac" was developed

Use note paper and scratch pads as you flesh out your idea, or use a note-taking or outlining program on your computer. Start with broad brush strokes, then think through each constituent multimedia element. Ultimately, you will generate a plan of action that will become your road map for production. Who needs this project? Is it worthwhile? Do you have the materials at hand to build it? Do you have the skills to build it? Your idea will be in balance if you have considered and weighed the proper elements:

- What is the essence of what you want to do? What is your purpose and message?

- How can you organize your project?

- What multimedia elements (text, sounds, and visuals) will best deliver your message?

- Do you already have content material with which you can leverage your project, such as videotape, music, documents, photographs, logos, advertisements, marketing packages, and other artwork?

- Is your idea derived from an existing theme that can be enhanced with multimedia, or will you create something totally new?

- What hardware is available for development of your project? Is it enough?

- How much storage space do you have? How much do you need?

- What hardware will be available to your end users?

- What multimedia software is available to you?

- What are your capabilities and skills with both the software and the hardware?

- Can you do it alone? Who can help you?

- How much time do you have?

- How much money do you have?

- How will you distribute the final project?

You can maintain balance between purpose and feasibility by dynamically adding and subtracting multimedia elements as you stretch and shape your idea. You can start small and build from minimum capabilities toward a satisfactory result in an additive way. Or you can shoot the moon with a heavy list of features and desired multimedia results, then discard items one-by-one because they are just not possible. Both additive and subtractive processes can work in concert. In the end, this process will yield very useful cost estimates and a production road map.

Consider the following scenario: You have a videotape with four head-and-shoulders testimonials that will be perfect for illustrating your message. So add motion video to your list. You will need to purchase a video digitizing board and digitizing software, so add those items and their cost to your list as well. But you want to make your product available at a Web site, which means people without high-speed connections will wait minutes for the video to play. Subtract motion video, but add tiny framed still images of the four talking heads (captured with your new video equipment) using short, one-sentence voice-overs of the speakers (recorded from the videotape). Subtract one of the four testimonials because you discover that particular executive is no longer with the firm. Add animation instead. Subtract. Add. Subtract. In this manner, you will flesh out your idea, adding and subtracting elements within the constraints of the hardware, software, and your budget of cost and expertise.

The time you spend defining your project in this way—reality-testing it against technology and your abilities—might be your most valuable investment, even before you boot up a computer. At any point, you can decide to go forward or bail out.

---

tip *Treat your multimedia idea like a business venture. As you visualize in your mind's eye what you want to accomplish, balance the project's profit potential against the investment of effort and resources required to make it happen.*

Pretesting

If you decide that your idea has merit, take it to the next step. Define your project goals in greater detail and spell out what it will take in terms of skills, content, and money to meet these goals. If you envision a commercial product, sketch out how you will sell it. Work up a prototype of the project on paper, with an explanation of how it will work. All of these steps help you organize your idea and test it against the real world.

Prototype Development

When you have decided that a project is worth doing, you should develop a working prototype. This is the point at which you begin serious work at the computer, building screen mock-ups and a human interface of menus and button clicks. Your messages and story lines will take shape as you explore ways of presenting them. For the prototype, sometimes called a proof-of-concept or feasibility study, you might select only a small portion of a large project and get that part working as it would in the final product. Indeed, after trying many different approaches in the course of prototyping, you may end up with several different approaches or candidates. Test your prototype along several fronts: technology (will it work on your proposed delivery platform(s)?), cost (can you do this project within budget constraints?), market (can you sell it or will it be properly used, if it is an in-house project?), and human interface (is it intuitive and easy to use?). At this point you may wish to arrange a focus group, where you watch potential end users play with your prototype and analyze their reactions. The purpose of any prototype is to test the initial implementation of your idea and improve on it based upon test results. So you should never feel committed or bound to any one option, and you should be ready and willing to change things!

Alpha Development

As you go forward, you should continually define the tasks ahead—like navigating a supertanker, you should be aware of the reefs and passages that will appear along your course and be prepared. With a prototype in hand and a commitment to proceed, the investment of effort will increase and, at the same time, become more focused. More people may become involved as you begin to flesh out the project as a whole.

Beta Development

By the time your idea reaches the beta stage of development, you will have committed serious time, energy, and money, and it is likely too late to bail out. You have gone past the point of no return and should see it through. But by now you have a project that is looking great! Most of the features are working, and you are distributing it to a wider arena of testers. In fact, you are on the downhill slope now, and your concern should be simply successfully steering the project to its well-defined goal.

Delivery

By the time you reach the delivery stage, you are "going gold." Your worries slide toward the marketplace. How will your project be received by its intended audience? And you must also deal with a great many practical details, such as who will answer the support hotline, or whether to co-locate a server or trust the current ISP to handle the predicted increased volume of hits. The Alpha, Beta, and final Gold stages of project delivery for CD-ROM and the Web are discussed in Chapter 19.

Hardware

Hardware is the most common limiting factor for realizing a multimedia idea: no sound board, no sound effects; no synthesizer, no MIDI composed by you on-site; no high-resolution color display, no pretty pictures; no modem or network, no Internet.

Begin by listing the hardware capabilities of the end user's computer platform (not necessarily the platform on which you will develop the project). If the capabilities are not enough, examine the cost of enhancing that delivery platform and balance those results against your purpose and resources.

---

tip *In the early days of multimedia development, most projects were designed for monitors set to a resolution of 640x480 pixels and 8-bit color depth (256 colors); this was the most common end-user hardware configuration. Today, designers commonly deliver projects, both on CD-ROM and for the Web, that require a minimum monitor resolution of 800x600 pixels and at least 16-bit color depth (thousands of colors). Hardware improvements and cost drops have increased the assumed available "real estate" or "geography," and use of undithered high-color images has greatly improved the end-user experience.*

Available Skills and Software

You should also list the skills and software capabilities available to you. This list is not as limiting as the hardware list because you can always budget for new and more powerful software and for the learning curve (or consultant fees) required to make use of it. Indeed, the software is usually necessary only for development of the project, not its playback or delivery, and should be a cost or learning burden not directly passed to end users.

The Paper Napkin

The very early idea processing and preliminary planning sketched on the working-lunch paper napkin shown in Figure 16-2 evolved into a complex multimedia project of many months duration.

FIGURE 16-2

The ideas on this luncheon napkin evolved into an animated guided tour for Lotus's Multimedia 1-2-3

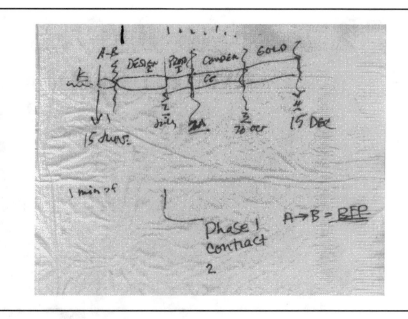

First, the idea was discussed, refined, and cultivated as a preliminary project plan. Then work began with the building of a prototype, shown as the A-B portion of the napkin notes, which quite literally answered the question "How do we get from A to B with this idea?" The prototype was then carefully examined in terms of projected work effort and the technology required to implement a full-blown version of the prototype. Based upon experience, a more complete plan and cost estimate for full implementation was then developed, and the project was launched in earnest. Figure 16-3 shows a screen from the final product.

Idea Management Software

Software such as SiteSpring (see Figure 16-4), Microsoft Project, Designer's Edge (see Figure 16-5), Screenplay System's Screenwriter and StoryView, outlining programs, and spreadsheets such as Excel can be useful for arranging your ideas and the many tasks, work items, employee resources, and costs required of your multimedia project. Project management tools provide the added benefit of built-in analysis to help you stay within your schedule and budget during the rendering of the project itself.

FIGURE 16-3

A screen from the guided tour for Lotus 1-2-3 for Windows with Multimedia SmartHelp, which is shipped on CD-ROM

FIGURE 16-4

SiteSpring from Macromedia is a professional solution for collaborative design and production management

FIGURE 16-5

Designer's Edge, an integrated pre-authoring idea management tool from Mentergy, generates helpful documents for instructional designers

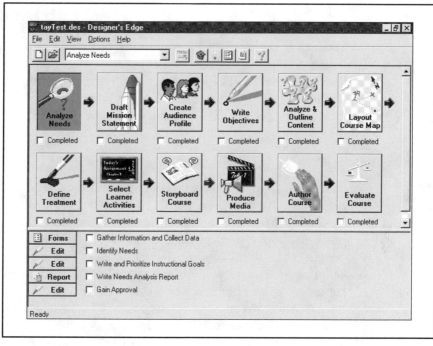

warning Budget your time if you are new to project management software. It may be difficult to learn and to use effectively.

First Person

Last time I took the red-eye home, the fat guy behind me was pretty ill, sneezing and hawking incessantly over my headrest on the full, hot plane. My glasses blurred with misty droplets, and I wiped the fog away with the damp cocktail napkin under my Coke. That trip cost me four days sick in bed, and I promised I would never fly night coach again to make a meeting, no matter how important.

Then I broke my promise and, after a sleepless night on the plane, found myself sitting in the muggy summer air on the bank of the Charles River, having lunch with Rob Lippincott and his multimedia team from Lotus. I pretended to be alert, but residual white noise from the plane ride beat in my ears, and my dry eyes wouldn't focus in the umbrella sunlight. Rob made intelligent notes with a ballpoint pen on a paper napkin while my own input to the creative process was reduced to grunts and short sentences. The smartest thing I did, though, was slip the paper napkin with its notes into my briefcase as we left the table. After some sleep, I was able to retrieve the napkin and craft those luncheon thoughts into the backbone of a rational project proposal and action plan. We launched the venture, and about ten months later it went gold, shipping with Lotus's new Multimedia 1-2-3 product.

Project management software typically provides Critical Path Method (CPM) scheduling functions to calculate the total duration of a project based upon each identified task, earmarking tasks that are critical and that, if lengthened, will result in a delay in project completion. Program Evaluation Review Technique (PERT) charts provide graphic representations of task relationships, showing what tasks must be completed before others can commence. Gantt charts depict all the tasks along a timeline.

Building a Team

Multimedia is an emerging technology requiring a set of skills so broad that multimedia itself remains poorly defined. Players in this technology come from all corners of the computer and art worlds as well as from a variety of other disciplines, so if you need to assemble a team, you need to know what people and skills it takes to make multimedia. (Refer to Chapter 3 for a description of the various skills and talents needed and how others have built successful teams.) Building a matrix chart of required skills is often helpful to describe the makeup of your team. Figure 16-6 shows a skill matrix developed when four medium-sized multimedia development companies came together to bid on a single, large CD-ROM project. If you are building a complex Web site, substitute Java/Perl programmer, HTML programmer, and Server Specialist into the proper row.

In a business where success and failure often depends upon our ability to monitor and anticipate emerging technology, job recruiters see multimedia as very challenging. Not only does the fledgling multimedia industry incorporate some of the hottest computer technology tools, it draws on talent that comes from outside the traditional boundaries of data processing and MIS recruitment. The ill-defined but very technical skills needed for multimedia provide us, the industry recruiters, an exceptional opportunity for creativity. Our clients, too, need to be open minded and flexible about the talent and skills required of multimedia developers.

Heinz Bartesch, Director of Sales and Marketing, The Search Firm (San Francisco)

Staying at the leading edge is important. If you remain knowledgeable about what's new and expected, you will be more valuable to your own endeavors, your team, and to your employer or prospective clients. But be prepared for steep learning curves and difficult challenges in keeping your own skills and those of your employees current and in demand. And don't neglect team morale as hours grow long, deadlines slip, and tempers flare.

16

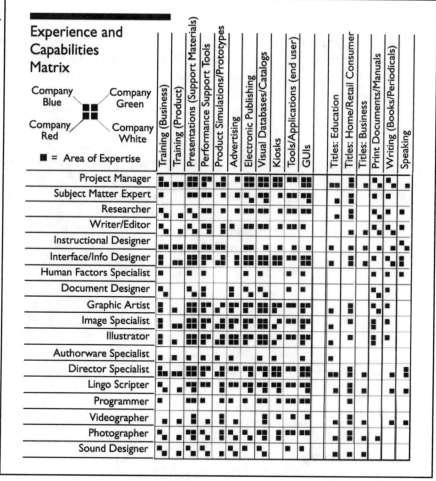

FIGURE 16-6

A matrix of available skills can assist you in planning for your project ■

tip *If you are looking for multimedia talent, try placing a Help Wanted ad in one of the job-hunting/help wanted areas on the Internet.*

http://www.lycos.net-temps.com
http://www.careerpath.com
http://www.monster.com/
http://www.hotjobs.com/
http://www.jobbankusa.com
http://www.dice.com
http://www.fedworld.gov/jobs/jobsearch.html

Places to find jobs

Pilot Projects and Prototyping

When organizing your multimedia project, it may be advisable to incorporate a proof-of-concept or pilot project phase. During this phase you can test ideas, mock up interfaces, exercise the hardware platform, and develop a sense about where the alligators live. These alligators are typically found in the swampy edges of your own expertise, in the dark recesses of software platforms that almost-but-not-quite perform as advertised, and in your misjudgment of the effort required for various tasks. The alligators will appear unexpectedly behind you and nip at your knees, unless you explore the terrain a little before you start out.

Persuade the client to spend a small amount of money and effort up front to let you build a skeletal version of the project, including some artwork, interactive navigation, and performance checks. Indeed, there may be some very specific technology issues that need thorough examination and proof before you can provide a realistic estimate of the work and cost required. The focused experience of this proof will allow both you and the client to assess the project's goals and the means to achieve them.

Build in your experimental pilot as the first phase of your project. At the pilot's conclusion, prepare a milestone report and a functional demo. You will be paid for the work so far, and the client will get real demonstration material that can be shown to bosses and managers. If your demo is good, it will be a very persuasive argument within the client's management hierarchy for completing the full-scale project. Figure 16-7 is excerpted from trial calculations that were the result of a prototype five-language CD-ROM project. In the prototyping, office staff read the voice-over script as a "scratch track," like using a stand-in for the real thing; later, professional talent was used in the recording studio. As a result of building a prototype, accurate estimates of required storage space on the disc were possible.

As part of your delivery at the end of the pilot phase, reassess your estimate of the tasks required and the cost. Prepare a written report and analysis of budgets and anticipated additional costs. This is also the proper time to develop a revised and detailed project plan for the client. It allows the client some flexibility and provides a reality check for you. At this point you can also finalize your budget and payment schedule for the continuation of the project, as well as ink a contract and determine overrun procedures.

Difficulties may arise if your client is disappointed in the quantity of material delivered or is otherwise not satisfied with your work. If you have kept good accounts of the time and effort spent during prototyping, you may be able to smooth the rough waters. Remember that developing multimedia is a "trying"

FIGURE 16-7

Trial calculations are possible after prototyping

■

Calculation Sheet

CD-ROM Project

Allocation of Disc Space

Note 1: The following trial calculations are based upon the file sizes yielded by an early voice rendering of the project's English script.

Note 2: File sizes for low-resolution images (72dpi) of 640×480 and 768×512 pixel dimensions are estimated at 768KB each.

Note 3: File sizes for high-resolution images (300dpi) may range from 3.7MB to 4.5MB, depending upon image complexity and compression rates. The conservative figure of 4.5MB per high-resolution image is used in these estimates.

Note 4: More accurate real estate estimates will be available following finalization of the script and recording of the English version narration.

Note 5: Firm count of low-resolution images and their pixel dimensions will be calculated upon script freeze.

SUMMARY: There is adequate room on the disc for both sound and images if each language recording is limited to no more than 9 minutes.

Scratch Track File (English)	Duration	Scratch Track File (English)	Duration
SNDE01A	18.369	SNDE12A	14.314
SNDE01B	9.180	SNDE13A	14.193
SNDE01C	9.295	SNDE14A	7.487
SNDE02A	17.609	SNDE15A	16.172
SNDE03A	17.932	SNDE16A	19.450
SNDE04A	11.156	SNDE17A	5.830
SNDE05A	18.035	SNDE18A	21.443
SNDE06A	8.050	SNDE19A	12.295
SNDE07A	12.790	Total	306.800 Seconds
SNDE08A	16.218		5.113 Minutes
SNDE09A	27.468	plus Intro Fanfare	30.0 Seconds
SNDE10A	5.658	(Shared by all languages)	
SNDE11A	23.856		

experience—try this, try that, then try this again a bit differently—and the creative process soaks up a lot of hours. Listen carefully to the client's reaction to your prototype; many problems might be quickly fixed, and all constructive comments can certainly be woven into the next phase of development.

First Person

Not every prototype segues naturally into a full-blown project. Sometimes a project is shut down at this milestone due to reality shock: the client chokes on cost-to-completion estimates. Sometimes it's the Reorg Alligator: new managers with new agendas axe the project. Sometimes the client just plain doesn't like your work. Then sometimes a project simply disappears like a dream forgotten by mid-morning.

We were invited to prepare the prototype for a large and intricate intranet site behind a corporate fire wall—potentially a two-year involvement. We proposed a first phase, an analysis and definition of the company's structure and information-gathering and dissemination needs so we could lock down major content areas and the navigation design. We wanted to know how many buttons to put on the main menu and what they would say, before we spent long hours creating the bitmaps and animated GIFs of a neat interface. "No, no," they said,

"our guys have put that together already."

So we negotiated for creation of artwork and HTML page styles that would provide a consistent look and feel throughout the site. We set a fixed price and provided a list of deliverables: (1) graphic style and GIF/JPEG elements for main home and sub pages; (2) a complete site structure and map with navigationally functional "under construction" pages based on the organizational charts they would provide; and (3) working demo pages for two of the company's departments.

Then we had our first team meeting, and it soon became clear they needed hand-holding while their own MIS people transitioned from other tasks and got up to speed in their new jobs as in-house intranet team and webmasters. None had coded a page of HTML, although some had used editors and builders to get pages working. The database guy was stopped dead by an undefined Java error when accessing his massive SQL database. The server guy was still getting set up. The HTML guy was learning his authoring tools.

There was neither a graphic artist nor a handy pool of company graphic art from which our own contribution might spring. OK, we thought, so they're on the learning curve. We can start from scratch. We took the group leader aside and quietly suggested that she consider bringing on a full-time graphics person to support her team.

During the next weeks, we developed a classy look and feel and theme. After a couple of feedback/change loops, they loved it. We worked up the more detailed bits and pieces of our deliverable and tightened up the organization of their proposed navigation map. By prototype deadline, we had spent all the hours we had estimated for the job, and they had the site up and working in test mode. We had gotten their motor running.

Last we saw of the SQL database programmer, on the afternoon we picked up our milestone check, he was removing shrinkwrap from a new copy of Photoshop, and the HTML guy was deep into Cold Fusion. We never heard from them again.

Task Planning

There may be many tasks in your multimedia project. Here is a brief checklist of action items for which you should plan ahead as you think through your project:

- ❏ Design Instructional Framework
- ❏ Hold Creative Idea Session(s)
- ❏ Determine Delivery Platform
- ❏ Determine Authoring Platform
- ❏ Assay Available Content
- ❏ Draw Navigation Map
- ❏ Create Storyboards
- ❏ Design Interface
- ❏ Design Information Containers
- ❏ Research/Gather Content
- ❏ Assemble Team
- ❏ Build Prototype
- ❏ Conduct User Test
- ❏ Revise Design
- ❏ Create Graphics
- ❏ Create Animations
- ❏ Produce Audio
- ❏ Produce Video
- ❏ Digitize Audio and Video
- ❏ Take Still Photographs
- ❏ Program and Author
- ❏ Test Functionality
- ❏ Fix Bugs
- ❏ Conduct Beta Test
- ❏ Create Golden Master
- ❏ Replicate
- ❏ Prepare Package
- ❏ Deliver or Install at Web Site
- ❏ Award Bonuses
- ❏ Throw Party

In a white paper about producing educational software, Mentergy has allocated the following percentages of effort:

Analyze need	3%
Draft mission statement	1%
Create audience profile	2%
Write objectives	2%
Analyze and outline content	6%
Lay out course map	2%
Define treatment	2%
Select learner activities	2%
Storyboard the course	19%
Author the course	28%
Evaluate the course	20%
Produce media	13%

Scheduling

When you have worked up a plan that encompasses the phases, tasks, and work items you feel will be required to complete your project, you need to lay out these elements along a timeline. To do this, you must estimate the total time required for each task and then allocate this time among the number of persons who will be asynchronously working on the project (see, for example, Figure 16-8). Again, the notion of balance is important: if you can distribute the required hours to perform a task among several workers, completion should take proportionally less time.

---

warning *Assigning twice as many people to work on a task may not cut the time for its completion precisely in half. Consider the administrative and management overhead of communication, networking, and necessary staff meetings required when additional staff is added.*

Scheduling can be difficult for multimedia projects because so much of the making of multimedia is artistic trial and error. A recorded sound will need to be edited and perhaps altered many times. Animations need to be run

FIGURE 16-8

Portion of a spreadsheet used to schedule manpower and project costs

PROJECT CALC SHEET			1			2					
c. 5 5	$112,000		MARCH			APRIL					MAY
		SALARY	1	2	3	4	5	6	7	8	9	10
1 CONTEN	ORIGINATION FEE	5										
	DIRECTOR	40	0.1	0.1	0.1	0.1	0.1	0.1	0.1	0.1	0.1	0.1
	cost		0.22	0.22	0.22	0.22	0.22	0.22	0.22	0.22	0.22	0.22
	EDITOR	20					1	1				
	cost		0.00	0.00	0.00	0.00	1.12	1.12	0.00	0.00	0.00	0.00
	WRITER A	40	1	1	1	1	1					
	cost		2.24	2.24	2.24	2.24	2.24	0.00	0.00	0.00	0.00	0.00
	RESEARCHER	16										
	cost		0.00	0.00	0.00	0.00	0.00	0.00	0.00	0.00	0.00	0.00
	subtotal number personnel		1.1	1.1	1.1	1.1	2.1	1.1	1.1	0.1	0.1	0.1
	cost		2.46	2.46	2.46	2.46	3.58	1.34	0.22	0.22	0.22	0.22
2 ART	DIRECTOR	35	1	1	1	1	1	1	1	1	1	1
	cost		1.40	1.40	1.40	1.40	1.40	1.40	1.40	1.40	1.40	1.40
	ART 1	18								1	1	1
	cost		0.00	0.00	0.00	0.00	0.00	0.00	0.00	1.01	1.01	1.01
	ART2	13										
	cost		0.00	0.00	0.00	0.00	0.00	0.00	0.00	0.00	0.00	0.00
	subtotal number personnel		1	1	1	1	1	1	1	2	2	2
	cost		1.40	1.40	1.40	1.40	1.40	1.40	1.40	2.41	2.41	2.41
3 TECHNICAL	DIRECTOR	35								1	1	1
	cost		0.00	0.00	0.00	0.00	0.00	0.00	0.00	1.40	1.40	1.40

again and again and adjusted so that they are smooth and properly placed. A QuickTime or MPEG movie may require many hours of editing and tweaking before it works in sync with other screen activities.

Scheduling multimedia projects is also difficult because the technology of computer hardware and software is in constant flux, and upgrades while your project is under way may drive you to new installations and concomitant learning curves. The general rule of thumb when working with computers and new technology under a deadline is that everything will take longer to do than you think it will.

In scheduling for a project that is to be rendered for a client, remember that the client will need to approve or sign off on your work at various stages. This approval process takes time, and it may also require revision of your submitted work. These client feedback loops depend upon factors beyond your control and can wreak havoc with your schedule.

tip *When you negotiate with your client, limit the number of revisions allowed (each revision costs time and money) before you rename the revisions as change orders and bill extra.*

Many times we have heard about the Feedback Alligator. Its mottled skin boasts an Escher-like pattern of lines and marks, showing apparently clear definition along the head and neck, but converging to a brown muddled wash at the tail. When the tail wags this alligator, all hell breaks loose, and multimedia contracts can be severely strained or lost altogether.

Feedback Alligators can appear when you throw a client into the mix of creative people... when necessary-for-client-satisfaction approval cycles can turn your project into an anorexic nightmare of continuing rework, change, and consequently diminished profit. These alligators typically slink out from the damps after you have locked down a contract and scope of work, when the creative guys are already being well paid to ply their craft.

For client protection, multimedia creative artists should be hired with a cap on budget and time. They should be highly skilled, efficient, and have a clear understanding of what a project's goals are, and they should be allowed to accomplish these goals with as much freedom as possible. But good multimedia artists should come close to the mark the first time.

They don't always. For example, you agree to compose background theme music to play whenever your client's logo shows on the screen. You master a sample cassette tape and pass it to the client. She doesn't quite like the sound but is not sure why. You go back to the MIDI sequencer and try again. The client still isn't sure that's it. Again, you make up a tape and pass it to her for review. No, maybe it needs a little more Sgt. Pepper... this is our logo, remember?

The process of client feedback can go on and on forever in a resonance of desire-to-please and creative uncertainty unless you have developed rules for limiting these cycles. While your client might always be right, you will still go broke working unlimited changes on a fixed budget.

So do two things to ward off the Feedback Alligator. First, make it clear up front (in your contract) that there will be only a certain number of review cycles before the client must pay for changes. Second, invite the client to the workstation or studio where the creative work is done. For sound, tickle the keyboard until the client says, "That's it!" Make 'em sign off on it. For artwork and animations, let the client spend an afternoon riding shotgun over the artist's shoulder, participating in color and design choices. Get the client involved.

If your client contact isn't empowered to make decisions but simply carries your work up to the bosses for "management approval," you are facing the unpleasant Son of Feedback Alligator. Demand a client contact who has budget and design authority.

Estimating

In production and manufacturing industries, it is a relatively simple matter to estimate costs and effort. To make chocolate chip cookies, for example, you need ingredients, such as flour and sugar, and equipment, such as mixers, ovens, and packaging machines. Once the process is running smoothly, you can turn out hundreds of cookies, each tasting the same and each made of the same stuff. You then control your costs by fine-tuning known expenses, negotiating deals on flour and sugar in quantity, installing more efficient ovens, and hiring personnel at a more competitive wage. In contrast, making multimedia is not a repetitive manufacturing process. Rather, it is by its very nature a continuous research and development effort characterized by creative trial and error—a "trying" experience, as described above. Each new project is somewhat different from the last, and each may require application of many different tools and solutions. Philosophers will counsel you that experience is something you get only after you need it!

In the area of professional services, let's consider some typical costs in the advertising community. Production of a storyboard for a 30-second commercial spot costs about $50,000. Postproduction editing time in a professional video studio runs upwards of $500 per hour. An hour of professional acting talent costs $350 or more at union scale. The emerging multimedia industry, on the other hand, does not have a track record long enough to have produced "going rates" for its services. A self-guided tour distributed with a software product, for example, may cost $15,000 for one client and $150,000 for another, depending upon the tour's length and polish. A short original musical clip may cost $50 or $500, based on the talent used and the nature of the music. A graphical menu screen might take 2 or 20 hours to develop, depending on its complexity and the graphic art talent applied. Without available going rates for segments of work or entire projects, you must estimate the costs of your multimedia project by analyzing the tasks that it comprises and the people who build it.

The first time you accomplish a multimedia task, it will demand great effort as you learn the software and hardware tools and the techniques required. The second time you do a similar task, you will already know where the tools are and how they work, and the task will require less effort. On the third take, you should be quite proficient.

tip *To recoup learning-curve costs when you first perform a task, you must factor extra time into your budget; later you can increase your billing rate to reflect your improved skill level.*

Be sure you include the hidden costs of administration and management. It takes time to speak with clients on the telephone, to write progress reports, and to mail invoices. In addition, there may be many people in your workforce who represent specialized skills, for example, a graphic artist, musician, instructional designer, and writer. In this case, you'll need to include a little extra buffer of time and expense in your estimate to pay for these artists' participation in project meetings and creative sessions.

As a general rule, there are three elements that can vary in project estimates: time, money, and people. As illustrated below, if you decrease any one of these elements, you'll generally need to increase one or both of the others. For example, if you have very little time to do a project (an aggressive schedule), it will cost more money in overtime and premium sweat, and it may take more people. If you have a good number of people, the project should take less time. By increasing the money spent, you can actually decrease the number of people required by purchasing efficient (but costly) experts; this may also reduce the time required.

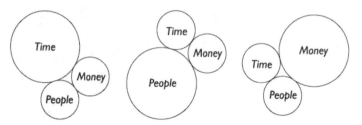

Do your best to estimate the amount of time it will take to perform each task in your plan. Multiply this estimate by your hourly billing rate. Sum the total costs for each task, and you now have an estimate of the project's total time and cost. Though this simple formula is easy, what is not so easy is diligently remaining within the budgeted time and money for each task. For this, you need good tracking and management oversight.

Billing Rates

Your billing rate should be set according to your cost of doing business plus a reasonable profit margin. Typical billing rates for multimedia production companies and Web designers range from $60 to $150 an hour, depending upon the work being done and the person doing it. If consultants or specialists are employed on a project, the billing rate can go much higher. You can establish a rate that is the same for all tasks, or you can specify different rates according to the person assigned to a task.

Everyone who contributes to a project should have two rates associated with their work: the employee's cost to the employer (including salary and benefits), and the employee's rate billed to the customer. The employee's cost, of course, is not included in your estimate, but you need to know this as part of your estimate—because your profit margin is the difference between the rate you charge the client and the cost to your company, less a proportion of overhead expenses (rental or leasing of space, utilities, phones, shared secretarial and administrative services, etc.). If your profit margin is negative, you should reconsider both your project plan and your long-term business plan.

Multimedia production companies and Web site builders with high billing rates claim their skillset and experience allow them to accomplish more work in a given amount of time, expertly, thus saving money, time, and enhancing the finished quality and reliability of a project. This is particularly the case with larger-scale, complex projects. Smaller and leaner companies that offer lower billing rates may claim to be more streamlined, hungry, and willing to perform extra services. Lower rates do not necessarily mean lower-quality work, but rather imply that the company either supports less overhead or is satisfied with a reduced profit margin. The business of making multimedia is a "low entry barrier" enterprise because all you need to get started is some (relatively) inexpensive computer hardware and software, not a 70,000 square foot factory or expensive tooling. You can make multimedia in a living room, basement, or garage. As more and more multimedia producers and Web developers enter this marketplace, the competition is increasing and the free hand of supply and demand is driving prices (down).

Purchasers of multimedia services must, however, thoroughly examine the qualifications of a prospective contracting person or company to ensure that the work required can be accomplished on time and within budget. There is no more difficult business situation than a half-completed job and an exhausted budget.

First Person

We were asked by a large institution to complete a project that had fallen on the floor. It was really worse than that—the project had actually slipped through the cracks in that floor. The single known copy of work—representing about $30,000 in paid billings—had been copied to 19 high-density floppy disks and stored in a file cabinet. Here, they were discovered by the secretarial pool and formatted, to be used for WordPerfect documents. The secretaries remembered the whole thing because the stored backups contained protected files, so the disks were unusually difficult to erase! Luckily, bits and pieces of the project were unearthed on the hard disk of a computer that had been disconnected and stored in the basement. We were able to reconstruct much of the artwork, but not the interactive links.

As we studied the leavings of the embarrassed progenitors, we discovered a trail of mistakes and errors. It became clear that the institution made a bad decision in hiring a well-qualified engineering firm at great expense (standard billing rates) to construct a difficult multimedia presentation. CAD/CAM drawings and finite element analysis were the forte of these engineers—not animated icons and colorful bitmaps with sound tracks. Furthermore, the engineering firm erred in selecting software that performed on the target hardware platform at about the speed of snails chasing a dog. Money had been spent, the product didn't work, and everyone involved was in gray limbo, slinking around, looking for a solution.

We determinedly pulled together the bits and pieces we could find, designed a snappy navigational structure we were proud of, and quickly fixed the big problem for a small fee (based upon our own standard billing rate). The institution, of course, was delighted and became a client of long standing.

First Person

I was downbound from Puget Sound to San Francisco, and the weather was up, with seas running heavy and winds gusting to 80 knots in our face. The Master and the First Mate were on the bridge, the old man sitting curled up in his upholstered high chair on the darkened starboard wing, the First pacing on the rubber mat behind the helmsman. The Third Mate was on watch, leaning over the radar screen and making fluorescent notes with a grease pencil. As I was a guest with no duties, I mostly hung out in the chart room while white water broke over the bows and the shuddering propeller came out of the sea; wind screamed in the vents on the roof of the bridge. There wasn't much conversation that night, but the Master slowed us to 5 knots, concerned about the containers lashed to the forward deck.

When the young Third Mate came into the chart room, I asked, "Where are we?" and he took a sharp pencil, made a fine point on the chart, and drew a tiny circle around the point; he smiled, proud to have good radar bearings. The First Mate came in about a half hour later, and when I asked the same question, he circled an area about the size of a walnut. As the Master left the bridge for his cabin, I asked him, too, where we were. He took his thumb and rubbed it on the chart in a rough oval about the diameter of his fist, saying, "Somewhere in here," and grinned at me as the ship heaved suddenly and we grabbed for the handholds.

The more experience these professionals had, the larger the circle they drew, and the less they relied upon pinpoint navigation. You should be prudent when costing a multimedia production; precision estimating can wreck your project.

Contractors and consultants can bring specialized skills such as graphic art, C and Java programming, database expertise, music composition, and video to your project. If you use these experts, be sure your billing rate is higher than theirs. Or, if you have a task the client has capped with a not-to-exceed cost, be sure your arrangement with the contractor is also capped. Contractors place no burden on your overhead and administration other than a few cups of coffee, and they should generate a generous profit margin for you during the course of your project. Be sure that contractors perform the majority of their work off-site, using their own equipment; otherwise, federal tax regulators may reclassify these freelancers as employees and require you to pay employee benefits. In 1998, in *Vizcaino v. Microsoft,* the U.S. Supreme Court required the Microsoft Corporation to pay employee benefits to hundreds of workers that the court determined were regular employees rather than independent contractors. There are about 20 factors, according to the IRS, in making a determination whether a worker is an employee or an independent contractor for tax purposes, and companies may be liable for all employment benefits, including (as Microsoft discovered) stock option and stock sharing plans, if the work arrangement is not carefully constructed.

Example Cost Sheets

Figure 16-9 contains groups of expense categories for producing multimedia. If you use these in your own work, be sure to temper your guesses with experience; if you are new to multimedia production, get some qualified advice during this planning stage.

16

FIGURE 16-9

There are many costs associated with producing multimedia
■

PROJECT DEVELOPMENT COSTS

Salaries
Client Meetings
Acquisition of Content
Communications
Travel
Research
Proposal & Contract Prep
Overhead

PRODUCTION COSTS
Management
  Salaries
  Communications
  Travel
  Consumables
Content Gathering
  Salaries
  Research Services
  Licenses
Graphics Production
  Salaries
  Hardware/Software
  Fees for Content Use
  Animation
  Consumables
Audio Production
  Salaries
  Hardware/Software
  Studio Fees
  Licenses

Consumables
Data Storage
Talent Fees
Video Production
  Salaries
  Hardware/Software
  Equipment Rental
  Talent Fees
  Location Fees
  Studio Fees
  Digital Capture & Editing
  Consumables
Authoring
  Salaries
  Hardware/Software
  Consumables

TESTING COSTS
Salaries
Focus Groups
Editing
Beta Program

DISTRIBUTION COSTS
Salaries
Documentation
Packaging
Manufacturing
Marketing
Advertising
Shipping

RFPs and Bid Proposals

Often, potential clients don't have a clue about how to make multimedia, but they have a vision or a mandate. You field a telephone call, a voice describes a need or a want, and you explain how you (and your company) can satisfy that need. Much of the talk may be instructional as you teach the client about the benefits and pitfalls of multimedia in all its forms. You seldom will glean enough information during this initial discussion to accurately estimate time or cost, so be prepared to answer these queries in vague terms while you present your available skillsets and capabilities in the most favorable light. If the client is serious and your instruction well received, in short time you may be able to guide this client into good choices and reasonable decisions, working together to conceive and design an excellent product. Discussions will soon turn into design meetings. Somewhere along the way, you will sign a contract.

Occasionally you may encounter a more formal Request for Proposal (RFP). These are typically detailed documents from large corporations who are "outsourcing" their multimedia development work. Figure 16-10 is an example of such a document that provides background information, scope of work, and information about the bidding process. Still, you should note that there is little "hard" information in this document; most bid proposals require contact with the client to fill in details prior to bidding.

A multimedia bid proposal will be passed through several levels of a company so that managers and directors can evaluate the project's quality and its price. The higher a bid proposal goes in the management hierarchy, the less chance it has of being read in detail. For this reason, you always want to provide an executive summary or overview as the first page of your proposal, briefly describing the project's goals, how the goals will be achieved, and the cost.

In the body of the proposal, include a section dealing with creative issues, and describe your method for conveying the client's message or meeting the graphic and interactive goals of the project. Also incorporate a discussion of technical issues, in which you clearly define the target hardware platform. If necessary, identify the members of your staff who will work on the project, and list their roles and qualifications.

The backbone of the proposal is the estimate and project plan that you have created up to this point. It describes the scope of the work. If the project is complicated, prepare a brief synopsis of both the plan and the timetable; include this in the overview. If there are many phases, you can present each phase as a separate section of the proposal.

Cost estimates for each phase or deliverable milestone, as well as payment schedules, should follow the description of the work. If this section is lengthy, it should also include a summary.

FIGURE 16-10
Some RFPs provide
great detail
∎

Smythe Industries
Request for Proposal

Summary: The objective is to produce a family of materials that will develop a unique personality and visual image for the Smythe Campus in Vancouver, British Columbia, home of multiple Smythe subsidiaries and divisions.

As background, Smythe Industries was launched in 1995 following the acquisition of Wilson Aluminum Foundries, Ltd. (Canada) and Fenwick Rolling Mills, Inc. (U.S.A.) and is based in Vancouver. The site is also the headquarters for Global Aluminum Research, a research and development subsidiary. In addition, there are discussions concerning the establishment of a special alloy research institute at the Vancouver campus.

Each of the entities has unique personality traits, management structures, and business cultures which will need to be recognized and incorporated into the design process.

Audience and Message
Potential Employees - "employer of choice"
Business Development - "partner of choice"
   Metals Companies
   Academic Institutions
Government/Community officials - "good neighbor/citizen"
Smythe Employees - "credible/proud"
Scientific/Engineering Organizations - "credible research/scientifically advanced"

Tone and Manner
Innovative, scientifically advanced, sophisticated, credible
Colorful: jewel colors/crisp/high contrast
Energetic, modern, innovative, cutting edge
Geometric lines and shapes (vs. free form)
A human element: photography, illustration, etc.
Personable, warm, intellectually inviting

Electronic Communications RFP

Multimedia Presentation Capabilities
Summary: The objective is to create a set of tools that will deliver key messages while positioning Smythe Vancouver as an innovative user of technology for communication. There will be two components to this project: a presentation format and a library of images. We would like to develop a library, including still imagery, audio, and QuickTime movies, that can be contained on a set of CDs. Note: all images should be created with the goal of repurposing across different mediums and projects.

The key purpose is to make core messages and the corporate personality come alive by utilizing sound and motion. These multimedia assets will be used for recruiting purposes at career centers, job fairs, and in-house for visiting recruits. They will also serve as presentation support material at scientific and engineering forums. Smythe will work with the multimedia design firm to create and identify existing television clips, video, and other material that can serve to reinforce key messages.

FIGURE 16-10

Some RFPs provide

great detail

(continued)

■

External Web Site
Summary: As the most visible element of Smythe's Vancouver identity, the Web site will set the stage for positioning the company in the research community as an employer of choice and a key player in esoteric alloy and metallurgical research. The Web site will provide easy navigation for users to reach the areas of greatest interest to them, e.g., a particular business division, academic papers, employment opportunities, etc.

The multimedia design firm will also be expected to create a library of images that can be utilized to update the site periodically. The design firm should also be prepared to provide input on ways to easily update and cost-effectively maintain the site. In addition, the Web site should be created so that audio and live imagery can be incorporated and downloaded easily by users who have the appropriate equipment.

Internal Web Site
Summary: The internal Web site is the primary medium for employee communication. It will be a usable, interesting tool for internal users and serve to reinforce corporate messages and the campus culture. Since the Web site represents and includes different business entities on campus, this internal site will also introduce employees to activities in which other business units and groups are involved.

The site will need to be designed with a template format so that it can be easily updated.

Production Elements for All Electronic Communications
Icons: Develop an illustrative style for a family of icons shared across the CD-ROM, internal Web site, and external Web site.

Interface Design: Develop an interface design that provides design parameters and a personality for the internal Web site and external Web site. (Note: Internal and external Web sites should carry a similar look and feel; however, it must be easy to distinguish between the two.)

Visual Image: Produce a library of visual images. This will require the additional production of video clips and sound clips.

Photography: A photo shoot schedule and plan will be developed with Smythe to most effectively maximize time and resources in shooting photos which can be used in print, in the Web sites, and in multimedia materials.

RFP Process
Quotations: Itemize quotes, e.g. project management, copy writing, editing, design, photography, illustrations, etc. Also provide three references.

Note: Smythe will write the HTML directives in-house and will also be posting to a server that is maintained in-house.

All quotes should be submitted to:
Suzanne Petruski
Project Manager
Smythe Industries
65 Silver Foil
Vancouver, BC, CANADA

tip *Make the proposal look good—it should be attractive and easy to read. You might also wish to provide an unbound copy so that it can be easily photocopied. Include separate, relevant literature about your company and qualifications. A list of clients and brief descriptions of projects you have successfully completed are also useful for demonstrating your capabilities.*

Finally, include a list of your terms. Contract terms may become a legally binding document, so have your terms reviewed by legal counsel. An example is shown in Figure 16-11. Terms should include the following:

- A description of your billing rates and invoicing policy.

- Your policy for billing out-of-pocket expenses for travel, telephone, courier services, and so forth.

- Your policy regarding third-party licensing fees for run-time modules and special drivers (the client pays).

- Specific statements of who owns what upon completion of the project. You may wish to retain the rights to show parts of the work for your own promotional purposes and to reuse in other projects segments of code and algorithms that you develop.

- An assurance to the client that you will not disclose proprietary information.

- Your right to display your credits appropriately within the work.

- Your unlimited right to work for other clients.

- A disclaimer for liability and damages arising out of the work.

It is a significant task to write a project proposal that creatively sells a multimedia concept, accurately estimates the scope of work, and provides realistic budget costs. The proposal often becomes a melting pot—you develop the elements of your idea during early conversations with a potential client and add the results of discussions on technique and approach with graphic artists and instructional designers. You blend what the client wants done with what you can actually do, given the client's budgetary constraints, and when the cauldron of compromise cools, your proposal is the result.

The Cover and Package

You have many options for designing the look and feel of your proposal. And though we are often warned to avoid judging a book by its cover, the

FIGURE 16-11

Sample contract

terms adapted from

language developed

by the HyperMedia

Group, Inc. (do not

use without

appropriate legal

counsel)

■

Sample Terms:

We will undertake this assignment on a time-and-expenses basis at our current hourly rate of $___ per hour for __job title__, $___ per hour for __job title__, $___ per hour for __job title__ , plus applicable taxes and reimbursement of authorized out-of-pocket expenses. Reasonable travel, express, freight, courier and telecommunication expenses incurred in relation to the project, will be considered pre-authorized. [Client] will be responsible for all licensing fees of third-party products incorporated (with [Client]'s knowledge and approval) into the final product. We will invoice [Client] either upon [Client]'s acceptance of the specified deliverables for each work phase specified above, or monthly, whichever is more often. [Client]'s authorization, either written or verbal, to commence a work phase will constitute acceptance of the previous phase's deliverables. Invoices are due and payable upon presentation. To commence work, we require a retainer in the amount of $_____, which will be deducted from the final invoice for the project.

Upon our receipt of final payment, [Client] shall own all rights, except those noted below, to the completed work delivered under this agreement, including graphics, written text, and program code. [Client] may at [Client]'s sole discretion copyright the work in [Client]'s name or assign rights to a third party. Ownership of material provided by third parties and incorporated in our work with [Client]'s knowledge and approval shall be as provided in any license or sale agreement governing said materials. We reserve the right to use in any of our future work for ourselves or any client all techniques, structures, designs and individual modules of program code we develop that are applicable to requirements outside those specified above. Further, our performance of this work for [Client] shall in no way limit us regarding assignments we may accept from any other clients now or at any time in the future.

We shall be allowed to show [Client]'s finished work, or any elements of it, to existing and prospective clients for demonstration purposes. If such demonstration showings would reveal information [Client] has identified to us as proprietary or confidential, we shall be allowed to create a special version for demonstrations which omits or disguises such information and/or [Client]'s identity as the client. We shall also be allowed to include a production credit display, e.g. "Produced by [Our Name]" or equivalent copy, on the closing screen or other mutually agreeable position in the finished work. Following [Client]'s acceptance of this proposal we shall also be allowed to identify [Client] as a client in our marketing communications materials.

In the event it is necessary in the course of this assignment for us to view or work with information of [Client]'s that [Client] identify to us as proprietary and confidential (possibly including customer lists, supplier data, financial figures and the like), we agree not to disclose it except to our principals, associates and contractors having confidentiality agreements with us.

We make no warranty regarding this work, or its fitness for a particular purpose, once [Client] accepts it following any testing procedures of [Client]'s choice. In any event, our liability for any damages arising out of this work, expressly including consequential damages, shall not exceed the total amount of fees paid for this work.

reality is that it takes about two seconds for executives to assess the quality of the document they are holding. Sometimes, they decide before even touching it. Size up the people who will read your proposal and ferret out their expectancies; tailor your proposal to these expectancies.

If your client judges from the cover of your proposal that the document inside is amateurish rather than professional, you are already fighting an uphill battle. There are two strategies for avoiding this negative first impression:

1. Develop your own special style for a proposal cover and package, including custom fonts, cover art and graphics, illustrations and figures, unique section and paragraph styles, and a clean binding. Do your proposal first class.

2. Make the entire package plain and simple, yet businesslike. The "plain" part of the approach means not fussing with too many fonts and type styles. This austerity may be particularly successful for proposals to government agencies, where 10-point Courier Elite or 12-point Pica may be not just a de facto standard, but a required document format. For the "simple" part of the approach, a stapled sheaf of papers is adequate. Don't try to dress up your plain presentation with Pee-Chee folders or cheap plastic covers; keep it lean and mean.

16

Table of Contents

Busy executives want to anticipate a document and grasp its content in very short order. A table of contents or index is a straightforward way to present the elements of your proposal in condensed overview. In some situations, you may also wish to include an Executive Summary—a prelude containing no more than a few paragraphs of pithy description and budget totals. The summary should be on the cover page or immediately following.

Needs Analysis and Description

In many proposals, it is useful to describe in some detail the reason the project is being put forward. This Needs Analysis and Description is particularly common in proposals that must move through a company's executive hierarchy in search of approval and funding.

Target Audience

All multimedia proposals should include a section that describes the target audience and target platform. When the end user's multimedia capabilities have a broad and uncertain range, it is very important to describe the hardware and software delivery platform you intend to provide. For instance, if your project requires a compact disc player but the end user platform has none, you will need to adjust your multimedia strategy by revising the design or by requiring the end user to acquire a player. Some clients will clearly control the delivery platform, so you may not need to provide detail regarding system components.

Creative Strategy

A Creative Strategy section—a description of the look and feel of the project itself—can be important to your proposal, especially if the executives reviewing your proposal were not present for creative sessions or did not participate in preliminary discussions. If you have a library of completed projects that are similar to your proposed effort, it is helpful to include them with your proposal, pointing the client to techniques and presentation methods that may be relevant. If you have designed a prototype, describe it here, or create a separate heading and include graphics and diagrams.

Project Implementation

A proposal must describe the way a project will be organized and scheduled. Your estimate of costs and expenses will be based upon this description. The Project Implementation section of your proposal may contain a detailed calendar, PERT and Gantt charts, and lists of specific tasks with associated completion dates and work hours. This information may be general or very detailed, depending upon the demands of the client. The Project Implementation section is not just about how much work there is, but how the work will be managed and performed. You may not need to specify time estimates in work hours, but rather in the amount of calendar time required to complete each phase.

Budget

The budget relates directly to the scope of work you have laid out in the Project Implementation section. Distill your itemized costs from the Project Implementation description and consolidate the minute tasks of each project phase into categories of activity meaningful to the client.

[Feedback loops and good communication between the design and production effort are critical to the success of a project.]

strengths and limitations

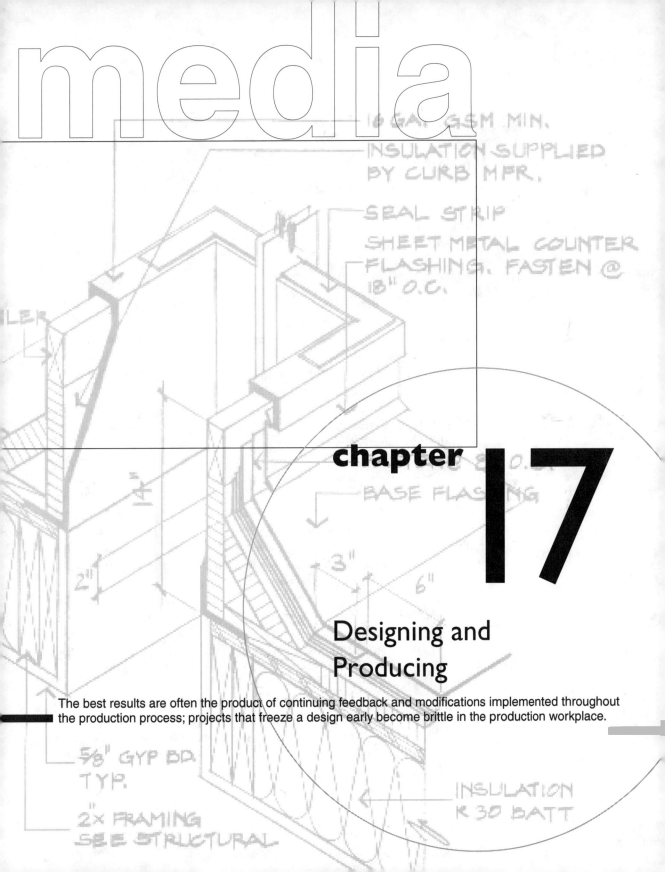

media

16 GA. GSM MIN.

INSULATION SUPPLIED
BY CURB MFR.

SEAL STRIP

SHEET METAL COUNTER
FLASHING, FASTEN @
18" O.C.

BASE FLASHING

chapter 17

3"

6"

Designing and
Producing

The best results are often the product of continuing feedback and modifications implemented throughout
the production process; projects that freeze a design early become brittle in the production workplace.

5/8" GYP BD.
TYP.

2× FRAMING
SEE STRUCTURAL

INSULATION
R 30 BATT

D ESIGNING and building multimedia projects go hand in hand. Indeed, design input to a project is never over until the product is actually frozen and shipped. The best products are often the result of continuing feedback and modifications implemented throughout the production process; projects that freeze a design too early become brittle in the production workplace, losing the chances for incremental improvement. But there is a danger: too much feedback and too many changes can kill a project, draining it of time and money. Always balance proposed changes against their cost to avoid the "creeping features" syndrome.

Just as the architect of a high-rise office tower must understand how to utilize the materials with which he or she works (lest the construction collapse on trusting clients), designers of multimedia projects must also understand the strengths and limitations of the elements that will go into their project. It makes no sense, for example, to design the audio elements of a multimedia project in memory-consuming 16-bit, 44.1 kHz stereo sound when the delivery CD-ROM will not have sufficient room for it; or to produce lengthy full-screen QuickTime movies to play at 30 frames per second over the Internet when end users connect with 28.8 Kbps modems; or to design 24-bit color graphics for elementary schools when that environment supports 8-bit graphics. Architects don't design inner-city parking garages with 14-foot ceilings and wide turning radii for 18-wheel big rigs, and they don't build them using wood or mud laid on a swampy foundation.

Designers must work closely with producers to ensure that their ideas can be properly realized, and producers need to confirm the results of their work with the designers. "These colors seem to work better—what do you think?" "It plays faster now, but I had to change the animation sequence..." "Doing the index with highlighted lines slows it down—can we eliminate this feature?" Feedback loops and good communication between the design and production effort are critical to the success of a project.

The idea processing (described in Chapter 16) of your multimedia project will have resulted in a detailed and balanced plan of action, a production schedule, and a timetable. Now it's time for implementation!

Designing

The design part of your project is where your knowledge and skill with computers, your talent in graphic arts, video, and music, and your ability to conceptualize logical pathways through information are all focused to create the real thing. Design is thinking, choosing, making, and doing. It is shaping, smoothing, reworking, polishing, testing, and editing. When you design your project, your ideas and concepts are moved one step closer to reality. Competence in the design phase is what separates amateurs from professionals in the making of multimedia.

---

t i p   *Never begin a multimedia project without first outlining its structure and content.*

Depending on the scope of your project and the size and style of your team, you can take two approaches to creating an original interactive multimedia design. You can spend great effort on the *storyboards,* or graphic outlines, describing the project in exact detail—using words and sketches for each and every screen image, sound, and navigational choice, right down to specific colors and shades, text content, attributes and fonts, button shapes, styles, responses, and voice inflections. This approach is particularly well suited for teams that can build prototypes quickly and then rapidly convert them into finished goods. Or you can use less-detailed storyboards as a rough schematic guide, exerting less design sweat up front and more effort actually rendering the product at a workstation.

The method you choose depends on whether the same people will do the whole thing (both designing and the implementing) or whether design and implementation are tasked to separate teams by other members, who of course need a more detailed specification (that is, detailed storyboard and sketches). Both approaches require the same thorough knowledge of the tools and capabilities of multimedia, and both demand a storyboard or a project outline. The first approach is often favored by clients who wish to tightly control the production process and labor costs. The second approach gets you more quickly into the nitty-gritty, hands-on tasks, but you may ultimately have to give back that time because more iterations and editing will be required to smooth the work in progress. In either case, the more planning on paper, the better and easier it will be to construct the project.

Designing the Structure

A multimedia project is no more than an arrangement of text, graphic, sound, and video elements (or *objects*). The way you compose these elements into interactive experiences is shaped by your purpose and messages.

How you organize your material for a project will have just as great an impact on the viewer as the content itself. With the explosive growth of the World Wide Web and proliferation of millions and millions of multimedia-capable HTML documents that can be linked to millions of other similar documents in the cyberspace of the Web, your designs and inventions may actually contribute to the new media revolution: other creators may discover your work and build upon your ideas and methods.

Navigation

Mapping the structure of your project is a task that should be started early in the planning phase, because navigation maps outline the connections or links among various areas of your content and help you organize your content and messages. A *navigation map* (or *site map*) provides you with a table of contents as well as a chart of the logical flow of the interactive interface. As a more detailed design document, it may show your multimedia objects and describe what happens when the user interacts.

Just as eight story plots might account for 99 percent of all literature ever written (boy meets girl, protagonist versus antagonist, etc.), a few basic structures for multimedia projects will cover most cases: linear, hierarchical, nonlinear, and composite. Figure 17-1 illustrates the four fundamental organizing structures used in multimedia projects, often in combination:

- *Linear:* Users navigate sequentially, from one frame or bite of information to another.

- *Hierarchical:* Users navigate along the branches of a tree structure that is shaped by the natural logic of the content.

- *Nonlinear:* Users navigate freely through the content of the project, unbound by predetermined routes.

- *Composite:* Users may navigate freely (nonlinearly), but are occasionally constrained to linear presentations of movies or critical information and/or to data that is most logically organized in a hierarchy.

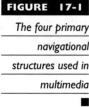

FIGURE 17-1

The four primary navigational structures used in multimedia

■

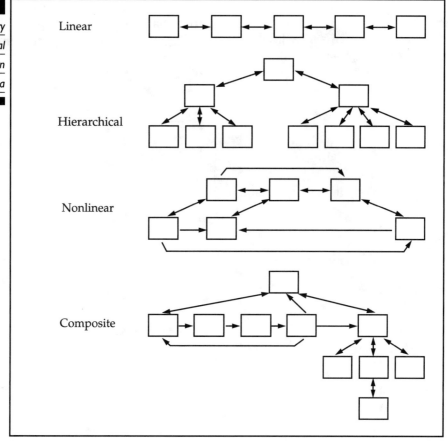

The method you provide to your viewers for navigating from one place to another in your project is part of the user interface. The success of the user interface depends not only upon its general design and graphic art implementations but also upon myriad engineering details—such as the position of interactive buttons or hot spots relative to the user's current activity, whether these buttons "light up," and whether you use standard Macintosh or Windows pull-down menus. A good user interface is critical to the overall success of your project.

Structural Depth   Professor Judith Junger from the Open University of the Netherlands in Amsterdam suggests that when you design your multimedia product you should work with two types of structure: *depth structure* and *surface structure*. Depth structure represents the complete navigation map and describes all the links between all the components of your project (see Figure 17-1). Surface structure, on the other hand, represents the structures actually realized by a user while navigating the depth structure. Thus the following depth structure

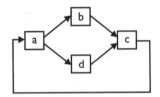

might be realized as the following surface structure:

Some surface structures generated by users might look like this:

Sequential structure with optional paths

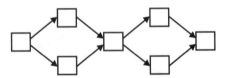

Sequential structure with alternative paths

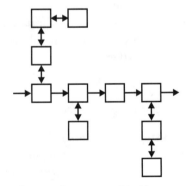

Sequential structure with sidesteps

The following depth structure for a quiz thus consists of three possible surface structures:

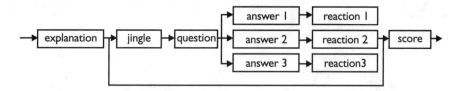

When you design your navigation map, it helps to think about surface structure—to view the product from a user's perspective. Surface structures are of particular interest to marketing firms in tracking users' routes through a Web site to determine the effectiveness of a Web site's design and to profile a user's preferences. When a user's preferences are known, a custom Web site experience can be dynamically tailored and delivered to that user. Acquisition and management of such profiling data is a hot topic, with privacy advocates claiming the personal information revealed in these surface structures is akin to a person's medical and health records.

Many navigation maps are essentially nonlinear. In these navigational systems, viewers are always free to jump to an index, a glossary, various menus, Help or About... sections, or even to a rendering of the map itself. It is often important to give viewers the sense that free choice is available; this empowers them within the context of the subject matter. Nonetheless, you should still provide consistent clues regarding importance, emphasis, and direction by varying typeface size and look, colorizing, indenting, or using special icons.

The architectural drawings for your multimedia project are the storyboards and navigation maps. The storyboards are married to the navigation maps during the design process.

Because all forms of information—including text, numbers, photos, video, and sound—can exist in a common digital format, they can be used simultaneously as people browse through an information stream, just as people use their various senses simultaneously to perceive the real world.

Bill Gates, Chairman, Microsoft Corporation

First Person

With regard to the creation of interactive fiction, what kinds of software engineering strategies would you recommend for creating stories that maintain a strong sense of cumulative action (otherwise known as plot) while still offering the audience a high frequency of interaction? In other words, how do you constrain the combinatoric explosion of the narrative pathways, while still maintaining the Aristotelian sense of a unity of plot?

   —Patrick Dillon, Atlanta, GA

   One and one-half T-shirts to Patrick Dillon! Would have been two for your invocation of a famous Greek philosopher, but then I couldn't find "combinatoric" in Webster's. Aristotle himself would have been pleased by the harmonious balance of your reward: you have asked a really good question.

   As multimedia and the power of computers begin to change our approach to literature and storytelling, new engineering strategies do need to be implemented.

   When fiction becomes nonlinear, and users can choose among alternative plot lines, the permutations can become staggering. To an author, this means each new plot pathway chosen by user interaction requires its own development, and one story may actually become several hundred or more. To constrain this fearsome explosion of narrative pathways, yet retain a high frequency of interaction, try designing your fiction around a single core plot that provides the cumulative action, and use arrays of returning branches for detail and illustration. In this way you can entirely avoid the permutations of alternative universes and still offer the adventure of interactive exploration.

   Dear Tay: I just read your answer to Patrick Dillon's question about interactive fiction in your column for March 1993. My response is difficult to contain: "Aaarrrrggghhhh!!!! You Ignorant Slut!" OK, perhaps I am overreacting, but you are refusing to let go of linearity. Why ever do you want to "constrain the combinatoric explosion of narrative pathways"? Good Lord, that's what makes the gametree bushy. This is exactly the kind of work that's well suited for a computer to perform—grinding out three billion story variations!

   —Chris Crawford,
   San Jose, CA

   Chris, I've been called a lot of things over the years (like Fay and Ray), and it's with a smile that I add your gift to my collection. Playing Jane Curtin to your Dan Aykroyd, I'll be happy to counter your counterpoint.

   Your challenge represents a serious subject for multimedia designers today. I agree that interactive stories with too few branches are disappointingly flat and shallow. When a plot is broadly nonlinear, however, the permutations of events and possible outcomes become staggering, and the story as a whole becomes difficult to visualize and manage. Producing such work is also an intellectual challenge and costly in time and effort.

   A truly open-ended "hypermedia" navigation system for consumer consumption risks death by shock caused by open arterial branches and loss of story pressure, where plot lines become too diffuse and users founder in trivia. Most users may, indeed, prefer a structured, organized, and well-defined story environment.

   The argument for simplicity is voiced by Steven Levy, the author of Hackers and Artificial Life, who says, "There's really something to be said for documents with a beginning, middle, and end."

   The shape of this new literature made possible by multimedia computers and wide-bandwidth cable and telephone delivery systems is

17

being born in the working designs of developers. The final test for successful multimedia design is the marketplace, where consumers will decide.

Your interesting "algorithms for interpersonal behavior,

personality models, artificial personality, languages of expression, and facial displays" represent, perhaps, a successful marriage of this computer power with literature containing malleable plots and seemingly endless variations.

Indeed, your forthcoming epic game, Le Morte D'Arthur, will surely break new ground and quite possibly prove your point. Can't wait to get a copy!

From correspondence in "Ask the Captain," a monthly column by Tay Vaughan in NewMedia *magazine.*

A simple navigation map is illustrated in Figure 17-2, where the subject matter of a small project is organized schematically. The items in boxes are not only descriptions of content but also active buttons that can take users directly to that content. At any place in the project, users can call up this screen and then navigate directly to their chosen subject.

A storyboard for this same project is organized sequentially, screen by screen, and each screen is sketched out with design notes and specifications before rendering. At the left of Figure 17-3 is part of the storyboard for this project; at the right are corresponding finished screens.

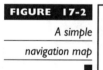

FIGURE 17-2

A simple navigation map

FIGURE 17-3

A storyboard on the left, with finished screen on the right

Multimedia provides great power for jumping about within your project's content. And though it is important to give users a sense of free choice, too much freedom can be disconcerting, and viewers may get lost. Try to keep your messages and content organized along a steady stream of the major subjects, letting users branch outward to explore details. Always provide a secure anchor, with buttons that lead to expected places, and build a familiar landscape to which users may return at any time.

17

Really good software products should be simple, hot, and deep. People need to get into your software in about 20 seconds and get immediate positive feedback and reward; then they are smiling and having a good time and they want to go further. Hot *means that you've got to be fully cooking the machine, with all its graphics and sound capabilities, conveying something dynamic and exciting that competes with what people are used to seeing in a movie or on TV. In terms of* deep, *it's kind of like the ocean where there are people of all ages: some kids will just wade out in a foot of surf, other guys with scuba gear go way out and way deep. Make it possible for me to go as deep as I want, but don't force it on me. Just let the depth of your product unfold to me in a very natural way.*

Trip Hawkins, Chairman & CEO, 3DO Company

Your content may not always be an assembly of discrete subjects as illustrated in Figure 17-2. If your material deals with a chronology of events occurring over time, for example, you may wish to design the structure as a linear sequence of events and then send users along that sequence, allowing them to jump directly to specific dates or time frames if desired (see Figure 17-4). A timeline will graphically show the positioning of your multimedia elements and can be helpful during the design phase: where there are overlapping events, you may wish to create cross-sectional paths or views for a "slice in time."

FIGURE 17-4

A chronological

navigation map

with active buttons

■

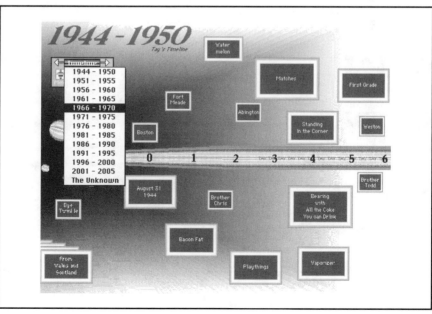

Even within a linear, time-based structure, you may still wish to sort events into categories regardless of when they occur. There is no reason you can't do this and offer more than one method of navigating through your content. Figure 17-5, for instance, illustrates a navigation map that accesses the same events from the timeline form of Figure 17-4, but arranged here instead into meaningful groups of events.

Hot Spots and Buttons

Most multimedia authoring systems allow you to make any part of the screen, or any object, into a button or hot spot. When users click a button at that location, something happens—this makes multimedia not just interactive, but also exciting. Your navigation design must provide buttons that make sense, so their actions will be intuitively understood by means of their icon or graphic representation, or via text cues. Do not force your viewers to learn many new or special icons; keep the learning curve to a minimum. It's also important to include buttons that perform basic housekeeping tasks, such as quitting the project at any given point, or canceling an activity.

There are three general categories of buttons: text, graphic, and icon. Text buttons and their fonts and styles are described in Chapter 8. Graphic buttons can contain graphic images or even parts of images—for example, a map of the world where each country is color coded, and a mouse click on a country yields further information. Icons are graphic objects designed specifically to be

FIGURE 17-5

A navigation map

based on events

that are active

buttons

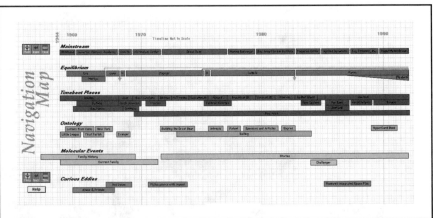

First Person

One day I launched an application named Disk Formatter on my Macintosh, just to see what it was about. Suddenly I was in a pretty scary user-interface predicament (Figure 17-6 is what I saw). I could tell from its name that the software erased and formatted hard disks and cartridges: my mounted hard disks were listed on the screen by SCSI number, and I was being prompted to select one of them. I looked over at the CPU and was pleased that the disk drive access light wasn't ticking away at sector-length intervals. I didn't know what the software was doing because I hadn't read the manual; I did know, however, what I wanted to do—back out and quit. Too much at stake to be fooling around here!

Well, there was no Cancel button and no Quit button, and OK was too risky with the radio button for my 200MB internal hard disk turned on. Did OK mean "OK, start formatting," or did it mean "OK, thanks for selecting that drive, now on to further options"? As a dialog box, the Disk Formatter application limited my choices to its own, and I didn't like any of them. I figured I would do an emergency power-down by pulling the plug on the CPU, and then I could restart. But before employing that ultimate solution for sticky-cursors, I tried ⌘-Q. This is the conventional Macintosh keyboard method to quit an application, and it worked. The screen went away.

I was pretty unhappy about the application's design, though, because there was no clear route to back out of the formatting activity, and OK implies going forward in most user interactions.

FIGURE 17-6

A user interface with no Cancel or Quit provision

Disk Formatter   Please Select The Required Drive

- ⊙ 0   MAXTOR LXT-200S   2.15
- ○ 1   SyQuest SQ555   F9K   g>   567323
- ○ 2   QUANTUM P105S 910-10-94xA.3
- ○ 3   No Device
- ○ 4   SONY   CD-ROM CDU-8001 3.2i
- ○ 5   No Device
- ○ 6   Mystery Box   MII SC23MSF300ZS SCANNERV3.2SCSI F/WV2.3

[Versions]   [Devices]   [OK]

meaningful buttons and are usually small (although size is, in theory, not a determining factor). Icons are fundamental graphic objects symbolic of an activity or concept:

Most authoring systems provide a tool for creating text buttons of various styles (radio buttons, check boxes, push buttons, animated buttons, and spin buttons), as well as graphic and icon buttons.

---

tip *Designing a good navigation system and creating original buttons appropriate for your project are not trivial artistic tasks. Be sure you budget sufficient time in your design process for many trials, so you'll be able to get your buttons looking and acting just right.*

---

cross platform *Windows does not manage icon resources in the same manner as Macintosh. Each Windows multimedia authoring tool allows for the construction and use of graphic buttons in its own way. If you are bringing Macintosh icons into a Windows tool, export them from the Macintosh as bitmaps, import them into your Windows authoring tool, and create appropriate mouse-clicking activities for highlighting and other effects.*

Highlighting a button or object is the most common method of distinguishing it as the object of interest when single-clicking. When a button is double-clicked, it should be highlighted before the intended activity occurs, to let the user know that the button was, indeed, clicked. Highlighting is usually accomplished by reversing the object's colors: changing black to white or vice versa, or otherwise altering its colors. Drop shadows placed slightly below and to the right of a button can give it a 3-D look and, depending upon how you arrange the highlighting, can make a button appear out (not pressed) or in (pressed). In Windows, when the Help button is pressed (clicked or selected), the perimeter shading is changed, and the text is offset to the right, as illustrated here:

HTML documents do not directly support interactive buttons that follow the rules of good interface design—by highlighting or otherwise confirming a mouse-down action. But you *can* make plain and animated buttons for your HTML documents on the Web using plug-ins such as Flash and Shockwave, or JavaScripts. A simple JavaScript in an HTML document can replace one image with another on mouseOver (see Chapter 15 for a code snippet that does this). The simplest buttons on the Web are the anchors that link a document to other documents—usually a browser indicates that text is a hot link by coloring/underlining the text so it stands out from the body. Default colors for anchor text are a user-defined preference, so you can override the default in the <BODY> tag.

Other common buttons found on the Web consist of small JPEG or GIF graphic images that are themselves anchor links. Browsers indicate that an image is hot by drawing a border around it. (You can remove this border by placing "BORDER="0" into the <IMG> tag.) Larger images may be sectioned into hot areas with associated links; these are called *image maps*. Figure 17-7 shows a graphic image of a village that has been programmed in HTML to have 32 hot spots with links (the document to open when clicked) and a JavaScript routine called "set" that will place an image into the frame at the left when the mouse rolls over that area. The code looks like this:

```
<AREA shape="rect" coords="180,85,230,135" href="../vendors/v25/index.html"
onmouseover="set('../vendors/v25/images/logomenu.gif');">
```

In most Web browsers, you know you have clicked on a button only after the cursor changes while the browser seeks another document and loads it. Ways to make interesting buttons and interactive graphical interfaces on the World Wide Web are described more fully in Chapter 15.

Designers will build screens where there are tiny little things going on all over it at different places, and everything has momentous significance. And then the user is supposed to be able to find these momentous things. So people just glaze over. If you want them to hit a button, put a big button right in the middle of the screen.

Trip Hawkins, Chairman & CEO, 3DO Company

Using a large image map and JavaScript embedded in a normal HTML Web page, when the mouse rolls over a house or barn, the content of that building is displayed as a separate graphic at the left. Users can actively explore this seaside village to discover what's hidden behind its doors

■

Icons

On the Macintosh, icons have a special meaning: they constitute a suite of image resources that can be linked to the Finder and used to identify an application or project. ResEdit, the resource editing tool from Apple, allows you to create and edit System icons. They are small (16×16 pixels) or large (32×32 pixels), may be colored, and may have a text label attached, as shown by some of the icons used by Microsoft Word98:

tip *For a quick and simple way to change a Macintosh icon, highlight any file's icon by clicking on it once, open the Get Info... dialog (⌘-I), click once on the icon shown at the top left of the Get Info panel to highlight it, and paste any 32x32-pixel bitmap from the Clipboard. The old icon is replaced with the new. You can also copy an icon to the Clipboard from the Get Info panel (⌘-C). With this trick, you can customize the look of your desktop.*

Icons can be embedded within a Macintosh application or project (in the resource fork) for use as buttons, but these icons are limited in size to 32×32 pixels. In Windows, you can change the icon used to represent an application or other file. Select My Computer, and then click on the following menus: View | Options... | File Types | New Type... | Change Icon.... You will then see the icons currently available in the system's SHELL32.DLL (see Figure 17-8). If you are building a multimedia project in Windows, you can create custom icons and store them as .ico files. Visual Basic, for example, ships with a library of more than 450 icons ready to use in the following categories: arrows and pointers, communication, computers, drag and drop, elements, flags, industry and transportation, mail, miscellaneous, office, traffic signs, and writing. These icons are quite useful simply as clip art, but they are either small (32×32 pixels) or smaller (16×16 pixels). These smaller icons are primarily used as mouse pointers or cursors.

Icons (and .ico files that contain icons) are created using an icon editor such as IconDraw (freeware) or another editor utility. Icons in Windows, however, relate to the Windows operating system and to Program Manager (as do

FIGURE 17-8

In Windows, many icons are installed with the system

Finder icons on the Macintosh), and these icons are typically not available for easy use within an authoring tool. If you want to use a system icon, it is best to capture it off the screen and place the icon into your project as a bitmap.

Designing the User Interface

The user interface of your multimedia product is a blend of its graphic elements and its navigation system. If your messages and content are disorganized and difficult to find, or if users become disoriented or bored, your project may fail. Poor graphics can cause boredom. Poor navigation aids can make viewers feel lost and unconnected to the content; or, worse, viewers may sail right off the edge and just give up and quit the program.

Novice/Expert Modes

Be aware that there are two types of end users: those who are computer literate and those who are not. Creating a user interface that will satisfy both types has been a design dilemma since the invention of computers. The simplest solution for handling varied levels of user expertise is to provide a *modal interface*—one where the viewer can simply click a Novice/Expert button and change the approach of the whole interface, to be either more or less detailed or complex. Modal interfaces are common on bulletin boards, for example, allowing novices to read menus and select desired activities, while experts can altogether eliminate the time-consuming download and display of menus and simply type an activity code directly into an executable command line. Both novices and experts alike may quickly learn to click the mouse and skip the annoying ragtime piece you chose for background music.

Unfortunately, in multimedia projects, modal interfaces are not a good answer. It's best to avoid designing modal interfaces because they tend to confuse the user. Typically, only a minority of users are expert, and so the majority are caught in between and frustrated. The solution is to build your multimedia project to contain plenty of navigational power, providing access to content and tasks for users at all levels, as well as a Help system to provide some hand-holding and reassurance. Present all this power in easy-to-understand structures and concepts, and use clear textual cues. Above all, keep the interface simple! Even experts will balk at a complex screen full of tiny buttons and arcane switches, and will appreciate having neat and clean doorways into your project's content.

Two readers didn't notice the screen had changed in different circumstances. This happened when the button they clicked on took them to a visually similar screen, and there was no visual effect as the screens changed. One reader was looking at the details of a hostel and clicked on the left-hand Next arrow. He arrived at a screen with details about another hostel, but did not notice he was looking at a different screen. He tried the right-hand Next arrow as well, and the screen changed back to the one he had been viewing initially, but again he did not notice the change and concluded the Next buttons did nothing. A visual effect or animation here would have provided a cue to make the screen changes more noticeable.

Lynda Hardman of the Scottish HCI Centre, after focus group
testing the "Glasgow Online" hypertext system

GUIs

The Macintosh and Windows graphical user interfaces (GUI, pronounced "gooey") are successful partly because their basic point-and-click style is simple, consistent, and quickly mastered. Both these GUIs offer built-in Help systems, and both provide standard patterns of activity that produce standard expected results. The following actions, for example, are consistently performed by similar keystrokes when running most programs on the Macintosh or in Windows:

Action	Macintosh Keystroke	Windows Keystroke
New file	⌘-N	ALT-F-N or CTRL-N
Open file	⌘-O	ALT-F-O or CTRL-O
Save file	⌘-S	ALT-F-S or CTRL-S
Quit	⌘-Q	ALT-F-X or CTRL-Q
Undo	⌘-Z	ALT-E-U or CTRL-Z
Cut	⌘-X	ALT-E-T or CTRL-X
Copy	⌘-C	ALT-E-C or CTRL-C
Paste	⌘-V	ALT-E-P or CTRL-V

For your multimedia interface to be successful, you, too, must be consistent in designing both the look and the behavior of your human interface. Multimedia authoring systems provide you with the tools to design and implement your own graphical user interface from scratch. Be prudent with all that flexibility, however. Unless your content and messages are bizarre or require special treatment, it's best to stick with accepted conventions for button design and grouping, visual and audio feedback, and navigation structure.

Vaughan's General Rule for Interface Design

The best user interface demands the least learning effort

Stick with real-world metaphors that will be understood by the widest selection of potential users. For example, consider using the well-known trash can for deleting files, a hand cursor for dragging objects, and a clock or an hourglass for pauses. If your material is time-oriented, develop metaphors for past, present, and future. If it is topic-oriented, choose metaphors related to the topics themselves. If it is polar (the pros and cons of an issue, for example), choose relevant contrasting images.

---

tip *Most multimedia authoring systems include tutorials and instructions for creating and using buttons and navigation aids. Typically, they also supply templates or examples of attractive backgrounds and distinctive buttons that serve as an excellent starting place. In a large project, you might want to use a different metaphor as the backbone of each major section, to provide a helpful cue for users to orient themselves within your content. For the Travel section, for example, you could use icons that are sailing ships with various riggings; for the Finance section, buttons that are coins of different denominations; and for the buttons of the International Business section, you could use colorful flags from various countries.*

Users like to be in control, so avoid hidden commands and unusual keystroke/mouse click combinations. Design your interface with the goal that no instruction manual or special training will be required to move through your project. Users do not like to have to remember keywords or special codes, so always make the full range of options easily available as interactive buttons or menu items. And finally, users do make mistakes, so allow them a chance to escape from inadvertent or dangerous predicaments ("Do you really want to delete? Delete/Escape"). Keep your interface simple and friendly.

Throw out your tried and true training or software development methodologies, and pretend that you're Spielberg or Lucas: think of what the viewer sees and hears and how the viewer interacts with the system you deliver. Create an "experience" for the viewer.

David A. Ludwig, Interactive Learning Designs

Graphical Approaches

Designing excellent computer screens requires a special set of fine art skills, and not every programmer or graduate in fine arts may be suited to creating computer graphics. Like programmers who must keep up with current operating systems and languages, computer graphic artists must also stay informed about the rapidly changing canvas of new features, techniques, applications, and creative tools.

Computer graphics is more left- and right-brained—and not so spontaneous as doing it by hand. The ramp time is tedious; I am used to instant gratification with my fine artwork.

Cornelia Atchley, a fine artist creating
multimedia art with computers, Washington, D.C.

The artist must make broad design choices: cartoon stick figures for a children's game, rendered illustrations for a medical reference, scanned bitmaps for a travel tour of Europe. The graphic artwork must be appropriate not only for the subject matter, but for the user as well. Once the approach is decided, then the artist has to put real pixels onto a computer screen and do the work. A multimedia graphic artist must always play the role of the end user during the design and rendering process, choosing colors that look good, specifying text fonts that "speak," and designing buttons that are clearly marked for what they do.

Things That Work   Here are some graphical approaches that get good results:

- Neatly executed contrasts: big/small, heavy/light, bright/dark, thin/thick, cheap/dear (see Figure 17-9)

FIGURE   17-9

Contrasts attract the eye—Bud Knight, PGA Junior Champion at the turn of the century, was made thick by stretching him in an image-editing program

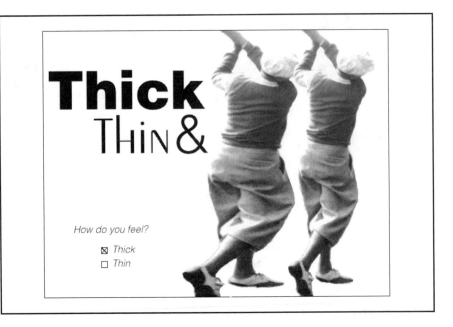

- Simple and clean screens with lots of white space (see Figure 17-10)
- Eye-grabbers such as Drop caps, or a single brightly colored object alone on a gray-scale screen

FIGURE   17-10

Use plenty of white space ("noninformation areas") in your screens

- Shadows and drop shadows in various shades

- Gradients

- Reversed graphics to emphasize important text or images

- Shaded objects and text in 2-D and 3-D

Things to Avoid   Here are some mistakes you will want to avoid in creating computer graphics:

- Clashes of color

- Busy screens (too much stuff)

- Trite humor in oft-repeated animations

- Clanging bells or squeaks when a button is clicked

- Frilly pattern borders

- Cute one-liners from famous movies

- Requiring more than two button clicks to quit

- Too many numbers (limit charts to about 25 numbers; if you can, just show totals)

- Too many words (don't crowd them; split your information into bite-sized chunks)

- Too many substantive elements presented too quickly

Most graphic artists will tell you that design is an "intuitive thing," but they will be hard pressed to describe the rules they follow in their everyday work. They know when colors are not "working" and will change them again and again until they're right, but they usually won't be able to explain why the colors work or don't work. A project with a good navigation design, though it may have been developed with good planning and storyboarding, is indeed more often the result of many hours of crafty finagling with buttons and editors.

Audio Interfaces

A multimedia user interface may include important sound elements that reflect the rhythm of a project and may affect the attitude of your audience. Sounds can be background music, special effects for button clicks, voice-overs, effects synced to animation, or they may be buried in the audio track of a video clip. The tempo and style of background music can set the "tone" of a project. Vivaldi or Bach might be appropriate for a banking or investment annual report delivered on CD-ROM. Comic laughs and screeching effects might be appropriate for a clothing web site aimed at pre-teens. Choose music that fits the content and the atmosphere you wish to create. In all cases, use special effects sparingly. Always provide a toggle switch to disable sound. And always test a project that contains sound with potential users. Many AOL users disable the "You've Got Mail!" voice.

A Multimedia Design Case History

This section presents an example of the design process for a simple multimedia project about the construction and launch of a 31-foot ocean-going sailboat. This project was initially crafted in SuperCard (a Macintosh-only page-based authoring tool), but it was later ported to Macromedia Director (a time-based tool) so that it could be played on both Mac and Windows platforms (see Chapter 7 for details about authoring systems).

Storyboarding a Project

The source material (all that was available) practically sorted itself into logical groups: a pile of old photographs, a magazine article and newspaper clippings, engineering drawings, official documents, and some cassettes with recorded sounds. The first storyboard was a simple hierarchical structure with branches to each subject area, as shown in Figure 17-11.

Putting It Together

The most eye-catching photograph was chosen as a background for the main menu, and, as shown in Figure 17-12, the main menu was planned to contain clearly labeled buttons navigating to linear presentations of each topic area. From every screen in the project, users would be able to return to the main menu. Where sound bites were appropriate, sounds would be played by buttons to be clicked on screens. And a Quit button was necessary, also on the main menu, so that users would never be more than two button clicks from exiting the project (back to the main menu, and then quit).

The 50 or so 4×5 photographs were old color prints that offered poor contrast and faded colors (due to a saltwater dunking in a storm off the Central American coastline). Digitized on a flat-bed scanner in gray-scale, however, they worked fine, and Photoshop was available to improve contrast. All the

FIGURE 17-11

The first storyboard

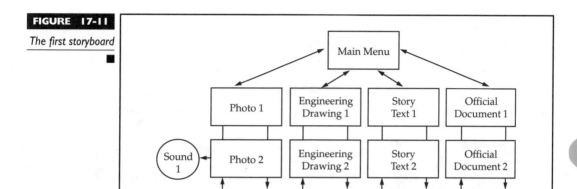

prints were scanned, cropped to the same dimension, optimized, and stored as bitmapped objects within Director. While at the scanner, merchant marine licenses and documents were also digitized, and the magazine article was scanned using OCR software to bring it into ASCII format. The story text was imported into the project.

After all the content was in Director's Cast (see Chapter 7), and work on the navigation system was under way, several issues emerged. First, it is terrifically boring to read a 3,000-word story by scrolling a long text field. Second, the photos were too small to be placed alone on a single screen. So it

FIGURE 17-12

Main menu screen

with relevant

artwork as

background

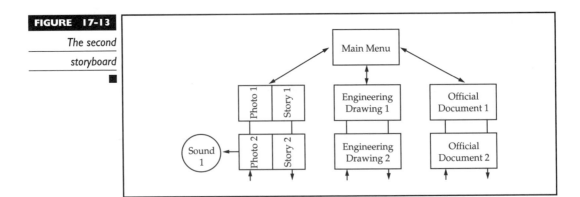

made sense to combine the story line with the images, even though they were not directly related; the story about launching the boat would progress from beginning to end as the boat was slowly built in the pictures. The storyboard changed to that shown in Figure 17-13.

The photo-essay-and-story combination worked out to 28 screens. The photos were placed into the score, and the text was cut and pasted into fields (see Figure 17-14). It became clear that users might want to scan rapidly through the photographs to watch the boat being built, ignoring the text of the story. So a special button was programmed to scan through the images until the mouse was clicked.

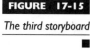

FIGURE 17-15

The third storyboard

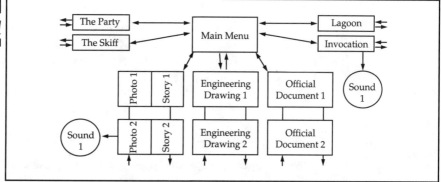

Images that did not fit into the photo essay about building the boat—for instance, the launching party with its roast pig, the long haul to the beach by trailer, and setting the mooring—were withdrawn from the pile of construction photographs; but because they were interesting, they were attached as separate branches accessible by button from the main menu. This was the third time the navigation changed, proving that you can continue to hang elements on a menu until the menu screen is too busy (and then you use submenus), or until you run out of material, as shown in Figure 17-15.

Next, the sound bites were recorded, digitized, and added to the project. Figure 17-16, the screen where the sounds were to play, shows the special button installed to play sound bites. It's simply a picture of a loudspeaker.

FIGURE 17-16

Sound is played

when the

loudspeaker icon is

clicked

The documents for the project included engineering drawings, highway permits, and licenses. The highway permit, for example, was 8.5×11 inches (portrait); but after some experimentation, once it was scaled to 480 pixels in height, it was (barely) readable and acceptable for this project. The licenses and drawings were in landscape orientation and fit more easily on the 640×480-pixel screen (see Figure 17-17).

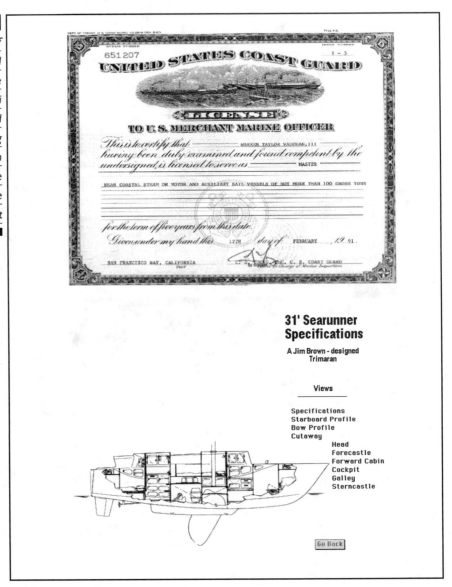

Reworking

The buttons on the main menu were the wrong color, so they were changed a few times until the color worked. Helvetica title text wasn't fancy enough, so it was reworked and a drop shadow was laid in. A special slider button was built and programmed to allow the construction sequence to go immediately to any of the pictures in the sequence. The backgrounds were tweaked a little, and the order of images changed somewhat. A small red car was animated to drive along the edge of the lagoon.

The project described here was simple and straightforward. With the exception of designing a few custom buttons for autoscanning through some of the images and designing the animations, the entire project was a progression of screens of information, with links activated by clicking buttons.

Producing

By the time you reach the development phases of your multimedia project and you start building, you should already have taken care to prepare your plan and to get organized. The project plan (see Chapter 16) now becomes your step-by-step instruction manual for building the product. For many multimedia developers, following this plan and actually doing the construction work—being down in the trenches of hands-on creation and production—is the fun part of any project.

Developing multimedia can be like taking a joy ride in a washer/dryer. When it's all over you feel like you've been washed, rinsed, spun, and tumble-dried.

Kevin McCarthy, Director of Business Development, Medius IV

Production is the phase when your multimedia project is actually rendered. During this phase you will contend with important and continuing organizing tasks. There will be times in a complex project when graphics files seem to disappear from the server, when you forget to send or cannot produce milestone progress reports, when your voice talent gets lost on the way to the recording studio, or when your hard disk crashes. So it's important to start out on the right foot, with good organization, and to maintain detailed management oversight during the entire construction process. This rule applies to projects large and small, projects for yourself or for a client, and projects with 1 or 20 people on staff. Above all, provide a good time-accounting system for everyone working on the project. At the end of the week, it's hard to remember how much time you spent on tasks done on Monday.

tip   *If your project is to be built by more than one person, establish a management structure in advance that includes specific milestones and production expectations for each contributor.*

Starting Up

Before you begin your multimedia project, it's important to check your development hardware and software and review your organizational and administrative setup, even if it is you working alone. This is a serious last-minute task. It prevents you from finding yourself halfway through the project with nowhere to put your graphics files and digitized movie segments when you're out of disk space, or stuck with an incompatible version of a critical software tool, or with a network that bogs down and quits every two days. Such incidents can take many days or weeks to resolve, so try to head off as many potential problems as you can before you begin.

- Desk and mind clear of obstructions?
- Fastest CPU and RAM you can afford?
- Time-accounting and management system in place?
- Biggest (or most) monitors you can afford?
- Sufficient disk storage space for all work files?
- System for regular backup of critical files?
- Conventions or protocols for naming your working files and managing source documents?
- Latest version of your primary authoring software?
- Latest versions of software tools and accessories?
- Communication pathways open with client?
- Breathing room for administrative tasks?
- Financial arrangements secure (retainer in the bank)?
- Expertise lined up for all stages of the project?
- Kick-off meeting completed?

First Person

At 18, I used to hang around with people who drove fast cars, and once volunteered to help an acquaintance prepare his Ferrari Berlinetta for a race at Watkins Glen. My job was to set the valves while my friend went over the suspension, brakes, and later, the carburetor. The car boasted 12 cylinders and 24 valves, and adjusting the clearance between tappet and rocker arm seemed to me akin to a jeweler's fine work. It required special wrenches and feeler gauges and an uncommon touch to rotate the high-compression engine so the cam was precisely at its highest point for each valve. I was blown away by the sheer quantity of moving parts under the Ferrari's long and shiny valve covers—my own fast car had only four cylinders and eight simple valves. It took me about seven exhausting hours (including double-checking) to get it right. As the sun came up, though, the engine sounded great!

Tuning up and preparing, I learned, is as important to the race as the race itself. My friend, however, learned a much tougher lesson: he spun out and rolled his Ferrari at the hairpin turn in the seventh lap. He crawled unhurt from the twisted wreckage, but all he was able to salvage from the car was the engine.

Working with Clients

Making multimedia for clients is a special case. Be sure that the organization of your project incorporates a system for good communication between you and the client as well as among the people actually building the project. Many projects have turned out unhappily because of communication breakdowns.

Client Approval Cycles

Provide good management oversight to avoid endless feedback loops—in this situation the client is somehow never quite happy, and you are forced to tweak and edit many times. Manage production so that your client is continually informed and formally approves artwork and other elements as you build them. Develop a scheme that specifies the number and duration of client approval cycles, and then provide a mechanism for change orders. For change orders, remember that the client should pay extra and changes are costly.

Data Storage Media and Transportation

It's important that the client be able to easily review your work. Remember that both you and the distant site need to have matching data transfer

First Person

We made up two sample musical tracks to play in the background and sent them off by overnight courier to the client. Four days later, the client phoned to say that both were good, but couldn't we make it sound a little more like Windham Hill. So we redid the music and sent two more samples. Five days later, the client said the samples were great, but the boss wanted something with a Sergeant Pepper feel. So we sent a fifth creation, this time with a note that they would have to either settle on one of the five styles submitted, supply the music themselves, or pay us more money to keep up the creative composition work. They chose the music the boss liked, but we wound up more than two weeks behind schedule and had spent significantly more money and effort on this task than originally budgeted.

Several months later, in the next job requiring original music composition, we specified a maximum of two review/feedback cycles and added a clause for cost overrun beyond that. The first sound we submitted to this new client was approved, and we stayed ahead of schedule and budget.

systems and media, or you need to provide a Web or FTP site for your project. Organize your system before you begin work, as it may take some time for both you and the client to agree on an appropriate system and on the method of transportation.

Because multimedia files are large, your means of transporting the project to distant clients is particularly important. Typically, both you and the client will have access to the Internet. If not, the most cost- and time-effective method for transporting your files is on CD-R or DVD-ROM by an overnight courier service (Fedex, DHL, Airborne Express, or U.S. Postal Service Express Mail). Material completed in time for an afternoon pickup will usually be at the client's site by the next morning. Sending an overnight letter-size package (with discs inside) usually costs less than $20.

If you use the Internet to deliver your multimedia to the client, be sure that you set up rules and conventions for naming files placed at an FTP site, and use codes in the subject headers of your e-mail to describe the content of the message. After a project has been under way for a while, there will be many files and many communications—keywords and clues will make life easier. This is another place where planning ahead pays off!

Tracking

Organize a method for tracking the receipt of material that you will incorporate into your multimedia project. Even in small projects, you will be dealing with many digital bits and pieces.

Develop a file-naming convention specific to your project's structure. Store the files in directories or folders with logical names. If you are working across platforms, develop a file identification system that uses the DOS file-naming convention of eight characters plus a three-character extension. Use this convention on files for the Macintosh as well as the PC; otherwise, files transferred from the Macintosh to the PC may receive default names with strange characters and extensions that are difficult to interpret. You may also need to set up a database with file names as eight-character codes matched to lengthier descriptive names, so you know what the codes mean.

17

---

warning *Even if you are working in Windows, avoid using long file names with characters like spaces, periods, or colons. Those names may not map properly to the other operating system.*

Version control of your files (tracking editing changes) is critically important, too, especially in large projects. If more than one person is working on a group of files, be sure that you always know what version is the latest and who has the current version. If storage space allows, archive all file iterations, in case you change your mind about something and need to go back to a prior rendering.

Copyrights

Macromedia Director, ToolBook, MetaCard, Visual Basic, and other commonly used authoring platforms may allow access to the software programming code or script that drives a particular project. The source code of HTML pages on the Web may also be easily viewed.

In such an open-code environment, are you prepared to let others see your programming work? Is your code neat and commented? Perhaps your mother cautioned you to wear clean underclothing in case you were suddenly on a table among strangers in a hospital emergency room—well, apply this rule to your code. You can insert a copyright statement in your project that clearly (and legally) designates the code as your intellectual property (see Figure 17-18), but the code, tricks, and programming techniques remain accessible for study, learning, and tweaking by others.

Hazards and Annoyances

Even experienced producers and developers commonly run into at least some light chop and turbulence during the course of a project's development. The experts, however, never crash when their vehicle shudders or loses some altitude. You can expect the going to get rough at any number of stages—from trying to design the perfect interface, to endless testing, to problems with client sign-off or payment. Expect problems beyond your control, and be prepared to accept them and solve them.

Small annoyances, too, can become serious distractions that are counter-productive. The production stage is a time of great creativity, dynamic intercourse among all contributors, and, above all, hard work. Be prepared to deal with some common irritants, for example:

- Creative coworkers who don't take (or give) criticism well

- Clients who cannot or are not authorized to make decisions

- More than two all-nighters in a row

- Too many custom-coded routines

- Instant coffee and microwaved corn dogs

- Too many meetings; off-site meetings

- Missed deadlines

If your project is a team effort, then it is critical that everyone works well together—or can at least tolerate one another's differences—especially when the going gets tough. Pay attention to the mental health of all personnel involved in your project, and be aware of the dynamics of the group and whether people are being adversely affected by individual personalities. If problems arise, deal with them before they become hazardous; the mix of special creative talents required for multimedia can be volatile. If you stay organized and flexible throughout, you will complete your project successfully. See Chapter 19 for the next step—how to deliver it!

17

First Person

In 1975, I was hired to deliver a 41-foot cruising sailboat from Fort Lauderdale to the British Virgin Islands for the charter trade. In three days I assembled a crew of strangers, provisioned the boat, and checked all the equipment. Then we took off across the Gulf Stream and into the Bermuda Triangle.

After two days it was clear that the cook was a bad apple. It wasn't just that she couldn't cook—she whined about everything: the stove wouldn't light, the boat heeled too much, her socks were wet, her sleeping bag tore on a cleat, her hair was tangled, she couldn't get her favorite radio station (now a few hundred miles astern). It was unending.

The whining began to envelop her in a smog-colored, onionlike layering, each new complaint accreting to the last one, like growing coral. By the fifth day, her unpleasant aura saturated the entire main cabin; the rest of us sought sanctuary in the cockpit or the small aft cabin. Efforts were made to solve this bizarre situation, but by then, nobody could get near her (or wanted to).

When we pulled into tiny Caicos Island for water and fresh stores, I paid her off and arranged for a room at the quaint waterfront hotel, where she could wait three days for the weekly airplane back to Florida. Everyone felt bad about her disappointment and how it all turned out—for about an hour. The rest of the voyage was jubilant.

Multi

Content is the information
and material that forms
the heart of your project...

Content comes from somewhere.

balance

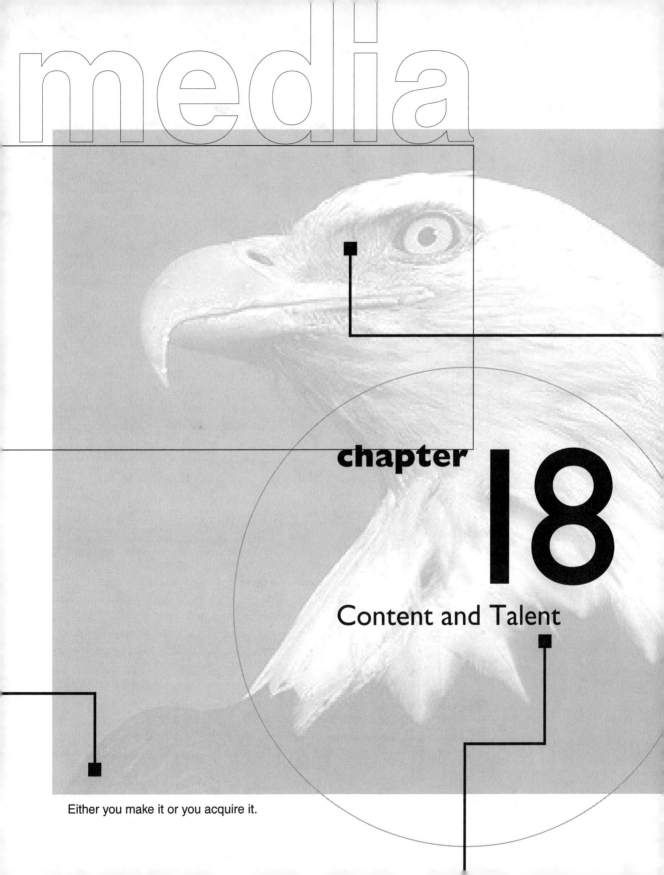

media

chapter 18

Content and Talent

Either you make it or you acquire it.

E VERY multimedia project includes content. It is the "stuff" from which you fashion your messages. It is also the information and material that forms the heart of your project—that defines what your project is about.

Practically, content can be any and all of the elements of multimedia. You might use your collection of wedding photographs and videotapes to create a special multimedia newsletter for family and relatives. Or you might edit portions of the audio track from these videotapes and capture still images to build a multimedia database of aunts, uncles, and cousins. This material is your project's content.

Content can have low and high *production value*. If you hire a team of professionals to shoot your wedding video, and then they digitize images and audio clips at broadcast quality, your content will have high production value. If you persuade Hillary Rodham Clinton to record the voice-over and Garry Trudeau, the "Doonesbury" artist, to retouch the images, it will have yet higher production value.

You must always balance the production value of your project against your budget and the desired result. For aerial photographs of the wedding reception, you would not likely commission the private launch of a spy satellite from Kennedy Space Center to achieve highest production value. Instead, you could rent a helicopter with paparazzi and still achieve good production value. Or you could photograph the wedding yourself from a neighboring rooftop and be satisfied with the lower production value. The production value of your project is a question of balance (see Vaughan's Law of Multimedia Minimums in Chapter 9).

Content comes from somewhere—either you make it or you acquire it. Whether you make it, borrow it, or buy it depends upon your project's needs, your time constraints, and your pocketbook. Content that is destined for sale to the public is also wrapped in numerous legal issues. Who owns the content? Do you have the proper rights to use it? Copyright laws, for example, protect literary works; musical works; dramatic works; pictorial, graphic, and sculptural works; motion pictures and other audiovisual works; and sound recordings. Do you have licenses and signed releases?

When the Vatican recently made a collection of artwork available on the World Wide Web, they made certain there was a digital "watermark" for each image; they would then know if the artwork was ripped off, without recourse to even higher laws. The Vatican is aware (as you should be) of the nature of the electronic revolution:

> In accordance with international regulations on Intellectual Property and Author's Rights, we inform our readers that the news items contained in the Vatican Information Service may be used in part or in their entirety, but only if the source (V.I.S., Vatican Information Service) is quoted. In the case of electronic retransmission (Internet, telematic networks, via PC-modem, fax, etc.), prior authorization from the Vatican Information Service is always required.

http://www.vatican.va
http://www.christusrex.org/www1/icons/index.html

Collections of hundreds of classical images

This chapter discusses some of the legal issues surrounding content and the use of talent in multimedia projects. It provides examples of contract terms and introduces you to some of the sources and providers of content and talent. Needless to say, always consult an attorney versed in intellectual property law when you negotiate the rights and ownership of content.

Acquiring Content

Content acquisition can be one of the most expensive and time-consuming tasks in organizing a multimedia project. You must plan ahead, allocating sufficient time (and money) for this task.

- If your project describes the use of a new piece of robotics machinery, for example, will you need to send a photographer to the factory for the pictures? Or can you digitize existing photographs?

- Suppose you are working with 100 graphs and charts about the future of petroleum exploration. Will you begin by collecting the raw data from reports and memos, or start with an existing spreadsheet or database? Perhaps you have charts that have already been generated from the data and stored as TIFF or PICT files?

- You are developing an interactive guide to the trails in a national park, complete with video clips of the wildlife that hikers might encounter on the trails. Will you need to shoot original video footage, or are there existing tapes for you to edit?

tip   Be sure to specify in your project plan the format and quality of content and data to be supplied to you by third parties. Format conversion and editing takes real time.

This is how you do things on a shoestring. Years ago, we created a basketball product starring Dr. J and Larry Bird. The first thing we knew we had to do was sign a contract with Dr. J. So we found a guy that knew his agent and we made a side deal with him to pay him to convince Julius to do it. And then we went to Julius and we made a deal where we gave him some stock in the company, rather than writing a huge check. And we convinced him of the educational value of what we were doing, instead of just trying to get it to be an arms-length financial deal. So we were able to sign him up with an advance of only $20,000. And he was quite easily the biggest name in basketball and one of the top two or three regarded professional athletes at the time. We got him for a royalty rate of 2 1/2 percent (not what you hear today in a lot of cases), so you don't have to do things that have really high royalty rates and advances. By the way, he made a killing on the stock!

Trip Hawkins, Chairman & CEO, 3DO Company

Using Content Created by Others

Since the late 1980s, investors in the multimedia marketplace have been quietly purchasing electronic rights to the basic building blocks of content—films, videos, photographic collections, and textual information bases—knowing that in the future these elements can and perhaps will be converted from their traditional form to computer-based storage and delivery. This is smart, but not easy; the many union-supported contract restrictions and performer and producer rights are not only complicated and difficult to trace but also very expensive to acquire.

18

---

warning   *If you negotiate ownership or rights to someone else's content, be sure to get the advice of a skilled copyright and contracts attorney.*

Obtaining the rights to content is not, however, a hopeless undertaking. For example, Amaze, Inc., acquired rights from several sources to produce a series of computer-based daily planners with a cartoon-a-day from Gary Larson's "The Far Side" or Cathy Guisewite's "Cathy"; a word-a-day from Random House; or a question-a-day from the Trivial Pursuit game. Random House and Brøderbund's Living Books Division negotiated the rights to the Dr. Seuss books for multimedia use. Multimedia rights to Elvis Presley historical material, to the movie *Jurassic Park*, and to a myriad of other content have been acquired by multimedia developers and publishers.

Depending on the type and source of your content, the negotiations for usage rights can be simple and straightforward, or they may require complicated contracts and a stack of release forms. Each potential content provider you approach will likely have his or her own set of terms that you need to look at carefully so that the terms are broad enough not to constrain the scope of your multimedia project.

Locating Preexisting Content

Preexisting content can come from a variety of sources: from a trunk of old photographs in your neighbor's attic or from a stock house or image bank offering hundreds of thousands of hours of film and video or still images, available for licensing for a fee.

If your needs are simple and fairly flexible, you may be able to use material from collections of clip art. Such collections of photographs, graphics, sounds, music, animation, and video are becoming widely available from many sources, for anywhere from fifty to several hundred dollars. Part of the value of many of these packages is that you are granted unlimited use, and you can be comfortable creating derivative versions tailored to your specific application. Carefully read the license agreement that comes with the collection before assuming you can use the material in any manner. In the six-point italicized type on the back of the agreement, you may discover that the licensor offers no guarantee that the contents of the collection are original works. Thus, the licensor bears no responsibility to indemnify you for inadvertently infringing on the copyrights of a third party. You may also discover that the collection comes with severe restrictions on the way material can be used, or that a royalty is required for use.

If your content needs are more specific or complex, a good place to start your search for material might be at a still photo library, a sound library, or a stock footage house. These resources may be public or private and may contain copyrighted works as well as materials that are in the public domain, meaning that its copyright protection has expired over time and not been renewed; you can use the material without a license.

The National Archives in Washington D.C. is a rich source of content, both copyrighted and in the public domain. Other public sources include the Library of Congress, NASA, U.S. Information Agency, and the Smithsonian Institution, all in Washington D.C. You cannot, however, safely assume that all material acquired from a public source is in the public domain. You remain responsible for ensuring that you do not infringe on a copyright.

In addition to public sources, there are many other repositories of content material. Commercial stock houses offer millions of images, video and film clips, and sound clips, and they often own the works outright—so you don't have to worry about copyright infringement. Some stock sources also specialize in certain subjects. For example, if you want a video clip of a shark, you might contact a stock footage house that specializes in underwater videos.

Copyrights

Copyright protection applies to "original works of authorship fixed in any tangible medium of expression." The Copyright Act of 1976, as amended (17 U.S.C.A. §101 et. seq.) protects the legal rights of the creator of an original work. Consequently, before you can use someone else's work in your multimedia project, you must first obtain permission from the owner of the copyright. If you do not do this, you may find yourself being sued for copyright infringement (unauthorized use of copyrighted material).

Works come under copyright protection as soon as they are created and presented in a fixed form. Works do not have to be registered with the U.S. Copyright Office to be protected. There are limited "fair use" exceptions in which copyrighted material can be used without permission, but you should consult an attorney before assuming this exception.

Owning a copy of a work does not entitle you to reproduce the work unless you have the permission of the copyright owner. If you buy a painting from an artist, the artist retains the copyright unless it is assigned to you. You do not have the right to reproduce the painting in any form, such as in postcards or a calendar, without permission.

http://www.timestream.com/info/license.html
http://www.timestream.com/info/mmlaw.html

This white paper about licensing still images and an intellectual property law primer for multimedia developers by Dianne Brinson and Mark Radcliffe provide useful insights into complex legal issues

For additional discussion about copyrights as they apply to original works created for a project, see "Using Content Created for a Project" later in this chapter, and visit the Library of Congress at http://lcweb.loc.gov/copyright/.

Obtaining Rights

You should license the rights to use copyrighted material before you develop a project around it. You may be able to negotiate outright ownership of copyrighted material. If the owner does not wish to give up or sell ownership rights, however, you may still be able to *license* the rights to use that material.

There are few guidelines for negotiating content rights for use in multimedia products. If you are dealing with content providers who are professionals familiar with electronic media, you may be given a standard rate card listing licensing fees for different uses, formats, and markets. Other content providers or owners may be less familiar with multimedia and electronic uses, and you will need to educate them.

::::::::::::::::::::::::::::::::

Explaining multimedia technology to people can be a challenge. Michelle, an eighth-grader, wanted to scan some 1920s photographs to use in the San Rafael Community Express, a multimedia magazine done for kids by kids. When Michelle asked the 80-year-old docent at the local museum if she could use the photographs for a computer project, the woman responded in horror that these were priceless pictures and that they couldn't be put in a computer—they'd be ruined. The team spent another 15 minutes explaining scanning to the woman by comparing a scanner to a copy machine and assuring her that the original photographs would be returned unharmed.

::::::::::::::::::::::::::::::::

John MacLeod, Publisher and Chief Pizza Provider for the San Rafael Community Express, a HyperStudio-based
interactive magazine created by seventh- and eighth-graders at Davidson Middle School, San Rafael, California

Some licensing agreements may be as simple as a signed permission letter or release form describing how you may use the material. Other agreements will specify in minute detail how, where, when, and for what purpose the content may be used. Ideally, you would seek rights to use the content any-time, anywhere, and in any way you choose; more likely, however, the final license would contain restrictions about how the material may be used. Try to retain the option to renegotiate terms in case you want to broaden the scope of use at a later date.

The following items are but a few of the issues you need to consider when negotiating for rights to use preexisting content:

- How will the content be delivered? If you limit yourself to CD-ROMs, for example, you may not be able to distribute your product over cable or telephone lines without renegotiation.

- Is the license for a set period of time?

- Is the license exclusive or nonexclusive? In an exclusive use arrangement, no one else would be able to use the material in the manner stipulated.

- Where will your product be distributed? There may be different rates for domestic and international distribution.

- Do you intend to use the material in its entirety, or just a portion of it?

- What rights do you need? You need to be sure you have the right to reproduce and distribute the material. In addition, you may wish to use the material in promotions for your product.

- Does the content owner have the authority to assign rights to you? It is important to ensure you will not be held liable if a third party later sues for copyright infringement.

- Do you need to obtain any additional rights to use the content? For example, if you use a clip from a movie, do you need to get separate releases from actors appearing in the clip or from the director or producer of the movie?

- Will the copyright owner receive remuneration for the license? If so, what form will it take? A one-time fee? Royalty? Or a simple credit attribution?

- In what format do you wish to receive the content? Specifying formats is particularly important with video dubbed from a master.

Derivative Works

Any text taken verbatim, or any image or music perfectly copied, clearly requires permission from its owner to incorporate it into your work. But there are some other, less clear-cut issues. For example, as a starter for your work, you may wish to incorporate but a tiny portion of an image owned by someone else, altering the image until the original is no longer recognizable. Is this legal? Indeed, how much of the original must you change before the product becomes yours? There are no simple answers to these tough questions.

Figure 18-1 shows an original photograph taken by Mark Newman, along with some artwork derived from it. Newman sold certain rights to 21st

FIGURE 18-1

The original photograph by Mark Newman was clipped and manipulated for use in a multimedia project. Who owns the resulting image?

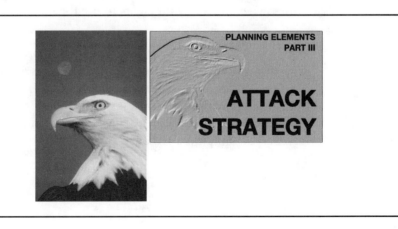

Century Media, Inc., which packages and sells assortments of stock photographs on CD-ROM to computer graphics and multimedia developers. The CD-ROM product contains these instructions:

> You may make copies of the digitized images contained on the Product for use in advertisements, public or private presentations, business communications, multimedia presentations, and other uses as long as the images are not used to create a product for sale. For example, you may not use the images to create calendars, posters, greeting cards, or books of image collections for sale. You may not use, in whole or in part, or alter a digitized image in any manner for pornographic use.

Suppose, however, that the image in Figure 18-1 were scanned from the pages of *National Geographic* or *Time*—what then? If you change 51 percent of the pixels, is the image yours? These questions of ownership will undoubtedly be resolved eventually in the courts.

There is a serious issue facing multimedia developers. Now that they have tools to creatively modify things, how much of someone else's image, music, or video clip needs to be modified before ownership changes? This is up for grabs. There is a law called "fair use," which comes into play in a very limited way here. But I think there needs to be a law called "fair modification."

Trip Hawkins, Chairman & CEO, 3DO Company

Use of images, sounds, and other resources from stock houses such as PhotoDisc or Index Stock Photography is perhaps the safest way to go, because ownership and your rights to use the material are clearly stated.

---

warning   *Beware of clip media claiming to be public domain (where no copyrights apply) that includes sounds from popular television shows or motion pictures.*

Permission must also be obtained to use copyrighted text. Figure 18-2 provides sample language for requesting permission to reprint copyrighted text material and sample terms that you might expect from the copyright owner.

FIGURE 18-2

Sample permission

request and terms

from a publisher for

use of copyrighted

text or images

■

Typical request to a large publishing company:

Dear Sirs:

I am currently producing a computer-based multimedia presentation with a working title of (Title). My publisher is (Publisher, Publisher's Address). The anticipated completion date of the work is (Month/Year). It will be used for (Use).

This letter is to request your permission to incorporate into this work a brief passage from: (Title, Author, Edition, ISBN, Page).

The text I wish to reproduce is: (Text).

Please process this request at your earliest convenience and use this letter or your own form to return your approval by mail or fax to: (Your Name/Address).

The undersigned, having full authority, hereby grants permission to (Your Name) to copy and reproduce the referenced text for use in the work cited above.

Signed:_____

Typical terms from a large publishing company:

1. To give full credit in every copy printed, on the copyright page or as a footnote on the page on which the quotation begins, or if in a magazine or a newspaper, on the first page of each quotation covered by the permission, exactly as "Reprinted with the permission of (Publisher) from (Title) by (Author). Copyright (Year) by (Publisher)."

2. To pay on publication of the work, or within 24 months of the date of granting the permission, whichever is earlier, a fee of: $_____.

3. To forward one copy of the work and payment on publication to the Permissions Department of (Publisher).

4. To make no deletions from, additions to, or changes in the text, without the written approval of (Publisher).

5. That the permission hereby granted applies only to the edition of the work specified in this agreement.

6. That permission granted herein is nonexclusive and not transferable.

7. That this permission applies, unless otherwise stated, solely to publication of the above-cited work in the English language in the United States, its territories and dependencies and throughout the world. For translation rights, apply to the International Rights Department of (Publisher).

8. That unless the work is published within two years from the date of the applicant's signature (unless extended by written permission of (Publisher)) or, if published, it remains out of print for a period of six months, this permission shall automatically terminate.

9. This permission does not extend to any copyrighted material from other sources which may be incorporated in the books in question, nor to any illustrations or charts, nor to poetry, unless otherwise specified.

10. That the work containing our selection may be reproduced in Braille, large type, and sound recordings provided no charge is made to the visually handicapped.

11. That unless the agreement is signed and returned within six months from the date of issue, the permission shall automatically terminate.

18

Using Content Created for a Project

In the process of developing your multimedia project, interfaces will be designed, text written, lines of code programmed, and original artwork, photographs, animations, musical scores, sound effects, and video may be produced. Each of these elements is an original work. If you are creating a project single-handedly and for yourself, you own the copyright outright. If other persons who are not your employees also contribute to the final product, they may own copyright of the element created by them or may share joint ownership of the product unless they assign or license their ownership rights to you.

The ownership of a project created by employees in the course of their employment belongs solely to the employer if the work fits the requirements of a "work made for hire." To meet the definition of a work made for hire, several factors must be weighed to determine whether the individual is legally an employee or an independent contractor. Among these factors are where the work is done, the relationship between the parties, and who provides the tools and equipment.

If the individual contributing to a project is not an employee, the commissioned work must fall within one of the following "work made for hire" categories: a contribution to a collective work, a work that is part of a motion picture or other audiovisual work, a translation, a supplementary work, a compilation, an instructional text, a test, answer material for a test, or an atlas (1976 Copyright Act, 17 U.S.C. § 201(b)). Even if the work falls within one of these categories, be sure to get an agreement in writing from every individual contributing to the work that it is being created as a work for hire. Figures 18-3 and 18-4 offer sample contracts with employees and contractors to precisely specify ownership issues.

The copyright ownership of works created in whole or in part by persons who fall under the definition of independent contractor may belong to that contractor unless the work is specially ordered or commissioned for use and qualifies as a work made for hire, in which case the copyright belongs to the entity commissioning the work.

A copyright can belong to a single individual or entity, or it may be shared jointly by several entities. Make sure that copyright ownership issues have been resolved, in writing, before people contribute to your project.

| FIGURE 18-3 | PROPRIETARY INFORMATION AND INVENTIONS AGREEMENT |

FIGURE 18-3

Sample employer/employee agreement covering intellectual property and inventions; consult an attorney when preparing your own legal document ■

PROPRIETARY INFORMATION AND INVENTIONS AGREEMENT

NOTICE:

This agreement does not apply to an invention which qualifies fully under the provisions of Section 2870 of the Labor Code of California as an invention for which no equipment, supplies, facility, or trade secret information of (Company) was used and which was developed entirely on the employee's own time, and (a) which does not relate (1) to the business of (Company) or (2) to (Company's) actual or demonstrably anticipated research or development, or (b) which does not result from any work performed by the employee for (Company).

Employee's Name _____

Address _____

Date of Hire _____

In consideration of my employment by (Company) or any of its subsidiary or affiliated companies (all called "the Company") and the compensation paid me by the Company, I agree as follows:

1. I understand that my employment results in a confidential relationship between myself and the Company. It is expected that I will receive, during and for purposes of my employment, information about the Company's products, processes, business, plans, research programs, and like Company information (all called "the Company business"), which information is the property of the Company. I may also conceive of or develop ideas and inventions related to the Company business during or for purposes of my employment. The information received from the Company and information which I conceive or develop pertaining to the Company business are the sole property of the Company and are valuable trade secrets of the Company. I agree to preserve their value as Company property, by complying with the following requirements.

2. Except as required in the course of my employment, I shall not disclose to anyone or use at any time, either during or after my employment, any information about the Company business which is either received from the Company or conceived or developed by me, unless I have the prior written consent of the Company.

3. I agree to disclose promptly to the Company all inventions, ideas or conceptions, developments, and improvements (whether or not patentable or subject to copyright) which are made or conceived by me, either alone or together with others, during or as a result of my employment, provided that they pertain to the Company business. I will keep complete records of such matter and will and hereby do assign such matter to the Company, whether or not it has been tested or reduced to practice. Included are all data processing communications, computer software systems, programs, and procedures, which pertain to the Company business. All such records are and shall be the property of the Company alone.

4. Upon request of the Company, either during or after my employment, I will assist in applying for Letters Patent, or for copyright or Inventors Certificate or other appropriate legal form, on all such Inventions and Ideas, in this and in foreign countries, and will execute all papers necessary thereto, including assignments as may be requested by the Company, without further compensation to me. Such applications shall be filed at the expense of and under the control of the Company.

5. All unpublished data and information relating to the Company business, whether reduced to writing or not, are understood and agreed to be confidential and the sole property of the Company. This extends to all confidential information or data I may receive from or about any of the Company's licensees, customers, or others with whom the Company has a business relationship. I will maintain all such information in confidence and not use it other than as expressly requested by the Company, either during or after my employment with the Company, unless and until such information is published without fault on my part.

6. Upon termination of my employment, I will surrender all records and material relating to the Company business.

7. I am aware of no prior obligations which would prevent my compliance with the terms and spirit of this agreement.

8. This agreement shall be binding upon me and my heirs, executors, administrators, and assigns. The Company shall have the right to assign this agreement to any successor to the business in which I am employed.

Signed at _____ , on _____ , 20___

Employee (Signature)

Witness (Signature)

(Address of Witness)

Confidential

(Date)

(Name and Address of Consultant)

Dear (Consultant):

This document, when accepted and agreed to by you, will confirm our mutual understanding and agreement concerning your engagement as an independent contractor to render consulting services to (Employer Name).

You will be engaged as an independent contractor to provide such advice, consultation, and other assistance as may, from time to time, be requested by (Employer Name) in furtherance of (Employer Name)'s business in general and particularly for:

(General Statement of Scope of Work)

During the term of this Consulting Agreement, you agree to provide consulting services to (Employer Name), on the terms and conditions contained in Attachment A, "Description of Services and Reimbursement." Twice monthly you will submit a statement, in a form satisfactory to (Employer Name), setting forth the milestone reached and any authorized expenses incurred to be reimbursed by (Employer Name). Payment will be made according to the schedule in Attachment A.

The consulting services that you will provide are to be rendered at such times and at such places as are mutually agreed upon by (Employer Name) and you. You agree that (Employer Name) shall own all intellectual property rights, including but not limited to copyrights, patents, trade secrets, and trademarks in any and all products of your work within the scope of this Agreement. Said products will be copyrighted by (Employer Name) or in such other name as (Employer Name) may designate. You further agree that any work provided hereunder shall be considered "work made for hire" within the meaning of 17 U.S.C. 2201(b). However, (Employer Name) will give proper credit to you in a manner to be mutually agreed upon as appropriate to the creative direction of the work.

In the performance of the consulting services herein contemplated, you are, and shall be deemed to be for all purposes, an independent contractor (and not an employee or agent of (Employer Name)) under any and all laws, whether existing or future, including without limitation, Social Security laws, state unemployment insurance laws, withholding tax laws, and the payments and reports of any taxes and/or contributions under such laws. You will not be entitled to participate in any employee benefits accruing to employees of (Employer Name). You will not be authorized to make any material representation, contract, or commitment on behalf of (Employer Name).

You agree to comply with applicable laws, rules, and regulations in respect to self-employment, including without limitation, the payment of all taxes required, and you agree to furnish (Employer Name) evidence of the payment of such taxes if requested. In addition, you agree to defend, indemnify, and hold (Employer Name) harmless against all losses, liabilities, claims, demands, actions and/or proceedings, and all costs and expenses in connection therewith, including attorney's fees, arising out of your failure to comply with this paragraph.

The term of this Consulting Agreement shall be for the period of time described in Attachment A, subject to the following limitations:

Upon five (5) days written notice, either you or (Employer Name) may terminate this Consulting Agreement. Such termination shall be effective at the conclusion of said five-day period.

This Consulting Agreement shall terminate on your death.

Notwithstanding anything herein to the contrary, (Employer Name) may, without liability, terminate this Consulting Agreement for cause at any time, and without notice, and thereafter (Employer Name)'s obligations hereunder shall cease and terminate. The term "cause" shall mean, by way of example, but not by way of limitation:

Misappropriating funds or property of (Employer Name);

Attempting to obtain any personal profit from any transaction related to THIS consulting work which is adverse to the interest of (Employer Name);

Unreasonable neglect or refusal to perform the consulting services agreed to be performed by you under this Consulting Agreement;

Being convicted of a felony;

Being adjudicated a bankrupt; or

A breach of any of the other provisions of this Consulting Agreement.

FIGURE 18-4

Sample employer/consultant agreement in the form of a letter; hire an attorney when preparing your own legal documents

(continued)
■

Upon termination of this Consulting Agreement, for any reason, you will be paid your consulting fee on a pro rata basis, and you will be reimbursed for authorized expenses, to and including the effective date of such termination.

You agree to hold all Confidential Information in trust and confidence for (Employer Name), and except as may be authorized by (Employer Name) in writing, you shall not disclose to any person, and you shall take such reasonable precautions as may be necessary to prevent the disclosure of, any Confidential Information at all times during and after the term of this Consulting Agreement. For the purposes of this Consulting Agreement, "Confidential Information" shall mean all information obtained by you, or disclosed to you by (Employer Name), at any time before or during the term hereof, which relates to (Employer Name)'s or (Employer Name)'s clients' past, present, and future research, development, and business activities, and any other trade secrets, records, engineering notebooks, data, formulae, computer code, specifications, inventions, customer lists, and other proprietary information and data concerning (Employer Name) or any client, provided that Confidential Information shall not include information that becomes part of the public knowledge or literature (not as a result of any action or inaction on your part) either prior or subsequent to your receipt of such information.

Upon termination or expiration of this Consulting Agreement, you agree to return to (Employer Name) all written or descriptive matter, including but not limited to drawings, blueprints, descriptions, drafts, computer code, computer files, hardware, software, or other papers or documents that contain any Confidential Information.

(Employer Name) does not desire to receive information in confidence from you under this Consulting Agreement.

You represent and warrant that you are under no obligation or restriction nor will you assume any obligation or restriction which would in any way interfere or be inconsistent with the services to be furnished by you under this Consulting Agreement. In that regard, this Consulting Agreement will in no way restrict you from freely entering into other similar consulting agreements with other firms in the field as long as the provisions herein are honored.

(Employer Name) shall have sole discretion to make other consulting arrangements with other persons concerning any or all of the consulting services to be rendered by you under this Consulting Agreement.

(Employer Name) acknowledges and understands that he is the author of the work you are hired to consult on and that he is therefore responsible for its contents. In the event of a third party action against (Employer Name), (Employer Name) agrees to indemnify and hold you harmless if you are made a party to such action; provided however that (Employer Name) shall have no such responsibility to you if such suit arises due to your misconduct or gross negligence. You promise to provide (Employer Name) with all reasonable cooperation and assistance in any such action or proceedings.

If any action at law is necessary to enforce or interpret the terms of this Consulting Agreement, the prevailing party shall be entitled to reasonable attorneys' fees, costs, and necessary disbursements, in addition to any other relief to which such party shall be entitled.

This letter shall constitute the entire agreement between the parties hereto with respect to the subject matter hereof. In the event of any unresolved dispute in respect thereof, the matter shall be submitted to arbitration in accordance with the rules and regulations of the American Arbitration Association, and the decision of the arbitrator(s) shall be final and binding on both parties hereto.

The validity of this Consulting Agreement and any of its terms and conditions, as well as the rights and duties of the parties hereunder, shall be interpreted and construed pursuant to and in accordance with the laws of the State of California.

(Employer Name)

(Employer Signature)

Accepted and agreed to this _____ day of _____, 20__.

Consultant's Signature: _____

Consultant's Social Security Number or EIN: _____

Attachment A to the Consulting Agreement of (Date)

between (Employer Name) and (Consultant)

Description of Services and Reimbursement

18

Using Talent

After you have tested everybody you know and you still have vacant seats in your project, you may need to turn to professional talent. Getting the perfect actor, model, or narrator's voice is critical. You don't want to settle for a voice or an actor who is not quite polished or is ill suited to the part, or your whole project may have an amateurish feel.

Professional voice-over talents and actors in the United States usually belong to a union or guild, either AFTRA (American Federation of Television and Radio Artists) or SAG (Screen Actors Guild). They are usually represented by a talent agent or agency that you can find in the Yellow Pages.

First Person

We put out a call for a multimedia acting job (male, mid-30s, credible voice, earnest smile), and 18 men showed up for tryouts at a local studio—17 were nonunion and 1 belonged to AFTRA. We videotaped each applicant as he read a prepared script, chatted with all of them, and asked them to walk around and jump up and down. The best choice by far, we thought at the end of a long day, was Dave Kazanjian, the union member.

"Oooh," we said to ourselves, "real union talent! This is going to cost us." So we got together with the client and ran tapes of half a dozen of the better actors trying out, without saying which was our favorite. The client's choice was the same as ours, because Dave was very polished and professional and simply perfect for the part. Paying union-scale wages to the actor would double what we had estimated in our original budget; we had naively assumed we could quickly and easily find the right talent from the

nonunion pool. We ran the new numbers past the client, implying that the second-choice actor was more affordable, even if he wasn't quite perfect. Then we showed Dave's clip next to the other guy, and repeated it a few times, until the difference was really apparent. The comparison was persuasive, and in the end, the client supported the extra cost.

We all learned again that you get what you pay for: Dave did a terrific job. In future proposals, we used union scale in estimating cost, whether we hired a union actor or not.

Locating the Professionals You Need

Before you can safely put a professional in front of a camera or a microphone, you have to find the talent first and then deal with hiring and union contracts.

Begin by calling a talent agency; explain what you need. The agency will probably suggest several clients who might fit your needs and send you a collection of videotapes or cassettes as samples of the actors' work. After reviewing the tapes, you can arrange auditions of the best candidates, at your office or at a studio. You can also get in touch with several agencies and put out a casting call for screen or audio auditions. Furthermore, you are not limited to using union talent, and if your call is posted on bulletin boards in public places (in the theater department of a local university, for example), you may find yourself with many applicants, both union and nonunion, who are eager for the work.

If you run your own audition, be sure you are organized for it. You will need sign-up sheets for names and phone numbers, a sample script for applicants to read, a video camera or tape recorder, tracking sheets so you can coordinate actors' names with their video or audio clips, and hospitable coffee and donuts.

Working with Union Contracts

The two unions, AFTRA and SAG, have similar contracts and terms for minimum pay and benefits. AFTRA has approved an Interactive Media Agreement to cover on- and off-camera performers on all interactive media platforms. Figure 18-5 shows some AFTRA definitions related to interactive media.

FIGURE 18-5

From the AFTRA Interactive Media Agreement (reprinted courtesy of AFTRA, 260 Madison Avenue, New York, NY 10016)

DEFINITIONS

"Material": includes all products (audio or visual) derived from the recordation of the live-action performances of performers, whether or not such performances are in corporated into the final version of the fully-edited Interactive Program produced hereunder by Producer.

"Interactive": Interactive describes the attribute of products which enables the viewer to manipulate, affect or alter the presentation of the creative content of such product simultaneous with its use by the viewer.

"Interactive Media" means: any media on which interactive product operates and through which the user may interact with such product including but not limited to personal computers, games, machines, arcade games, all CD-interactive machines and any and all analogous, similar or dissimilar microprocessor-based units and the digitized, electronic or any other formats now known or hereinafter invented which may be utilized in connection therewith;

"Performers": Persons whose performances are used as on or off-camera, including those who speak, act, sing, or in any other manner perform as talent in material for Interactive Media.

The AFTRA and SAG contracts are lengthy and detailed. Both share language and job descriptions (such as principal, voice-over performer, extra, singer, and dancer). Also, both unions have approximately the same wage scales for these jobs. In 2001, AFTRA's minimum wage for an on-camera principal performer for interactive media was $540 for one eight-hour day, $1,367 for three days, or $1,876 for a week. The minimum wage for a voice-over performer doing up to three voices in a four-hour day was $540; each additional voice would be $180 more. Of course, an actor can always negotiate more than minimum wage.

If your talent needs are simple, you can usually get good contract advice directly from the union representative in your area or from the actors themselves. If your needs are elaborate or undefined, you may wish to consult an attorney or agent who specializes in this area and who can oversee the many required clauses and details of the contract.

Talent contracts are filled with quirky details and complicated formulas. Consider, for example, Article I.17.A.4(c)(i) of the AFTRA Interactive Media Agreement, which reads:

> If a solo or duo is called upon to step out of a group to sing up to fifteen (15) cumulative bars during a session, the solo/duo shall be paid an adjustment of fifty percent (50%) of the solo/duo rate in addition to the appropriate group rate for that day.

Although the concept of *stepping out* may be more in keeping with an MTV video project than with your own multimedia work, you need to keep an eye out for buried clauses that do apply to your project.

---

warning *If you create a multimedia product that incorporates union talent under contract, you will be restricted to using the material only for its initial primary use. Later, if you wish to spin off bits and pieces for other purposes (such as a commercial or as part of a product for sale to the public), you must then negotiate again with the talent and the union and pay for this expanded and supplemental use.*

Acquiring Releases

A union talent contract explicitly states what rights you have to the still and motion images and voices you make and use. If, however, your talent is non-union (a co-worker in your office, perhaps, or a neighbor's child, student actor, waitress, or tugboat captain), be sure to require the person to sign a release form. This form grants to you certain permissions and specifies the terms under which you can use the material you make during a recording session.

Sometimes it is very difficult to do certain things because of previous rights that have been given out. For example, not too long ago I asked an executive from a media company if it would be possible to take some of his film footage and put it into a copyright library, to have something available for multimedia software developers to freely use in their interactive products? He said, "Well, we couldn't use a single frame of any film that was ever shot by a director who was a member of the Directors Guild of America." The bottom line is that there are so many rights attached to so many of these things, with so many different people involved, that it is very complicated even to figure out if you have the right to use it in any way, and again that's too bad because again, that is just going to slow us down.

Trip Hawkins, Chairman & CEO, 3DO Company

Figure 18-6 is a sample release form that covers most situations in a multimedia project and provides nearly perfect rights to the producer. Because such

FIGURE 18-6

Sample release form; consult an attorney when preparing your own legal document

Release Form

This is a release and authorization to use the name, voice, sounds, image and likeness, and writings of the undersigned ("Model"), as obtained in the photography / filming / video / audio session / creative session taking place

_____ at, _____ ("the Session"), for commercial purposes by _____ and his respective successors and assigns (collectively, "Producer").

For valuable consideration, Model hereby authorizes the unlimited use in perpetuity by Producer of all recorded images, likenesses, voice and recorded sounds, and writings of Model obtained during the Session, and of Model's name in connection with such use. Model grants producer the rights to use such sounds, images, and likenesses in any and all media and forms now known or hereafter devised throughout the universe without limitation as to territory or term, including but not limited to advertising, literature, computer demonstrations, and packaging, whether in the form of photography, magnetic or electronic data storage, or any other form, both as obtained and as modified at Producer's sole discretion to suit business purposes of Producer. The compensation stated above shall be the sole compensation for all such use, and no further compensation, including but not limited to royalties, residuals, or use fees, shall be payable at any time.

Model further transfers and assigns all copyrights and all other rights in the recordings, sounds, images and likeness, and writings obtained at the Session to Producer. Producer shall have the right to register the copyright to these in the name of its choice and shall have the exclusive right to dispose of these in any manner whatsoever. This agreement constitutes the sole, complete, and exclusive agreement between Model and Producer.

Name: _____   SIGNATURE: _____

Address:_____   SOCIAL SECURITY NO.: _____

_____   DATE: _____

Phone:_____

forms are legal documents, always consult an attorney to be sure that the specific language of your own release document meets your requirements.

---

warning   *Do not include in your multimedia project any images or voices of people—even if you yourself recorded and edited the material—unless you have their written consent to use it; it is in the public domain; you are reporting it as news, commentary, or parody ("fair use"); or it is work unarguably made for hire.*

Multi

Test it, then test it again;
that's the unavoidable rule.

It's critical that you take the time
to thoroughly exercise your project
and fix both big and little problems...

test and review

media

Alpha...

chapter

19

...in the end,
you will save yourself
a great deal of agony!

Delivering

...Beta

T E S T it, then test it again; that's the unavoidable rule. You must test and review your project or Web site to ensure that it is bug free, accurate, operationally and visually on target, and that the client's requirements have been met, even if that client is you.

Do this before the work is finalized and released for public or client consumption. A bad reputation earned by premature product release can destroy an otherwise excellent piece of work representing thousands of hours of effort. If you need to, delay the release of the work to be sure that it is as good as possible. It's critical that you take the time to thoroughly exercise your project and fix both big and little problems; in the end, you will save yourself a great deal of agony!

One of the major difficulties you face in testing the operation of your multimedia project is that its performance depends on specific hardware and system configurations and, in the case of the Internet, on end users' connection speeds. If you cannot control the end user's platform, or if the project is designed to be shown in many different environments, you must fully test your project on as many platforms as possible, including heavily loaded, highly expanded systems.

warning   *Remember to budget for obtaining the hardware test platforms, as well as for the many hours of effort that testing will require.*

Few computer configurations are identical. Even identical hardware configurations may be running dissimilar software that can interact with your program in unexpected ways. The Macintosh environment is well known for its sensitivity to certain *extensions* (drivers and other parts of system software) that conflict with some software applications. Mac OS-X is at its core different from OS 9.1, the last of the traditional Macintosh operating systems, and not all authoring systems work in this newer OS. During Apple's transition to this OS, users typically install *both* operating systems.

Windows uses its registry database to store configuration information and settings, and still uses the WIN.INI and SYS.INI files to hold custom information that may be different for each installation. If your project depends on the Windows Multimedia Extensions, you will discover a great variety of options and implementations. If your project depends on QuickTime and will be delivered for Windows platforms, you will need to be sure the end user can install QuickTime from your CD or can download the QuickTime plug-in for use with Netscape's or Microsoft's Web browser.

---

tip   *If you are working for a client, clearly specify the intended delivery platform and its hardware and software configuration, and provide a clause in your agreement or contract that you will test only to that platform.*

19

Because any element of a computer's configuration may be the cause of a problem or a bug, you will spend a good portion of testing time configuring platforms and additional time reproducing reported problems and curing them. It is very difficult for even a well-equipped developer to test every possible configuration of computer, software, and third-party add-on boards. With this in mind, Apple Computer, for example, makes available to developers an elaborate testing facility at its corporate offices in Cupertino, California, where all of Apple's computer models and most variations of hardware and software are available.

---

warning   *Not everyone can test software. It takes a special personality to slog through this process. Every feature and function must be exercised, every button clicked. Then the same tests must be repeated again and again with different hardware and under various conditions.*

Testing

The terms *alpha* and *beta* are used by software developers to describe levels of product development when testing is done and feedback is sought. Alpha releases are typically for internal circulation only and are passed among a select group of mock users—often just the team working on the project. These versions of a product are often the very first working drafts of your project, and you can expect them to have problems or to be incomplete. Beta releases, on the other hand, are sent to a wider but still select audience with the same caveat: this software may contain errors, bugs, and unknown alligators that slither out of the swamp at day's end to bite startled designers from behind. Because your product is now being shown and used outside the privacy of its birth nest, its reputation will begin to take form during beta phase; thankfully, beta-level bugs are typically less virulent than alpha bugs.

Alpha Testing

Remain flexible and amenable to changes in both the design and the behavior of your project as you review the comments of your alpha testers. Beware of alpha testing groups made up of kindly friends who can provide positive criticism. Rather, you need to include aggressive people who will attack all aspects of your work. The meaner and nastier they are, the more likely they will sweat out errors or uncertainties in your product's design or navigation system. In the testing arena, learn to skillfully utilize friend and enemy alike. You will undoubtedly discover aspects of your work that, despite even the most insightful planning, you have overlooked.

Beta Testing

The beta testing group should be representative of real users and should not include persons who have been involved in the project's production. Beta testers must have no preconceived ideas. You want them to provide commentary and reports in exchange for getting to play with the latest software and for recognition as part of this "inside" process.

Managing beta test feedback is critical. If you ignore or overlook testers' comments, the testing effort is a waste. Ask your beta testers to include a very detailed description of the hardware and software configuration at the time the problem occurred, and a step-by-step recounting of the problem, so that you can re-create it, analyze it, and repair it. You should also solicit general comments and suggestions. Figure 19-1 presents the search page from a Web-based bug reporting system that is database driven and capable of managing thousands of reports about a complicated application in a meaningful way. (Apache is the most widely used HTTP daemon for serving Web pages.)

FIGURE 19-1

This page from a
Web-based bug
reporting system
seeks precise and
reproducible
descriptions of
problems. In testing
complex
applications,
thousands of bug
reports may be
received, and a
dedicated quality
control team may
be tasked to deal
with them

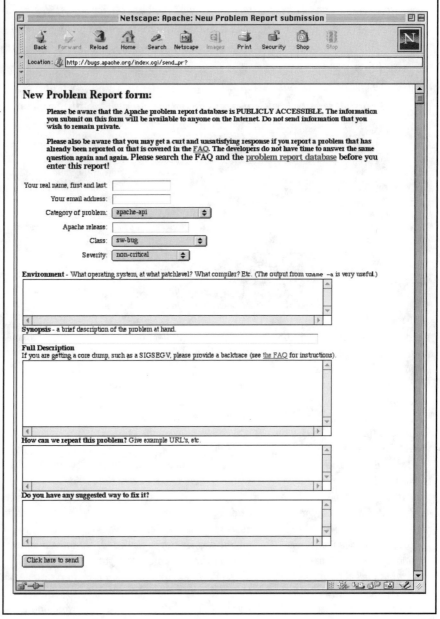

....

From a letter with enclosed disk, delivered by overnight courier to 240 testers around the world:

"We had a bit of a scare on this Beta. Here is the replacement copy for the infected B5 program disk. For your info, the virus that got past me was a strain of nVir. It was dormant and fooled Virus Detective, Virex, and Interferon. Virex 1.1 listed it as a harmless "Stub" that was left over from a previous cleanup. It wasn't until late yesterday that we discovered that it was real. I must apologize for letting this slip past me and thank the people in our tech support department for their help in calling all the members of the Beta test team and alerting them to this problem. If they didn't get hold of you, it was certainly not for lack of trying."

....

Ben Calica, letter author and a product manager who claims
this product shortened his life span by two years.

First Person

We beat on the bronze version of the program right up to the last day, when we had to send a golden master to the duplicator by overnight courier. They were prepared to make 40,000 disks in a matter of hours and then hand-carry them directly to a trade show.

Like kids with sticks at a piñata birthday party, we did everything we could to make all the bugs tumble out of the program. Every time a bug appeared, we killed it. As we pounded and tested, fewer and fewer bugs fell out, until none appeared for about six hours straight, under every condition we could dream up. As the deadline for the courier's airport facility neared, we were ready to apply the finishing touches to the product and stamp it gold. One of the guys waited in his car with engine running, ready for the sprint through commuter traffic to the airport.

We were saving the program every three minutes and nervously backing it up on different media about every ten minutes. We had built in a hidden software routine for debugging this project, and when the product manager clicked Save for the last time, he forgot to reset the program for normal use—we didn't know the master was flawed. Handling the disk like a uranium fuel rod traveling through heavy water, we packed it up and got it to the waiting car. An hour later, our postpartum celebration was interrupted by a painful cry from down the hall—someone had discovered the flaw. By then the courier flight had departed.

We fixed it. Faced with the appalling possibility of 40,000 bad disks being invoiced to us instead of the client, we sent the exhausted product manager out on the midnight flight, without a chance even to go home and clean up. He had a golden master disk in his briefcase, one in his shirt pocket, one in his pants pocket, and one in a manila envelope that would never see an airport X-ray machine.

Polishing to Gold

As you move through alpha and beta testing, then through the debugging process toward a final release, you may want to use terms that indicate the current version status of your project: *bronze* when you are close to being finished, *gold* when you have determined there is nothing left to change or correct and are ready to reproduce copies from your golden master. Some software developers also use the term *release candidate* (with a version number) as they continue to refine the product and approach a golden master. *Going gold*, or announcing that the job is finished, and then shipping, can be a scary thing. Indeed, if you examine the file creation time and date for many software programs, you will discover that many went gold at two o'clock in the morning.

Preparing for Delivery

If your completed multimedia project will be delivered to consumers or to a client who will install the project on many computers, you will need to prepare your files so they can be easily transferred from your media to the user's platform. Simply copying a project's files to the user's hard disk is often not enough for proper installation; frequently, you will also need to install special system and run-time files.

So that end users can easily and automatically set up your project or application on their own computers, you may need to provide a single program that acts as an installation routine. Mindvision's Installer Vise and Aladdin's InstallerMaker package for the Macintosh simplify the creation of an integrated, simple package.

http://www.aladdinsys.com
http://www.blue-sky.com
http://www.mindvision.com

Software and information about installer and help programs

w a r n i n g   *The task of writing a proper installation routine is not a trivial one. Be sure you set aside adequate time in your schedule and money in your programming budget for writing and testing the installation program for your project platforms.*

It is important to provide well-written documentation about the installation process so that users have a clear step-by-step procedure to follow. That documentation must include a discussion of potential problems and constraints related to the full range of your target platforms. Because you likely will not have control over the specification and configuration of the user's platform, it is critical that you include appropriate warnings in your installation document, like these examples:

- Must have at least 128MB of RAM
- Will not run unless QuickTime is installed
- 3MB available disk drive space
- Disable all screen savers before running
- On Macs, turn off extensions before installing
- Back up older versions before installing this update

Often a file named README.TXT or ReadMeFirst is a good thing to include on the distribution disk of your project. This file can be a simple ASCII text file accessible by any text editor or word processing application. It should contain a description of changes or bugs reported since the documentation was printed and may also contain a detailed description of the installation process.

The clearer and more detailed your installation instructions are, the fewer frustrated queries you will receive from your project's users. If your project is designed for wide distribution, installation problems can cause you many headaches and a great deal of time and expense in providing answers and service over the telephone. Set up a product-related Web site with pages for registering the software, bug reporting, technical support, and program upgrades.

```
Date: Mon, 16 Jun 1997 13:09:12 +0200
From: Christopher Yavelow <Christopher@yav.com>
Subject: The case of the keyboardless kiosk

About ten days ago I posted an announcement to the list about our interactive
kiosk installation at the new Netherlands Museum of Science and Technology
(press release at: http://www.yav.com/docs/YMEMIMpr.html).
```

Now I've discovered that science museums at this level are the target of bands of teenage hackers that try to crash all the exhibits. Our exhibit fell prey to such a band last Friday.

Although the software is running inside of a kiosk built into a larger "The Music is the Message" exhibit housing AND the museum visitor has only a trackball and single push button to operate the exhibit AND there is *no* way to quit the software without issuing a command-Q from a keyboard which is double-locked inside the guts of the exhibit housing, some kids were able to get back to the desktop and delete the 60 MB of files associated with the exhibit... and they did so in such a way that Norton Utils (3.5) could not find them for un-erasing (I had to bring over a CD-ROM version and re-install the entire exhibit).

How did they do it? Is there a way to get back to the desktop in such a scenario: a (for all practical purposes) keyboardless kiosk with only a trackball and single button interface and no on-screen option to quit the application? There are no menus, the menubar is hidden, there are no quit buttons, AllowInterrupts is set to false, etc., etc.

Christopher Yavelow
YAV Interactive Media
Brederodestraat 47
2042 BB Zandvoort
The Netherlands
eMail: Christopher@yav.com
wSite: http://www.yav.com

Scary message found at an Internet newsgroup for multimedia programmers

File Archives

Shareware and commercial utility programs for compressing and decompressing files have been in wide use in both the Macintosh and DOS environments for some time. These have been particularly popular with users of bulletin boards, the Internet, and online services such as America Online because compressed files take less time to transmit by modem than do uncompressed files. Most software that involves uploading and downloading online files automatically handles compression/decompression. Netscape and Explorer, for example, use "helper" applications to decompress documents downloaded from the Web:

One or more of the files in your project can be compressed into a single file, called an archive. When that archive is then decompressed, or the files are expanded or extracted, each file in the archive is "reconstituted." Figure 19-2 shows the Translate menu of a StuffIt archive, which contains options for converting several archive types. Archives are usually identified by file name extensions representing the compression software that was used, as shown in Table 19-1.

Compression Software	Extension	Platform
PKZIP	.zip	DOS/Windows
ARC	.arc	DOS/Windows
PAK	.pak	DOS/Windows
Windows Install	.xx__	Windows
StuffIt	.sit	Macintosh
PackIt	.pit	Macintosh
DiskDoubler	.dd	Macintosh
CompactPro	.cpt	Macintosh
AppleLink	.pkg	Macintosh
Self-extracting	.sea	Macintosh
Self-extracting	.exe	DOS/Windows
BinHex	.hqx	Internet
Uuencode	.uu	Internet
Tar	.tar	Internet, Unix
Compress	.z	Internet, Unix
Gzip	.gz	Internet, Unix

TABLE 19-1 *Common File Name Extensions for Compression Software* ■

Self-extracting archives are useful for delivering projects on disks in compressed form. On the Mac, these files typically carry the DOS-like file name extension .sea. On DOS platforms, these archives are executable files with an .exe file name extender. With self-extracting archives, the user simply runs the executable archive, and the compressed files are automatically decompressed and placed on the hard disk. DiskDoubler and StuffIt Deluxe both create self-extracting archives on the Macintosh; WinZip creates them in Windows environments. StuffIt Deluxe, while running on the Macintosh (as shown in Figure 19-2), will also decompress .arc, .pak., .zip, and other files, and convert text that was originally created on a PC or a Unix system.

19

FIGURE 19-2

An archive can contain many compressed files

Some compression applications allow you to compress, split, and store large files on several floppy disks or Zip disks; the segments of these files are then automatically rejoined during installation.

Most compression utilities also provide an encryption or security feature, so that people who have access to disks containing private archive files cannot read them without authorization. This helps hide classified data.

First Person

I recently discovered a group of computer scientists and programmers fully dedicated to exploring and improving the techniques and algorithms used for compression of digital data. These folks are from around the world and hang out on bulletin boards, where they have lengthy and arcane electronic conversations.

Programmers and mathematicians such as Huffman, Lempel, and Ziv have been made famous on these services.

The greatest contribution this group has made to computer technology may not be in the area of information condensation, but in the creative spin-off of peculiar new words such as freshen, pack, crunch, squash, shrink, crush, implode, distill, squeeze, stuff, and garble. When you throw a few atoms and bestGuesses into this potpourri of words, the language of data compression joins that of modern physics, with its own quarks, gluons, and happy and sad particles. It's a creative and inventive place in the day-to-day forward motion of human endeavor, this place of strange and beautiful compression algorithms.

Delivering on CD-ROM

The majority of multimedia products sold into retail and business channels are delivered on CD-ROM. While the very first users of CD-ROMs were owners of large databases like library catalogs, reference systems, and parts lists, today all computers are shipped with a CD-ROM drive, and software that is not downloadable from the Internet is packaged on CD-ROMs.

Compact Disc Technology

A compact disc, or CD, is a thin wafer of clear polycarbonate plastic and metal measuring 4.75 inches (120 mm) in diameter, with a small hole, or *hub*, in its center. The metal layer is usually pure aluminum, sputtered onto the polycarbonate surface in a thickness measurable in molecules. As the disc spins in the CD player, the metal reflects light from a tiny infrared laser into a light-sensitive receiver diode. These reflections are transformed into an electrical signal and then further converted to meaningful bits and bytes for use in digital equipment.

Pits on the CD, where the information is stored, are 1 to 3 microns long, about 1/2 micron wide, and 1/10 micron deep. (By comparison, a human hair is about 18 microns in diameter.) A CD can contain as many as 3 miles of these tiny pits wound in a spiral pattern from the hub to the edge. A layer of lacquer is applied to protect the surface, and artwork from the disc's author or publisher is usually silk-screened on the back side.

Compact discs are made in what is generally referred to as a *family* process. The glass master is made using the well-developed photolithographic techniques created by the microchip industry: First an optically ground glass disc is coated with a layer of photoresist material 1/10 micron thick. A laser exposes (*writes*) a pattern of pits onto the surface of the chemical layer of material. The disc is developed (the exposed areas are washed away) and is silvered, resulting in the actual pit structure of the finished master disc. The master is then electroplated with layers of nickel one molecule thick, one layer at a time, until the desired thickness is reached. The nickel layer is separated from the glass disc and forms a metal negative, or *father*.

In cases where low runs of just a few discs are required, the father is used to make the actual discs. Most projects, though, require several *mothers,* or positives, to be made by plating the surface of the father.

In a third plating stage, *sons,* or *stampers,* are made from the mother, and these are the parts that are used in the injection molding machines. Plastic pellets are heated and injected into the mold or stamper, forming the disc with the pits in it. The plastic disc is coated with a thin aluminum layer for reflectance and protective lacquer for protection, given a silk-screened label for marketing, and packaged for delivery. Most of these activities occur in a particle-free clean room, because one speck of dust larger than a pit can ruin many hours of work. The mastering process alone takes around 12 hours.

CD-R

CD-R (compact disc-recordable) is an excellent method for distributing multimedia projects. CD-R writers and blank CD-R discs are inexpensive, and for short runs of a product, it is more cost effective to *burn* your work onto CD-Rs and custom label them with your own printer than to have the discs mastered and *pressed* using the expensive father and son method described above. Many services with autoloading equipment and 24-hour turnarounds can make short runs.

CD-R blanks that can hold as much as 84 minutes of Red Book sound (see below) or more than 700MB of data are made of a polycarbonate core coated with layers of reflective metals and special photosensitive organic dyes (see Figure 19-3). During the "burning" process, laser light hits the layer of dye, bakes it, and forms a pit.

Compact Disc Standards

In 1979, Philips and Sony together launched CD technology as a digital method of delivering sound and music (audio) to consumers (see Chapter 9). This collaboration resulted in the Red Book standard (named for the color of the document's jacket), officially called the Compact Disc Digital Audio Standard. The Red Book standard defines the audio format for CDs available in music stores today; the Yellow Book is for CD-ROM; the Green Book is for CD-I (Interactive); the Orange Book is for write-once, read-only (WORM) CD-ROMs; and the White Book is for Video CD (Karaoke CD). These and other CD formats are discussed in the following sections.

The Red, Yellow, Green, Orange, and White Books

Red Book remains the basis for recent standards that define more elaborate digital data formats for computers and other digital devices. Audio CDs can provide up to 76 minutes of playing time, which is enough for a slow-tempo

FIGURE 19-3

As a CD or DVD disc spins, laser light is beamed along a groove or track of lands (high points) and pits (low points). The difference in reflected light as the beam passes over these tiny spots is interpreted as binary data. ∎

rendition of Beethoven's Ninth Symphony. This was reported to be Philips's and Sony's actual criterion during research and development for determining the size of sectors and ultimately the physical size of the CD itself.

A CD may contain one or more *tracks*. These are areas normally allocated for storing a single song in the Red Book format. CDs also contain lead-in information and a table of contents. Each track on the CD may use a different format; this allows you to create a mixed-mode disc that combines, for example, high-quality CD-Audio with Macintosh HFS CD-ROM or ISO 9660 data formats. Figure 19-4 illustrates the track layouts for Red Book, Yellow Book, Green Book, mixed mode, and for Kodak's PhotoCD Orange Book layout, discussed later. Both Macintosh and Windows support commands to access both Red Book Audio and data tracks on a CD, but you cannot access both at the same time.

Though a CD contains tracks, the primary logical unit for data storage on a CD is a *sector,* which is 1/75 second in length. Each sector of a CD contains 2,352 bytes of data. After every sector are another 882 bytes consisting of two layers of error-detecting and error-correcting information (EDC and ECC) and timing control data. A CD actually requires, then, 3,234 bytes to store 2,352 bytes of data. EDC and ECC allow a scratched or dirty data sector to be reconstructed by software fast enough to avoid dropout of music. Timing codes are used to display song-playing time on an audio CD player.

19

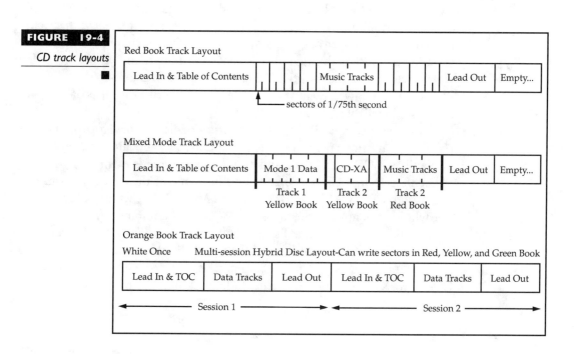

FIGURE 19-4
CD track layouts

The disc spins at a constant linear velocity (CLV), so data can be read at a constant density and spacing. This means the rotational speed of the disc may vary from about 200 rpm when the read head is at the outer edge, to 530 rpm when it is reading near the hub. This translates to about 1.3 meters (51 inches) of travel along the data track each second. CD players use very sensitive motors so that no matter where the read head is on the disc, approximately the same amount of data is read in each second.

The CD's rotational speed and the density of the pits and lands on the CD allow data to be read at a sustained rate of 150K per second in a *single-speed* reader. This is sufficient for good audio, but it is very slow for large image files, motion video, and other multimedia resources, especially when compared to the high data-transfer rates of hard disk drives. New drives that spin many times faster when reading computer data, and slower for Red Book Audio, have been designed specifically for computers. In any case, CD access speed and transfer rate from CD-ROM is much slower than from a hard disk.

Philips and Sony developed the Yellow Book to provide an established standard for data storage and retrieval. Yellow Book adds yet another layer of error checking to accommodate the greater reliability required of computer data, and it provides two modes: one for computer data and the other for compressed audio and video/picture data.

The most common standard currently used for CD-ROM production evolved from the Yellow Book, with Microsoft joining the collaboration, and it was approved by the International Standards Organization as ISO 9660 (see the next section). Later, other standards were developed to deal with specific user requirements, such as synchronized interleaving of compressed audio and visual data in interactive digital movies (Green Book), and with formats for write-once and magneto-optical CD technologies (Orange Book).

The Red, Yellow, Green, and Orange books describe the types of compact discs listed in Table 19-2.

Within each standard, there are variations called modes, forms, and levels. These variations pertain to the method used to allocate the 2,352 bytes available in a CD data sector and how the player reads them.

Each track on a CD can be one and only one of the following formats: CD-Audio, CD-ROM Mode 1, CD-ROM Mode 2, CD-ROM/XA, or CD-I. The whole track must be the same type. When you combine different types of tracks on the same disc, the disc is called a *mixed-mode* disc—for example, track 1 might be CD-ROM Mode 1 data, and all subsequent tracks might be audio data. This is the most common layout for CD-ROM Mode 2, CD-ROM/XA, or CD-I, but each whole track must be the same type.

Name	Description	Comment
CD-Audio or CD-DA	Digital audio	Consumer audio discs
CD-ROM High Sierra	Read-only memory	Vestigial standard, seldom used
CD-ROM ISO 9660	Read-only memory	MS-DOS and Macintosh files
CD-ROM HFS	Read-only memory	Macintosh HFS files
CD-ROM/XA	Read-only memory	Extended Architecture
CD-I or CD-RTOS	Interactive	Philips Interactive motion video
CD-I Ready	Interactive/Ready	Audio CD with features for CD-I player
CD-Bridge	Bridge	Allows XA track to play on CD-I player
CD-MO	Magneto-optical	Premastered area readable on any CD player
CD-WO or CD-R	Write-once recordable	May use multiple sessions to fill disc
CD+G	Mixed mode	CD+Graphics - MTV on disc
CDTV	ISO 9660 variant	Commodore proprietary system
PhotoCD	Compressed images	Kodak multisession XA system
Video CD or Karaoke CD	Bridge	Karaoke full-motion MPEG video
DVD	Digital Versatile Disc	MPEG video, surround sound, and interactive multimedia

TABLE 19-2   *Compact Disc Formats* ■

t i p   *Because there is built-in error correction on CDs, small scratches may not affect playback, particularly when the scratch runs in a straight line from center to edge. To really wreck a CD, scratch it in an easy arc from the center to the rim; error correction won't keep up.*

Note that the CD-ROM/XA format uses an additional subheader that tells the reading software what type of data to expect in that sector: either computer data or compressed audio data interleaved with picture data. (CD-ROM/XA is discussed further in a later section.) Additional hardware is required to play a CD-ROM/XA disc, but these XA-capable players, and players that can read Kodak's PhotoCD multisession XA discs, have become standard. These players can also play Red Book and Yellow Book formats.

19

ISO 9660

The most widely used format for storing digital data in files on CDs is ISO 9660. This standard originated at a famous meeting of industry representatives at Del Webb's High Sierra Hotel & Casino in Reno, Nevada. At that meeting, a common file structure for CDs specifically used by computers was defined. By the time it was processed as an international standard many months later, enhancements had been added, and the "High Sierra" format became outdated.

ISO 9660 file-naming conventions follow the MS-DOS style of eight characters, a period, and three extender characters. Directory names are limited to eight characters, and directories may not be nested more than eight deep. Acceptable characters for names are the capital letters A–Z, the digits 0–9, and the underscore character.

An executable program file designed for the PC will not run on a Macintosh (and vice versa). You can, however, access all files on the CD from either platform. On the Macintosh, you need the Apple CD-ROM extension, and the files named Foreign File Access and ISO 9660 File Access must be in the System folder. On MS-DOS or Windows computers, a device driver supplied by the player manufacturer must be called from the CONFIG.SYS file, and the file MSCDEX.EXE (the Microsoft CD-ROM Extensions) or equivalent (such as Corel's CDX Extension) must be run during boot-up. The ISO 9660 CD-ROM is viewed by either operating system as just another storage device containing directories or folders, and files.

Many multimedia developers place both Macintosh files and PC files on the same CD in a *hybrid* format, letting the user launch the proper applications for the appropriate platform. You can hide the files of either platform when you make the hybrid disc so that users are not confused by the files belonging to the other platform. Graphics, text, and data files written in common formats such as DOC, TIF, PIC, DBF, and WKS can be read from an ISO 9660 CD and imported into your application, whether the file was generated on a Macintosh or a PC.

Macintosh HFS

The Hierarchical File System (HFS) is Apple's method for managing files and folders on the Macintosh desktop, although with System 8.1, a newer format was introduced to optimize hard disk space. Apple has developed its own drivers for Yellow Book Mode 1 CDs, and the HFS driver for CD-ROMs (the default driver built into Apple CD-ROM) provides Macintosh users with the expected comfort of the familiar Apple desktop, complete with

32-character, mixed-case file names. HFS does not, however, comply with the international ISO 9660 standard. If your project is destined only for Macintosh platforms, the HFS format is the preferred choice.

It is easy to produce a Macintosh HFS-formatted CD. Just organize all your files and folders on a hard disk or removable cartridge, test that all paths are correct and your software works, and submit the disk to a CD-ROM manufacturing house. They will copy your disk contents to an HFS CD-ROM with no muss or fuss. When you then mount the disk on a Macintosh, it will look just like the submitted hard disk. With the popularity of CD-R devices (see Chapter 4), most developers "burn" their own test CDs using software like Toast or Easy CD Creator and submit these directly to the manufacturer for mastering.

CD-ROM/XA (Sony)

A standard of great interest to multimedia developers is CD-ROM/XA (Extended Architecture), which is an extension to the Yellow Book standard. XA defines a sector format to allow computer data (Form 1), as well as compressed audio data and video/image information (Form 2), to be read and played back apparently simultaneously. Computer data can be interleaved or mixed with audio and images. In effect, XA provides audio synchronization, similar to QuickTime or AVI.

Special enabling hardware is required on board a CD-ROM/XA player because the audio must be separated from the interleaved data, decompressed, and then output to speakers—while the computer data is sent onward to the computer. XA audio can be digitized and played back at two quality levels; though it falls short of Red Book quality, it is still adequate. Production of a CD-ROM/XA disc requires extensive premastering, because the data and audio/video information must be properly interleaved from your original material. You can still have high-quality Red Book tracks on your XA disc.

PhotoCD

In the summer of 1992, Eastman Kodak Company pioneered a well-planned and heavily financed effort to establish early market share in worldwide electronic photo-imaging systems for consumers. Designed to protect Kodak's investment in the photo-processing industry, its vast sales and technology infrastructure, and to allow gradual consumer transition from film-based cameras to digital cameras over the next decades, the new technology is a marriage of silver halide wet processing and digital processing and display techniques. Kodak has named this venture PhotoCD.

Customers present an exposed 35 mm roll of color film for wet processing and purchase a PhotoCD for an additional charge. The source images (negatives) are then processed by a technician who scans each image at an imaging workstation. The images (a *session*) are written onto PhotoCD write-once media, a color index of thumbnails of all the images is printed, and the PhotoCD is returned to the consumer in a CD jewel case with the printed thumbnails inserted as an attractive cover. The customer may return that same PhotoCD to have more images written onto it, creating a multisession disc. A PhotoCD can contain 125 or more high-resolution images.

PhotoCD images may be viewed using a CD-ROM/XA-capable player (most CD players are XA capable) connected to a computer. In this way, desktop publishing and multimedia production houses have access to images and libraries of images distributed on PhotoCD. Kodak has also created a method for viewing PhotoCD images over the World Wide Web—with a PhotoCD-enabled browser, you can use options such as zoom in, zoom out, and enlarge to view images.

Philips CD-I

The Green Book, published in 1988, specifies an Extended Architecture format and operating system (CD-RTOS) for Philips's proprietary CD-I (Interactive) environment. Like PhotoCD, CD-I discs are designed to play on a consumer-grade player connected to a television set. To prevent users from playing a CD-I track on an audio player (which produces maximum-volume noise and can damage eardrums), the CD-I tracks are not listed in the disc's table of contents. CD-I uses XA Form 1 and Form 2 data formats.

CD-I-ready discs are Red Book Audio discs with special information stored just ahead of track 1, in an area called the *pregap*. These discs are designed specifically to work with Philips CD-I players, allowing special pictures and text to be loaded into the player's memory before the Red Book Audio tracks begin to play. The disc can also be played on a standard CD-Audio player without interference from the additional information stored on the disc.

CD-Bridge discs are also designed to accommodate the Philips CD-I proprietary player system, and they conform to both the CD-I and CD-ROM/XA specifications. This format—which assigns two separate disc label locations, one for each format—allows a CD-ROM/XA track to be played on a CD-I player. Kodak PhotoCD discs are playable on Philips CD-I players because they are Bridge discs.

During the early 1990s, Philips, Kodak, Commodore, Tandy, Sega, NEC, Nintendo, Panasonic, and Sony entered the consumer electronics marketplace with television-based systems that allow users to dynamically interact with sound and displayed graphical information. The Commodore CDTV and Tandy VIS ventures never caught on in the retail marketplace of the United States, however, and were abandoned by 1994.

Video CDD White Book

Originally called Karaoke CD, the White Book format was developed in a joint effort by Philips and the Victor Company of Japan, Ltd. (better known as JVC). It is also supported by Matsushita (Panasonic) and Sony. As a Bridge format CD, these discs can be played on most players using CD-ROM/XA. Specialized consumer players that hook up to television sets have been developed for the Karaoke market, and they take advantage of the Video CD format's implementation of MPEG.

19

---

warning *It is possible to damage your speakers if you play the digital track of a CD-ROM on your audio CD player. The digital data is decoded as full-volume noise by players that do not check for a data flag in the control field of the Q subchannel.*

DVD

Digital Versatile Disc (DVD) CDs employ a different (multilayer, high-density) manufacturing process than current 74-minute (about 640MB) audio and data CDs, and this technology provides 4.7 gigabytes of storage on a disc of the same diameter. The DVD format itself is a product of broad support from most of the industry's leading manufacturers. DVD is discussed in greater detail in Chapter 4.

Wrapping It Up

Packaging is an important area where sales and marketing issues extend the process of making multimedia into the real world of end users. Like the cover of a book, people will judge your work based upon the impression it makes.

If your project is for your own use, you may not need the pretty cover, cardboard box, and shrink-wrap that is required for over-the-counter software sold to consumers. If your project is for a client or for the Web, you may simply need to deliver it on any sufficient storage media or upload it to a server. But if your project is headed for wider distribution within a large company or organization or into retail channels, you will need to think about packaging.

If your project is destined to be sold into the consumer retail channel, then you have made a *title*. Software titles are most often distributed on CD-ROM. The software itself may, indeed, be only one item (the most important one) in a package that includes a user's manual, a registration card, quick reference guides, hardware adapters, and collateral marketing material from you or other parties with whom you have arrangements.

Retailers claim that consumers typically relate the finish of a package to quality and price of the product inside. The fancier, bigger, and heavier the package, the higher its perceived value. Software manufacturers juggle the elements of this equation when they determine the cost of goods and shipping/freight add-ons and set the product's price point. Many big software boxes are shipped with plenty of sailboat fuel inside, and with cardboard or open-cell foam to hold the thin CD and manuals in place.

The art for your cover should reflect the content and function of the enclosed product; it should also follow normal rules for good design layout. Your company's logo should be prominent, and if this is one of a series of titles, the artwork should conform to the coordinated look or style you are using throughout that series or product line.

When your product reaches the retail channel, it may be displayed on shelves or racks, in kiosks, or it may be hung on brackets. You should be sure to put the name of your title on the front face and on the spine of the package. Use photo-quality images and high-caliber artwork for the front, because this is the most visible face of your package. Many packages are shrink-wrapped with thin plastic to protect them from fingerprints and pilferage at the retail outlet. Even after the shrink-wrap is on your package, there is room for additional artwork: bright stickers can be effective eye-catchers. And some vendors apply specially made holographic stickers to identify their product and to prevent unauthorized bootleg copies from reaching the marketplace.

Some vendors have developed unique or special solutions to make their product stand out. Authorware, for example, was once shipped in a custom-designed briefcase with carry handle. An expensive software package, this briefcase was easily absorbed in the purchase price. Fractal Design Painter from MetaCreations is shipped in a metal paint can with a colorful paper wrapper, and AlienSkin's Eye Candy special effects for After Effects comes in a metal movie reel case (see Figure 19-5). But package size and

FIGURE 19-5

Some software

comes in interesting

packages

■

19

shape options are, more often than not, limited by the common constraints of the floor and shelf space found in retailing outlets and by the expense of fabricating a nonstandard container.

Most industrial cities boast more than one packaging specialist with whom you can consult. These outfits can supply cardboard and plastic boxes, printing, cutting, folding, and wrapping services. Environmentally responsible packaging, especially for compact discs, is becoming popular, and special sleeves and cardboard containers are available. Be sure to consider the weight and bulk of your package—an ounce of extra weight that pushes you over a zone or destination boundary might increase your shipping costs significantly. The outside wrap for shipping should be plain because pilferage, especially for international destinations and customs zones, can be a problem. Look for volume discounts and price breaks.

The current trend in software packaging is toward simplification. Indeed, as the information revolution takes hold, more software and documentation will be available for purchase and downloading directly from the Web, and today's boxes and bright packages will become quaint collector's items.

Delivering on the World Wide Web

Delivering multimedia projects built for the World Wide Web can be as simple as renaming a directory or transferring a group of files to a Web server. Servers and networked systems are discussed in Chapters 4 and 13. On the face of it, the mechanics of actually putting a project on the Web are trivial, particularly because you have likely been designing, building, and testing within "Web space" throughout the development of your project, anyway. But delivery of your project and *activation* of your pages by making them available to your intended audience on the Web, whether to the general public or to an intranet of select users behind a fire wall, should be approached with caution. Here there are many technical considerations that, while outside the topic of multimedia per se, should be understood if you want your project to be a success.

If you own or *host* the delivery Web server yourself, you will have better security control, better integration of your project into your internal LAN or intranet, and you can fine-tune the server's configuration parameters and specify and install any special software you need. On the other hand, you will likely need a full-time webmaster to be in charge, and you will pay for a high-bandwidth connection directly to the Internet. When you have control of the server, you can provide secure commerce services for credit card transactions, encryption and passwords, special databases, and custom CGI programming. Server-side setup for plug-ins is discussed in Chapter 14. For multimedia projects requiring streaming technologies such as RealAudio or video conferencing, you can purchase and install the necessary software on the server.

If your project will reside at a site hosted by an Internet Service Provider (ISP) or a service such as America Online or MSN, you must discover during the planning phase of your project what your service's limitations might be and design your project within those limitations. It does no good to include PhotoCD image pacs, ToolVox meta voice files, or complex Java scripts in your Web page, only to find that your ISP does not or will not support the MIME type or purchase and install the necessary server software for you.

Internet directories like Yahoo, and search engines like Lycos, Google, and AltaVista, are important components of the Web's "how-to-find-it" functionality and power: using meta tags, be sure your project will register with the search engines and can be easily found.

A few years ago I taught a student of mine about HTML, just before she went off to a summer internship working on a traditional book publisher's Web site. She returned to school three months later and demonstrated to me how one might use the Web to generate profits—at a time when many doubted it was easy to do. Working for the publisher, she was assigned the job of marketing a book for college students. She did her research and discovered how advertising in the search engines works: by "buying" the word "college" on a few of them, she was able to place an ad on search results that were related to colleges; visitors who clicked on her ad were linked to the publisher's Web site, where they could purchase the book online. While explaining the process, she checked the online sales of her book: over 5,000 copies had been sold online within a month of publication—eight of them during the last hour!

Panagiotis Takis Metaxas
Associate Professor of Computer Science, Wellesley College

19

Index

INTERNATIONAL CONTACT INFORMATION

AUSTRALIA
McGraw-Hill Book Company Australia Pty. Ltd.
TEL +61-2-9417-9899
FAX +61-2-9417-5687
http://www.mcgraw-hill.com.au
books-it_sydney@mcgraw-hill.com

CANADA
McGraw-Hill Ryerson Ltd.
TEL +905-430-5000
FAX +905-430-5020
http://www.mcgrawhill.ca

**GREECE, MIDDLE EAST,
NORTHERN AFRICA**
McGraw-Hill Hellas
TEL +30-1-656-0990-3-4
FAX +30-1-654-5525

MEXICO (Also serving Latin America)
McGraw-Hill Interamericana Editores S.A. de C.V.
TEL +525-117-1583
FAX +525-117-1589
http://www.mcgraw-hill.com.mx
fernando_castellanos@mcgraw-hill.com

SINGAPORE (Serving Asia)
McGraw-Hill Book Company
TEL +65-863-1580
FAX +65-862-3354
http://www.mcgraw-hill.com.sg
mghasia@mcgraw-hill.com

SOUTH AFRICA
McGraw-Hill South Africa
TEL +27-11-622-7512
FAX +27-11-622-9045
robyn_swanepoel@mcgraw-hill.com

**UNITED KINGDOM & EUROPE
(Excluding Southern Europe)**
McGraw-Hill Education Europe
TEL +44-1-628-502500
FAX +44-1-628-770224
http://www.mcgraw-hill.co.uk
computing_neurope@mcgraw-hill.com

ALL OTHER INQUIRIES Contact:
Osborne/McGraw-Hill
TEL +1-510-549-6600
FAX +1-510-883-7600
http://www.osborne.com
omg_international@mcgraw-hill.com

About the CD

This book's CD-ROM contains a variety of software demos for PC and Macintosh users from Macromedia®, Inc.

BY USING THE SOFTWARE ON THIS CD, YOU ARE AGREEING TO BECOME BOUND TO THE TERMS OF THE END-USER LICENSE AGREEMENT THAT IS INCLUDED ON THE CD.

To use the CD

Please follow the instructions below:
Insert the CD into your CD drive.

On a PC

Select File | Run from the Start Menu, type in the letter of your CD drive, and press ENTER.

You will be presented with a window that shows different folders for each of the Macromedia product demos. Select the folder for the product you are interested in, and double-click on that folder's Setup file to run the installer Wizard. Follow the instructions on your screen to demo the products.

On a Macintosh

Double-click the CD icon on your desktop. You will be presented with a window that shows folders for each of the product demos. Select the folder for the product you are interested in, and double-click on that folder's Setup file to run the installer Wizard. Follow the instructions on your screen to demo the products.